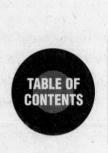

TABLE OF CONTENTS

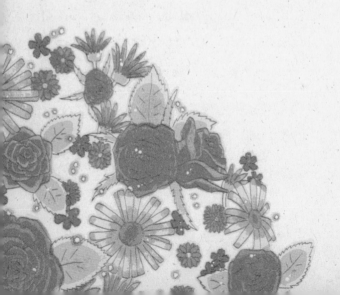

Honorifics Explained

Throughout the Del Rey Manga books, you will find Japanese honorifics left intact in the translations. For those not familiar with how the Japanese use honorifics and, more important, how they differ from American honorifics, we present this brief overview.

Politeness has always been a critical facet of Japanese culture. Ever since the feudal era, when Japan was a highly stratified society, use of honorifics—which can be defined as polite speech that indicates relationship or status—has played an essential role in the Japanese language. When addressing someone in Japanese, an honorific usually takes the form of a suffix attached to one's name (e.g. "Asuna-san"), or as a title at the end of one's name, or in place of the name itself (example: "Negi-sensei," or simply "Sensei!").

Honorifics can be expressions of respect or endearment. In the context of manga and anime, honorifics give insight into the nature of the relationship between characters. Many English translations leave out these important honorifics, and therefore distort the feel of the original Japanese. Because Japanese honorifics contain nuances that English honorifics lack, it is our policy at Del Rey not to translate them. Here, instead, is a guide to some of the honorifics you may encounter in Del Rey Manga.

-san: This is the most common honorific and is equivalent to Mr., Miss, Ms., Mrs. It is the all-purpose honorific and can be used in any situation where politeness is required.

-sama: This is one level higher than -san and it is used to confer great respect.

-dono: This comes from the word *"tono,"* which means "lord." It is even a higher level than "-sama" and confers utmost respect.

-kun: This suffix is used at the end of boys' names to express familiarity or endearment. It is also sometimes used by men amongst friends, or when addressing someone younger or of a lower station.

-chan: This is used to express endearment, mostly toward girls. It is also used for little boys, pets, and even among lovers. It gives a sense of childish cuteness.

Bozu: This is an informal way to refer to a boy, similar to the English terms "kid" or "squirt."

Sempai/
Senpai: This title suggests that the addressee is one's senior in a group or organization. It is most often used in a school setting, where underclassmen refer to their upperclassmen as "sempai." It can also be used in the workplace, such as when a newer employee addresses an employee who has seniority in the company.

Kohai: This is the opposite of "-sempai," and is used toward underclassmen in school or newcomers in the workplace. It connotes that the addressee is of a lower station.

Sensei: Literally meaning "one who has come before," this title is used for teachers, doctors, or masters of any profession or art.

-[blank]:   This is usually forgotten in these lists, but it is perhaps the most significant difference between Japanese and English. The lack of honorific means that the speaker has permission to address the person in a very intimate way. Usually, only family, spouses, or very close friends have this kind of permission. Known as *yobisute,* it can be gratifying when someone who has earned the intimacy starts to call one by one's name without an honorific. But when that intimacy hasn't been earned, it can be very insulting.

A Note from the Author

Artist, Minoru Toyoda

I'm going on a trip.

See you.

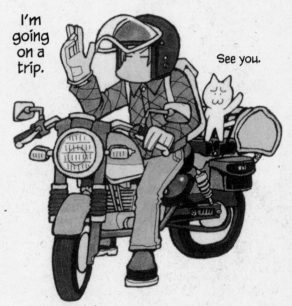

Thank you. Thank you.
Thank you very much!!!

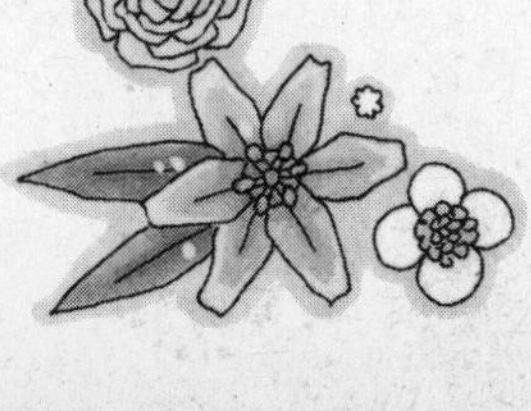

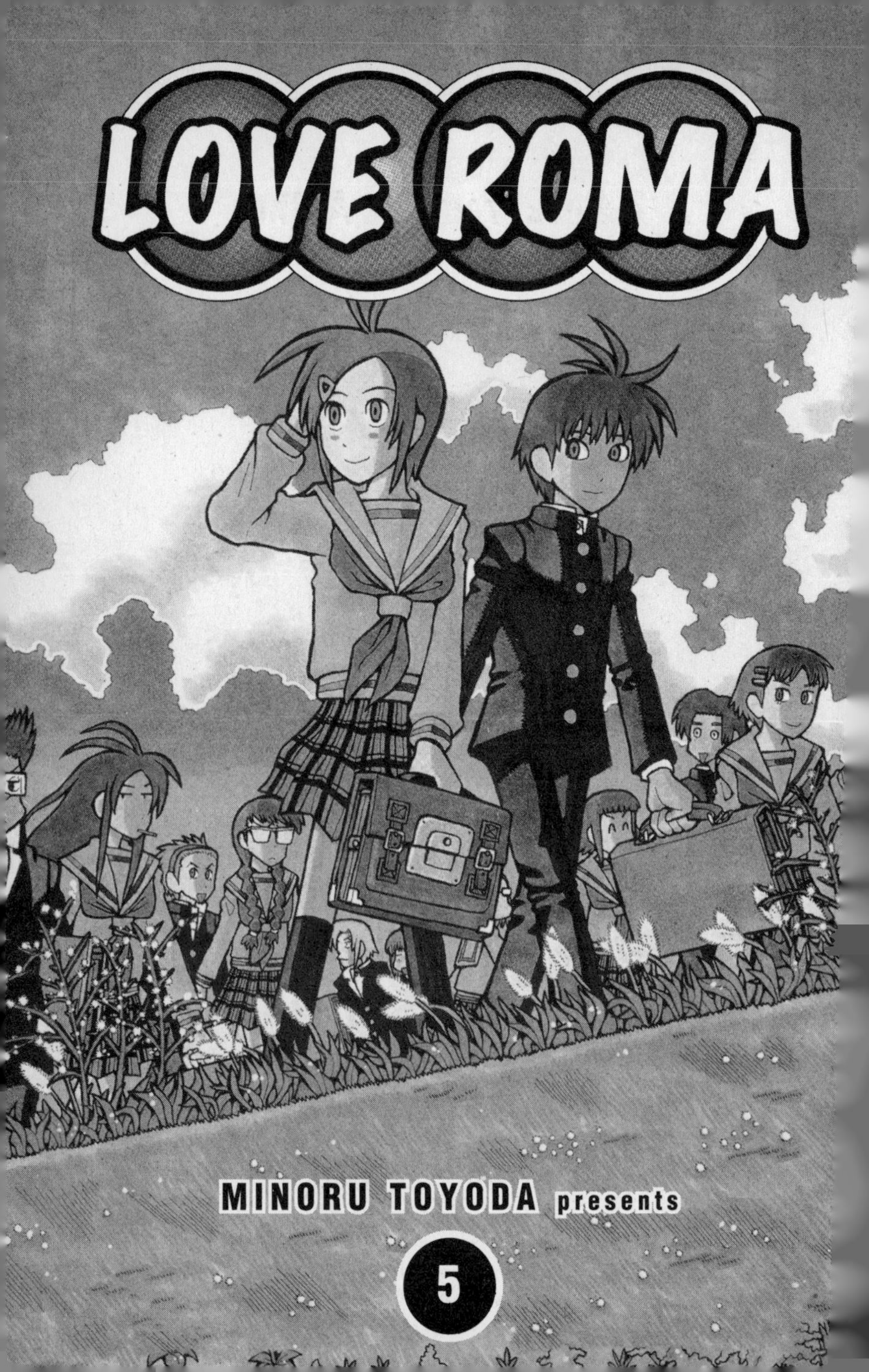
LOVE ROMA
MINORU TOYODA presents
5

CONTENTS

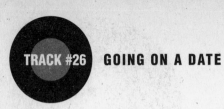

TRACK #26 GOING ON A DATE

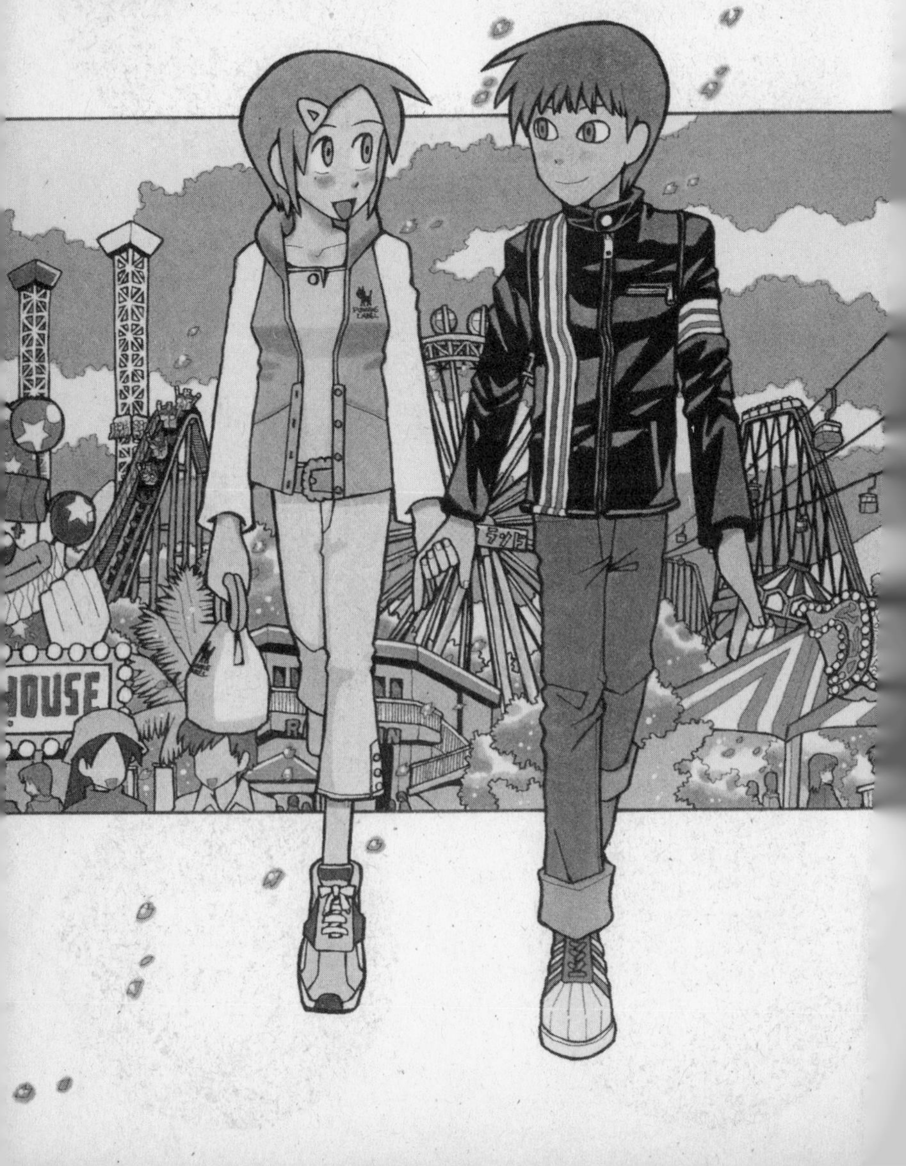

LINER NOTES

LOVE ROMA WILL BE ENDING WITH THIS VOLUME.

THIS WAS AN EXTRA PAGE SO I'M USING IT TO INTRODUCE SOME COLOR ILLUSTRATIONS FOR ADS FROM PREVIOUS VOLUMES.

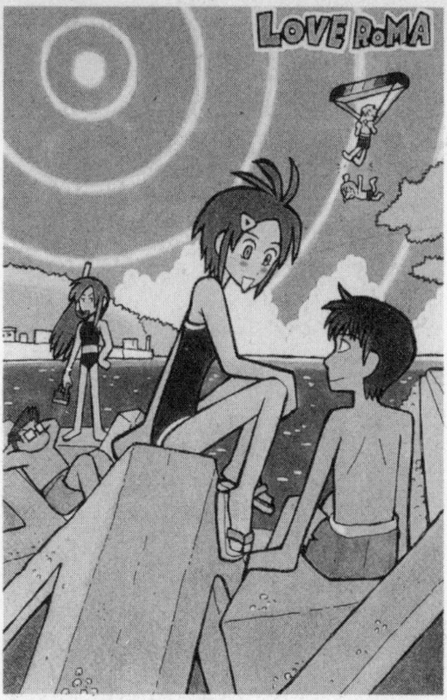
LOVE RoMA

▲ SUMMER, 2004
THIS IS A POSTCARD FOR THE AFTERNOON KC FESTIVAL. I STILL REMEMBER MY EDITOR PUSHED ME TO DRAW NEGISHI-SAN DRESSED IN HER SCHOOL SWIMSUIT.

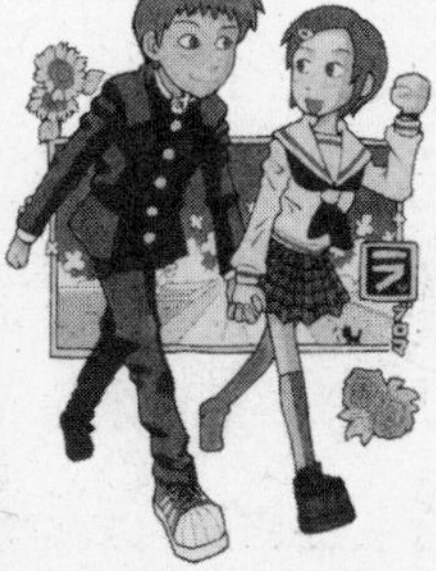

▲ SPRING, 2003
PREVIEW FOR THE NEW LOVE ROMA SERIES.

WINTER, 2002
THIS IS A PREVIEW FOR THE COMPLETE STORY "HOW TO KISS"
▼

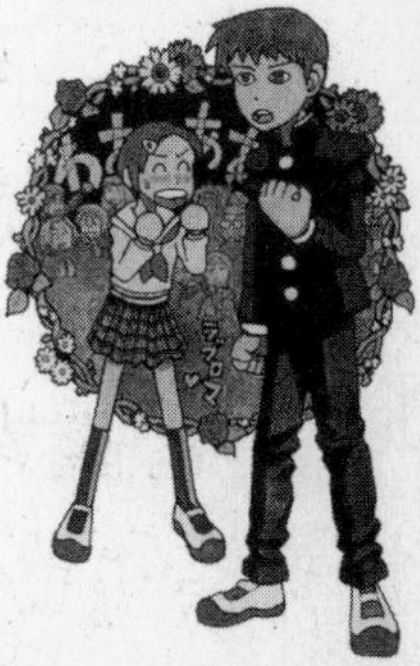

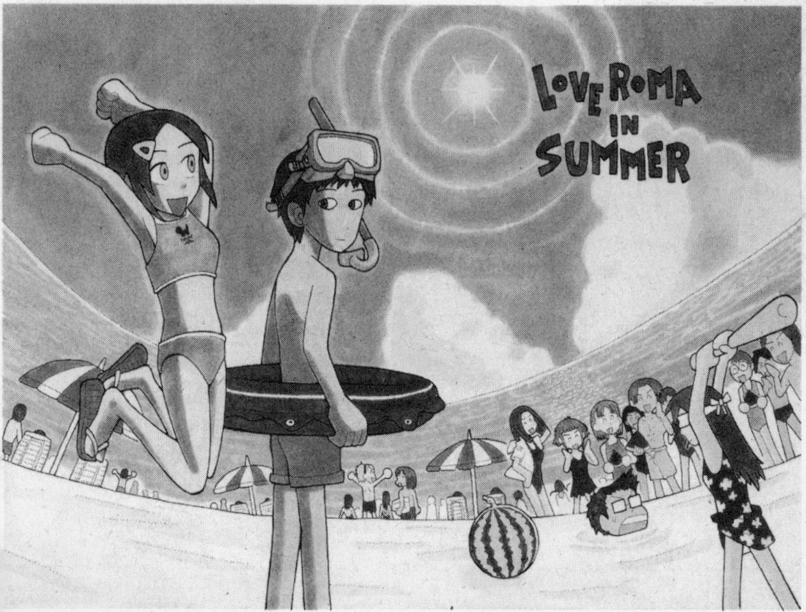
LoVE RoMA IN SUMMER

▲ SUMMER, 2003
THIS IS A POSTER INSERT THAT CAME WITH THE CD-ROM FROM AFTERNOON.

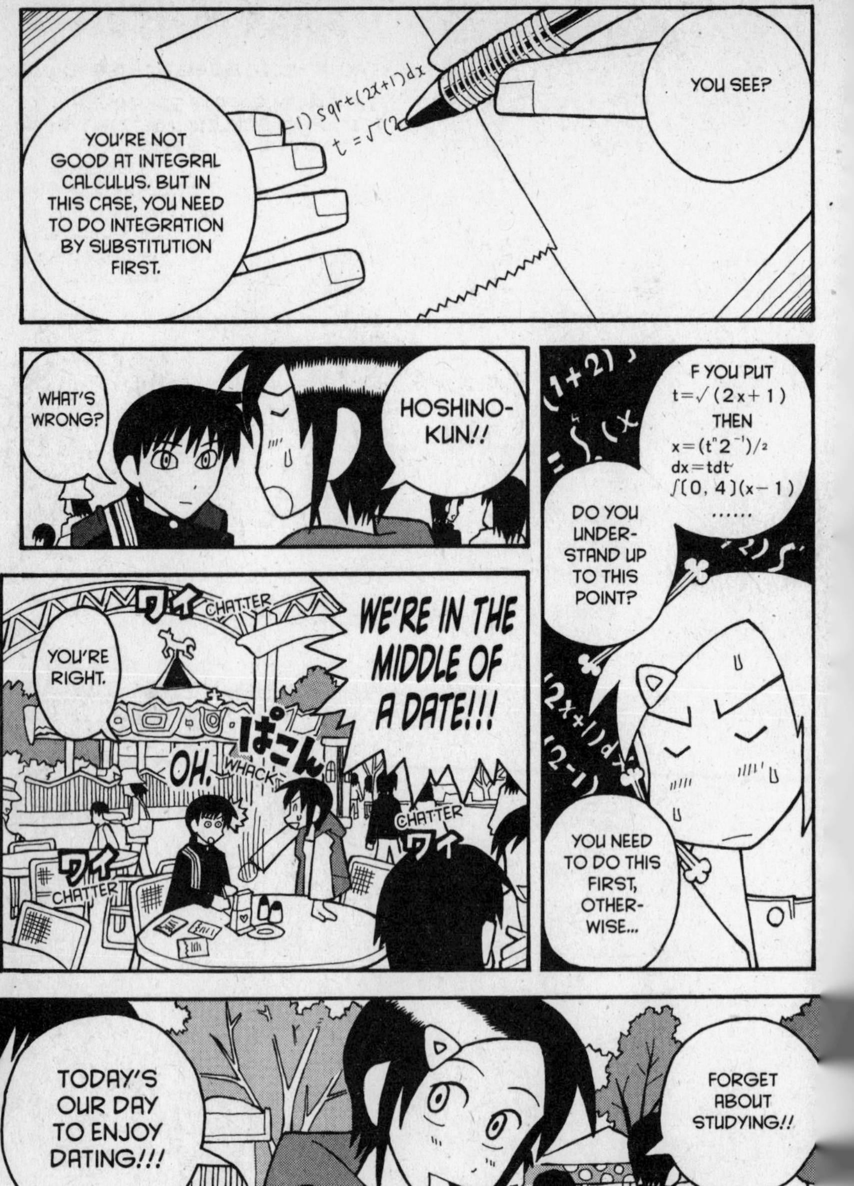
YOU SEE?
YOU'RE NOT GOOD AT INTEGRAL CALCULUS. BUT IN THIS CASE, YOU NEED TO DO INTEGRATION BY SUBSTITUTION FIRST.
-1) sqrt(2x+1)dx
t = √(2
F YOU PUT t=√(2x+1) THEN x=(t"2 -1)/2 dx=tdt ∫(0, 4)(x−1) ......
DO YOU UNDERSTAND UP TO THIS POINT?
YOU NEED TO DO THIS FIRST, OTHERWISE...
HOSHINO-KUN!!
WHAT'S WRONG?
WE'RE IN THE MIDDLE OF A DATE!!!
ワイ
CHATTER
YOU'RE RIGHT.
ぱこん
WHACK
OH.
ワイ
CHATTER
ワイ
CHATTER
FORGET ABOUT STUDYING!!
TODAY'S OUR DAY TO ENJOY DATING!!!

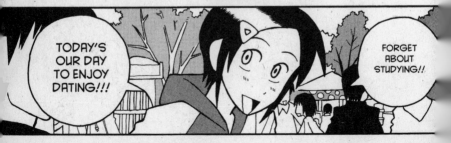

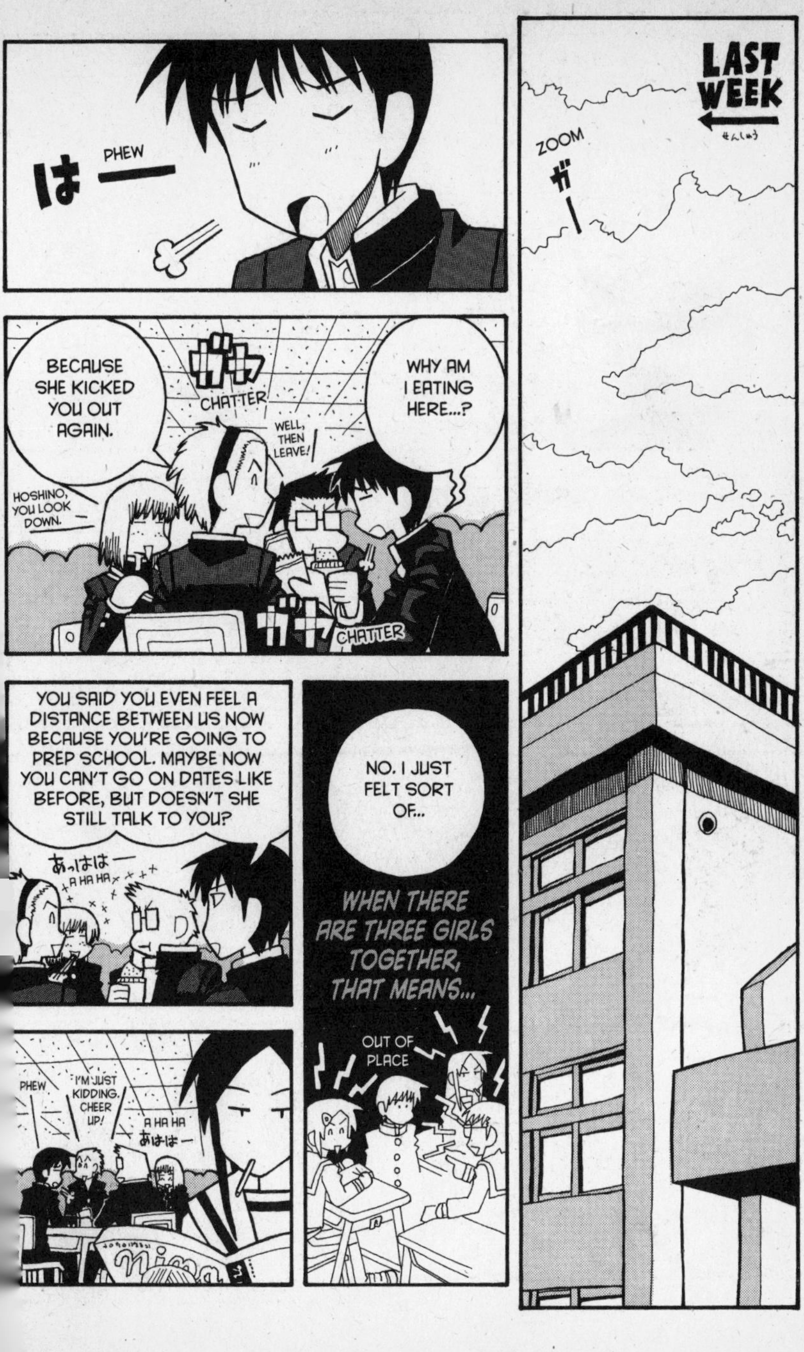
LAST WEEK
せんしゅう
ZOOM
ガー
はー
PHEW
WHY AM I EATING HERE...?
CHATTER
BECAUSE SHE KICKED YOU OUT AGAIN.
WELL, THEN LEAVE!
HOSHINO, YOU LOOK DOWN.
CHATTER
NO. I JUST FELT SORT OF...
WHEN THERE ARE THREE GIRLS TOGETHER, THAT MEANS...
OUT OF PLACE
YOU SAID YOU EVEN FEEL A DISTANCE BETWEEN US NOW BECAUSE YOU'RE GOING TO PREP SCHOOL. MAYBE NOW YOU CAN'T GO ON DATES LIKE BEFORE, BUT DOESN'T SHE STILL TALK TO YOU?
あっはは ー
A HA HA
I'M JUST KIDDING. CHEER UP!
A HA HA
あははー
PHEW

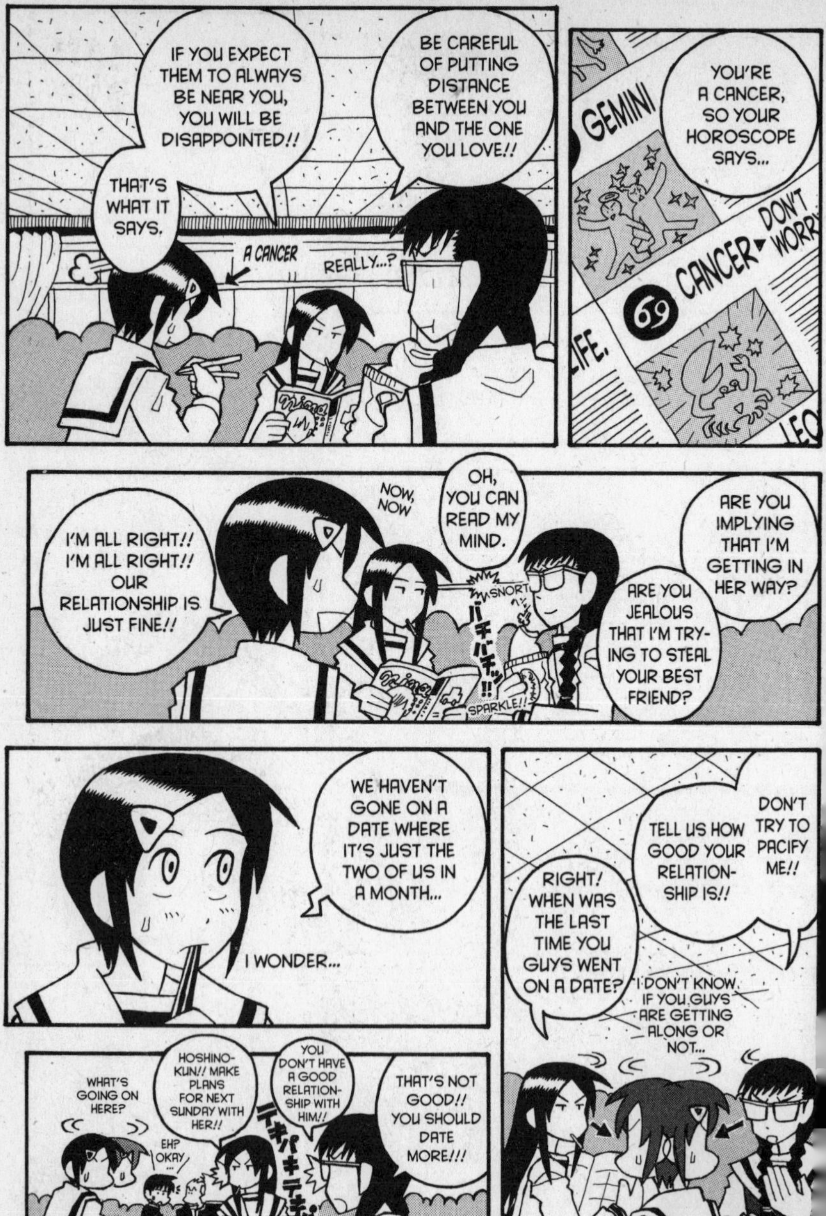

YOU'RE A CANCER, SO YOUR HOROSCOPE SAYS...
GEMINI
DON'T WORRY
CANCER
69
LIFE.
LEO
BE CAREFUL OF PUTTING DISTANCE BETWEEN YOU AND THE ONE YOU LOVE!!
IF YOU EXPECT THEM TO ALWAYS BE NEAR YOU, YOU WILL BE DISAPPOINTED!!
THAT'S WHAT IT SAYS.
REALLY...?
A CANCER
ARE YOU IMPLYING THAT I'M GETTING IN HER WAY?
ARE YOU JEALOUS THAT I'M TRY-ING TO STEAL YOUR BEST FRIEND?
OH, YOU CAN READ MY MIND.
SNORT
バチバチッ!!
SPARKLE!!
NOW, NOW
I'M ALL RIGHT!! I'M ALL RIGHT!! OUR RELATIONSHIP IS JUST FINE!!
DON'T TRY TO PACIFY ME!!
TELL US HOW GOOD YOUR RELATION-SHIP IS!!
RIGHT! WHEN WAS THE LAST TIME YOU GUYS WENT ON A DATE?
I DON'T KNOW IF YOU GUYS ARE GETTING ALONG OR NOT...
THEY CHANGED THEIR TARGET TO ATTACK
WE HAVEN'T GONE ON A DATE WHERE IT'S JUST THE TWO OF US IN A MONTH...
I WONDER...
THAT'S NOT GOOD!! YOU SHOULD DATE MORE!!!
テキパキテキパキ
PREACHY
YOU DON'T HAVE A GOOD RELATION-SHIP WITH HIM!!
HOSHINO-KUN!! MAKE PLANS FOR NEXT SUNDAY WITH HER!!
EH? OKAY...
WHAT'S GOING ON HERE?

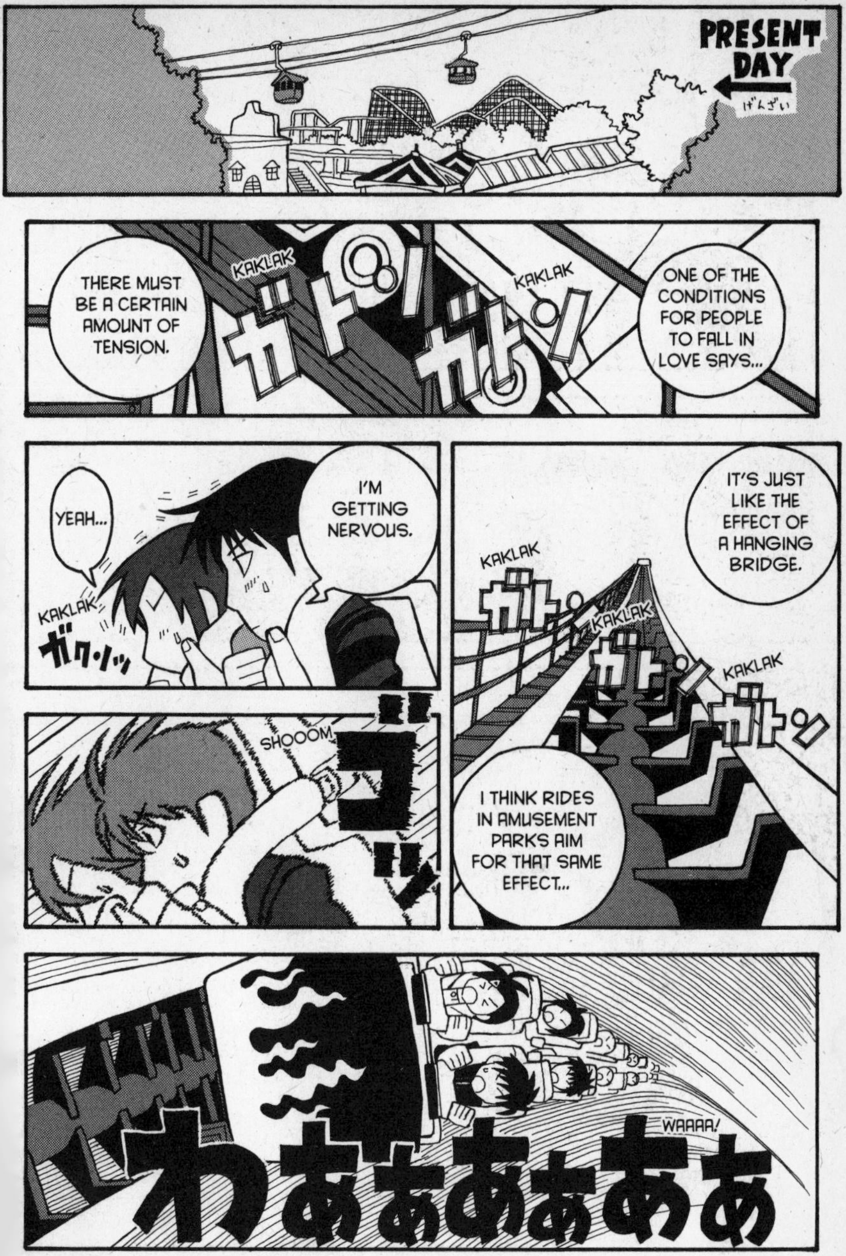
PRESENT DAY
げんざい
ONE OF THE CONDITIONS FOR PEOPLE TO FALL IN LOVE SAYS...
KAKLAK
ガトン
KAKLAK
ガトン
THERE MUST BE A CERTAIN AMOUNT OF TENSION.
IT'S JUST LIKE THE EFFECT OF A HANGING BRIDGE.
KAKLAK
ガトン
KAKLAK
ガトン
KAKLAK
ガトン
I THINK RIDES IN AMUSEMENT PARKS AIM FOR THAT SAME EFFECT...
I'M GETTING NERVOUS.
YEAH...
KAKLAK
ガクッ
SHOOOM
ゴゴゴ
WAAAA!
わあぁあぁああ

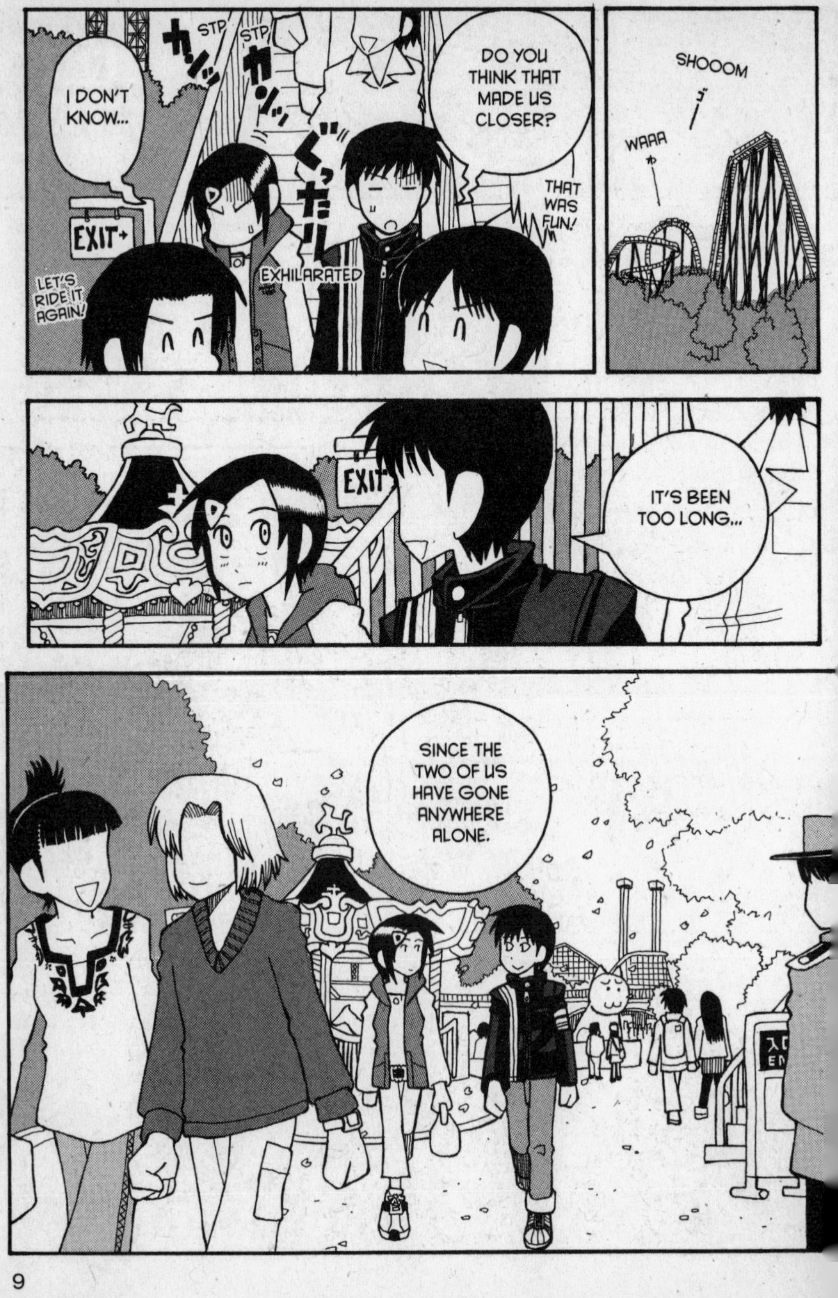
SHOOOM
ゴー
WAAA
わー
DO YOU THINK THAT MADE US CLOSER?
THAT WAS FUN!
STP
STP
ぐったり
EXHILARATED
I DON'T KNOW...
EXIT
LET'S RIDE IT AGAIN!
IT'S BEEN TOO LONG...
EXIT
SINCE THE TWO OF US HAVE GONE ANYWHERE ALONE.

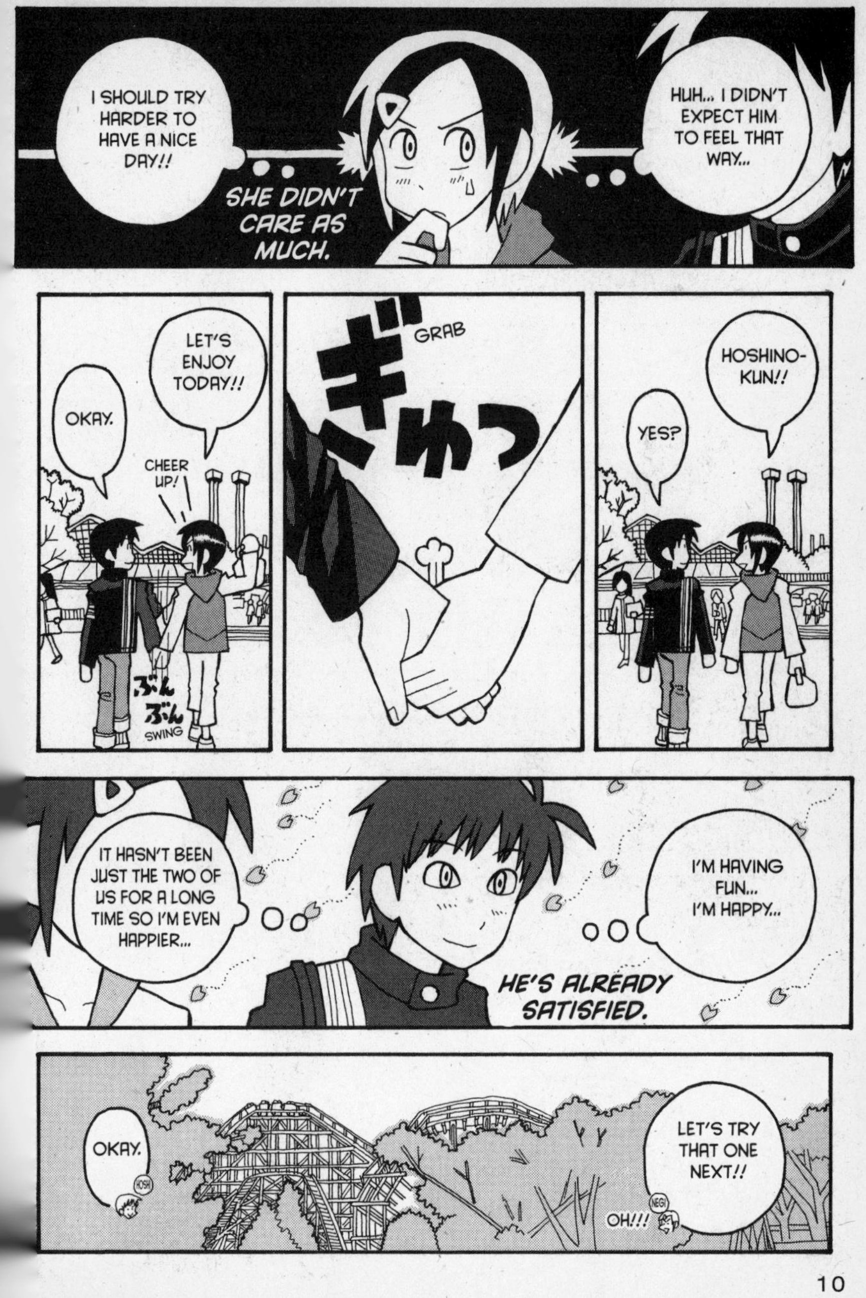
HUH... I DIDN'T EXPECT HIM TO FEEL THAT WAY...
I SHOULD TRY HARDER TO HAVE A NICE DAY!!
SHE DIDN'T CARE AS MUCH.
HOSHINO-KUN!!
YES?
ぎゅっ
GRAB
LET'S ENJOY TODAY!!
OKAY.
CHEER UP!
ぶんぶん
SWING
I'M HAVING FUN... I'M HAPPY...
IT HASN'T BEEN JUST THE TWO OF US FOR A LONG TIME SO I'M EVEN HAPPIER...
HE'S ALREADY SATISFIED.
LET'S TRY THAT ONE NEXT!!
NEGI
OH!!!
OKAY.
HOSH

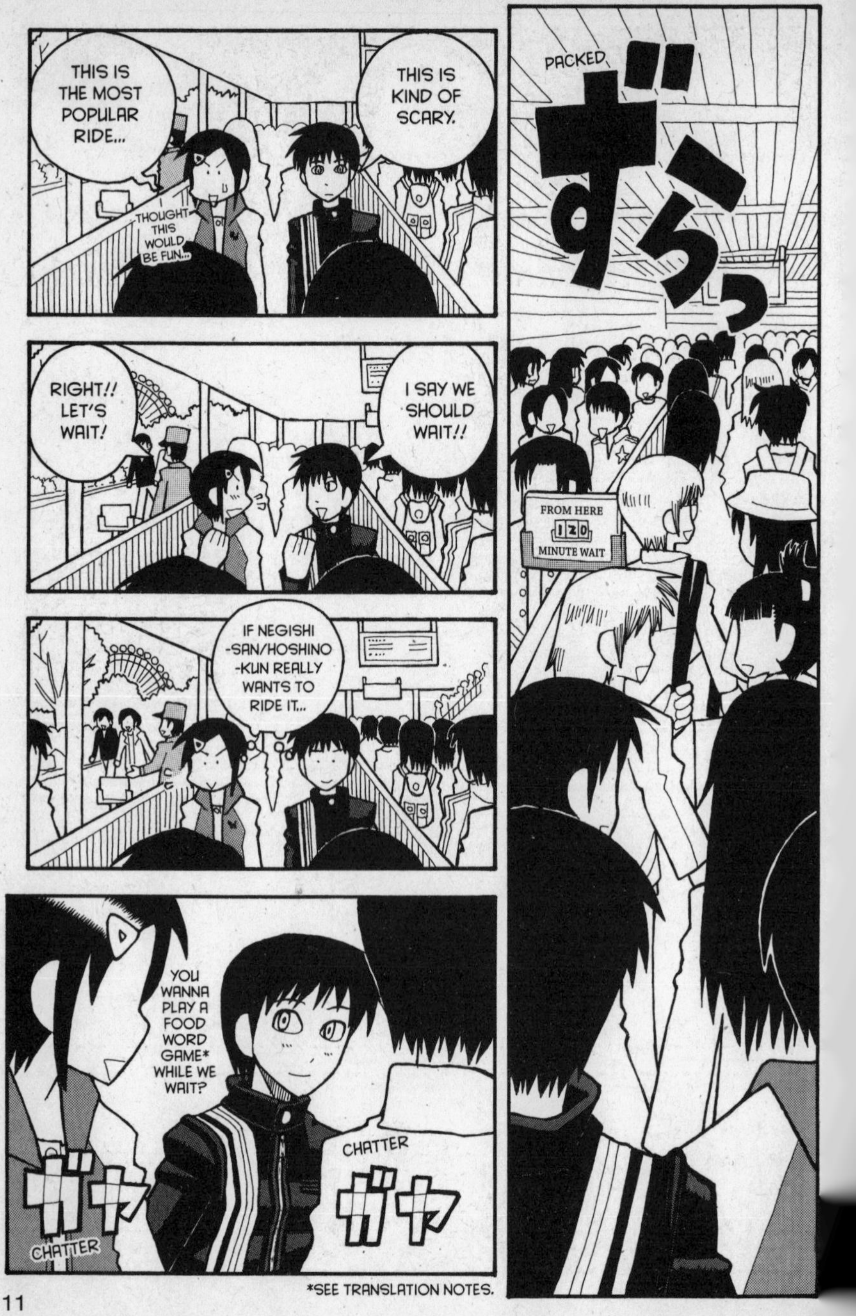
PACKED
ずらっ
FROM HERE
120
MINUTE WAIT
THIS IS KIND OF SCARY.
THIS IS THE MOST POPULAR RIDE...
I THOUGHT THIS WOULD BE FUN...
I SAY WE SHOULD WAIT!!
RIGHT!! LET'S WAIT!
IF NEGISHI-SAN/HOSHINO-KUN REALLY WANTS TO RIDE IT...
YOU WANNA PLAY A FOOD WORD GAME* WHILE WE WAIT?
CHATTER
ガヤ
ガヤ
CHATTER

*SEE TRANSLATION NOTES.

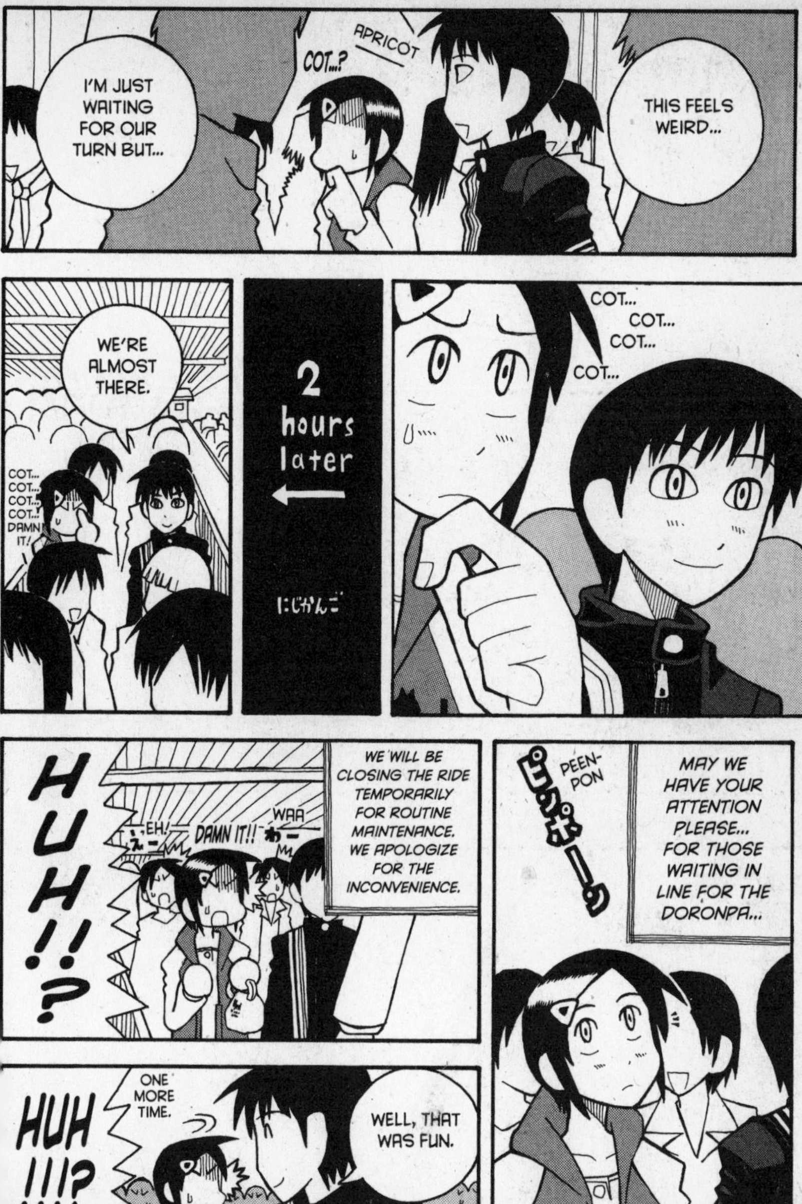
THIS FEELS WEIRD...
APRICOT
COT...?
I'M JUST WAITING FOR OUR TURN BUT...
COT... COT... COT... COT...
2 hours later
にじかんご
WE'RE ALMOST THERE.
COT... COT... COT... COT...! DAMN IT!
PEEN-PON
ピンポーン
MAY WE HAVE YOUR ATTENTION PLEASE... FOR THOSE WAITING IN LINE FOR THE DORONPA...
WE WILL BE CLOSING THE RIDE TEMPORARILY FOR ROUTINE MAINTENANCE. WE APOLOGIZE FOR THE INCONVENIENCE.
WAA
わー
DAMN IT!!
EH!
えー
HUH!!?
WELL, THAT WAS FUN.
ONE MORE TIME.
HUH!!!?

*SEE TRANSLATION NOTES.

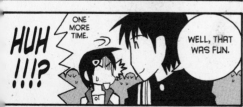

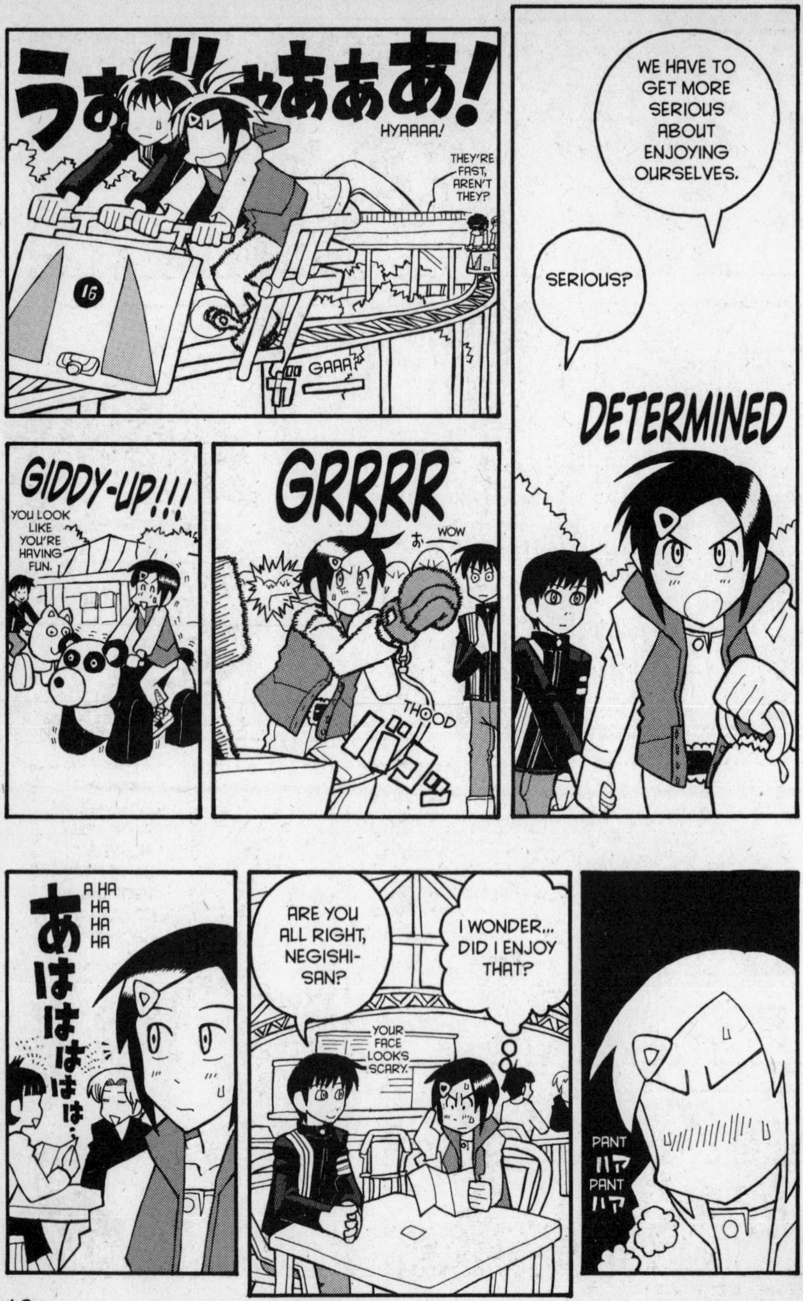

WE HAVE TO GET MORE SERIOUS ABOUT ENJOYING OURSELVES.
SERIOUS?
DETERMINED
HYAAAA!
THEY'RE FAST, AREN'T THEY?
GAAA
GRRRR
WOW
THOOD
GIDDY-UP!!!
YOU LOOK LIKE YOU'RE HAVING FUN.
PANT
ハア
PANT
ハア
I WONDER... DID I ENJOY THAT?
ARE YOU ALL RIGHT, NEGISHI-SAN?
YOUR FACE LOOKS SCARY.
A HA HA HA HA

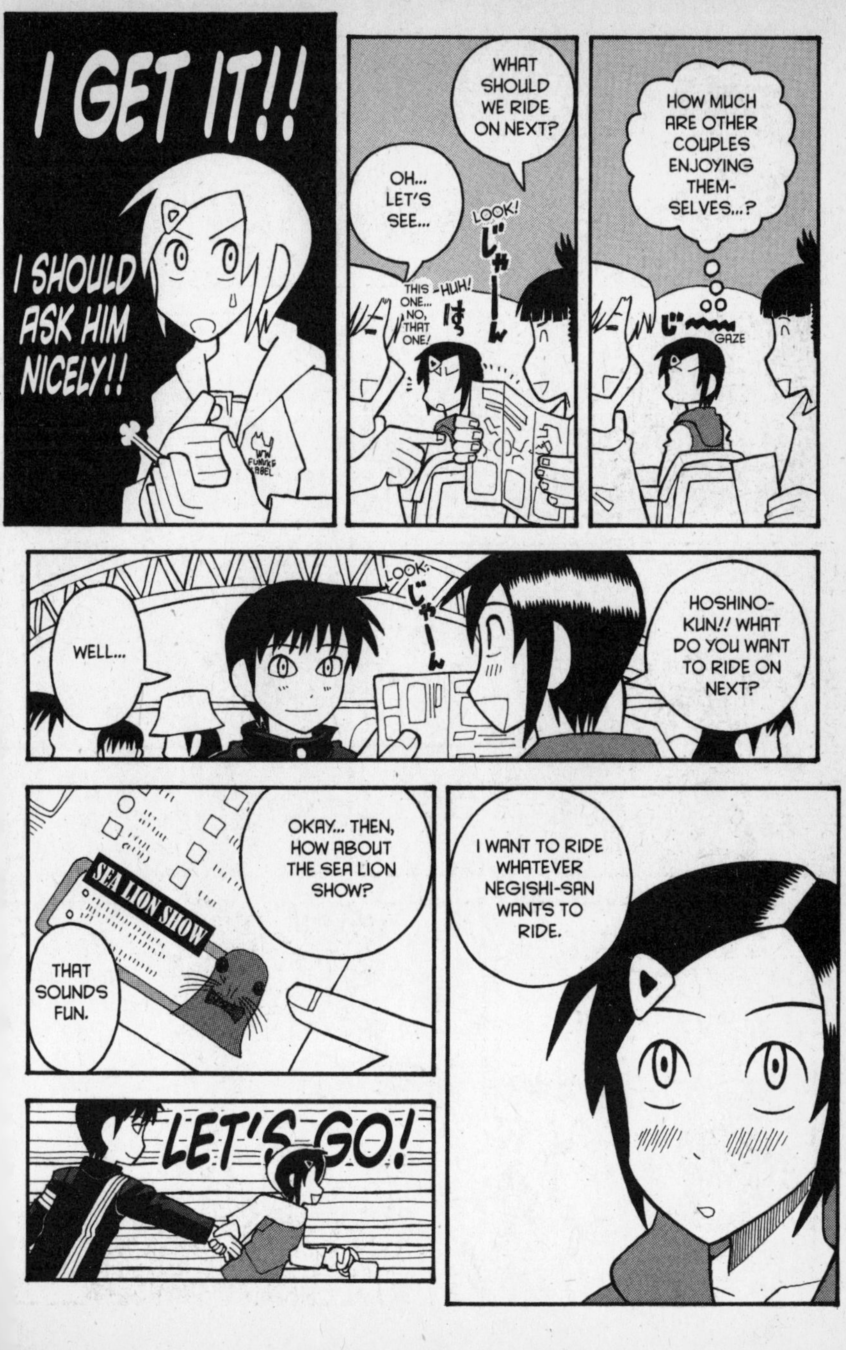
HOW MUCH ARE OTHER COUPLES ENJOYING THEMSELVES...?
じ〜
GAZE
WHAT SHOULD WE RIDE ON NEXT?
LOOK!
じゃーん
OH... LET'S SEE...
HUH!
はっ
THIS ONE... NO, THAT ONE!
I GET IT!!
I SHOULD ASK HIM NICELY!!
HOSHINO-KUN!! WHAT DO YOU WANT TO RIDE ON NEXT?
LOOK!
じゃーん
WELL...
I WANT TO RIDE WHATEVER NEGISHI-SAN WANTS TO RIDE.
OKAY... THEN, HOW ABOUT THE SEA LION SHOW?
SEA LION SHOW
THAT SOUNDS FUN.
LET'S GO!

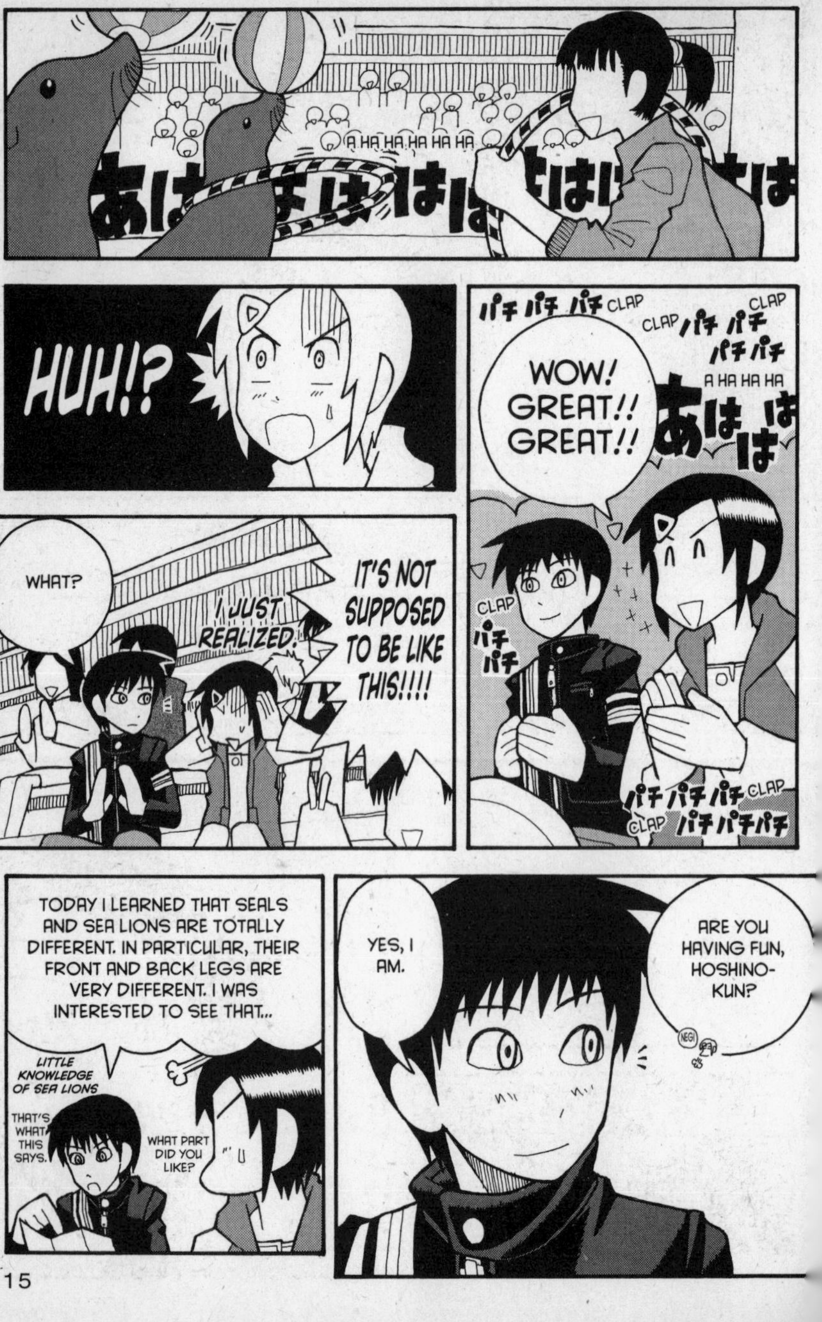
A HA HA HA HA HA
あははははははは
パチ パチ パチ CLAP
CLAP
CLAP パチ パチ
パチ パチ
A HA HA HA
あははは
WOW! GREAT!! GREAT!!
CLAP
パチ パチ
パチ パチ パチ CLAP
CLAP パチ パチ パチ
HUH!?
IT'S NOT SUPPOSED TO BE LIKE THIS!!!!
I JUST REALIZED.
WHAT?
ARE YOU HAVING FUN, HOSHINO-KUN?
NEGI
YES, I AM.
TODAY I LEARNED THAT SEALS AND SEA LIONS ARE TOTALLY DIFFERENT. IN PARTICULAR, THEIR FRONT AND BACK LEGS ARE VERY DIFFERENT. I WAS INTERESTED TO SEE THAT...
LITTLE KNOWLEDGE OF SEA LIONS
WHAT PART DID YOU LIKE?
THAT'S WHAT THIS SAYS.

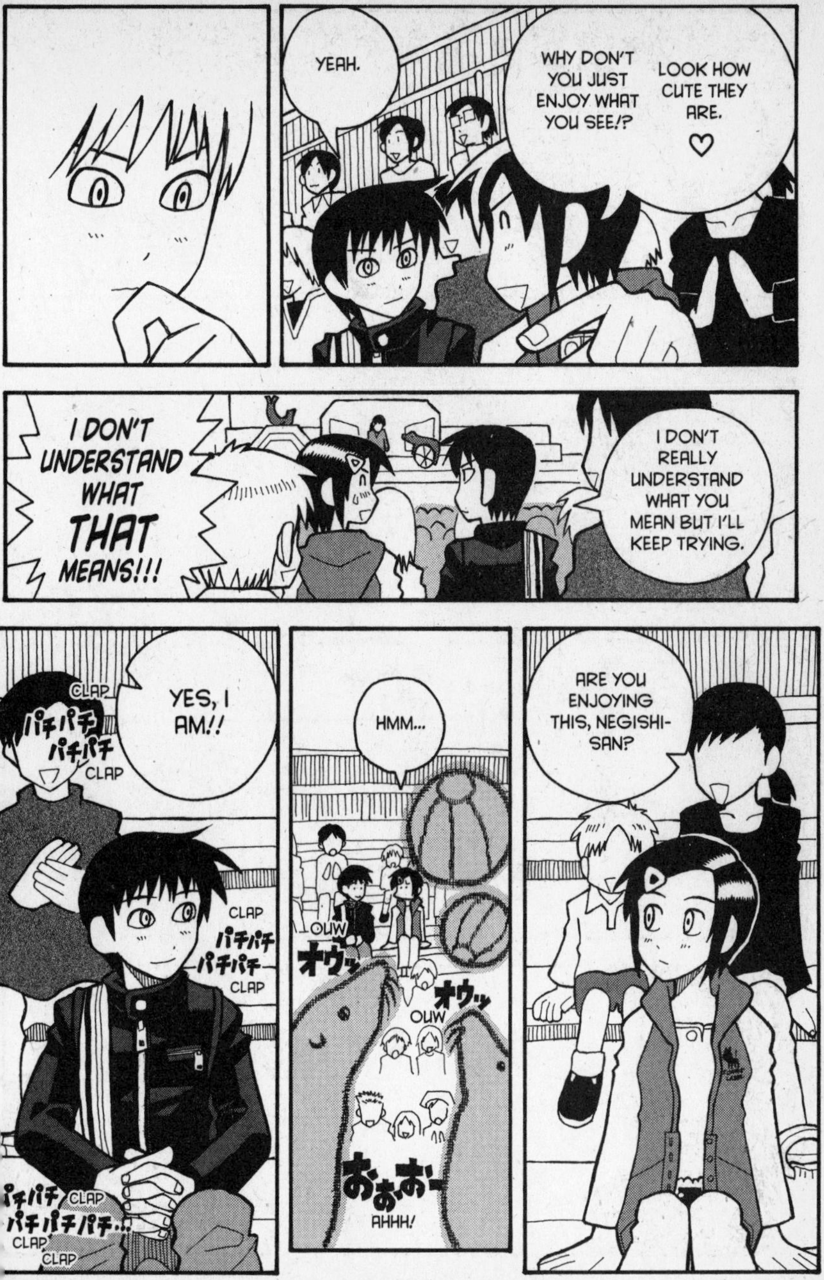
LOOK HOW CUTE THEY ARE. ♡
WHY DON'T YOU JUST ENJOY WHAT YOU SEE!?
YEAH.
I DON'T REALLY UNDERSTAND WHAT YOU MEAN BUT I'LL KEEP TRYING.
I DON'T UNDERSTAND WHAT THAT MEANS!!!
ARE YOU ENJOYING THIS, NEGISHI-SAN?
HMM...
オウッ OUW
オウッ OUW
おぉおー AHHH!
YES, I AM!!
パチパチ CLAP
パチパチ CLAP
CLAP パチパチ
パチパチ CLAP
パチ CLAP
パチパチパチ... CLAP
CLAP

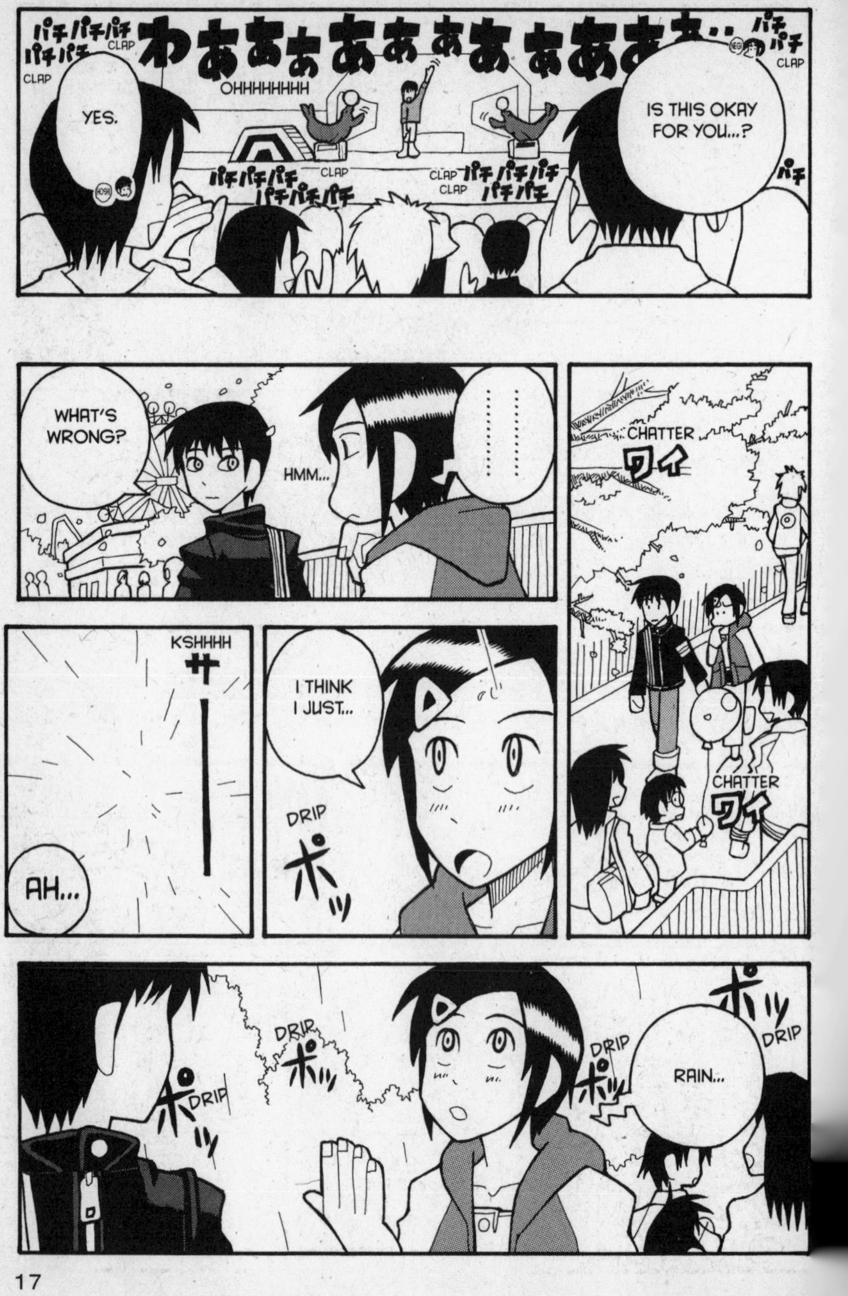
パチパチ
CLAP
IS THIS OKAY FOR YOU...?
パチ
わあああああああああああ…
OHHHHHHHHH
パチパチパチ
パチパチ
CLAP
YES.
CLAP
パチパチパチ
パチパチパチ
CLAP
CLAP CLAP
パチパチパチ
パチパチパチ
CHATTER
ワイ
CHATTER
ワイ
......
HMM...
WHAT'S WRONG?
I THINK I JUST...
DRIP
ポッ
KSHHHH
サー
AH...
ポツ
DRIP
RAIN...
DRIP
ポツ
DRIP
ポツ
ポ
DRIP
ツ

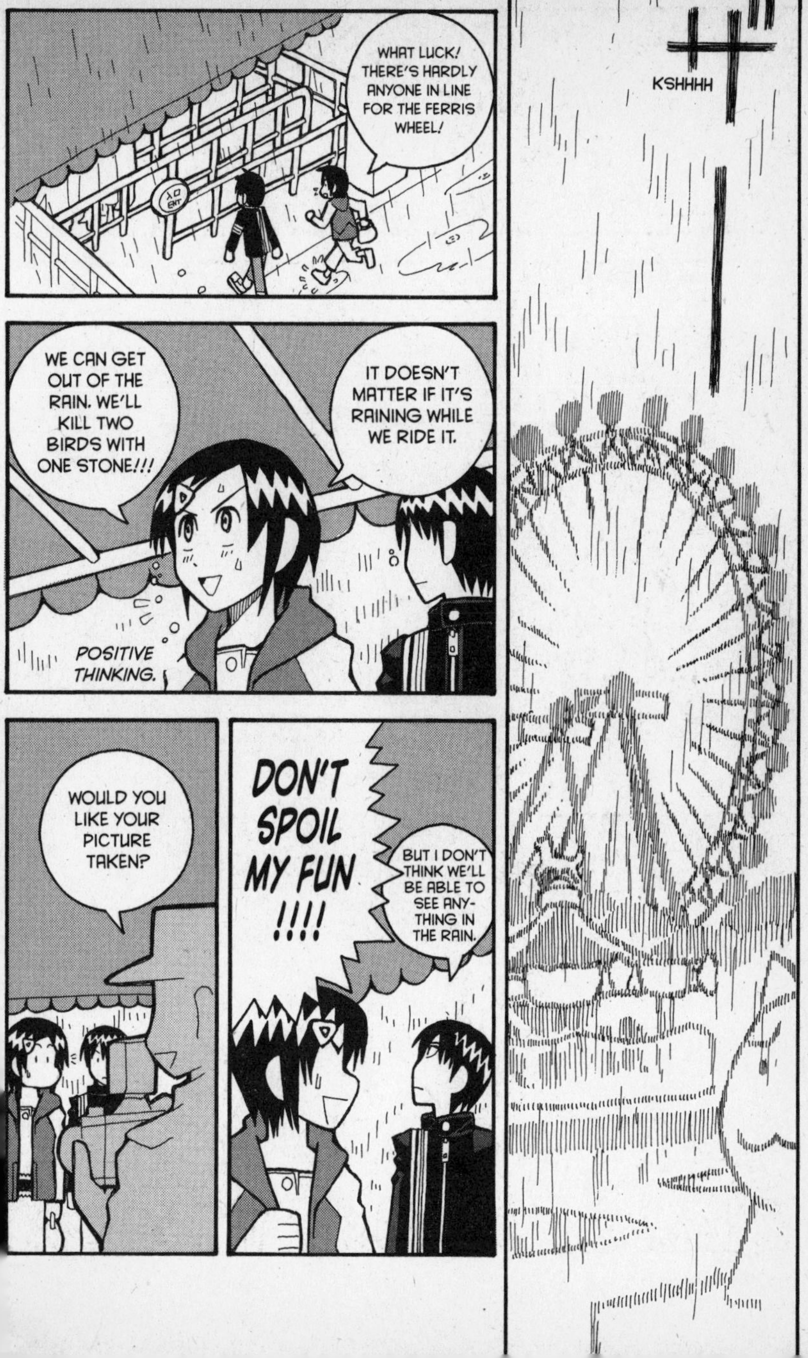
KSHHHH
WHAT LUCK! THERE'S HARDLY ANYONE IN LINE FOR THE FERRIS WHEEL!
IT DOESN'T MATTER IF IT'S RAINING WHILE WE RIDE IT.
WE CAN GET OUT OF THE RAIN. WE'LL KILL TWO BIRDS WITH ONE STONE!!!
POSITIVE THINKING.
BUT I DON'T THINK WE'LL BE ABLE TO SEE ANY-THING IN THE RAIN.
DON'T SPOIL MY FUN !!!!
WOULD YOU LIKE YOUR PICTURE TAKEN?

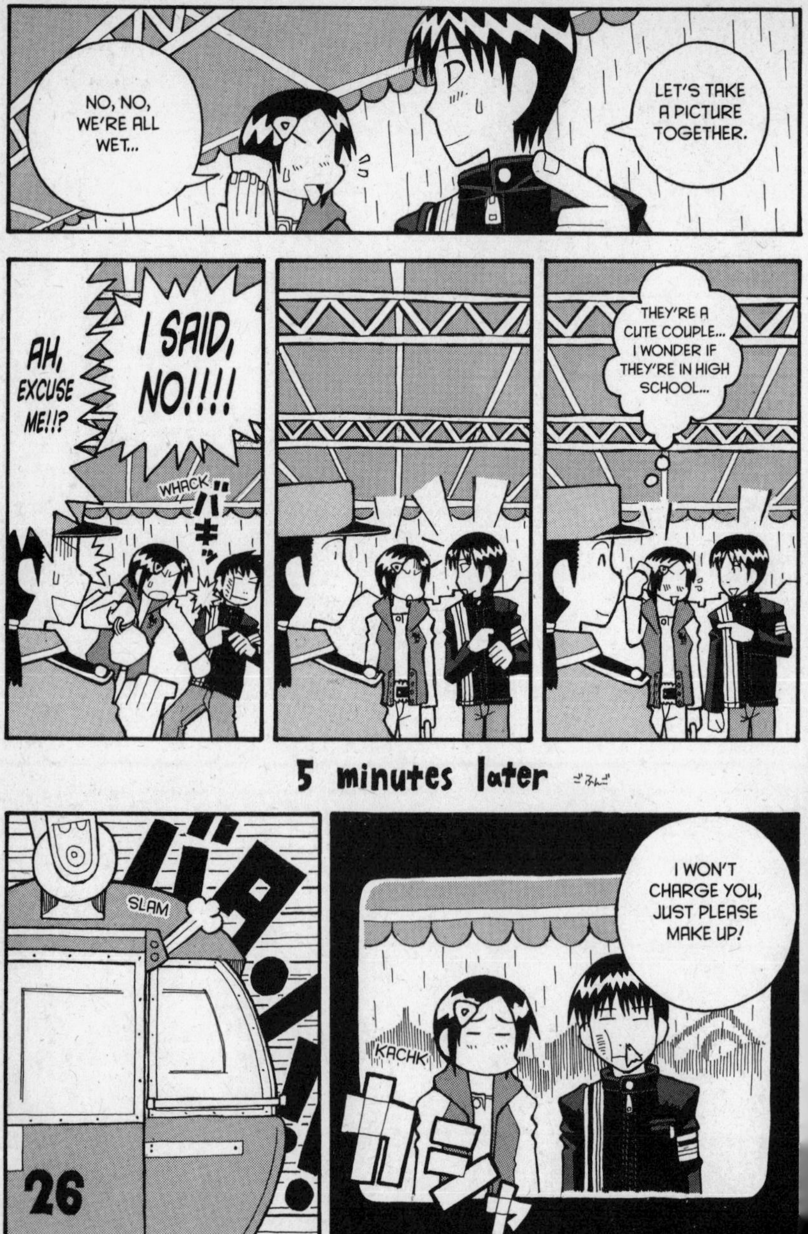
LET'S TAKE A PICTURE TOGETHER.
NO, NO, WE'RE ALL WET...
THEY'RE A CUTE COUPLE... I WONDER IF THEY'RE IN HIGH SCHOOL...
I SAID, NO!!!!
AH, EXCUSE ME!!?
WHACK
バキッ
5 minutes later
I WON'T CHARGE YOU, JUST PLEASE MAKE UP!
KACHK
SLAM
26

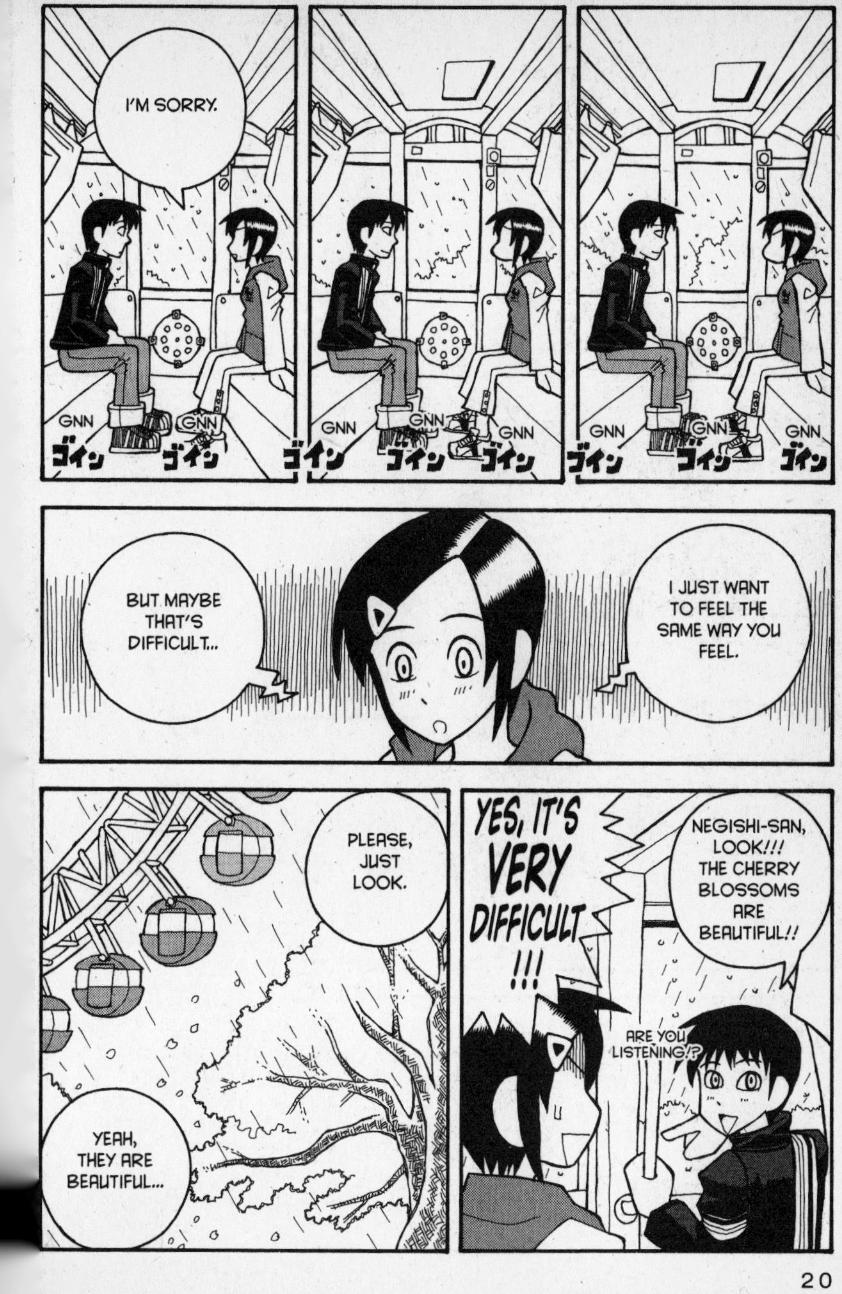
GNN
ゴイン
GNN
ゴイン
GNN
ゴイン
GNN
ゴイン
GNN
ゴイン
GNN
ゴイン
I'M SORRY.
GNN
ゴイン
GNN
ゴイン
ゴイン
I JUST WANT TO FEEL THE SAME WAY YOU FEEL.
BUT MAYBE THAT'S DIFFICULT...
NEGISHI-SAN, LOOK!!! THE CHERRY BLOSSOMS ARE BEAUTIFUL!!
YES, IT'S VERY DIFFICULT !!!
ARE YOU LISTENING!?
PLEASE, JUST LOOK.
YEAH, THEY ARE BEAUTIFUL...

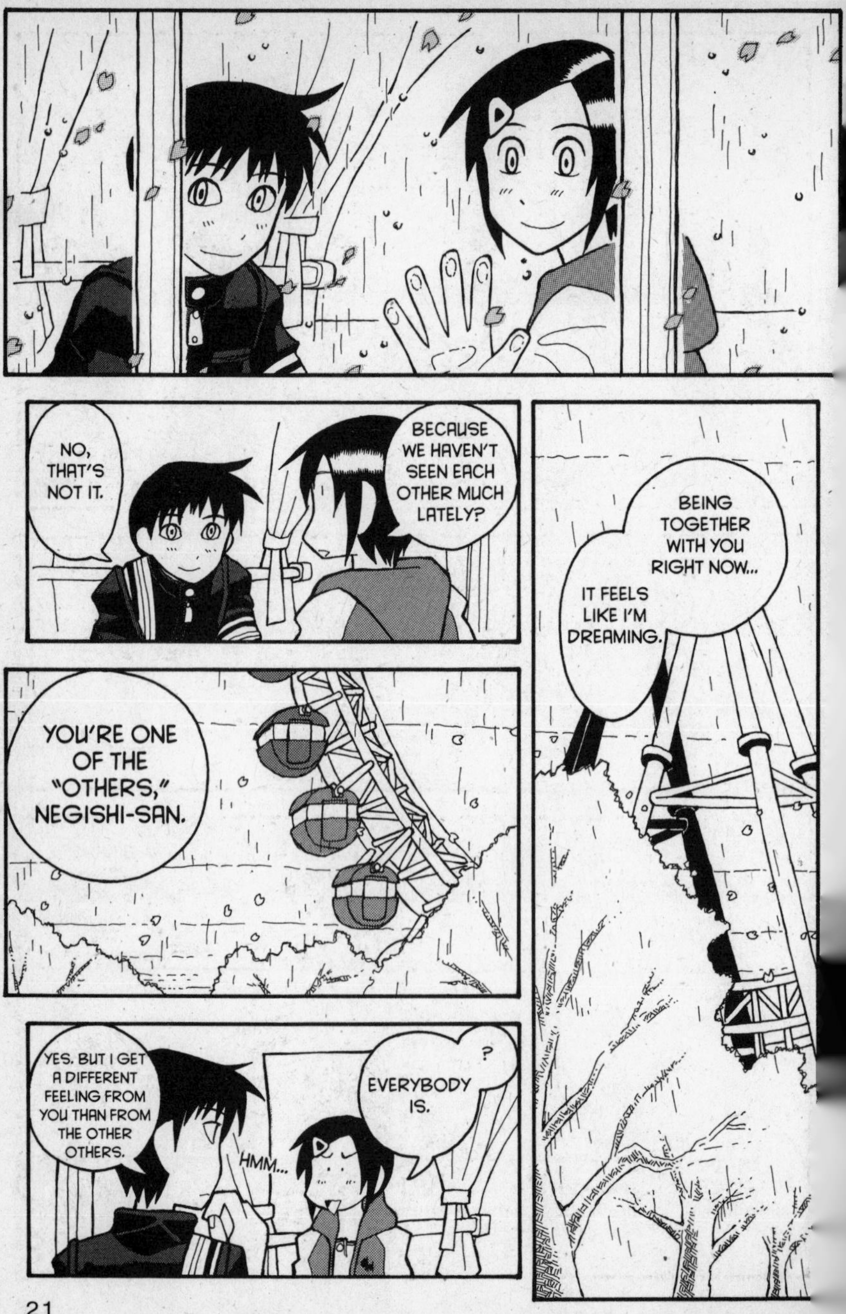
BEING TOGETHER WITH YOU RIGHT NOW...
IT FEELS LIKE I'M DREAMING.
BECAUSE WE HAVEN'T SEEN EACH OTHER MUCH LATELY?
NO, THAT'S NOT IT.
YOU'RE ONE OF THE "OTHERS," NEGISHI-SAN.
?
EVERYBODY IS.
HMM...
YES. BUT I GET A DIFFERENT FEELING FROM YOU THAN FROM THE OTHER OTHERS.

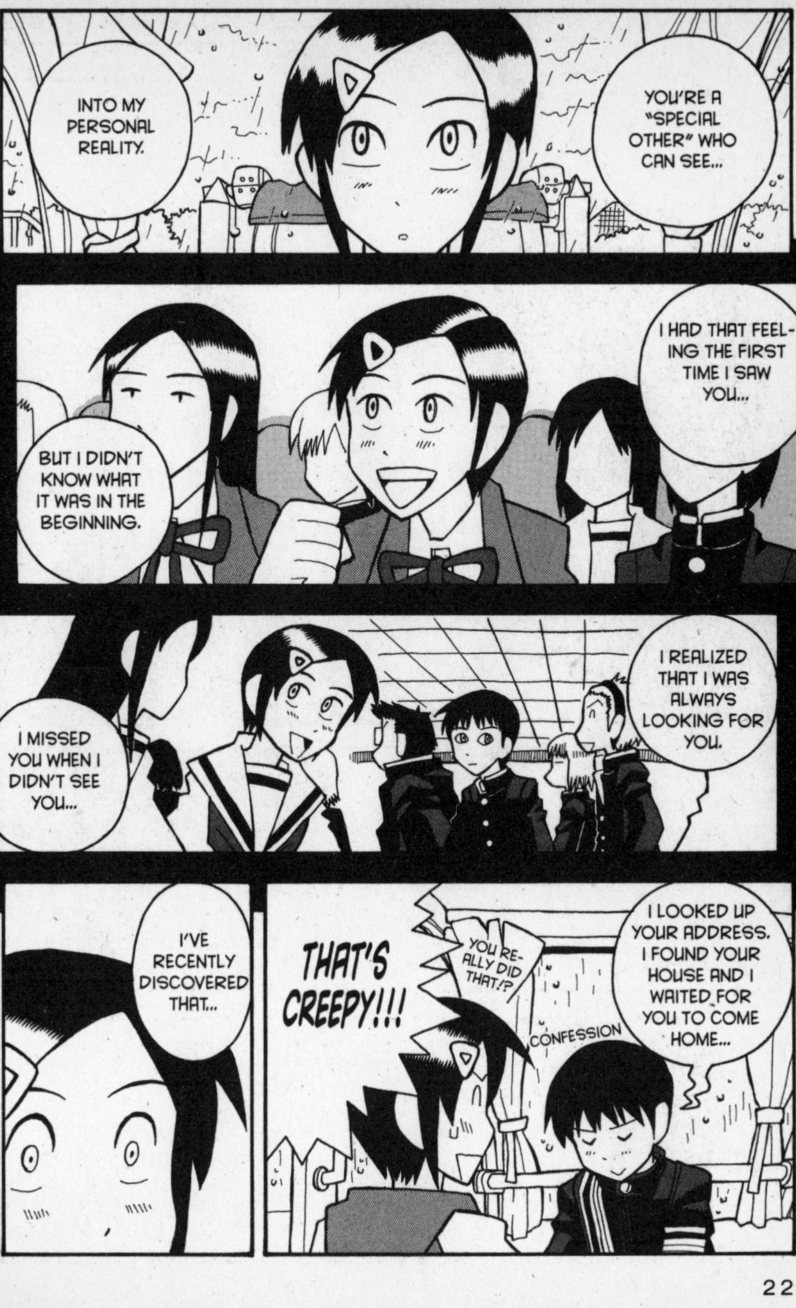
YOU'RE A “SPECIAL OTHER” WHO CAN SEE...
INTO MY PERSONAL REALITY.
I HAD THAT FEELING THE FIRST TIME I SAW YOU...
BUT I DIDN'T KNOW WHAT IT WAS IN THE BEGINNING.
I REALIZED THAT I WAS ALWAYS LOOKING FOR YOU.
I MISSED YOU WHEN I DIDN'T SEE YOU...
I LOOKED UP YOUR ADDRESS. I FOUND YOUR HOUSE AND I WAITED FOR YOU TO COME HOME...
CONFESSION
YOU REALLY DID THAT!?
THAT'S CREEPY!!!
I'VE RECENTLY DISCOVERED THAT...

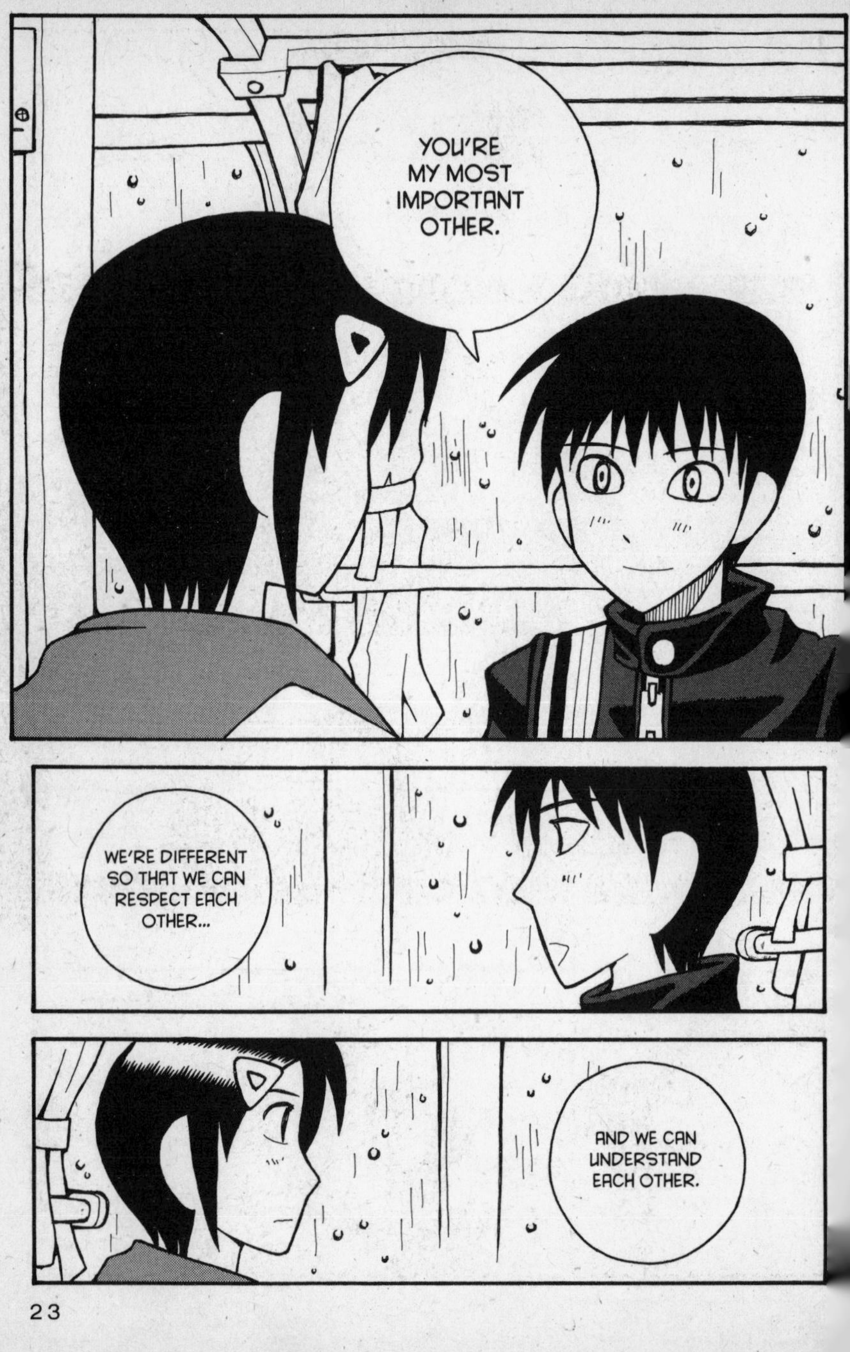
YOU'RE MY MOST IMPORTANT OTHER.
WE'RE DIFFERENT SO THAT WE CAN RESPECT EACH OTHER...
AND WE CAN UNDERSTAND EACH OTHER.

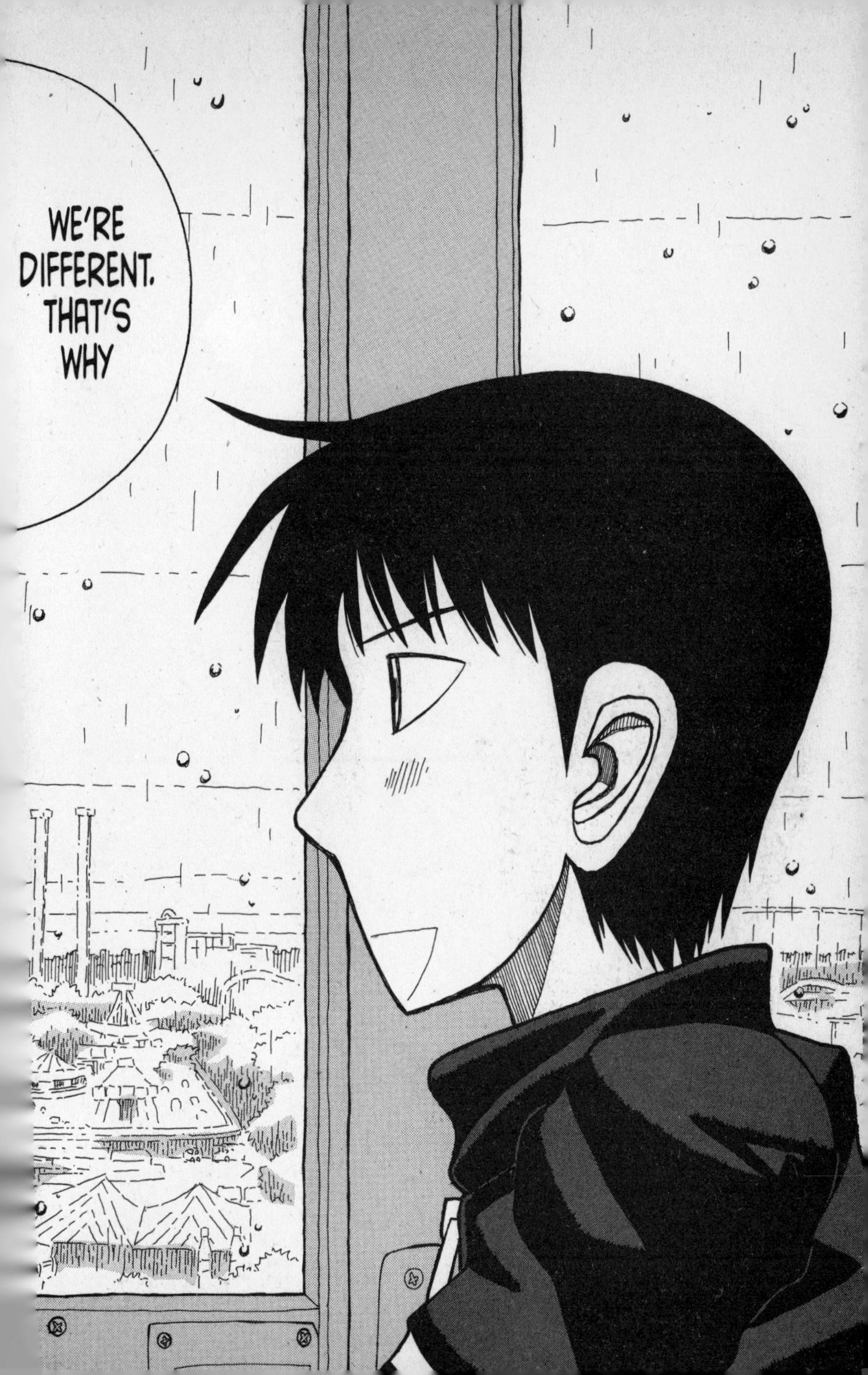
WE'RE DIFFERENT. THAT'S WHY

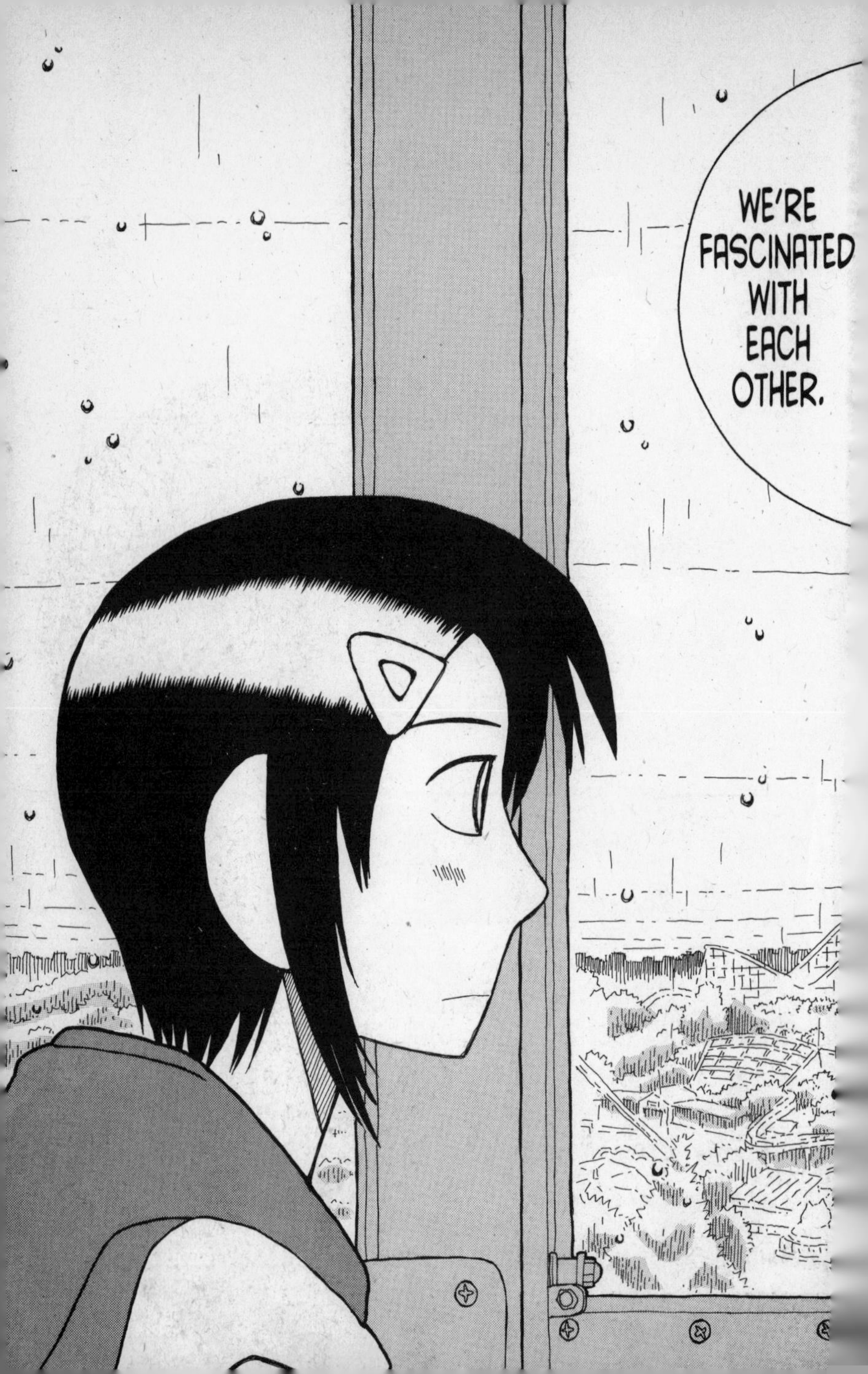
WE'RE FASCINATED WITH EACH OTHER.

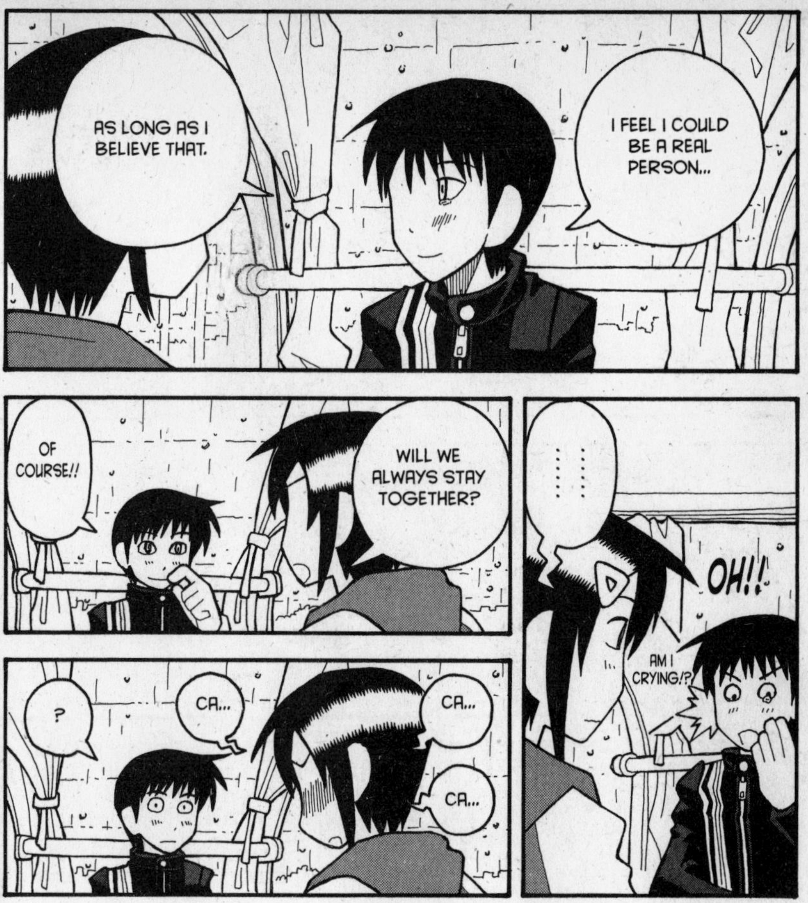
I FEEL I COULD BE A REAL PERSON...
AS LONG AS I BELIEVE THAT.
......
OH!!
AM I CRYING!?
WILL WE ALWAYS STAY TOGETHER?
OF COURSE!!
CA...
CA...
CA...
?

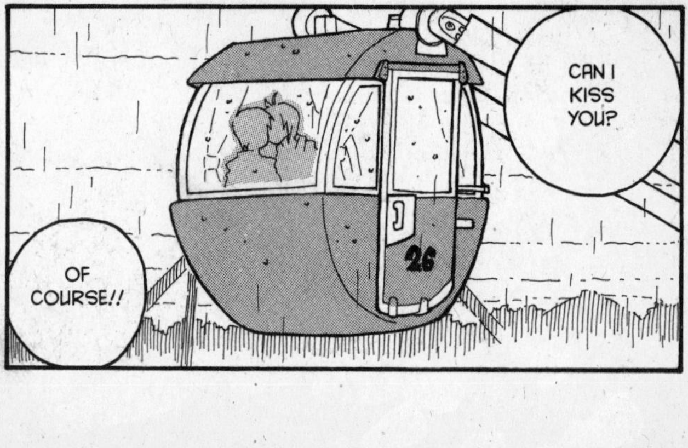
CAN I KISS YOU?
OF COURSE!!
26

TRACK 26 THE END

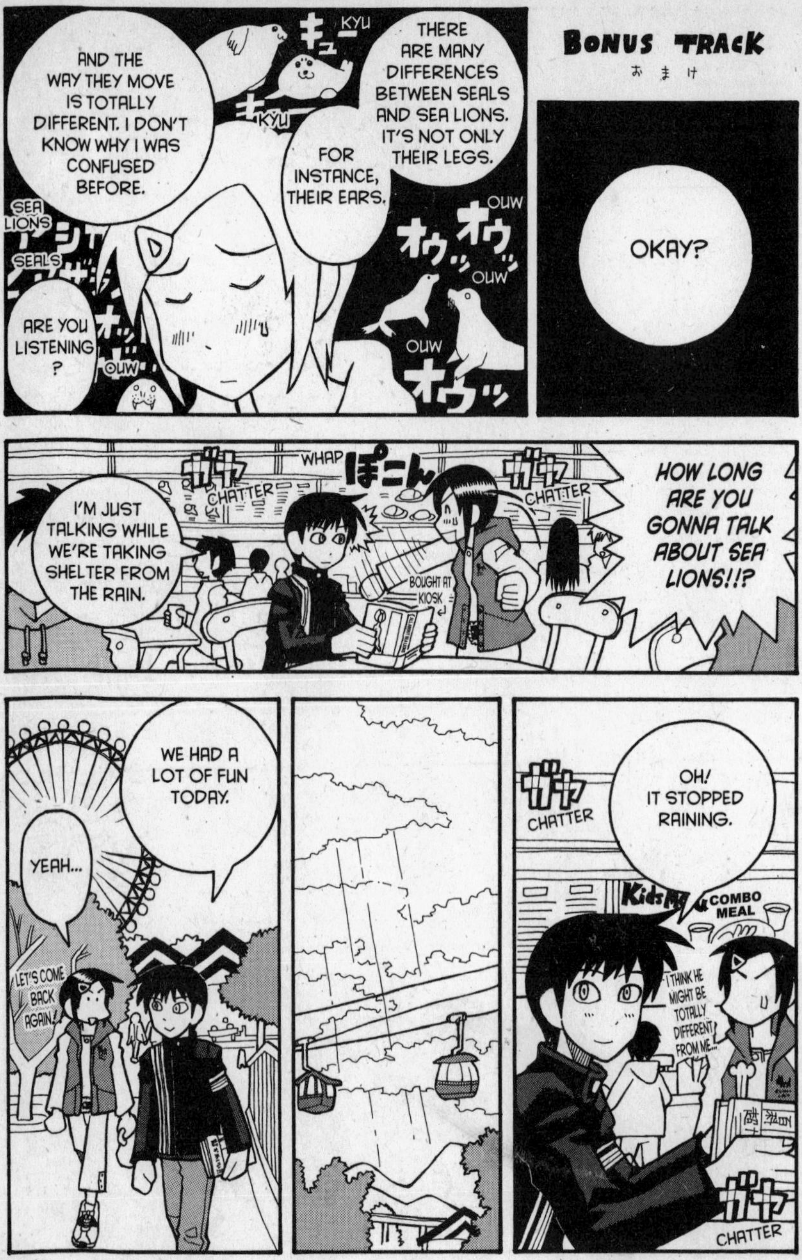
BONUS TRACK
おまけ
OKAY?
THERE ARE MANY DIFFERENCES BETWEEN SEALS AND SEA LIONS. IT'S NOT ONLY THEIR LEGS.
KYU
KYU
FOR INSTANCE, THEIR EARS.
AND THE WAY THEY MOVE IS TOTALLY DIFFERENT. I DON'T KNOW WHY I WAS CONFUSED BEFORE.
OUW
OUW
OUW
SEA LIONS
SEALS
ARE YOU LISTENING?
OUW
HOW LONG ARE YOU GONNA TALK ABOUT SEA LIONS!!?
CHATTER
WHAP
BOUGHT AT KIOSK
CHATTER
I'M JUST TALKING WHILE WE'RE TAKING SHELTER FROM THE RAIN.
OH! IT STOPPED RAINING.
CHATTER
COMBO MEAL
I THINK HE MIGHT BE TOTALLY DIFFERENT FROM ME...
CHATTER
WE HAD A LOT OF FUN TODAY.
YEAH...
LET'S COME BACK AGAIN.

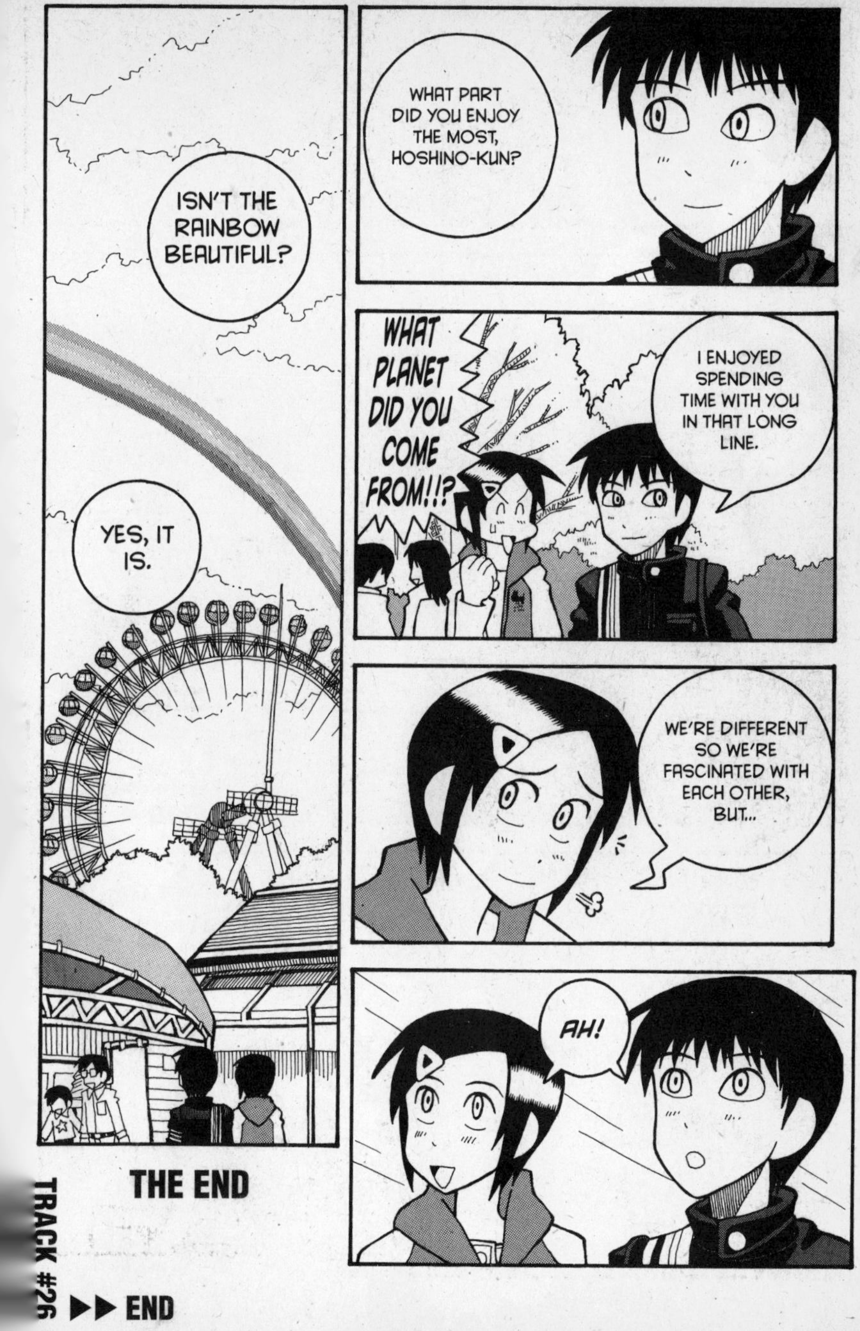
WHAT PART DID YOU ENJOY THE MOST, HOSHINO-KUN?
I ENJOYED SPENDING TIME WITH YOU IN THAT LONG LINE.
WHAT PLANET DID YOU COME FROM!!?
WE'RE DIFFERENT SO WE'RE FASCINATED WITH EACH OTHER, BUT...
AH!
ISN'T THE RAINBOW BEAUTIFUL?
YES, IT IS.

THE END

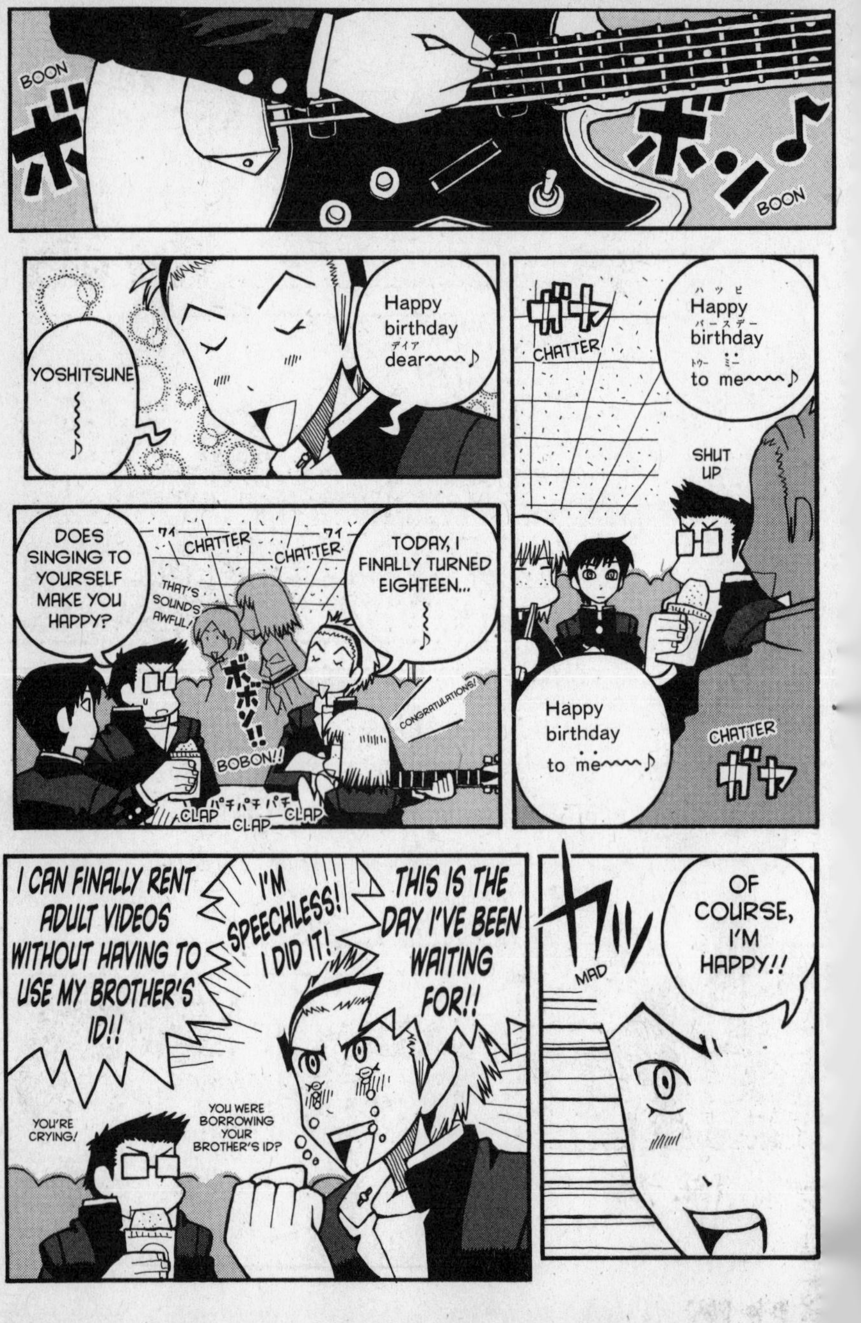

ボン♪
BOON
BOON
ボ
ハッピ Happy バースデー birthday トゥー ミー to me~♪
ガヤ
CHATTER
SHUT UP
Happy birthday to me~♪
CHATTER
ガヤ
Happy birthday デイア dear~♪
YOSHITSUNE~♪
TODAY, I FINALLY TURNED EIGHTEEN...~♪
ワイ
CHATTER
CHATTER
ワイ
DOES SINGING TO YOURSELF MAKE YOU HAPPY?
THAT'S SOUNDS AWFUL!
CONGRATULATIONS!
ボボン!!
BOBON!!
パチパチパチ
CLAP
CLAP
CLAP
OF COURSE, I'M HAPPY!!
カッ
MAD
THIS IS THE DAY I'VE BEEN WAITING FOR!!
I'M SPEECHLESS! I DID IT!
I CAN FINALLY RENT ADULT VIDEOS WITHOUT HAVING TO USE MY BROTHER'S ID!!
YOU WERE BORROWING YOUR BROTHER'S ID?
YOU'RE CRYING!

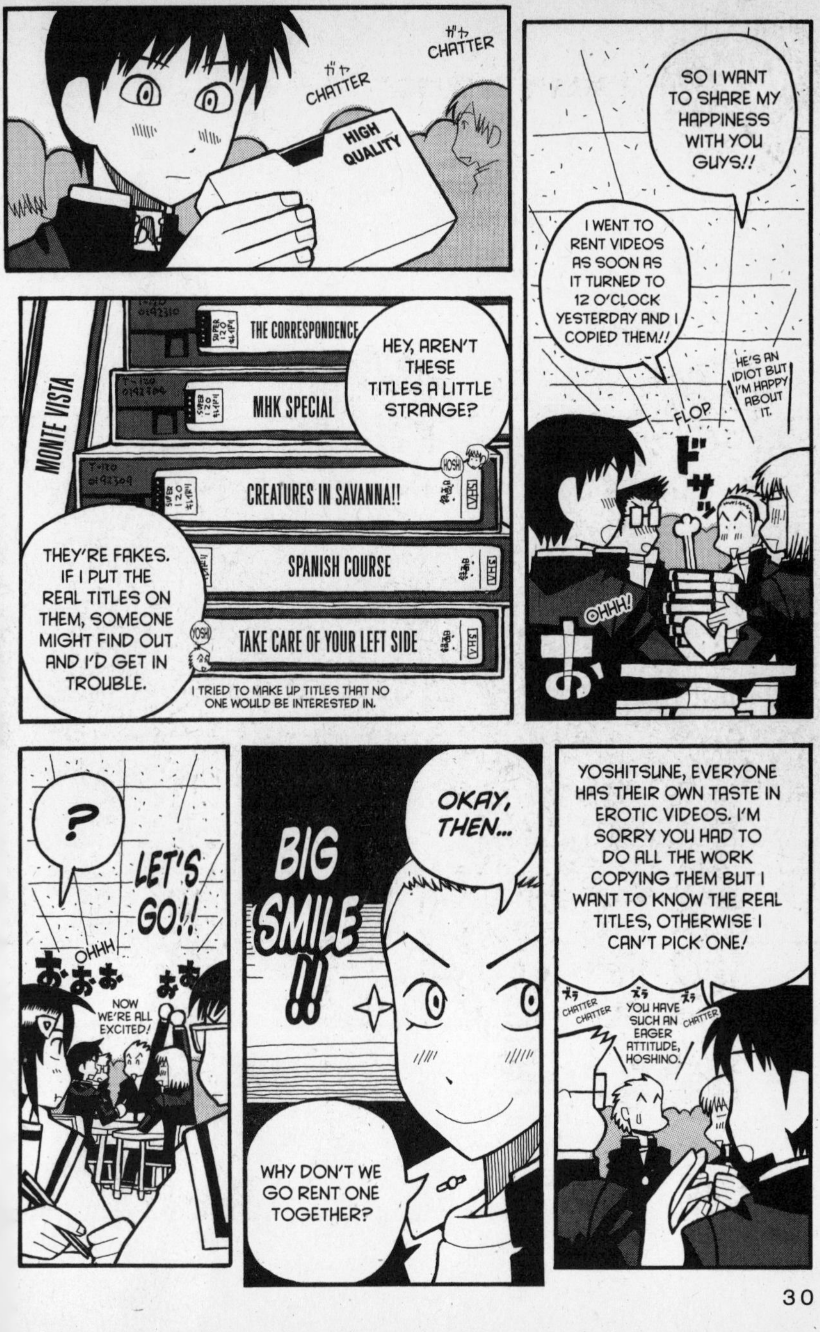
SO I WANT TO SHARE MY HAPPINESS WITH YOU GUYS!!
I WENT TO RENT VIDEOS AS SOON AS IT TURNED TO 12 O'CLOCK YESTERDAY AND I COPIED THEM!!
HE'S AN IDIOT BUT I'M HAPPY ABOUT IT.
FLOP
ドサッ
OHHH!
おぉ
ガヤ
CHATTER
ガヤ
CHATTER
HIGH QUALITY
HEY, AREN'T THESE TITLES A LITTLE STRANGE?
HOSHI
THE CORRESPONDENCE
MHK SPECIAL
MONTE VISTA
CREATURES IN SAVANNA!!
SPANISH COURSE
TAKE CARE OF YOUR LEFT SIDE
THEY'RE FAKES. IF I PUT THE REAL TITLES ON THEM, SOMEONE MIGHT FIND OUT AND I'D GET IN TROUBLE.
YOSHI
I TRIED TO MAKE UP TITLES THAT NO ONE WOULD BE INTERESTED IN.
YOSHITSUNE, EVERYONE HAS THEIR OWN TASTE IN EROTIC VIDEOS. I'M SORRY YOU HAD TO DO ALL THE WORK COPYING THEM BUT I WANT TO KNOW THE REAL TITLES, OTHERWISE I CAN'T PICK ONE!
ズラ
CHATTER
ズラ
YOU HAVE SUCH AN EAGER ATTITUDE, HOSHINO.
ズラ
CHATTER
OKAY, THEN...
BIG SMILE!!
WHY DON'T WE GO RENT ONE TOGETHER?
?
LET'S GO!!
OHHH
おおお
おお
NOW WE'RE ALL EXCITED!

TRACK #27 A MAN'S FEELINGS

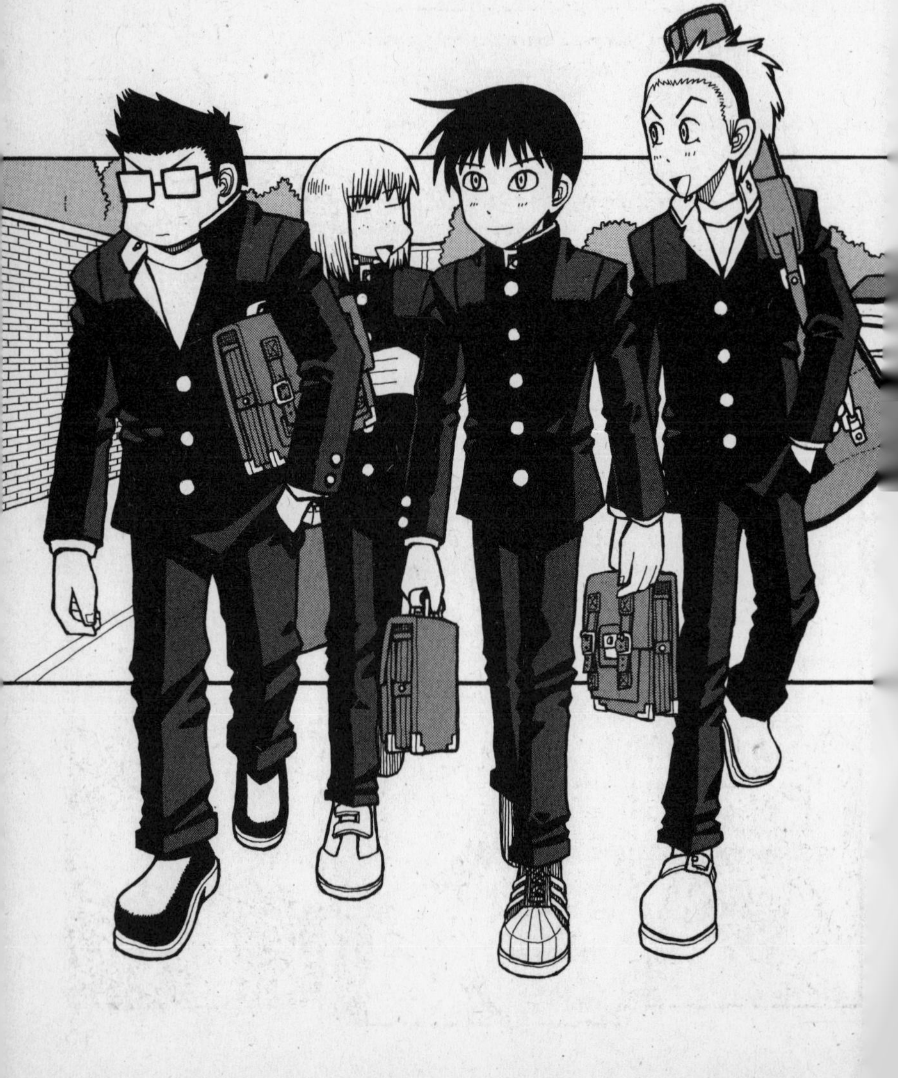

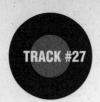

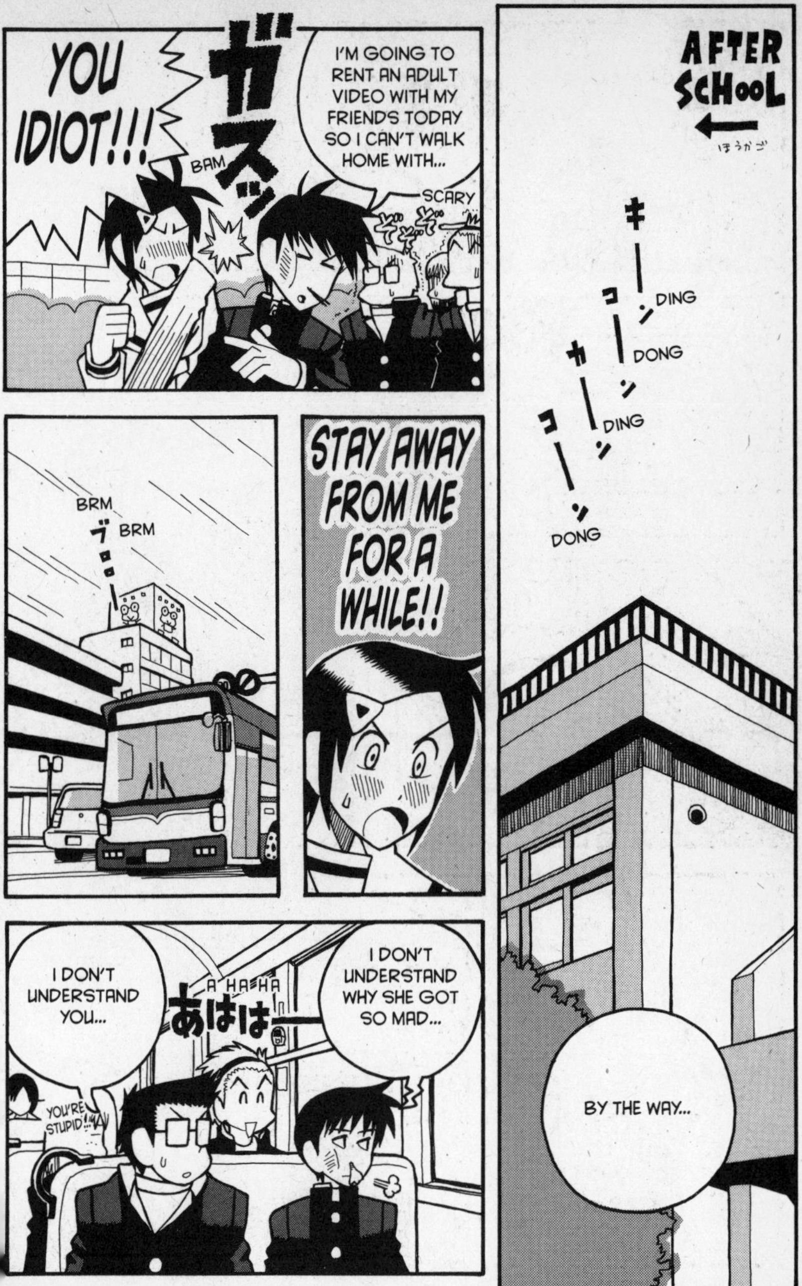
AFTER SCHOOL
ほうかご
キーンコーンカーンコーン
DING
DONG
DING
DONG
BY THE WAY...
I'M GOING TO RENT AN ADULT VIDEO WITH MY FRIENDS TODAY SO I CAN'T WALK HOME WITH...
SCARY
ガスッ
BAM
YOU IDIOT!!!
STAY AWAY FROM ME FOR A WHILE!!
ブロロー
BRM
BRM
I DON'T UNDERSTAND WHY SHE GOT SO MAD...
あはは
A HA HA
I DON'T UNDERSTAND YOU...
YOU'RE STUPID!...

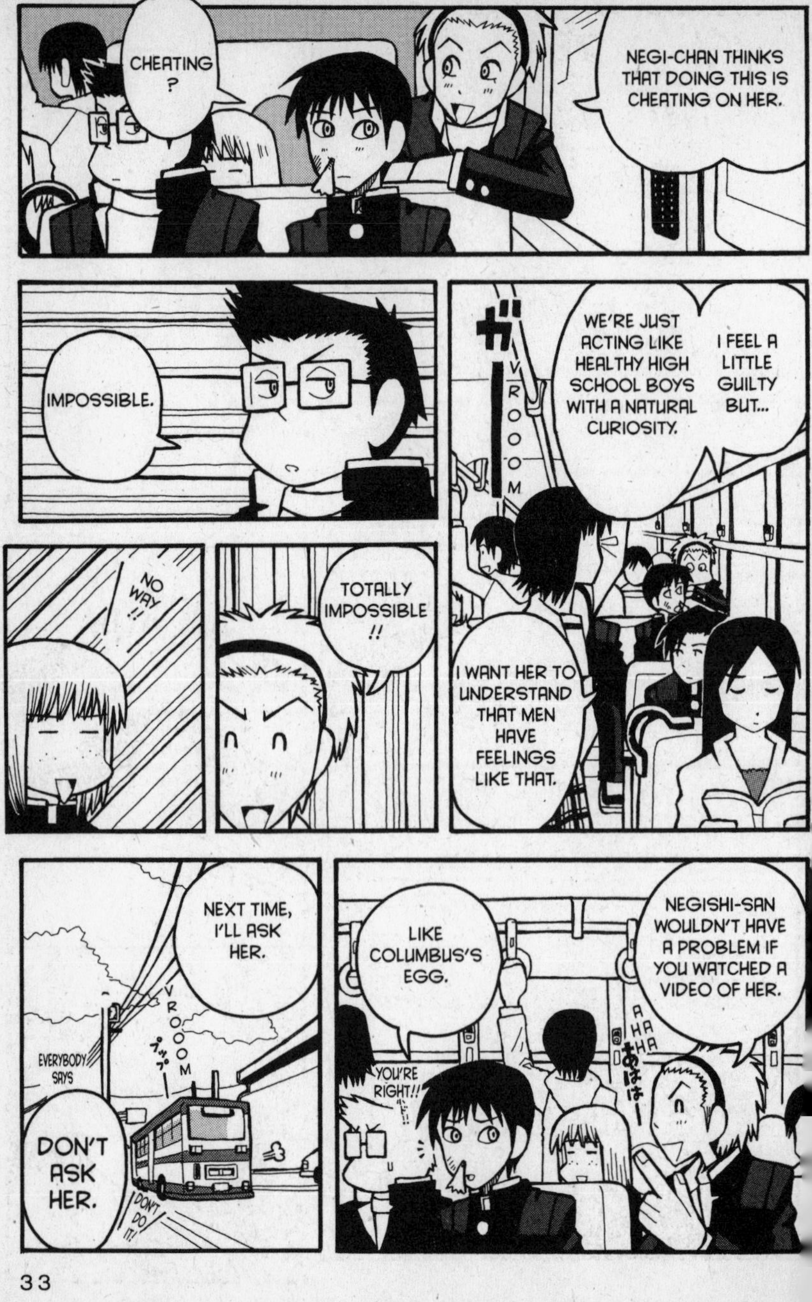
NEGI-CHAN THINKS THAT DOING THIS IS CHEATING ON HER.
CHEATING ?
I FEEL A LITTLE GUILTY BUT...
WE'RE JUST ACTING LIKE HEALTHY HIGH SCHOOL BOYS WITH A NATURAL CURIOSITY.
ガー
VROOOOM
I WANT HER TO UNDERSTAND THAT MEN HAVE FEELINGS LIKE THAT.
IMPOSSIBLE.
TOTALLY IMPOSSIBLE !!
NO WAY !!
NEGISHI-SAN WOULDN'T HAVE A PROBLEM IF YOU WATCHED A VIDEO OF HER.
AHAHA
あはは—
LIKE COLUMBUS'S EGG.
YOU'RE RIGHT!!
NEXT TIME, I'LL ASK HER.
VROOOM
プップー
EVERYBODY SAYS
DON'T ASK HER.
DON'T DO IT!

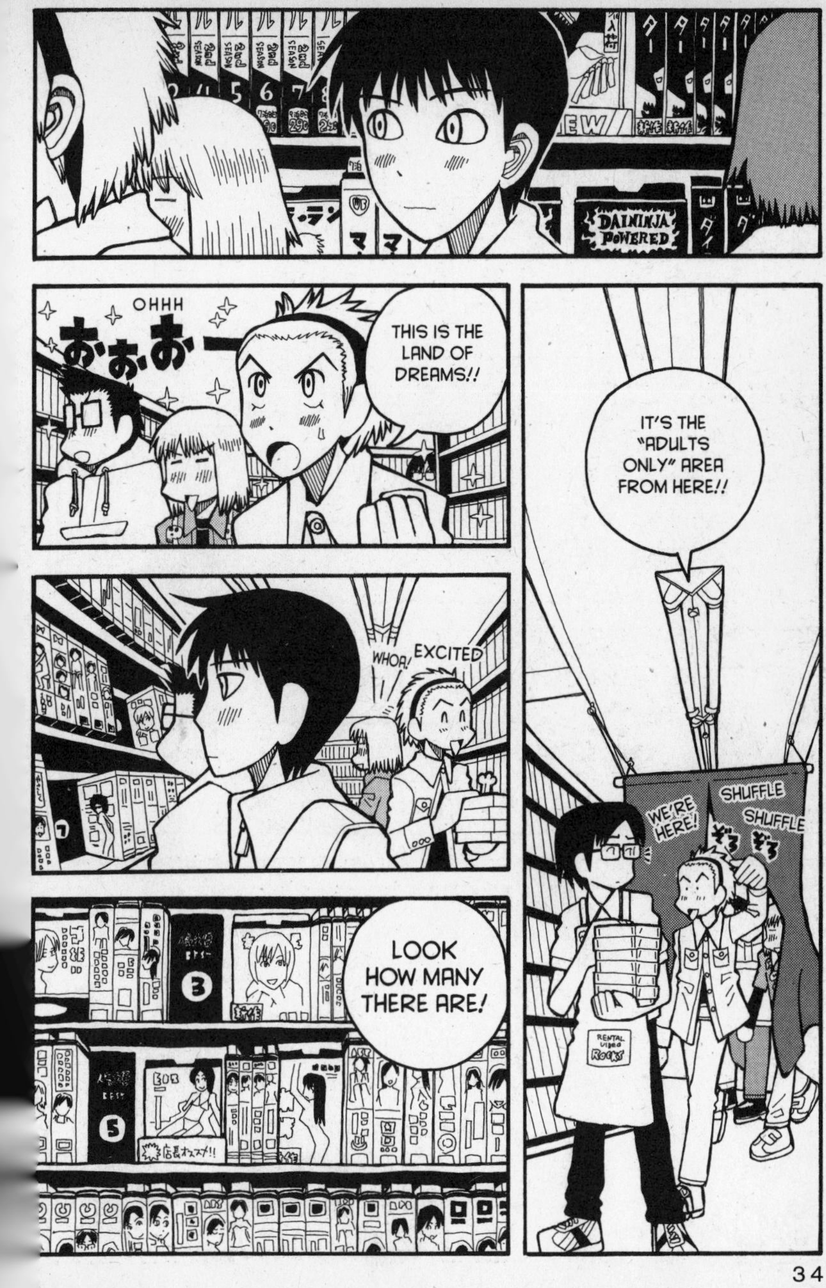
DAININJA POWERED
IT'S THE "ADULTS ONLY" AREA FROM HERE!!
WE'RE HERE!
SHUFFLE SHUFFLE
ぞろぞろ
OHHH
おおおー
THIS IS THE LAND OF DREAMS!!
EXCITED
WHOA!
LOOK HOW MANY THERE ARE!
RENTAL VIDEO ROCKS

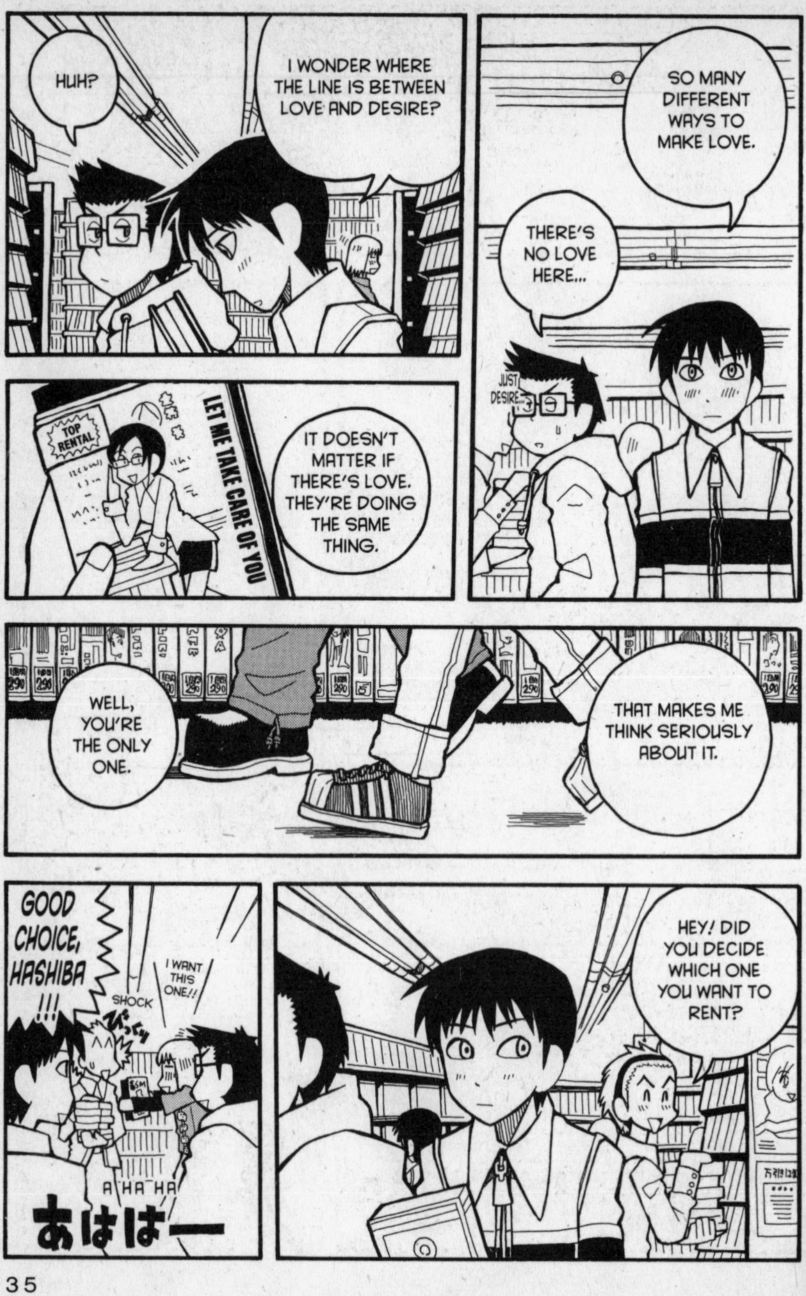
SO MANY DIFFERENT WAYS TO MAKE LOVE.
THERE'S NO LOVE HERE...
JUST DESIRE...
I WONDER WHERE THE LINE IS BETWEEN LOVE AND DESIRE?
HUH?
IT DOESN'T MATTER IF THERE'S LOVE. THEY'RE DOING THE SAME THING.
LET ME TAKE CARE OF YOU
TOP RENTAL
THAT MAKES ME THINK SERIOUSLY ABOUT IT.
WELL, YOU'RE THE ONLY ONE.
HEY! DID YOU DECIDE WHICH ONE YOU WANT TO RENT?
I WANT THIS ONE!!
SHOCK
GOOD CHOICE, HASHIBA!!!
A HA HA
あははー

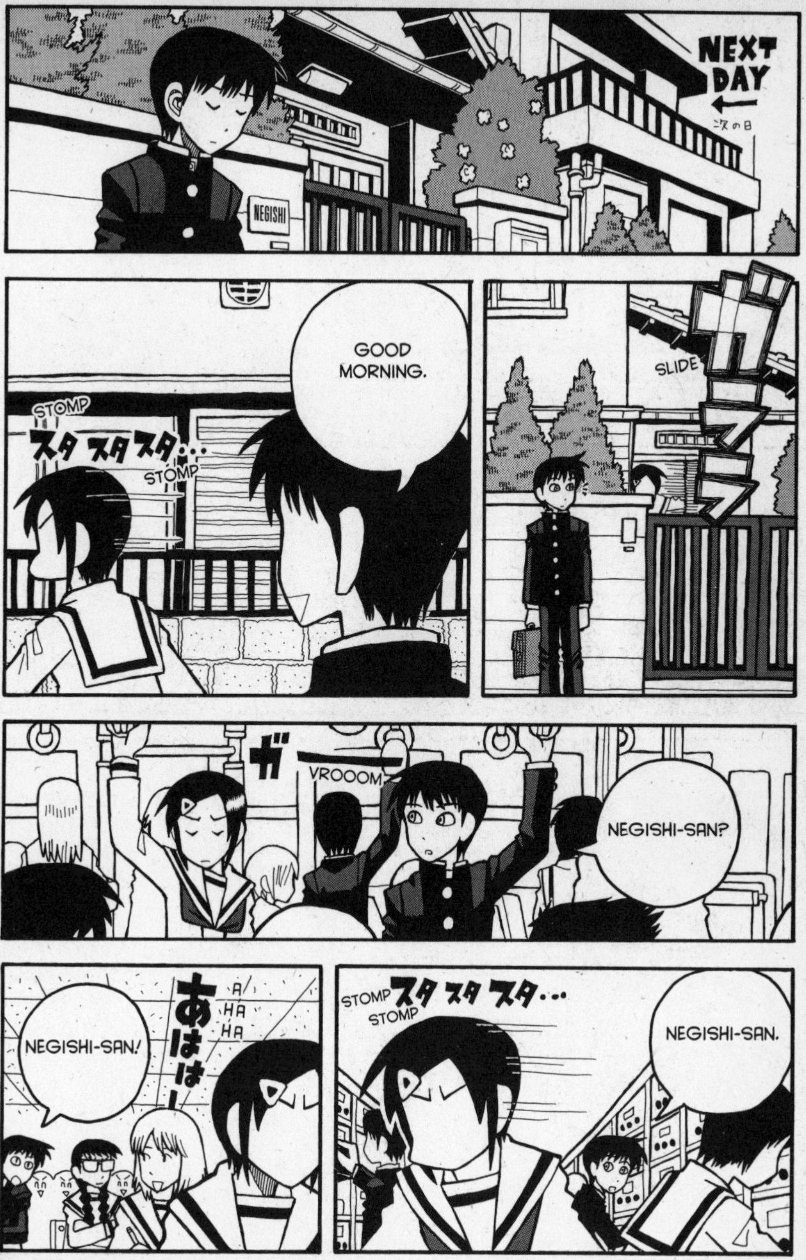
NEXT DAY
次の日
NEGISHI
SLIDE
GOOD MORNING.
スタ スタ スタ...
STOMP
STOMP
NEGISHI-SAN?
ガー
VROOOM
NEGISHI-SAN.
スタ スタ スタ...
STOMP
STOMP
あはは
A HA HA
NEGISHI-SAN!

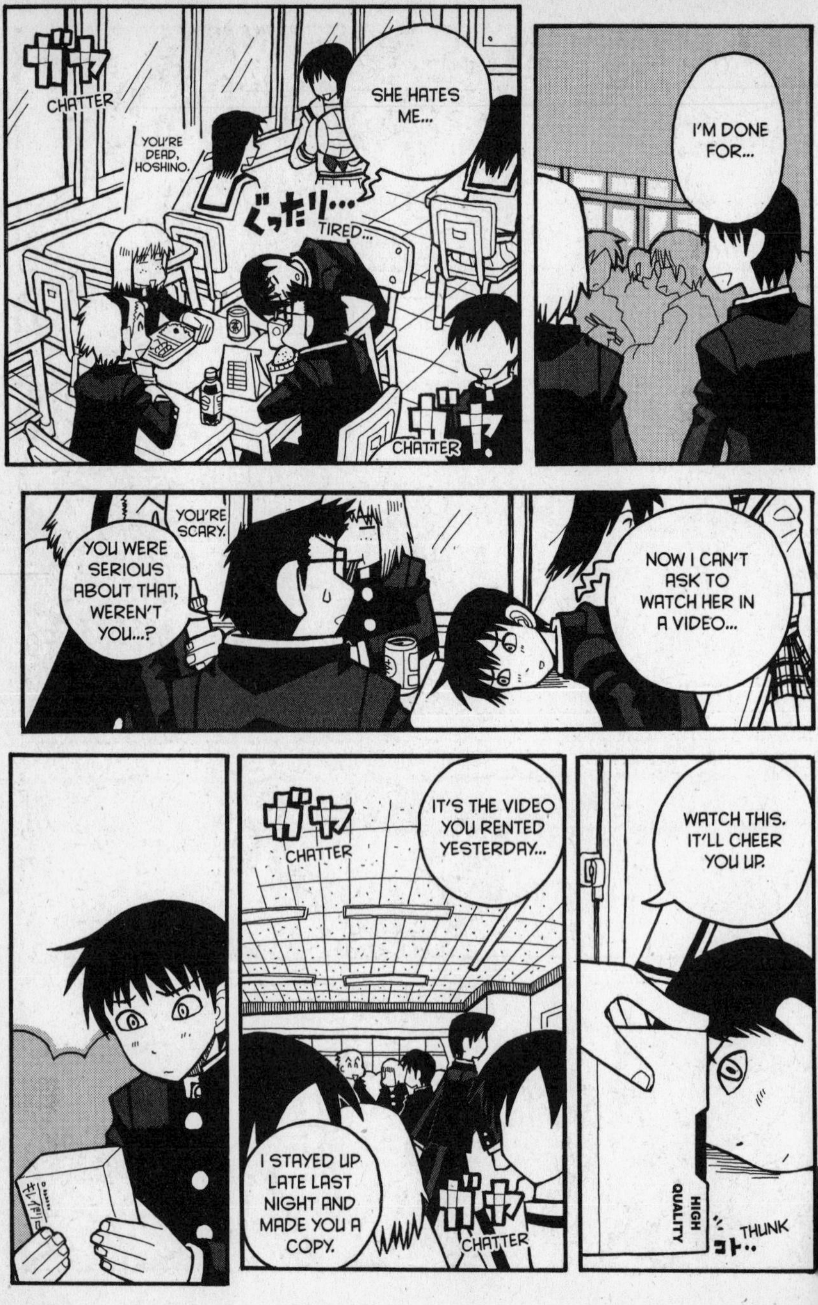
I'M DONE FOR...
SHE HATES ME...
ガヤ
CHATTER
YOU'RE DEAD, HOSHINO.
ぐったり…
TIRED...
ガヤ
CHATTER
NOW I CAN'T ASK TO WATCH HER IN A VIDEO...
YOU'RE SCARY.
YOU WERE SERIOUS ABOUT THAT, WEREN'T YOU...?
WATCH THIS. IT'LL CHEER YOU UP.
HIGH QUALITY
コト‥
THUNK
IT'S THE VIDEO YOU RENTED YESTERDAY...
ガヤ
CHATTER
I STAYED UP LATE LAST NIGHT AND MADE YOU A COPY.
ガヤ
CHATTER

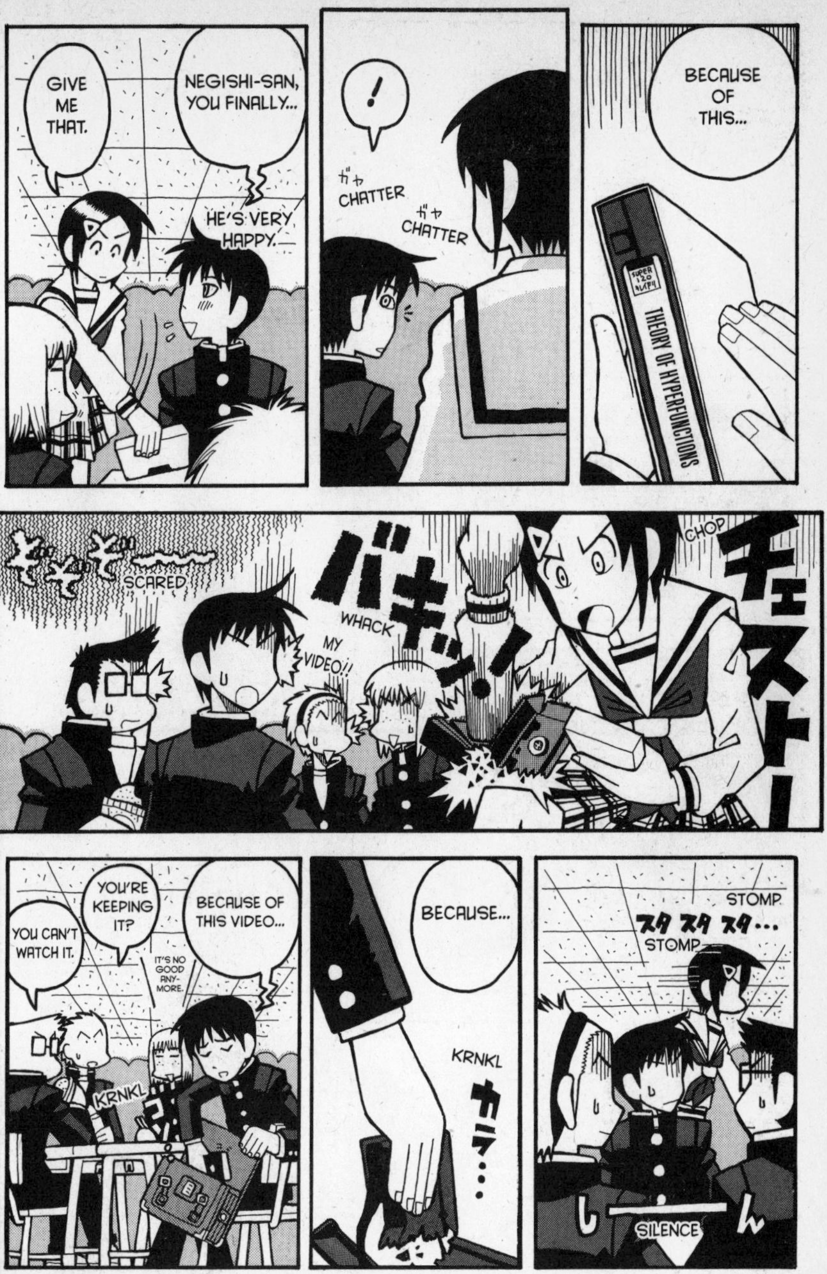
BECAUSE OF THIS...
THEORY OF HYPERFUNCTIONS
!
ガヤ CHATTER
ガヤ CHATTER
NEGISHI-SAN, YOU FINALLY...
GIVE ME THAT.
HE'S VERY HAPPY.
CHOP
チェスト!
バキッ
WHACK
MY VIDEO!!
SCARED
STOMP
スタ スタ スタ...
STOMP
しーーん
SILENCE
BECAUSE...
KRNKL
カラ...
BECAUSE OF THIS VIDEO...
YOU'RE KEEPING IT?
YOU CAN'T WATCH IT.
IT'S NO GOOD ANYMORE.
KRNKL

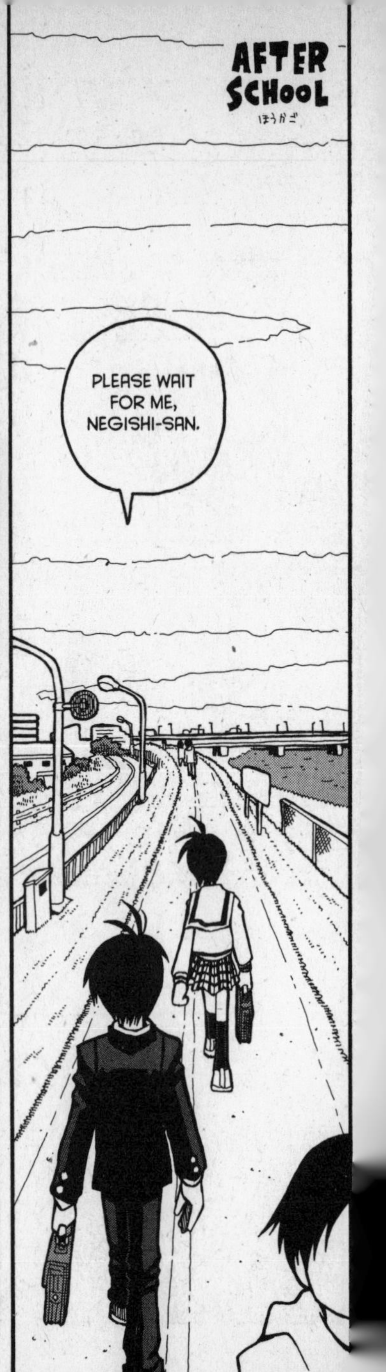
AFTER SCHOOL
ほうかご
PLEASE WAIT FOR ME, NEGISHI-SAN.

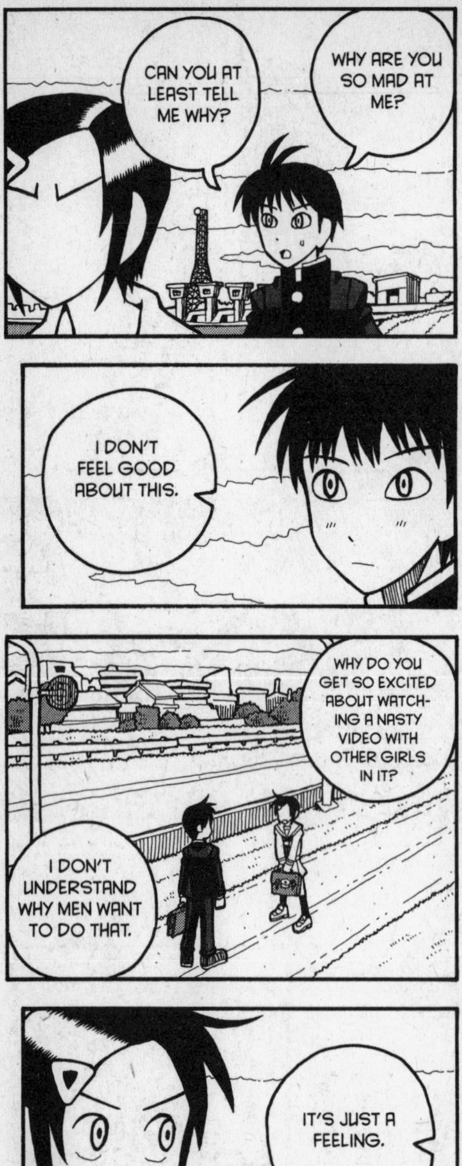
WHY ARE YOU SO MAD AT ME?
CAN YOU AT LEAST TELL ME WHY?
I DON'T FEEL GOOD ABOUT THIS.
WHY DO YOU GET SO EXCITED ABOUT WATCHING A NASTY VIDEO WITH OTHER GIRLS IN IT?
I DON'T UNDERSTAND WHY MEN WANT TO DO THAT.
IT'S JUST A FEELING.

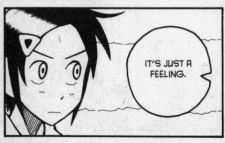

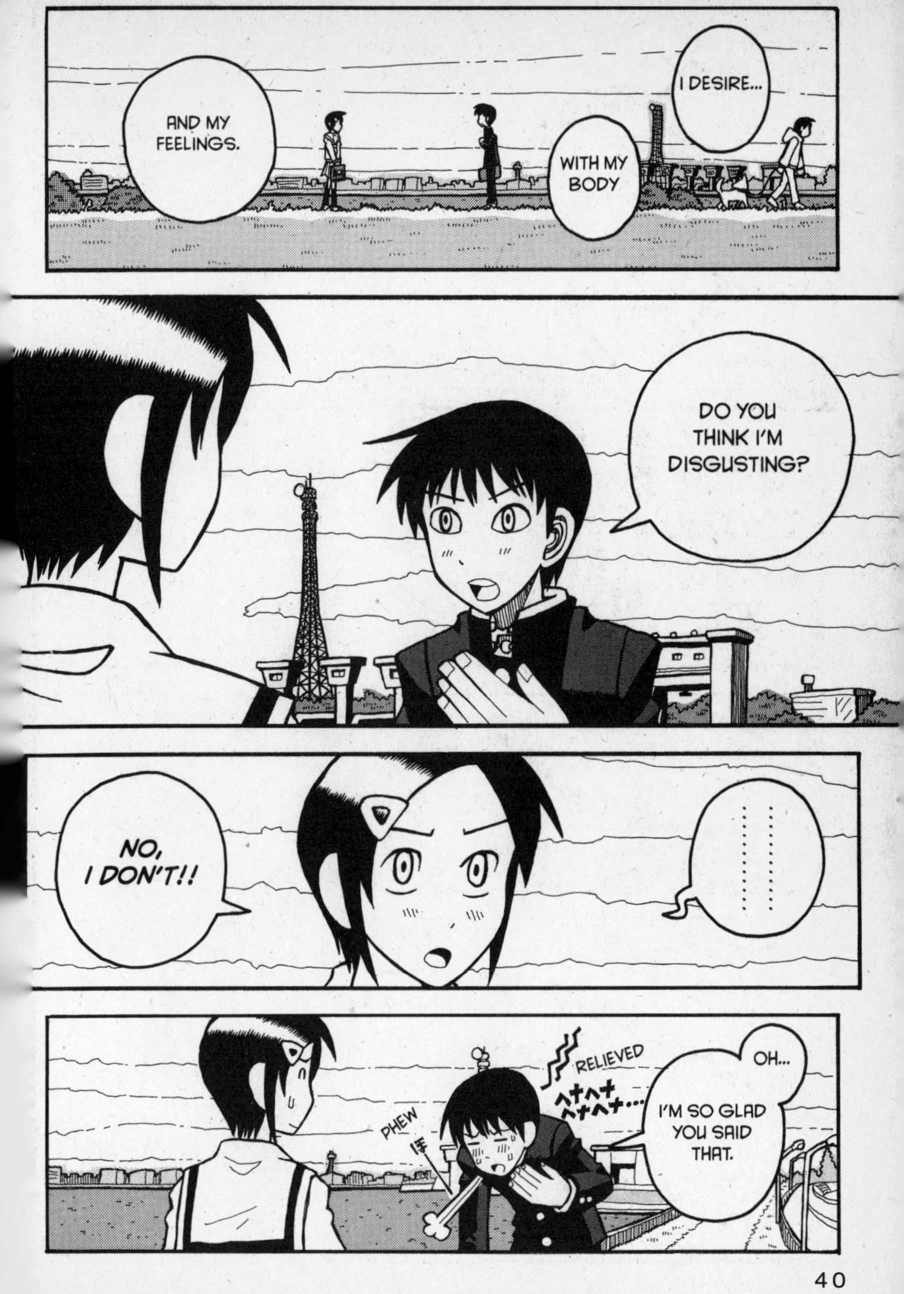
I DESIRE...
WITH MY BODY
AND MY FEELINGS.
DO YOU THINK I'M DISGUSTING?
......
NO, I DON'T!!
OH...
I'M SO GLAD YOU SAID THAT.
RELIEVED
ヘナヘナ ヘナヘナ...
PHEW
ほ

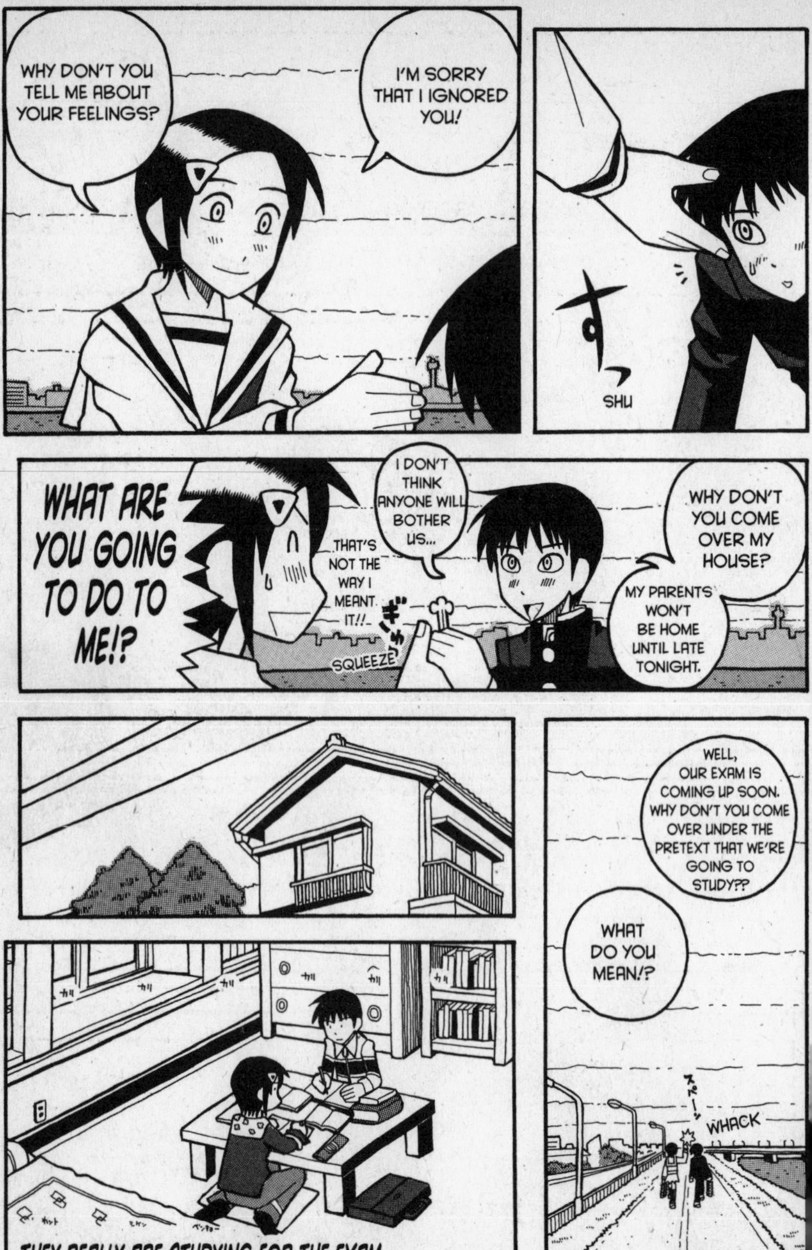
SHU
I'M SORRY THAT I IGNORED YOU!
WHY DON'T YOU TELL ME ABOUT YOUR FEELINGS?
WHY DON'T YOU COME OVER MY HOUSE?
MY PARENTS WON'T BE HOME UNTIL LATE TONIGHT.
I DON'T THINK ANYONE WILL BOTHER US...
SQUEEZE
THAT'S NOT THE WAY I MEANT IT!!
WHAT ARE YOU GOING TO DO TO ME!?
WELL, OUR EXAM IS COMING UP SOON. WHY DON'T YOU COME OVER UNDER THE PRETEXT THAT WE'RE GOING TO STUDY??
WHAT DO YOU MEAN!?
WHACK
THEY REALLY ARE STUDYING FOR THE EXAM.

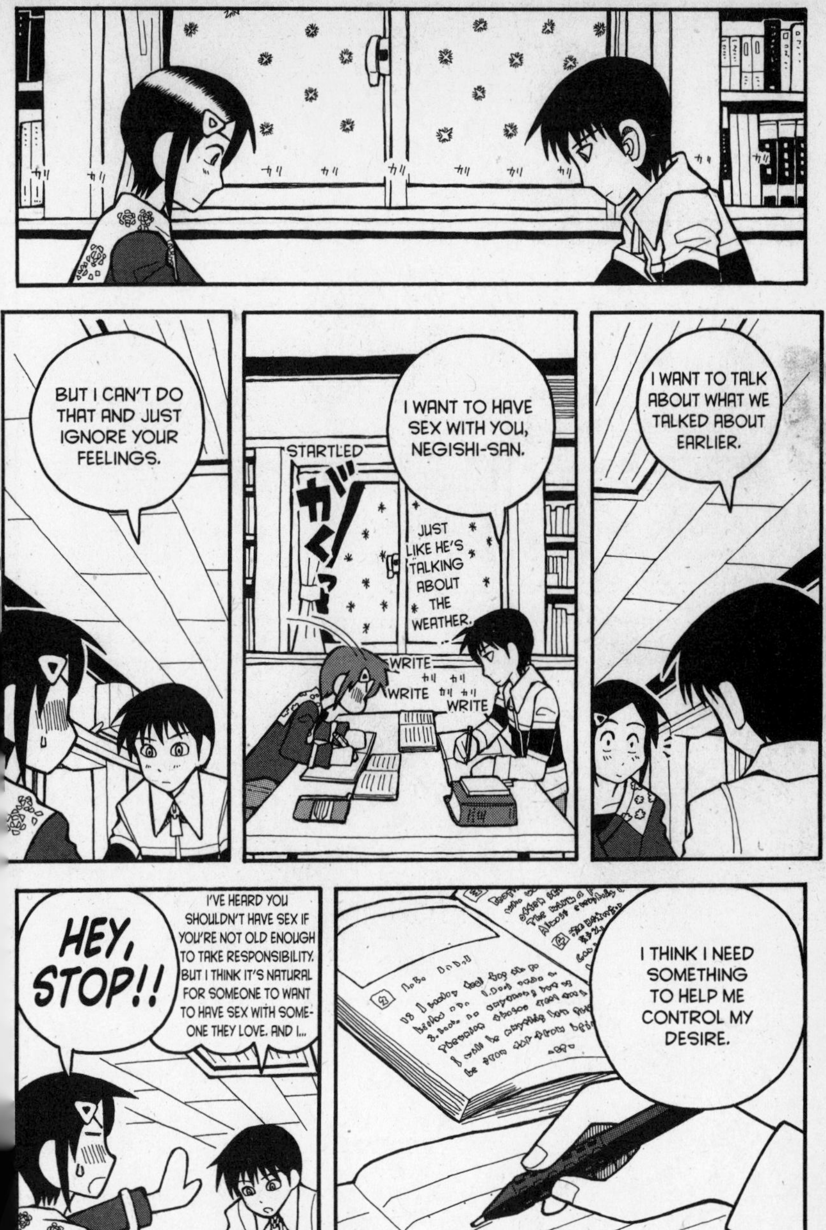
I WANT TO TALK ABOUT WHAT WE TALKED ABOUT EARLIER.
I WANT TO HAVE SEX WITH YOU, NEGISHI-SAN.
STARTLED
JUST LIKE HE'S TALKING ABOUT THE WEATHER.
WRITE
WRITE
WRITE
BUT I CAN'T DO THAT AND JUST IGNORE YOUR FEELINGS.
I THINK I NEED SOMETHING TO HELP ME CONTROL MY DESIRE.
I'VE HEARD YOU SHOULDN'T HAVE SEX IF YOU'RE NOT OLD ENOUGH TO TAKE RESPONSIBILITY. BUT I THINK IT'S NATURAL FOR SOMEONE TO WANT TO HAVE SEX WITH SOME-ONE THEY LOVE. AND I...
HEY, STOP!!

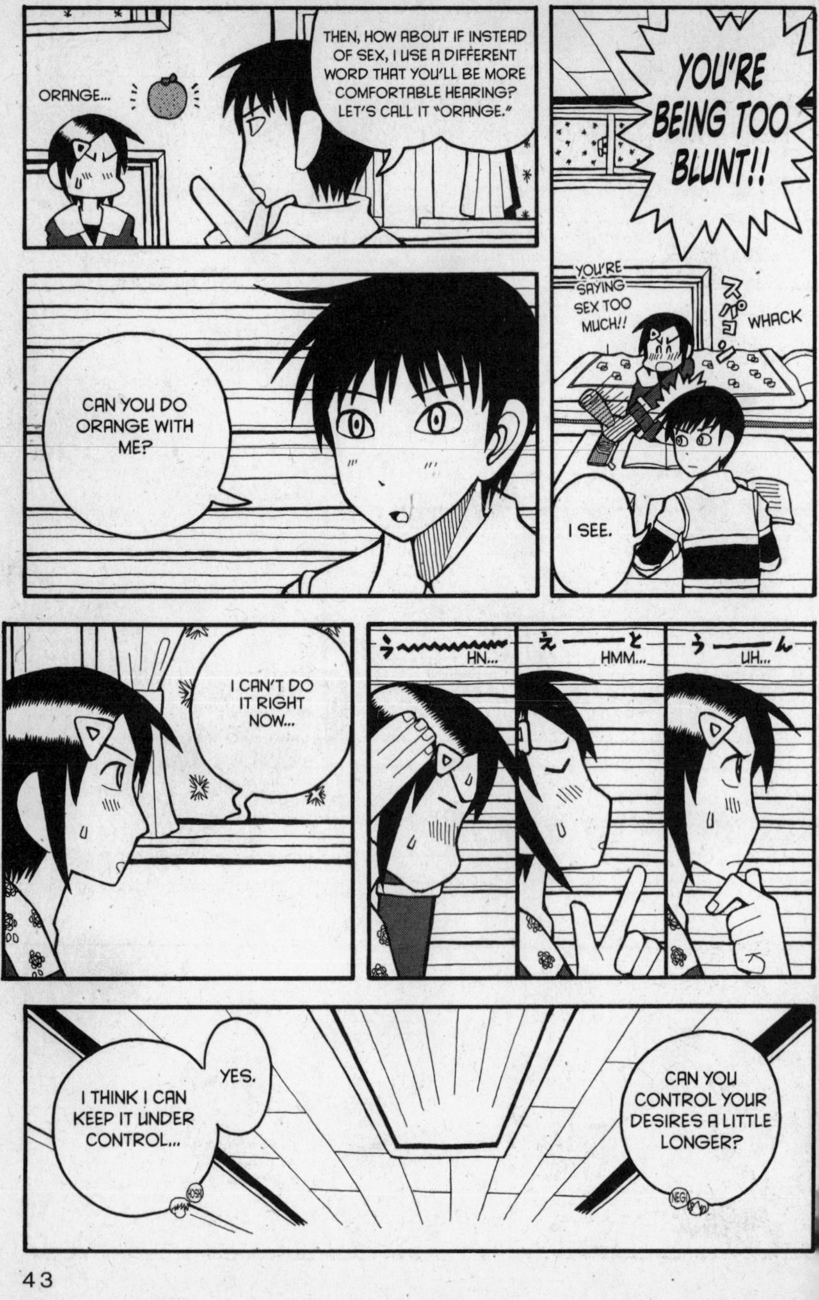
YOU'RE BEING TOO BLUNT!!
YOU'RE SAYING SEX TOO MUCH!!
WHACK
I SEE.
THEN, HOW ABOUT IF INSTEAD OF SEX, I USE A DIFFERENT WORD THAT YOU'LL BE MORE COMFORTABLE HEARING? LET'S CALL IT "ORANGE."
ORANGE...
CAN YOU DO ORANGE WITH ME?
う――ん
UH...
え――と
HMM...
う~~~~
HN...
I CAN'T DO IT RIGHT NOW...
CAN YOU CONTROL YOUR DESIRES A LITTLE LONGER?
NEGI
YES.
I THINK I CAN KEEP IT UNDER CONTROL...

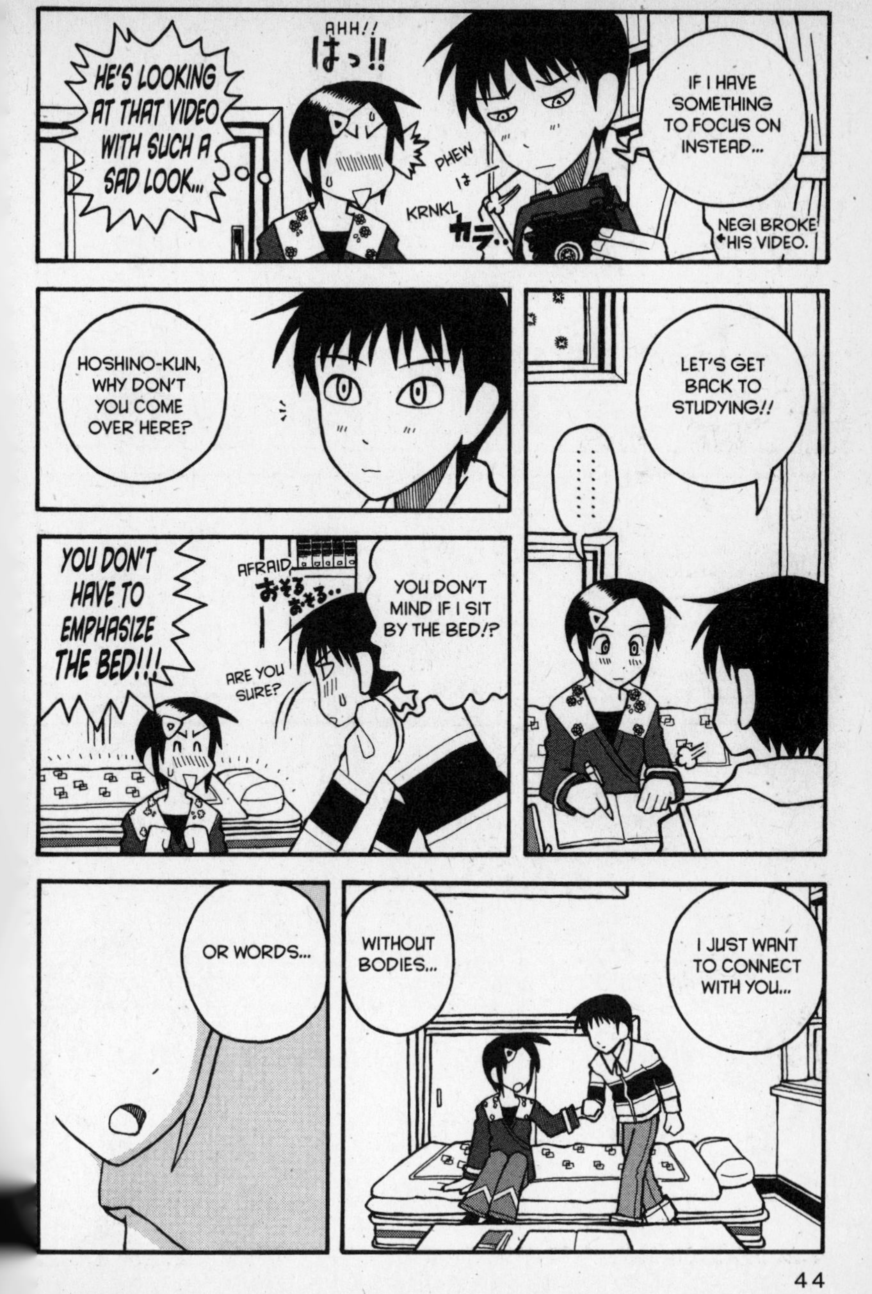
IF I HAVE SOMETHING TO FOCUS ON INSTEAD...
NEGI BROKE HIS VIDEO.
KRNKL
カラ..
PHEW
は—
AHH!!
はっ!!
HE'S LOOKING AT THAT VIDEO WITH SUCH A SAD LOOK...
LET'S GET BACK TO STUDYING!!
HOSHINO-KUN, WHY DON'T YOU COME OVER HERE?
YOU DON'T MIND IF I SIT BY THE BED!?
ARE YOU SURE?
AFRAID
おそるおそる..
YOU DON'T HAVE TO EMPHASIZE THE BED!!!
I JUST WANT TO CONNECT WITH YOU...
WITHOUT BODIES...
OR WORDS...

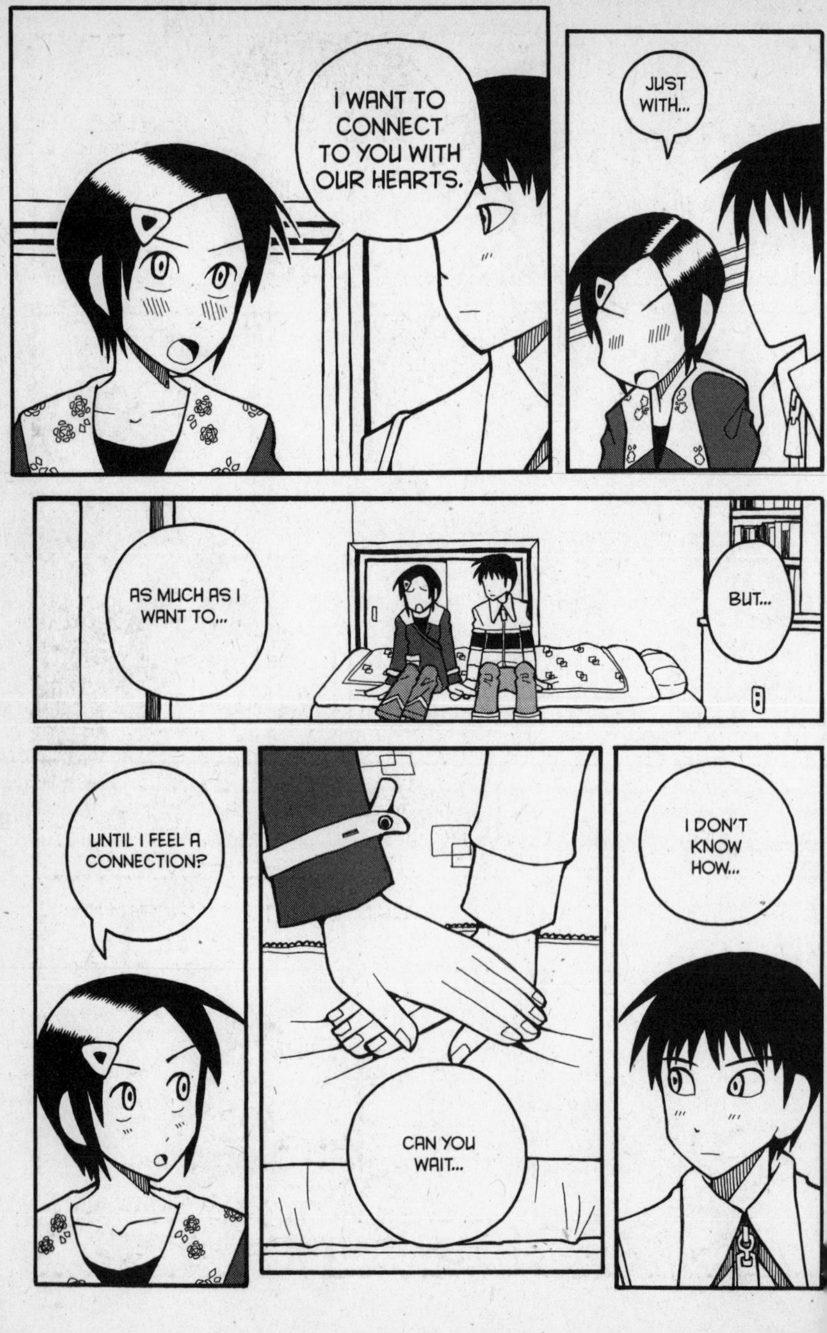
JUST WITH...
I WANT TO CONNECT TO YOU WITH OUR HEARTS.
BUT...
AS MUCH AS I WANT TO...
I DON'T KNOW HOW...
CAN YOU WAIT...
UNTIL I FEEL A CONNECTION?

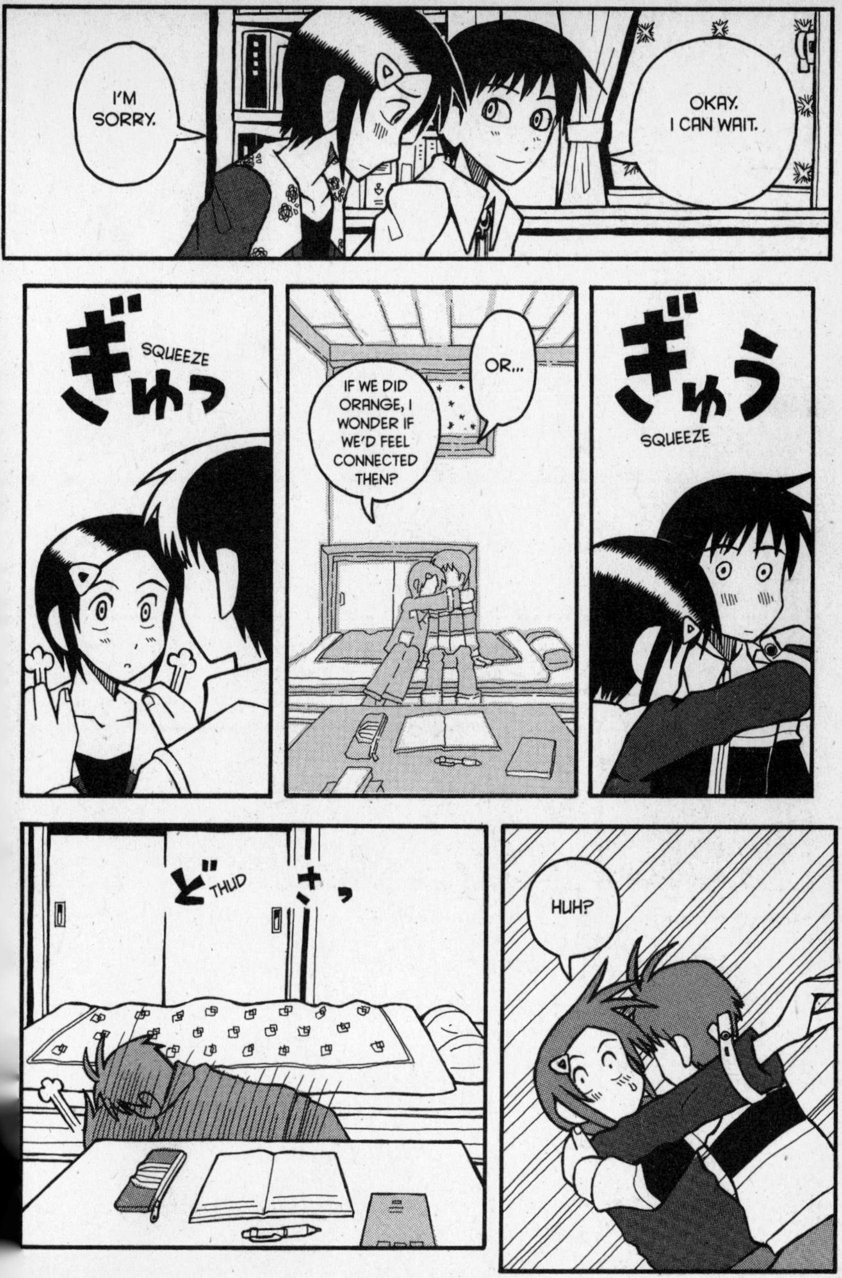

OKAY. I CAN WAIT.
I'M SORRY.
ぎゅう
SQUEEZE
OR...
IF WE DID ORANGE, I WONDER IF WE'D FEEL CONNECTED THEN?
ぎゅっ
SQUEEZE
HUH?
さっ
ど THUD

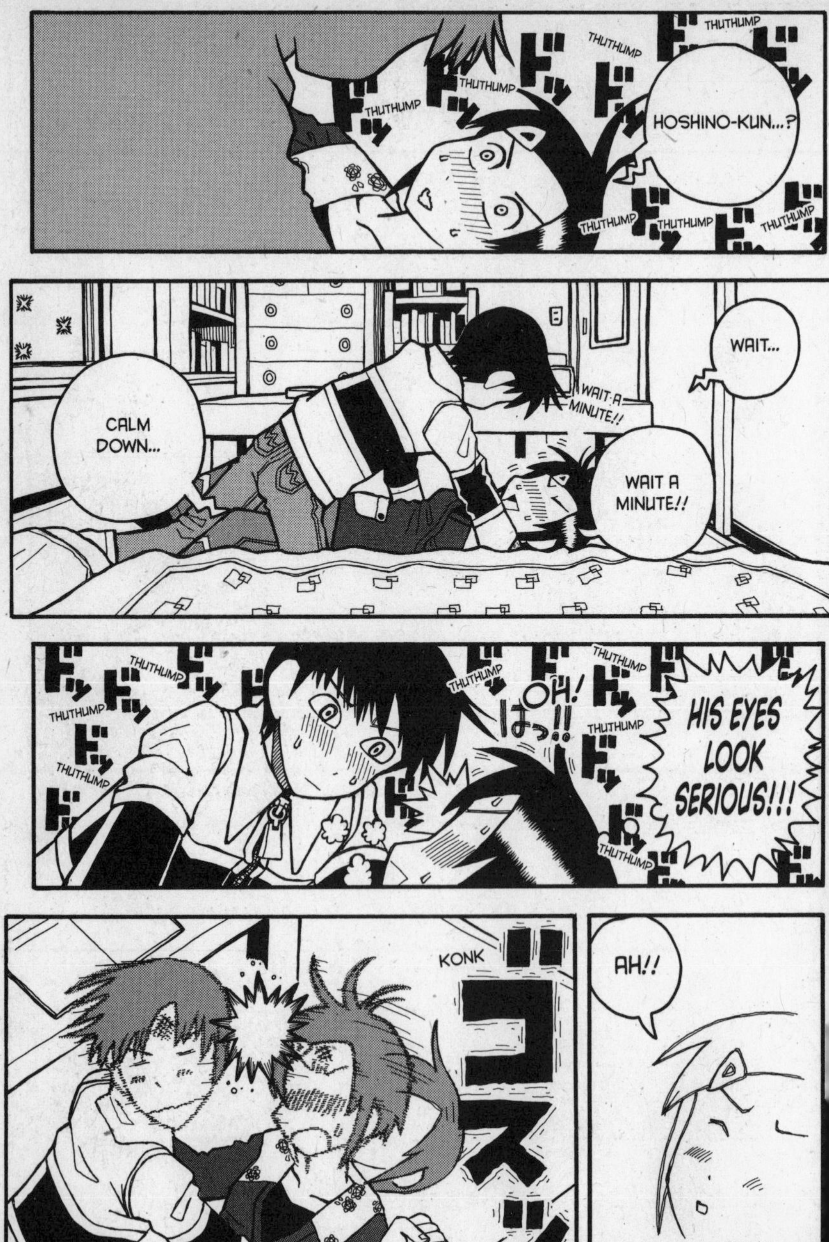
THUTHUMP
HOSHINO-KUN...?
THUTHUMP
THUTHUMP
THUTHUMP
THUTHUMP
THUTHUMP
THUTHUMP
WAIT...
WAIT A MINUTE!!
WAIT A MINUTE!!
CALM DOWN...
THUTHUMP
HIS EYES LOOK SERIOUS!!!
THUTHUMP
THUTHUMP
OH!
はっ!!
THUTHUMP
THUTHUMP
THUTHUMP
THUTHUMP
AH!!
KONK

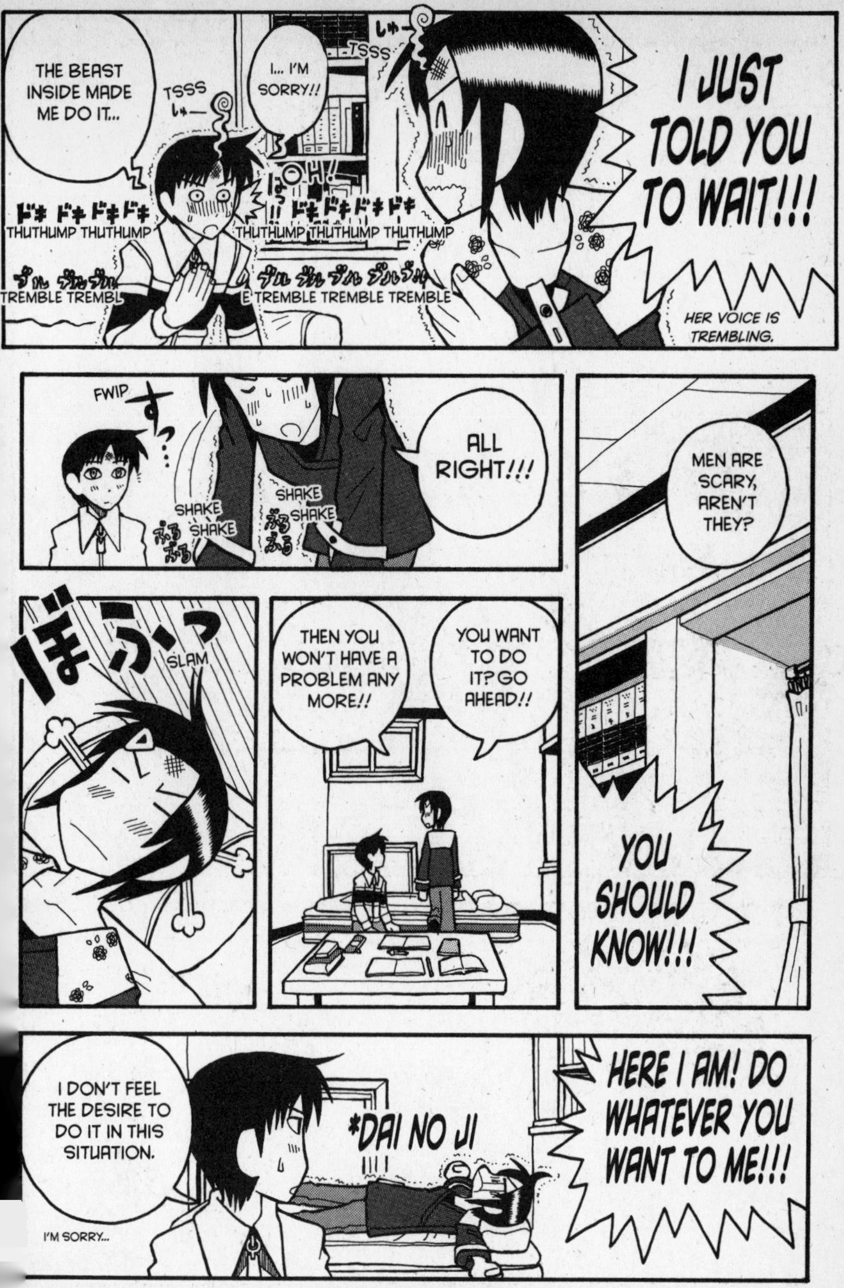
I JUST TOLD YOU TO WAIT!!!
HER VOICE IS TREMBLING.
TSSS
I... I'M SORRY!!
OH!
THUTHUMP THUTHUMP THUTHUMP
E TREMBLE TREMBLE TREMBLE
THE BEAST INSIDE MADE ME DO IT...
TSSS
THUTHUMP THUTHUMP
TREMBLE TREMBL
MEN ARE SCARY, AREN'T THEY?
YOU SHOULD KNOW!!!
ALL RIGHT!!!
SHAKE SHAKE
SHAKE SHAKE
FWIP
YOU WANT TO DO IT? GO AHEAD!!
THEN YOU WON'T HAVE A PROBLEM ANY MORE!!
SLAM
HERE I AM! DO WHATEVER YOU WANT TO ME!!!
*DAI NO JI
I DON'T FEEL THE DESIRE TO DO IT IN THIS SITUATION.
I'M SORRY...

*SEE TRANSLATION NOTES.

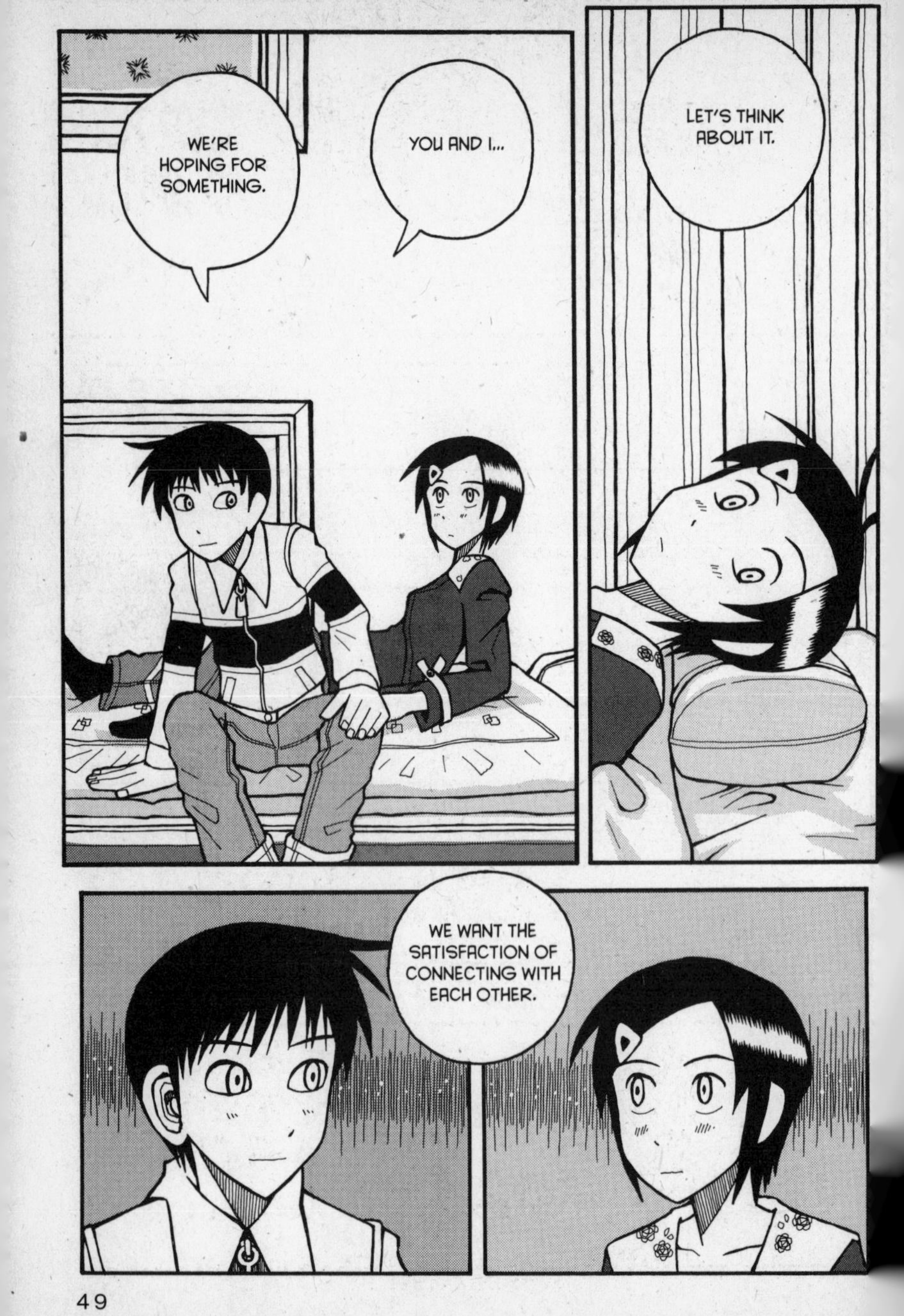
LET'S THINK ABOUT IT.
YOU AND I...
WE'RE HOPING FOR SOMETHING.
WE WANT THE SATISFACTION OF CONNECTING WITH EACH OTHER.

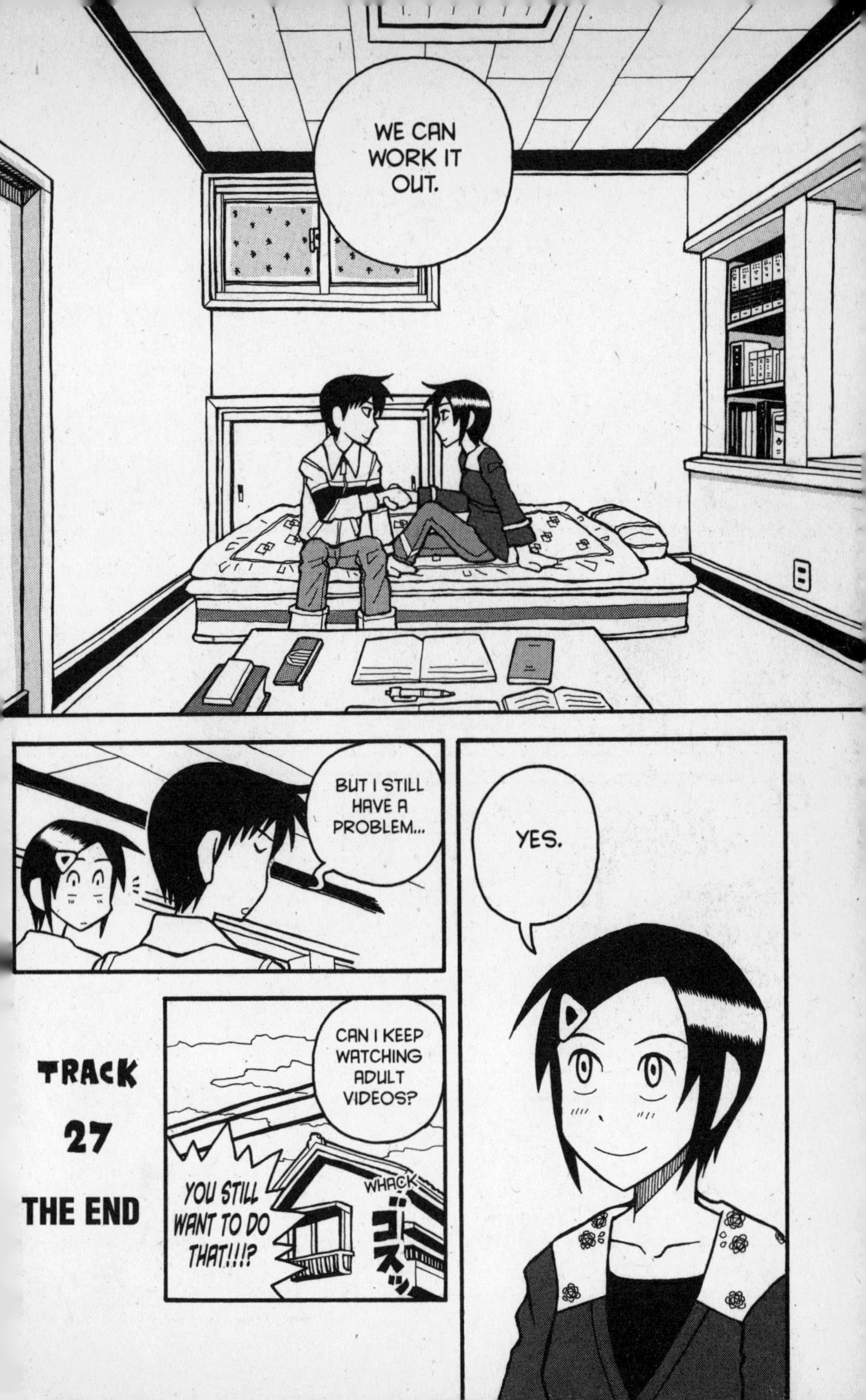
WE CAN WORK IT OUT.
YES.
BUT I STILL HAVE A PROBLEM...
CAN I KEEP WATCHING ADULT VIDEOS?
YOU STILL WANT TO DO THAT!!!?
WHACK
ゴスッ

TRACK 27 THE END

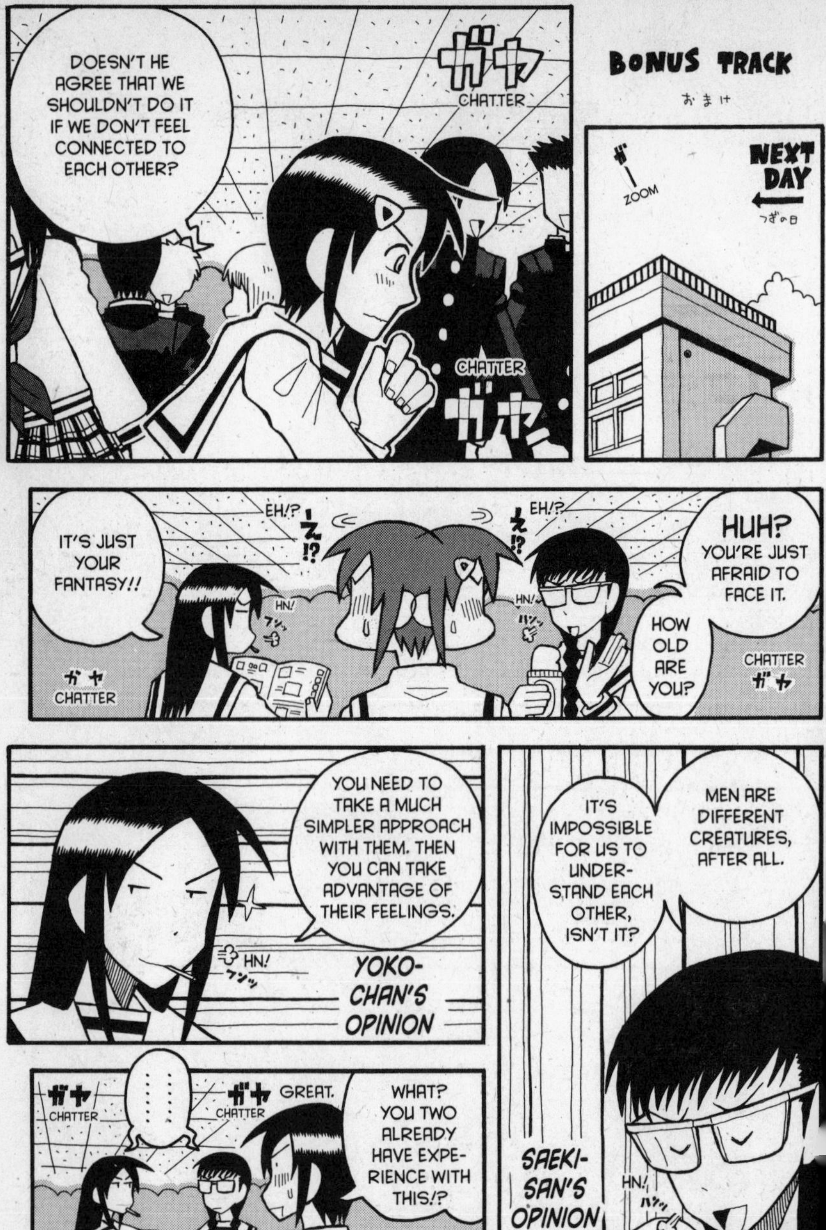
BONUS TRACK
おまけ
NEXT DAY
つぎの日
ZOOM
ガヤ
CHATTER
DOESN'T HE AGREE THAT WE SHOULDN'T DO IT IF WE DON'T FEEL CONNECTED TO EACH OTHER?
CHATTER
ガヤ
HUH? YOU'RE JUST AFRAID TO FACE IT.
HOW OLD ARE YOU?
CHATTER
ガヤ
HN!
EH!?
え!?
EH!?
え!?
HN!
IT'S JUST YOUR FANTASY!!
ガヤ
CHATTER
MEN ARE DIFFERENT CREATURES, AFTER ALL.
IT'S IMPOSSIBLE FOR US TO UNDER-STAND EACH OTHER, ISN'T IT?
HN!
SAEKI-SAN'S OPINION
YOU NEED TO TAKE A MUCH SIMPLER APPROACH WITH THEM. THEN YOU CAN TAKE ADVANTAGE OF THEIR FEELINGS.
HN!
YOKO-CHAN'S OPINION
WHAT? YOU TWO ALREADY HAVE EXPE-RIENCE WITH THIS!?
GREAT.
ガヤ
CHATTER
......
ガヤ
CHATTER

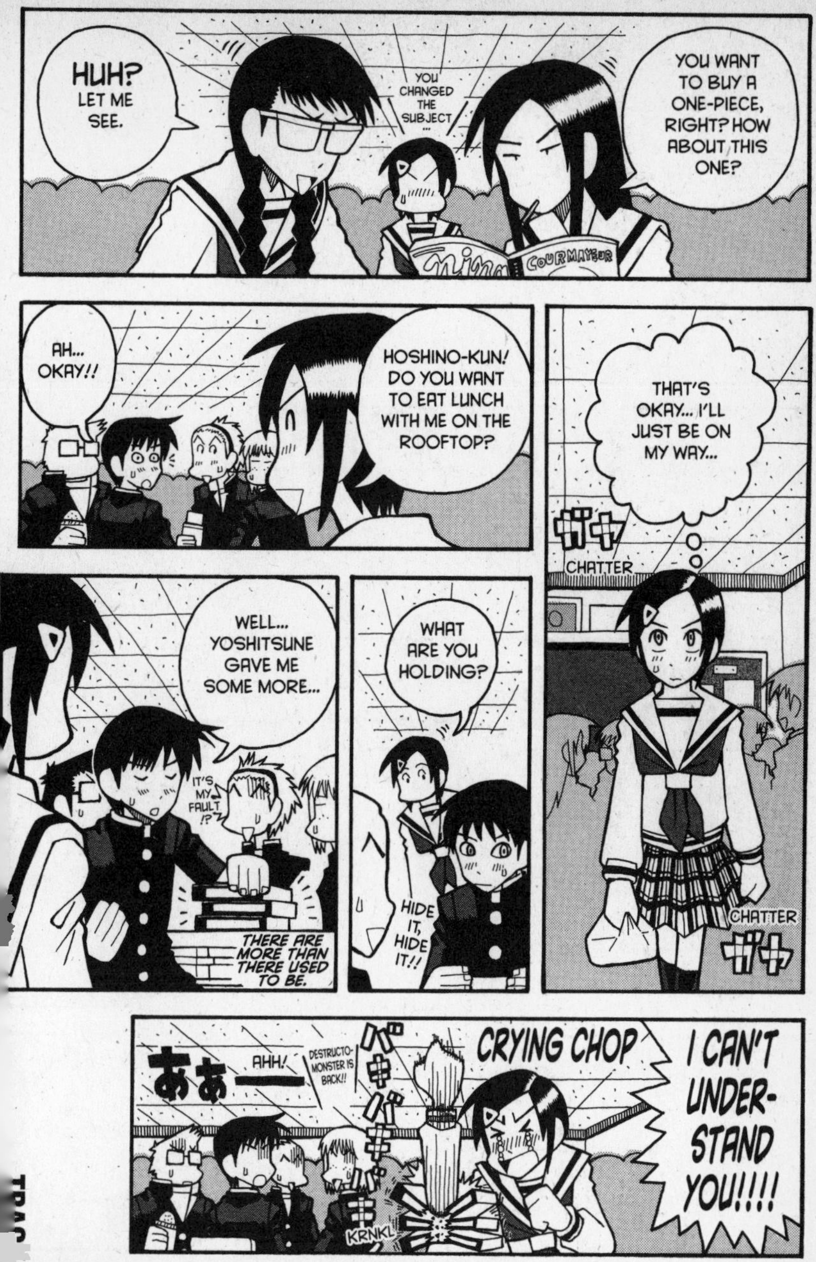
YOU WANT TO BUY A ONE-PIECE, RIGHT? HOW ABOUT THIS ONE?
COURMAYEUR
YOU CHANGED THE SUBJECT ...
HUH? LET ME SEE.
THAT'S OKAY... I'LL JUST BE ON MY WAY...
ガヤ
CHATTER
CHATTER
ガヤ
HOSHINO-KUN! DO YOU WANT TO EAT LUNCH WITH ME ON THE ROOFTOP?
AH... OKAY!!
WHAT ARE YOU HOLDING?
HIDE IT, HIDE IT!!
WELL... YOSHITSUNE GAVE ME SOME MORE...
IT'S MY FAULT!?
THERE ARE MORE THAN THERE USED TO BE.
I CAN'T UNDER-STAND YOU!!!!
CRYING CHOP
バキバキ
KRNKL
DESTRUCTO-MONSTER IS BACK!!
AHH!
あぁー

▶▶ END

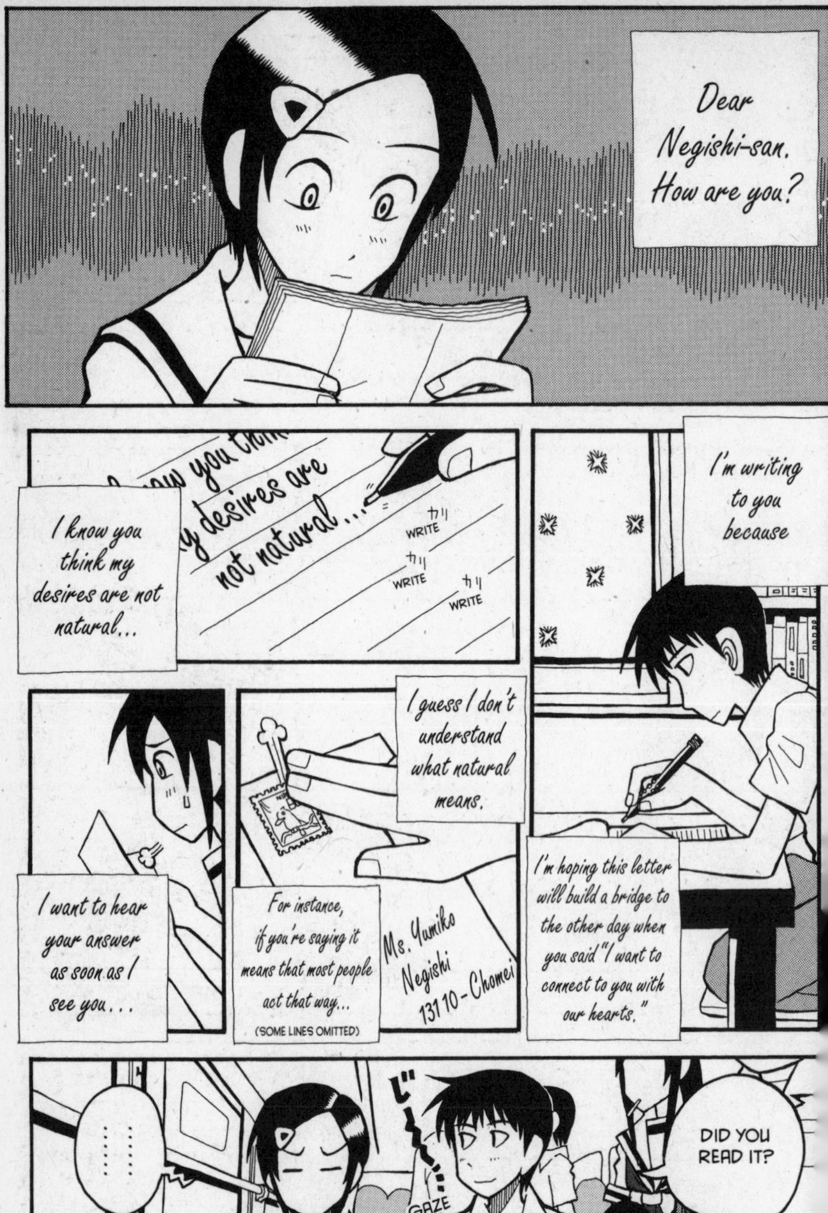
Dear Negishi-san. How are you?
I'm writing to you because
I'm hoping this letter will build a bridge to the other day when you said "I want to connect to you with our hearts."
desires are
not natural...
カリ WRITE
カリ WRITE
カリ WRITE
I know you think my desires are not natural...
I guess I don't understand what natural means.
For instance, if you're saying it means that most people act that way...
(SOME LINES OMITTED)
Ms. Yumiko Negishi 131 10-Chomei
I want to hear your answer as soon as I see you...
DID YOU READ IT?
GAZE
......

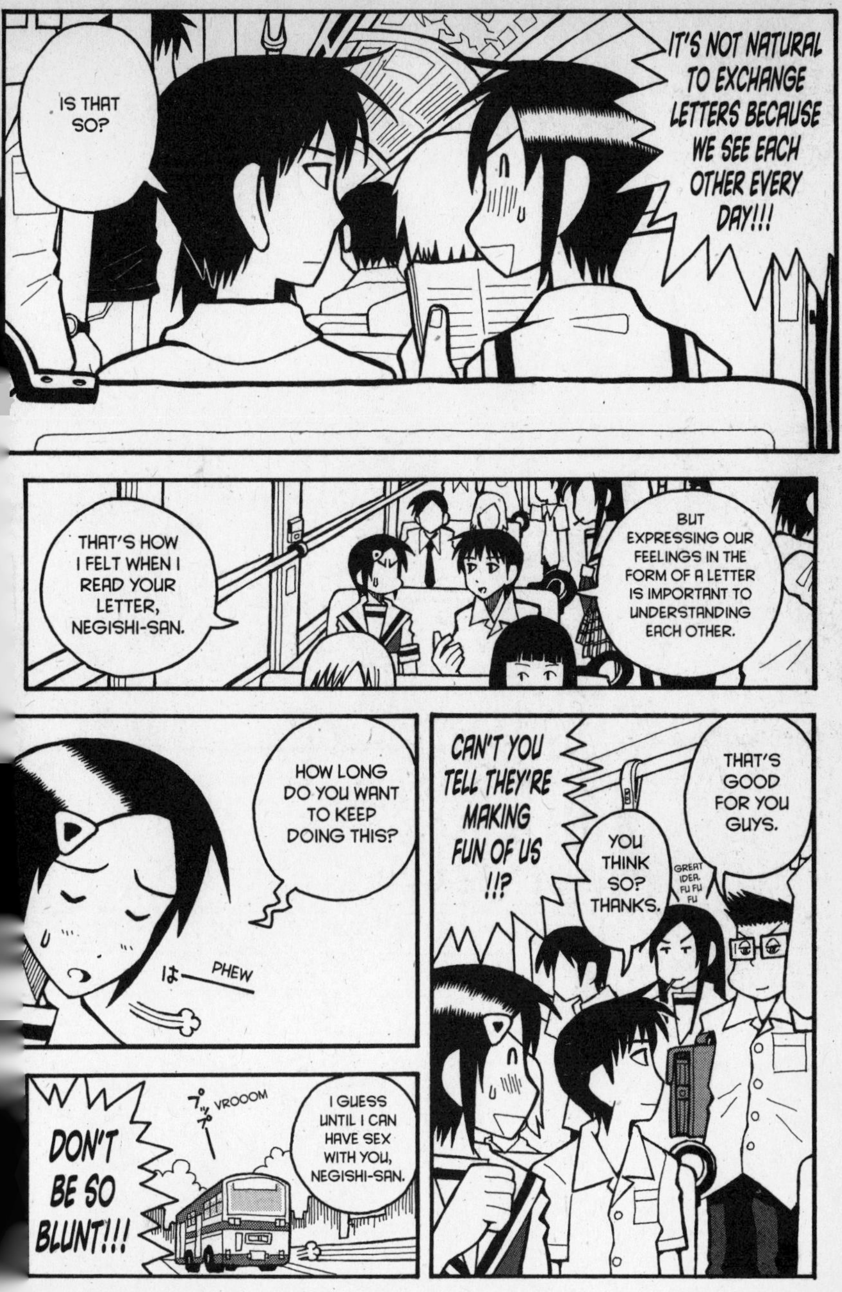
IT'S NOT NATURAL TO EXCHANGE LETTERS BECAUSE WE SEE EACH OTHER EVERY DAY!!!
IS THAT SO?
BUT EXPRESSING OUR FEELINGS IN THE FORM OF A LETTER IS IMPORTANT TO UNDERSTANDING EACH OTHER.
THAT'S HOW I FELT WHEN I READ YOUR LETTER, NEGISHI-SAN.
THAT'S GOOD FOR YOU GUYS.
GREAT IDEA. FU FU FU
YOU THINK SO? THANKS.
CAN'T YOU TELL THEY'RE MAKING FUN OF US !!?
HOW LONG DO YOU WANT TO KEEP DOING THIS?
は PHEW
I GUESS UNTIL I CAN HAVE SEX WITH YOU, NEGISHI-SAN.
プップ VROOOM
DON'T BE SO BLUNT!!!

TRACK #28 DEAR HOSHINO-KUN

NEGISHI

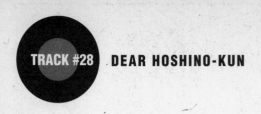

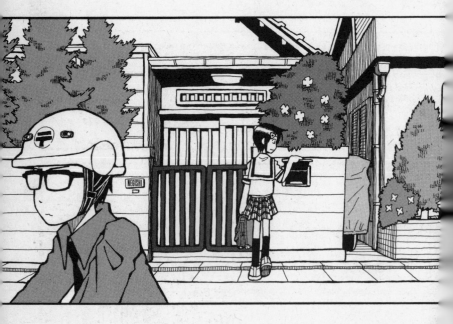

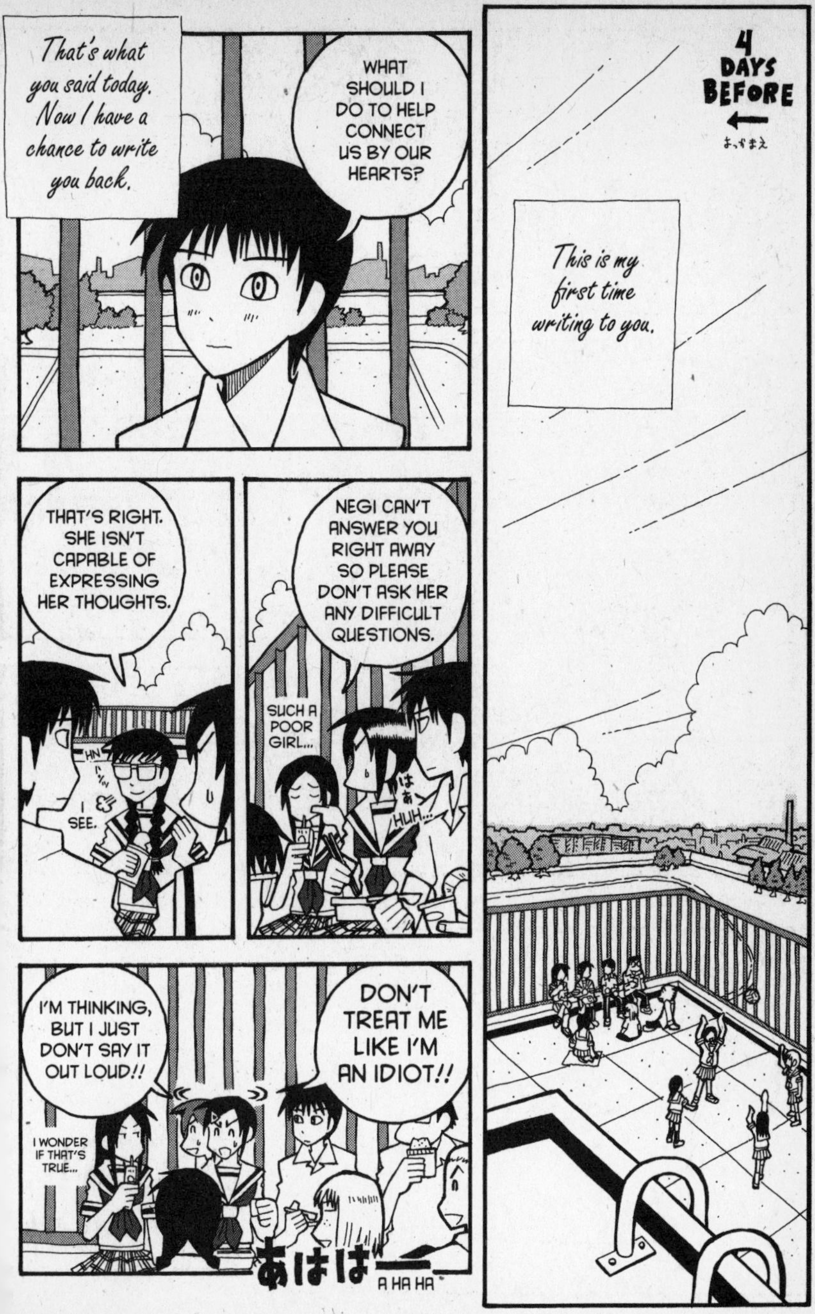
4 DAYS BEFORE
This is my first time writing to you.
That's what you said today. Now I have a chance to write you back.
WHAT SHOULD I DO TO HELP CONNECT US BY OUR HEARTS?
NEGI CAN'T ANSWER YOU RIGHT AWAY SO PLEASE DON'T ASK HER ANY DIFFICULT QUESTIONS.
SUCH A POOR GIRL...
HUH...
THAT'S RIGHT. SHE ISN'T CAPABLE OF EXPRESSING HER THOUGHTS.
HN
I SEE.
DON'T TREAT ME LIKE I'M AN IDIOT!!
I'M THINKING, BUT I JUST DON'T SAY IT OUT LOUD!!
I WONDER IF THAT'S TRUE...
あはは
A HA HA

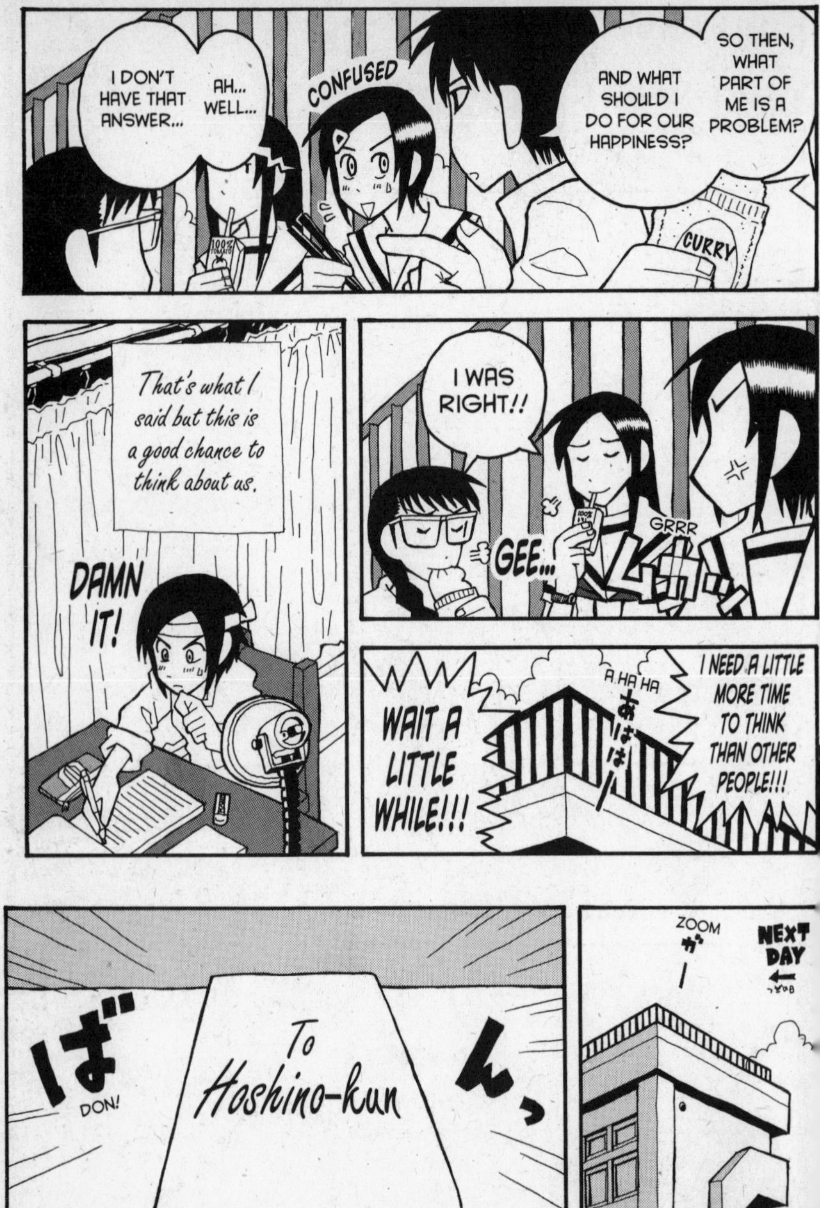
SO THEN, WHAT PART OF ME IS A PROBLEM?
AND WHAT SHOULD I DO FOR OUR HAPPINESS?
CONFUSED
AH... WELL...
I DON'T HAVE THAT ANSWER...
CURRY
100% TOMATO
I WAS RIGHT!!
GRRR
GEE...
I NEED A LITTLE MORE TIME TO THINK THAN OTHER PEOPLE!!!
A HA HA
あははー
WAIT A LITTLE WHILE!!!
That's what I said but this is a good chance to think about us.
DAMN IT!
NEXT DAY
つぎの日
ZOOM
ガー
ばんっ
DON!
To Hoshino-kun

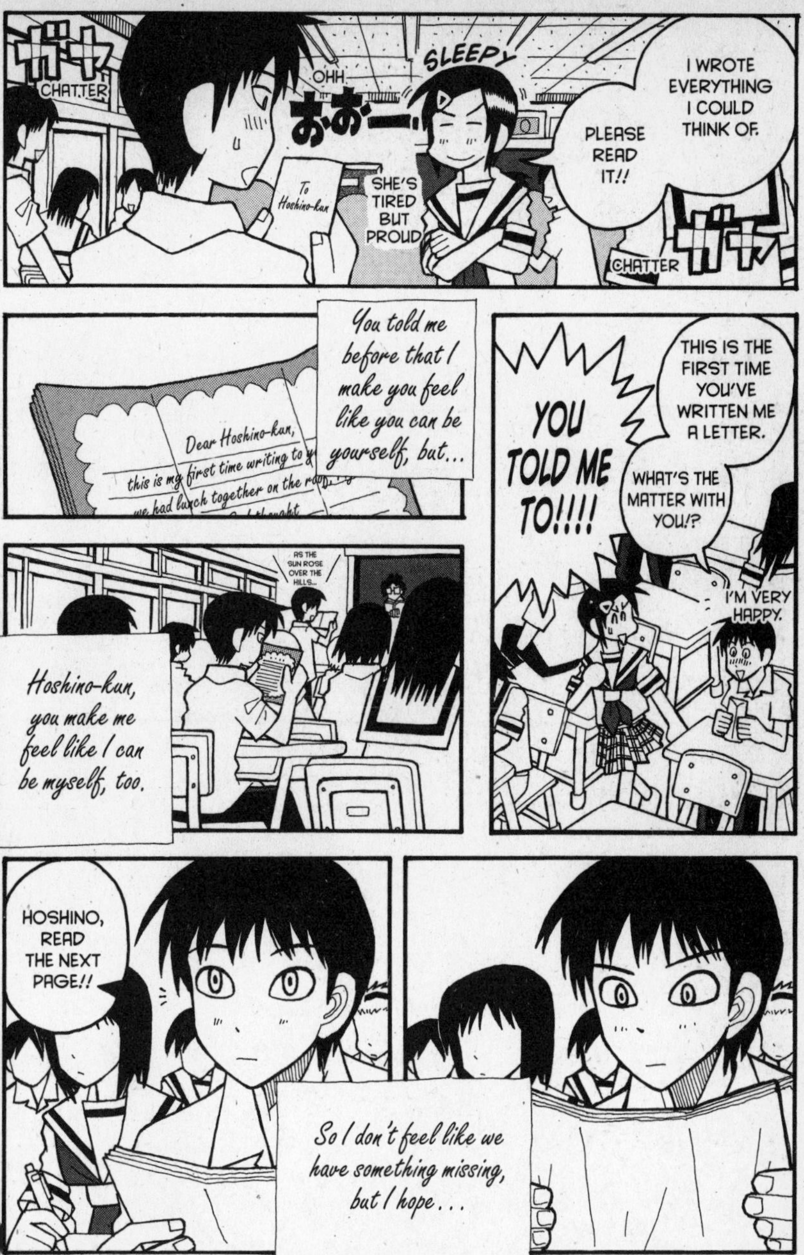
I WROTE EVERYTHING I COULD THINK OF.
PLEASE READ IT!!
SLEEPY
おぉー
OHH.
ガヤ
CHATTER
SHE'S TIRED BUT PROUD
To Hoshino-kun
ガヤ
CHATTER
THIS IS THE FIRST TIME YOU'VE WRITTEN ME A LETTER.
YOU TOLD ME TO!!!!
WHAT'S THE MATTER WITH YOU!?
I'M VERY HAPPY.
You told me before that I make you feel like you can be yourself, but...
Dear Hoshino-kun,
this is my first time writing to
we had lunch together on the
AS THE SUN ROSE OVER THE HILLS...
Hoshino-kun, you make me feel like I can be myself, too.
HOSHINO, READ THE NEXT PAGE!!
So I don't feel like we have something missing, but I hope...

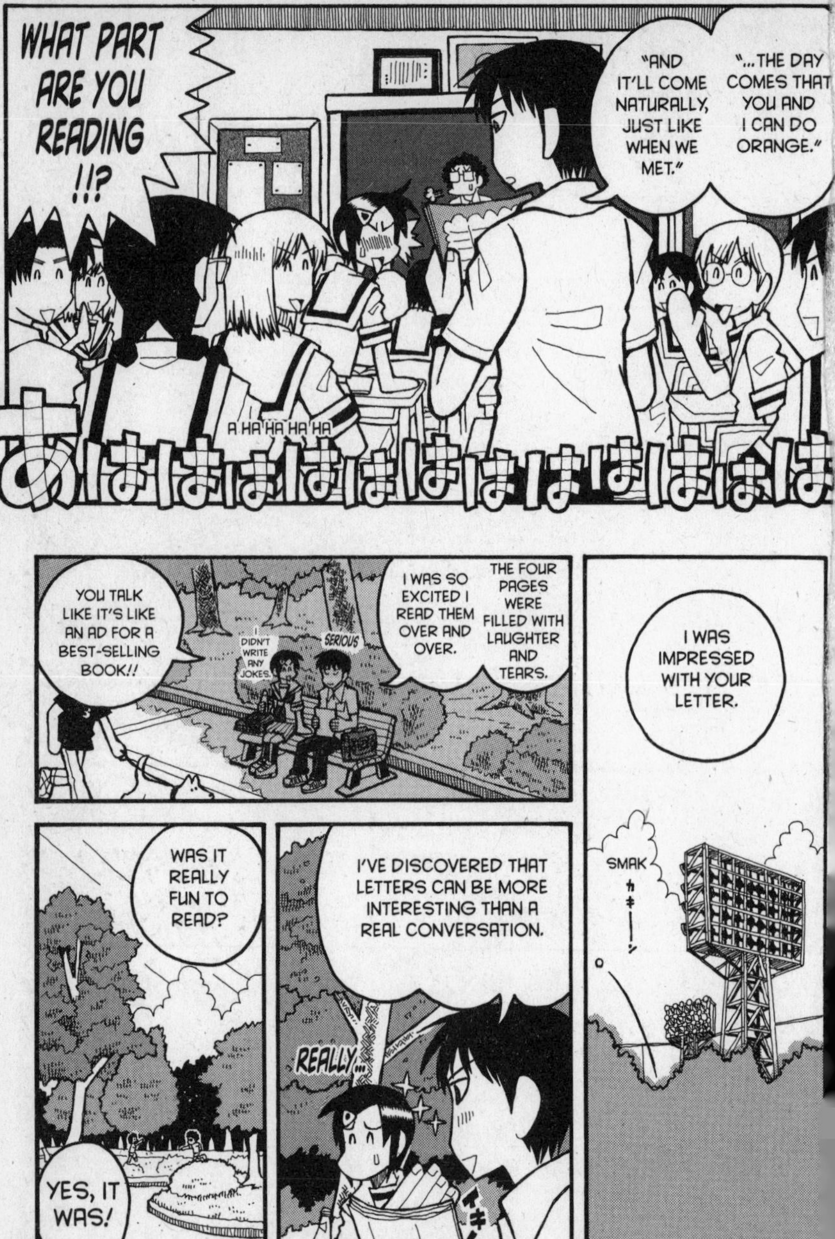
"...THE DAY COMES THAT YOU AND I CAN DO ORANGE."
"AND IT'LL COME NATURALLY, JUST LIKE WHEN WE MET."
WHAT PART ARE YOU READING !!?
A HA HA HA HA
あはははははははははは
I WAS IMPRESSED WITH YOUR LETTER.
THE FOUR PAGES WERE FILLED WITH LAUGHTER AND TEARS.
I WAS SO EXCITED I READ THEM OVER AND OVER.
SERIOUS
I DIDN'T WRITE ANY JOKES.
YOU TALK LIKE IT'S LIKE AN AD FOR A BEST-SELLING BOOK!!
SMAK
カキーン
I'VE DISCOVERED THAT LETTERS CAN BE MORE INTERESTING THAN A REAL CONVERSATION.
REALLY...
CHEERFULLY
イキイキ
WAS IT REALLY FUN TO READ?
YES, IT WAS!

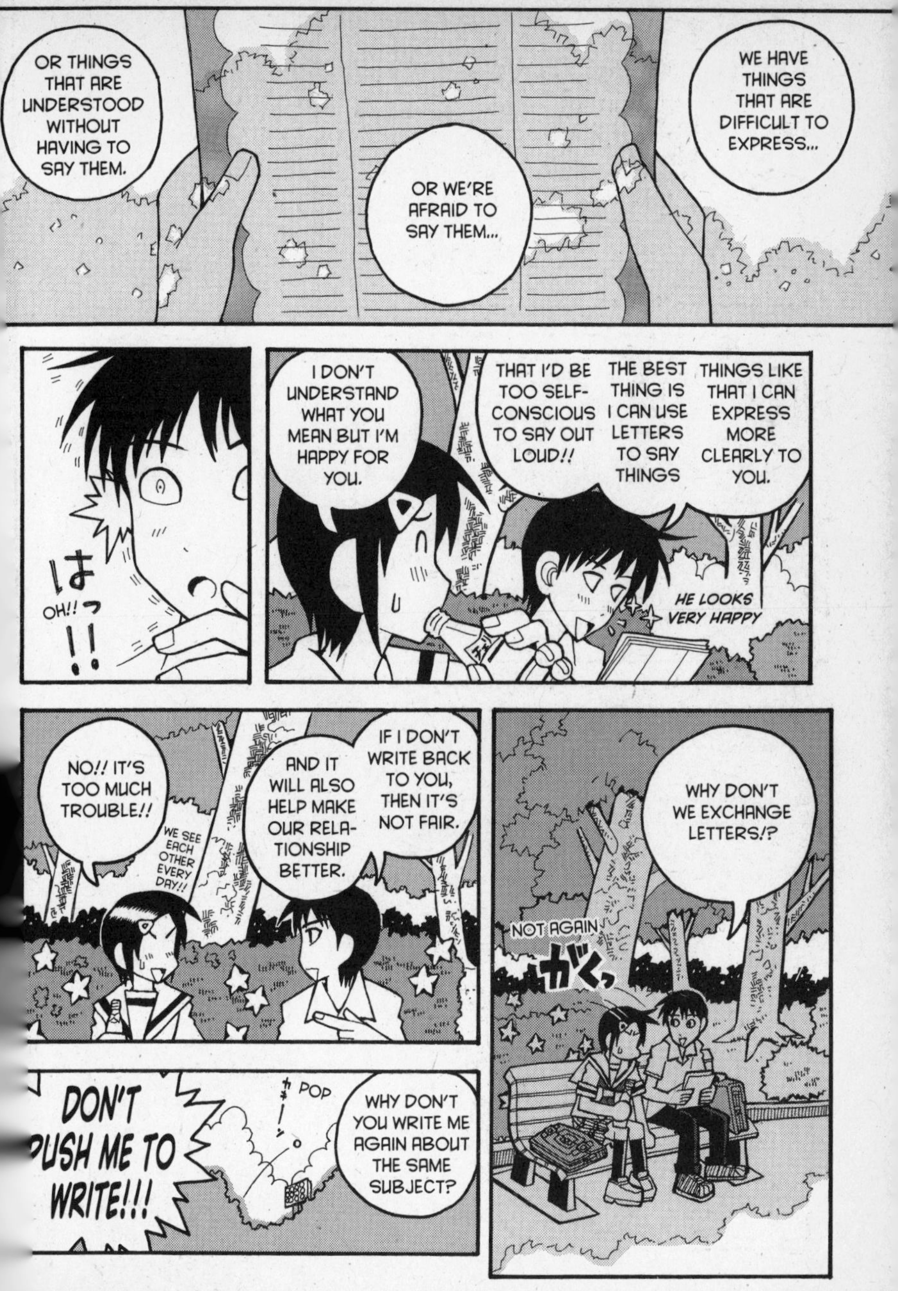
WE HAVE THINGS THAT ARE DIFFICULT TO EXPRESS...
OR WE'RE AFRAID TO SAY THEM...
OR THINGS THAT ARE UNDERSTOOD WITHOUT HAVING TO SAY THEM.
THINGS LIKE THAT I CAN EXPRESS MORE CLEARLY TO YOU.
THE BEST THING IS I CAN USE LETTERS TO SAY THINGS
THAT I'D BE TOO SELF-CONSCIOUS TO SAY OUT LOUD!!
I DON'T UNDERSTAND WHAT YOU MEAN BUT I'M HAPPY FOR YOU.
HE LOOKS VERY HAPPY
はっ!!
OH!!
WHY DON'T WE EXCHANGE LETTERS!?
NOT AGAIN
がくっ
IF I DON'T WRITE BACK TO YOU, THEN IT'S NOT FAIR.
AND IT WILL ALSO HELP MAKE OUR RELATIONSHIP BETTER.
NO!! IT'S TOO MUCH TROUBLE!!
WE SEE EACH OTHER EVERY DAY!!
WHY DON'T YOU WRITE ME AGAIN ABOUT THE SAME SUBJECT?
カキーン
POP
DON'T PUSH ME TO WRITE!!!

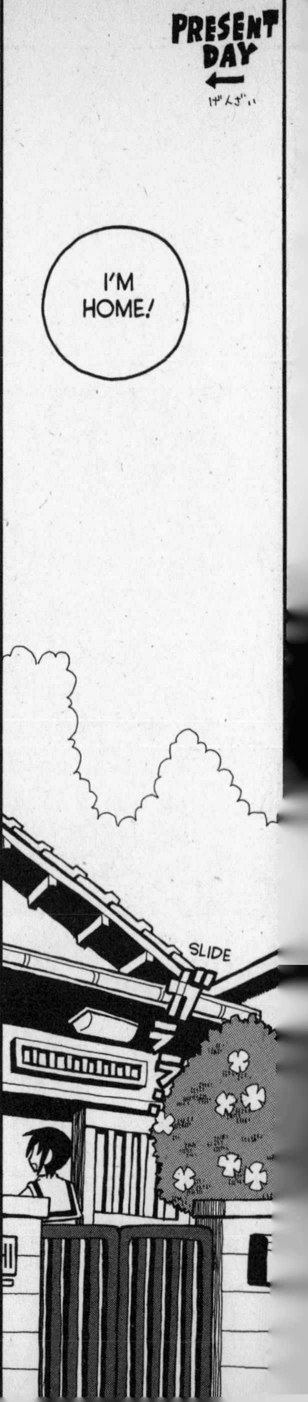
PRESENT DAY
I'M HOME!
SLIDE

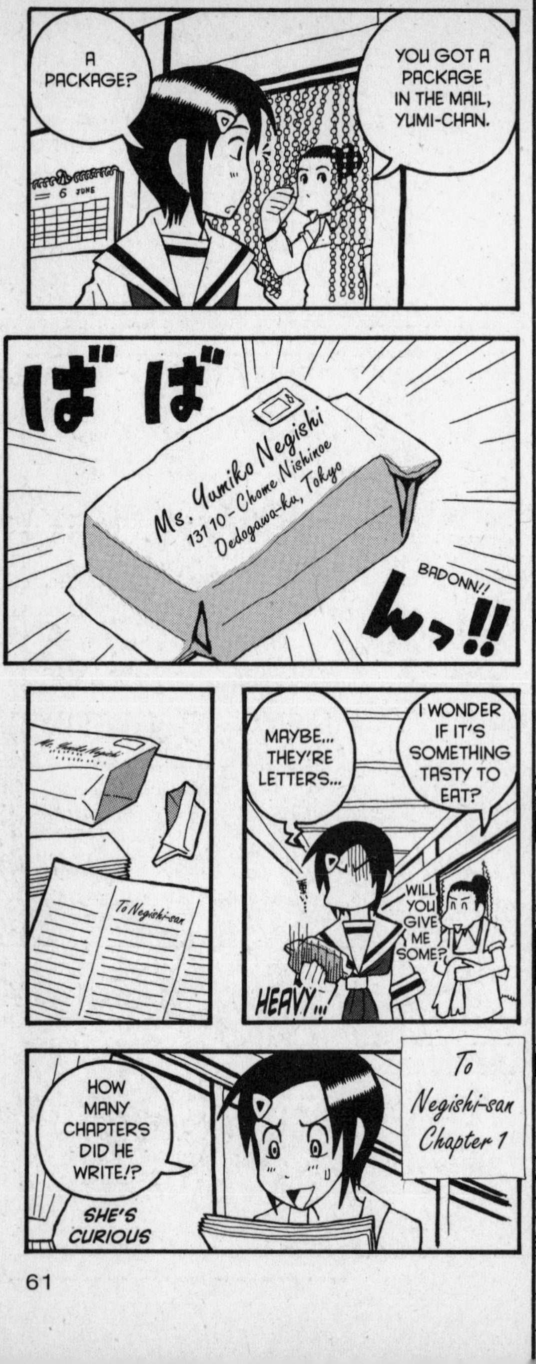
YOU GOT A PACKAGE IN THE MAIL, YUMI-CHAN.
A PACKAGE?
6 JUNE
Ms. Yumiko Negishi
131 10-Chome Nishinoe
Oedogawa-ku, Tokyo
BADONN!!
んっ!!
ばば
I WONDER IF IT'S SOMETHING TASTY TO EAT?
MAYBE... THEY'RE LETTERS...
WILL YOU GIVE ME SOME?
HEAVY...!
To Negishi-san
To Negishi-san Chapter 1
HOW MANY CHAPTERS DID HE WRITE!?
SHE'S CURIOUS

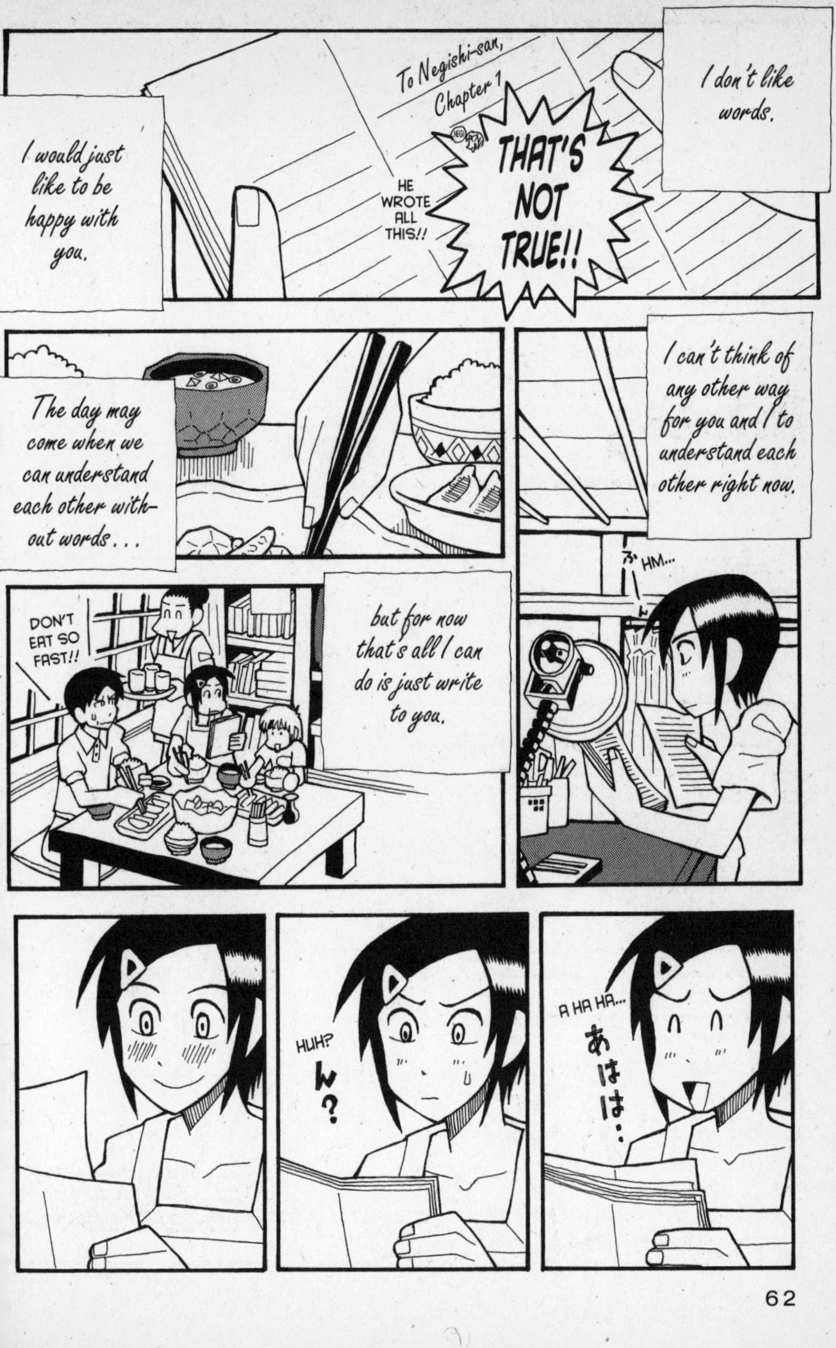

I don't like words.
To Negishi-san, Chapter 1
THAT'S NOT TRUE!!
HE WROTE ALL THIS!!
I would just like to be happy with you.
I can't think of any other way for you and I to understand each other right now.
ぶーん
HM...
The day may come when we can understand each other with-out words . . .
but for now that's all I can do is just write to you.
DON'T EAT SO FAST!!
A HA HA...
あはは・・
HUH?
ん?

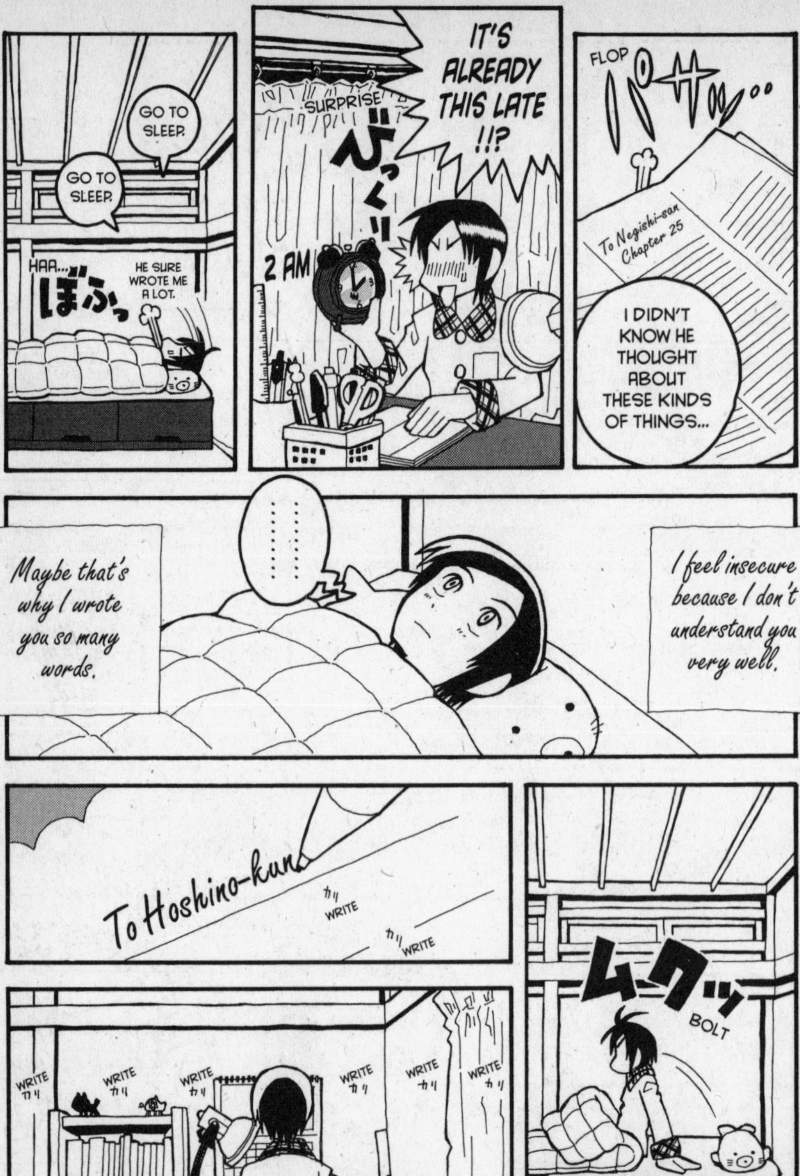

FLOP
パサッ…
To Negishi-san
Chapter 25
I DIDN'T KNOW HE THOUGHT ABOUT THESE KINDS OF THINGS...
IT'S ALREADY THIS LATE !!?
SURPRISE
びっくりッ
2 AM
GO TO SLEEP.
GO TO SLEEP.
HAA...
ぼふっ
HE SURE WROTE ME A LOT.
I feel insecure because I don't understand you very well.
......
Maybe that's why I wrote you so many words.
ムクッ
BOLT
To Hoshino-kun
カリ
WRITE
カリ
WRITE
WRITE
カリ
WRITE
カリ
WRITE
カリ
WRITE
カリ
WRITE
カリ
WRITE
カリ

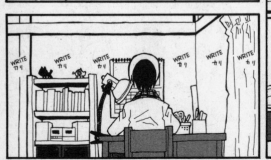

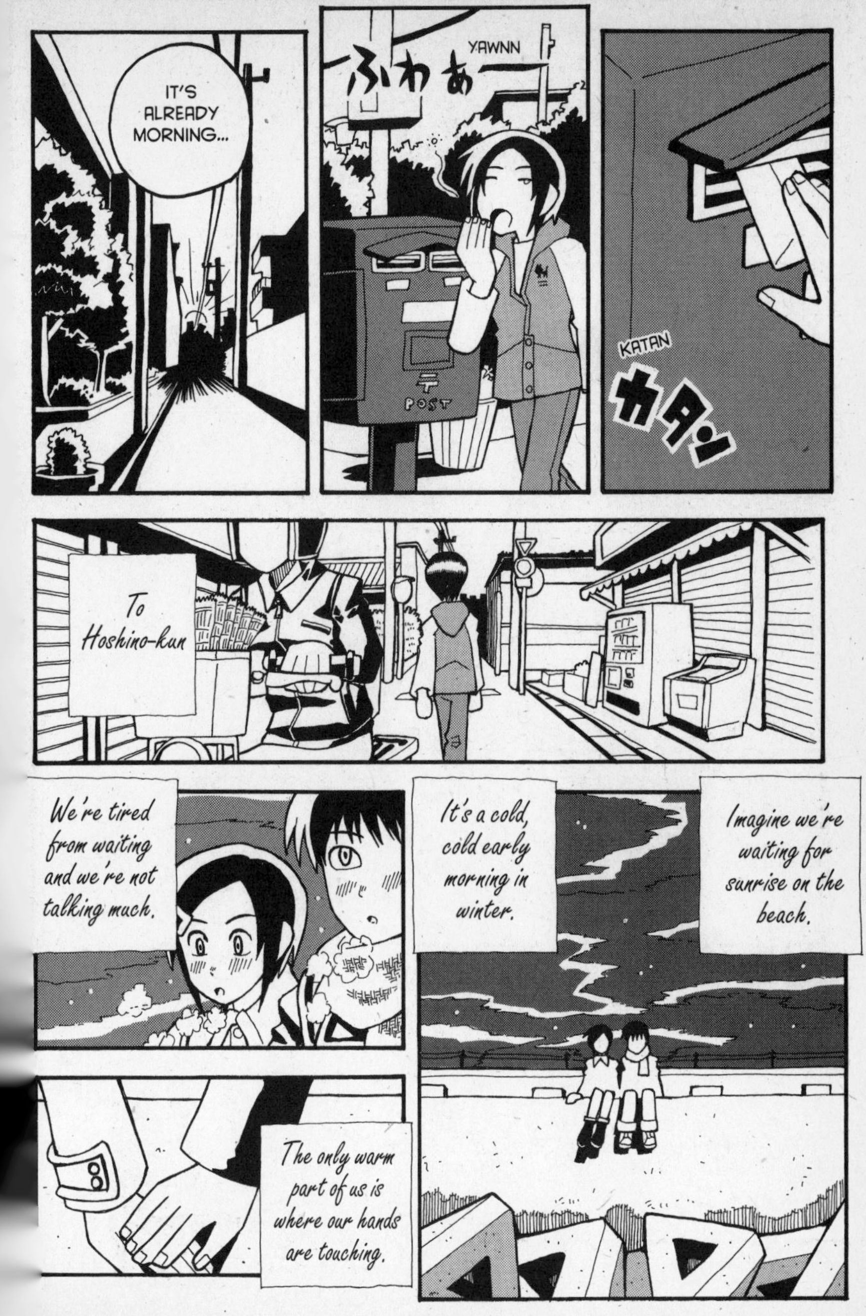
KATAN
カタン
YAWNN
ふわあー
IT'S ALREADY MORNING...
To Hoshino-kun
Imagine we're waiting for sunrise on the beach.
It's a cold, cold early morning in winter.
We're tired from waiting and we're not talking much.
The only warm part of us is where our hands are touching.

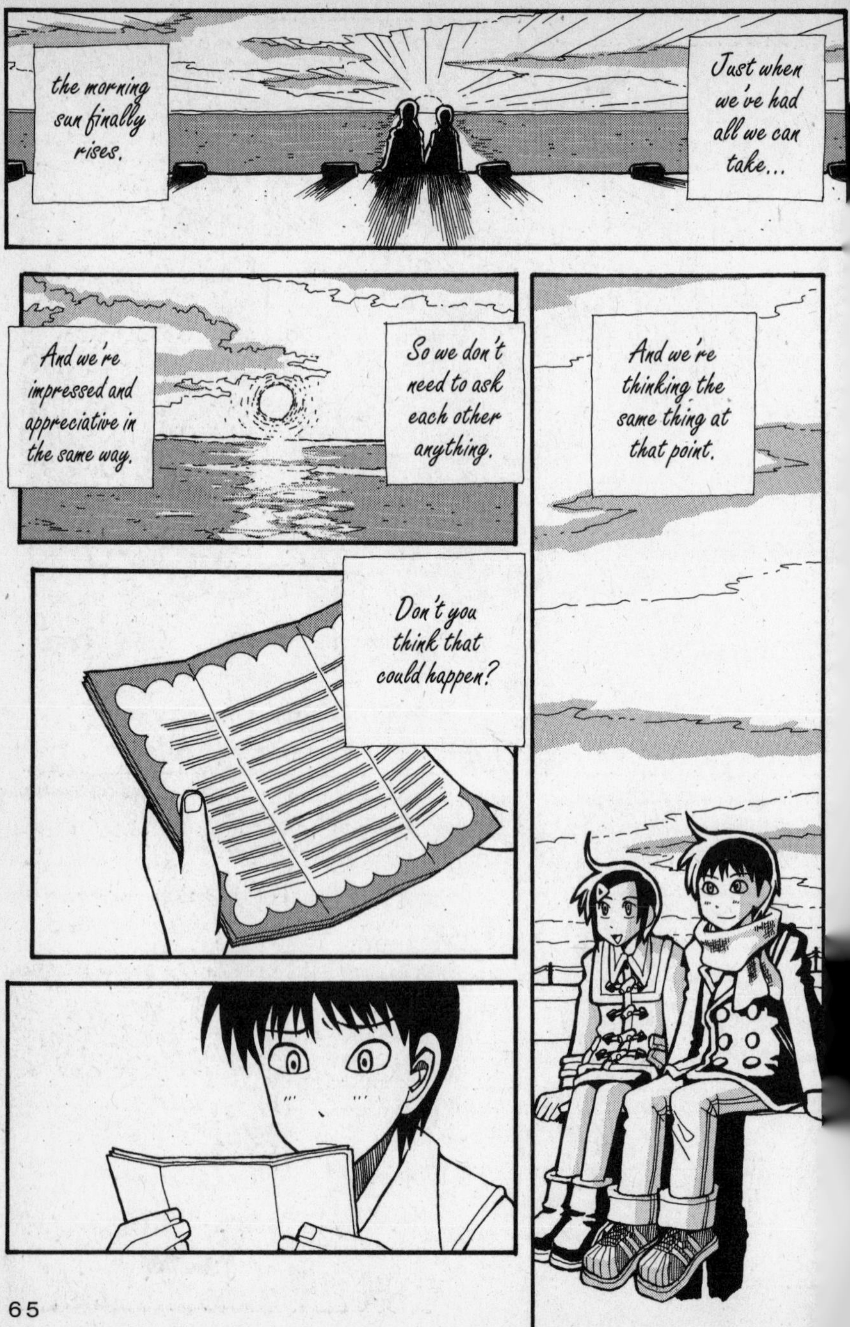
Just when we've had all we can take...
the morning sun finally rises.
And we're thinking the same thing at that point.
So we don't need to ask each other anything.
And we're impressed and appreciative in the same way.
Don't you think that could happen?

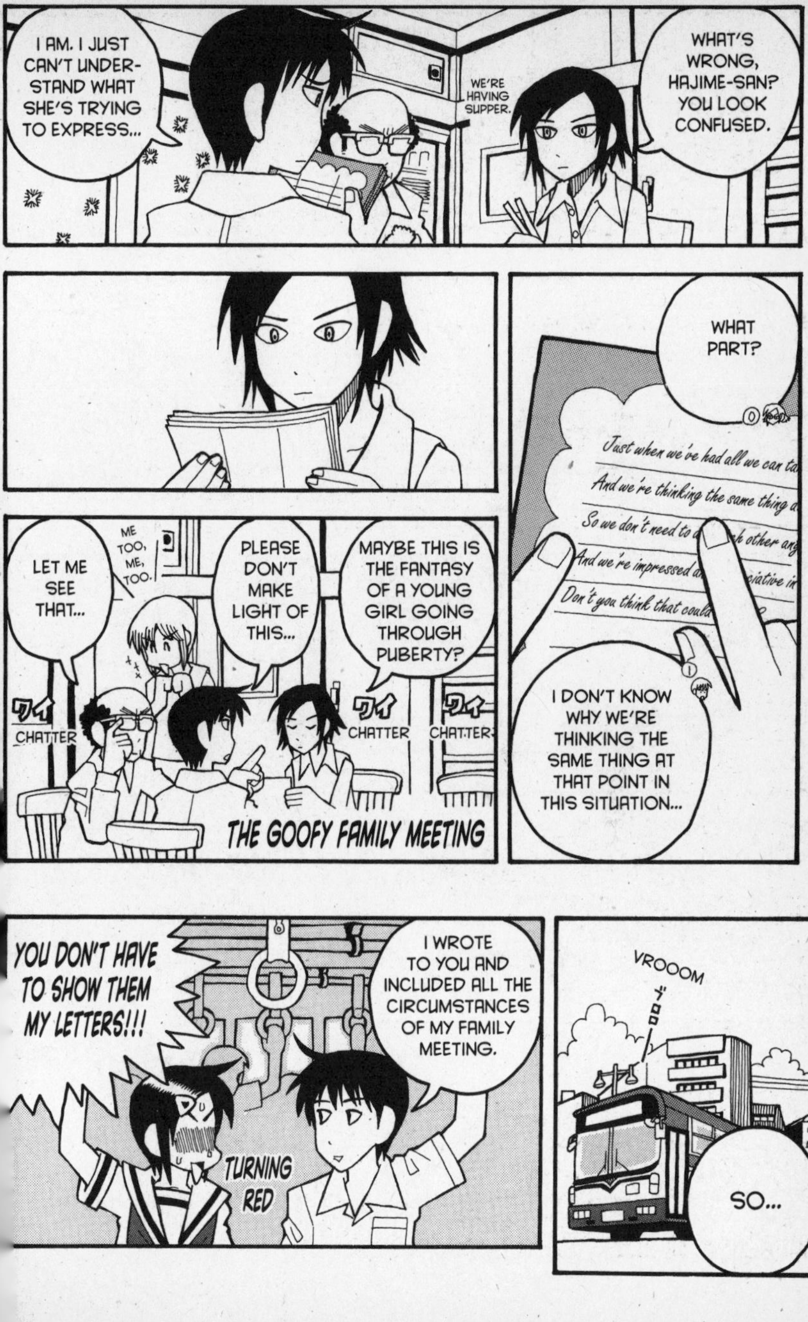
WHAT'S WRONG, HAJIME-SAN? YOU LOOK CONFUSED.
WE'RE HAVING SUPPER.
I AM. I JUST CAN'T UNDERSTAND WHAT SHE'S TRYING TO EXPRESS...
WHAT PART?
Just when we've had all we can ta
And we're thinking the same thing a
So we don't need to
h other an
And we're impressed a
iative in
Don't you think that coul
I DON'T KNOW WHY WE'RE THINKING THE SAME THING AT THAT POINT IN THIS SITUATION...
MAYBE THIS IS THE FANTASY OF A YOUNG GIRL GOING THROUGH PUBERTY?
PLEASE DON'T MAKE LIGHT OF THIS...
ME TOO, ME, TOO.
LET ME SEE THAT...
CHATTER
CHATTER
CHATTER
THE GOOFY FAMILY MEETING
VROOOM
SO...
I WROTE TO YOU AND INCLUDED ALL THE CIRCUMSTANCES OF MY FAMILY MEETING.
YOU DON'T HAVE TO SHOW THEM MY LETTERS!!!
TURNING RED

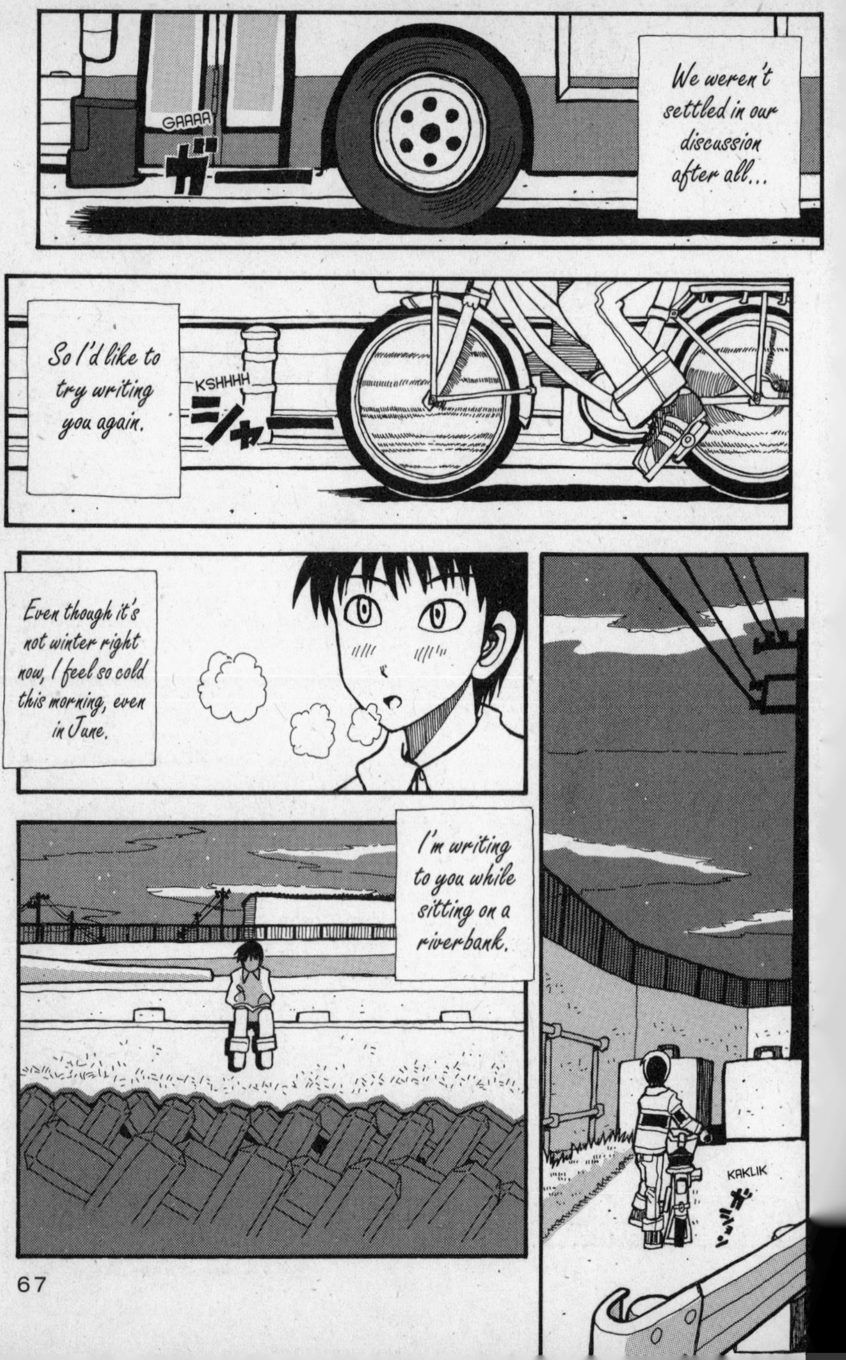
GAAAA
ガー
We weren't settled in our discussion after all...
KSHHHH
シャー
So I'd like to try writing you again.
KAKLIK
Even though it's not winter right now, I feel so cold this morning, even in June.
I'm writing to you while sitting on a riverbank.

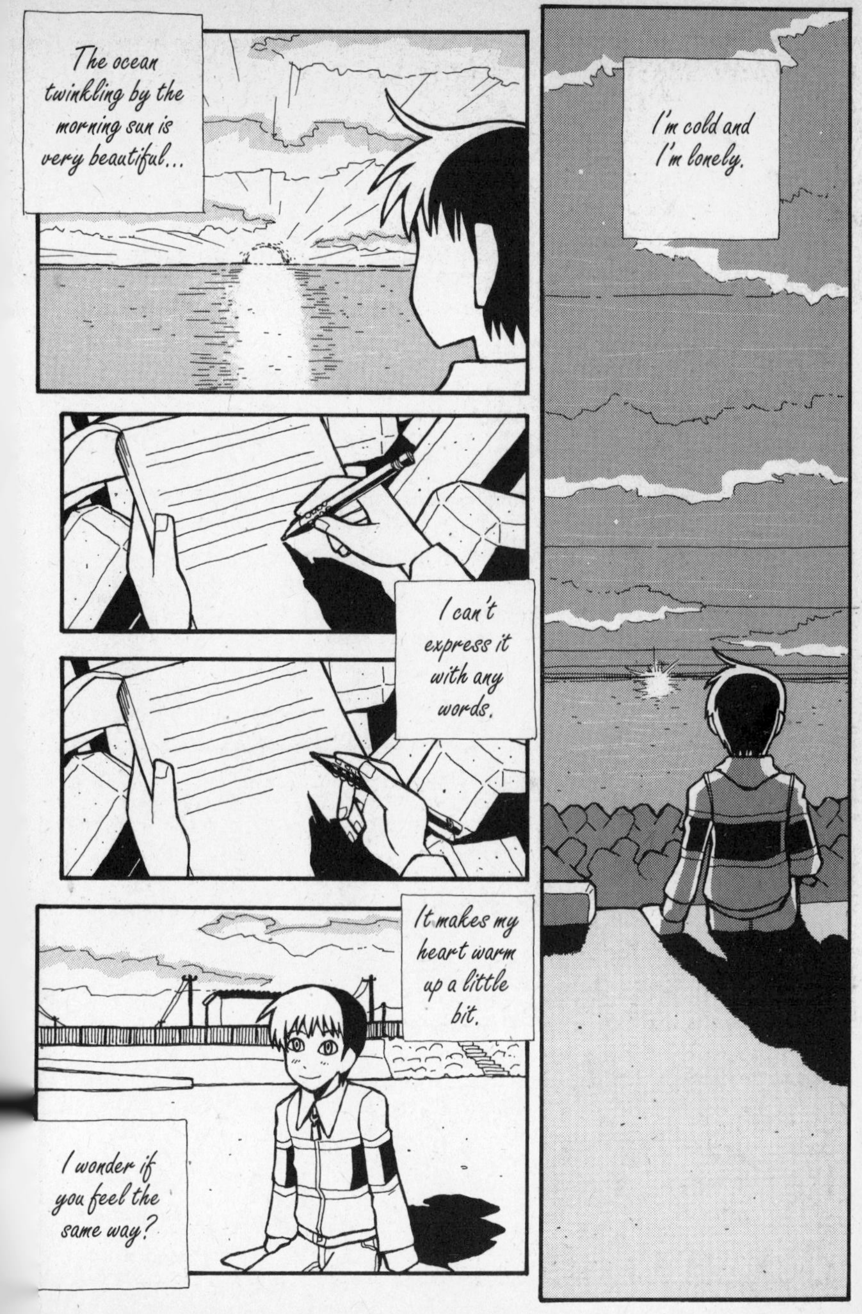
I'm cold and I'm lonely.
The ocean twinkling by the morning sun is very beautiful...
I can't express it with any words.
It makes my heart warm up a little bit.
I wonder if you feel the same way?

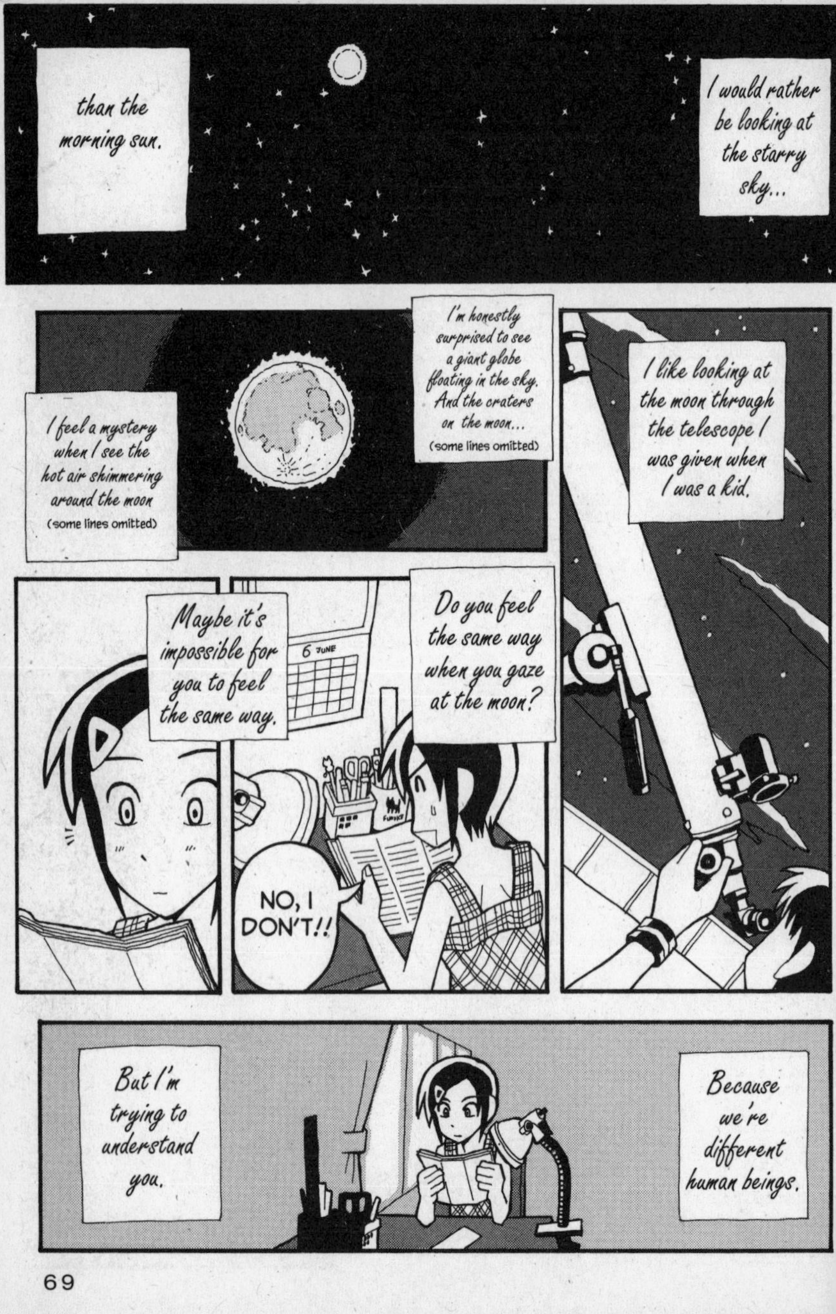
I would rather be looking at the starry sky...
than the morning sun.
I like looking at the moon through the telescope I was given when I was a kid.
I'm honestly surprised to see a giant globe floating in the sky. And the craters on the moon... (some lines omitted)
I feel a mystery when I see the hot air shimmering around the moon (some lines omitted)
Do you feel the same way when you gaze at the moon?
6 JUNE
NO, I DON'T!!
Maybe it's impossible for you to feel the same way.
Because we're different human beings.
But I'm trying to understand you.

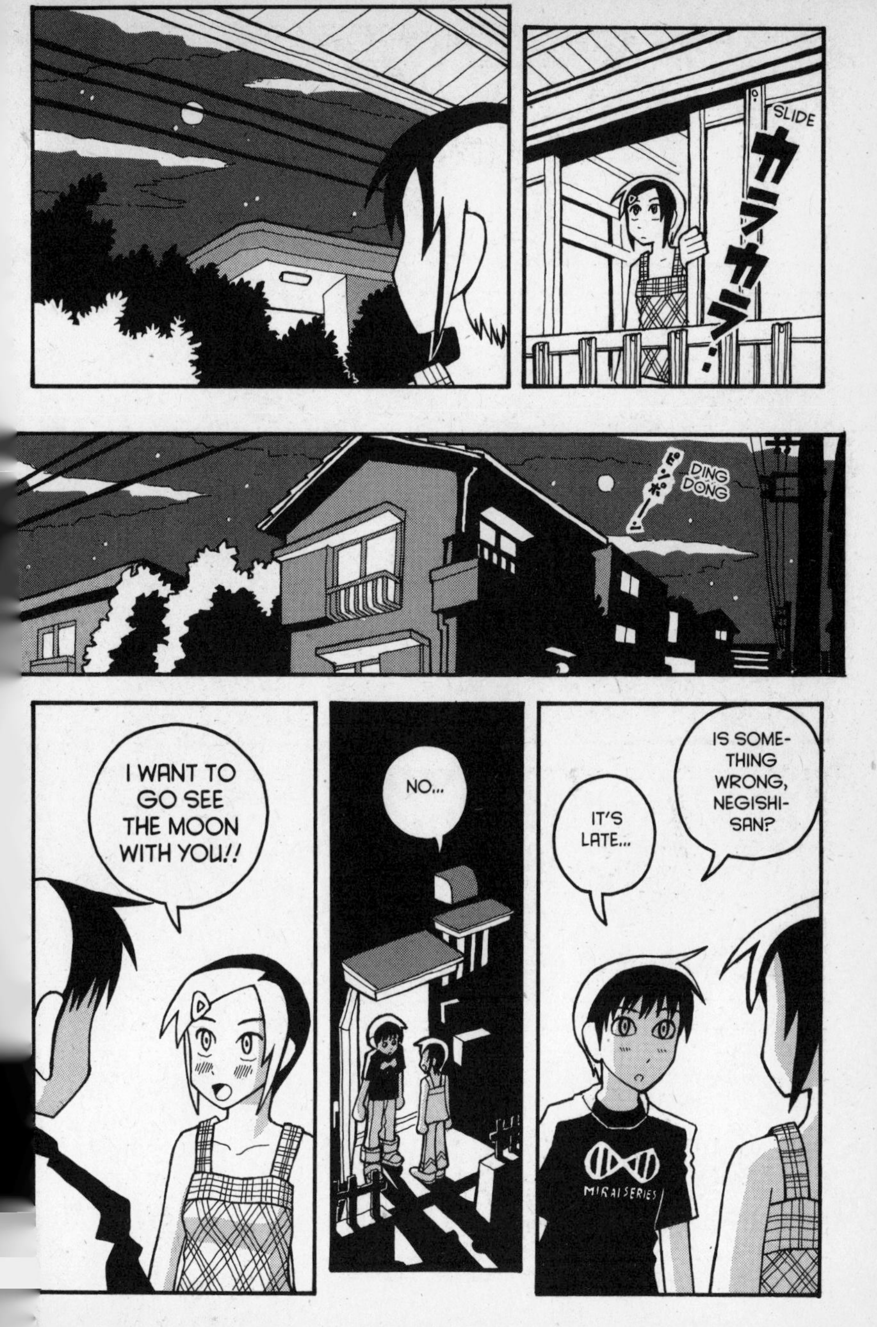
SLIDE
カラカラ…
ピンポーン
DING DONG
IS SOMETHING WRONG, NEGISHI-SAN?
IT'S LATE...
MIRAI SERIES
NO...
I WANT TO GO SEE THE MOON WITH YOU!!

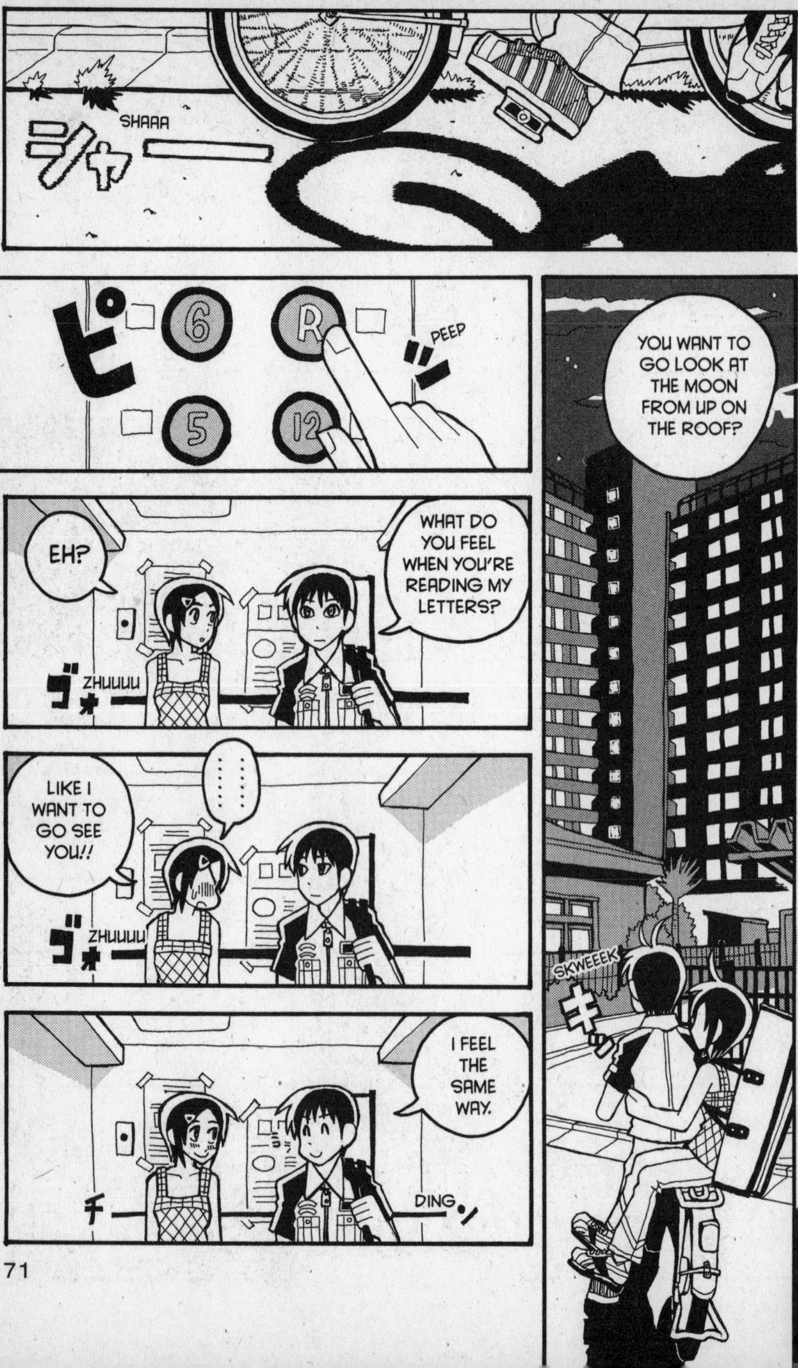
SHAAA
YOU WANT TO GO LOOK AT THE MOON FROM UP ON THE ROOF?
SKWEEEK
PEEP
WHAT DO YOU FEEL WHEN YOU'RE READING MY LETTERS?
EH?
ZHUUUU
. . . . . .
LIKE I WANT TO GO SEE YOU!!
ZHUUUU
I FEEL THE SAME WAY.
DING

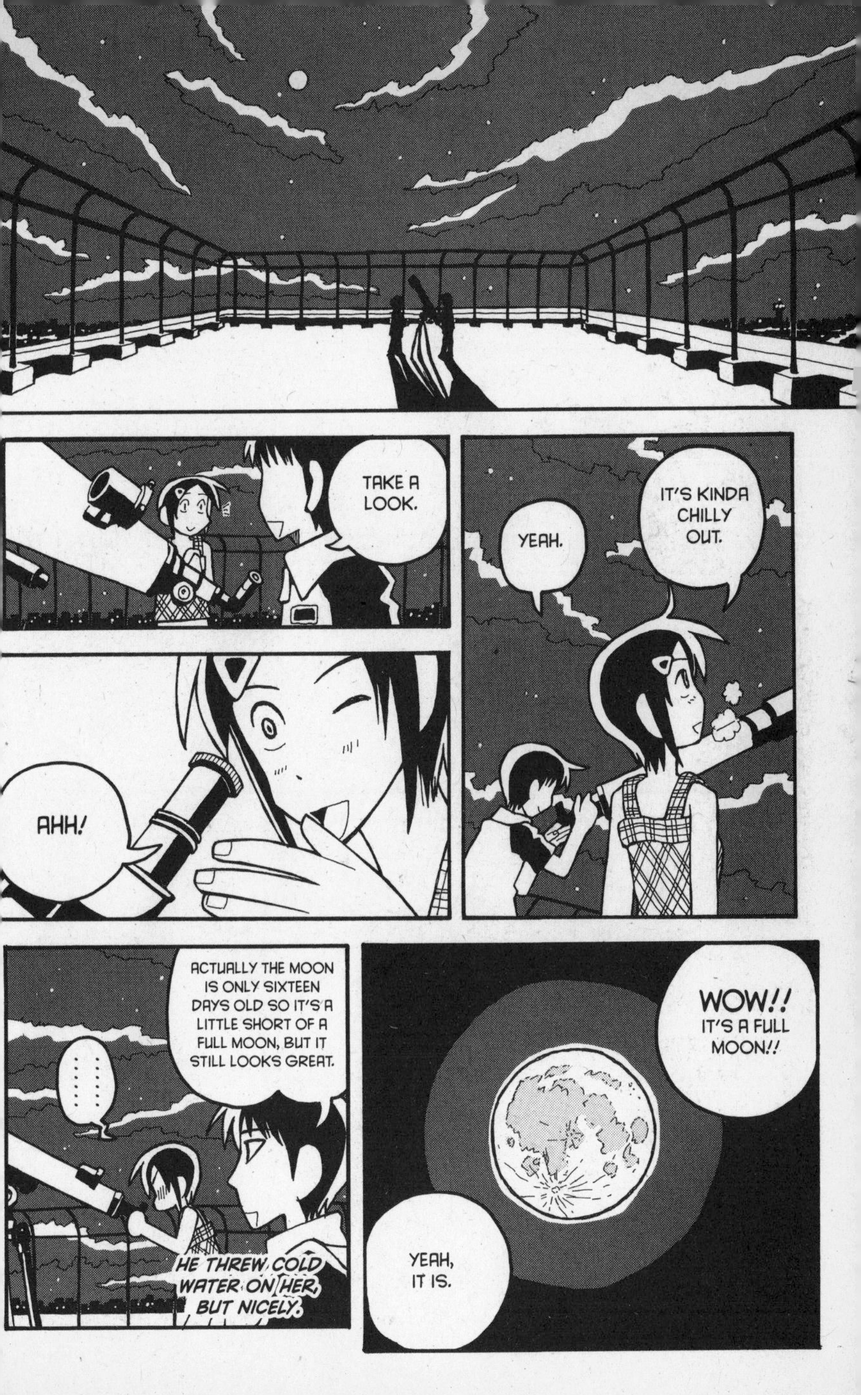
IT'S KINDA CHILLY OUT.
YEAH.
TAKE A LOOK.
AHH!
WOW!! IT'S A FULL MOON!!
YEAH, IT IS.
ACTUALLY THE MOON IS ONLY SIXTEEN DAYS OLD SO IT'S A LITTLE SHORT OF A FULL MOON, BUT IT STILL LOOKS GREAT.
......
HE THREW COLD WATER ON HER, BUT NICELY.

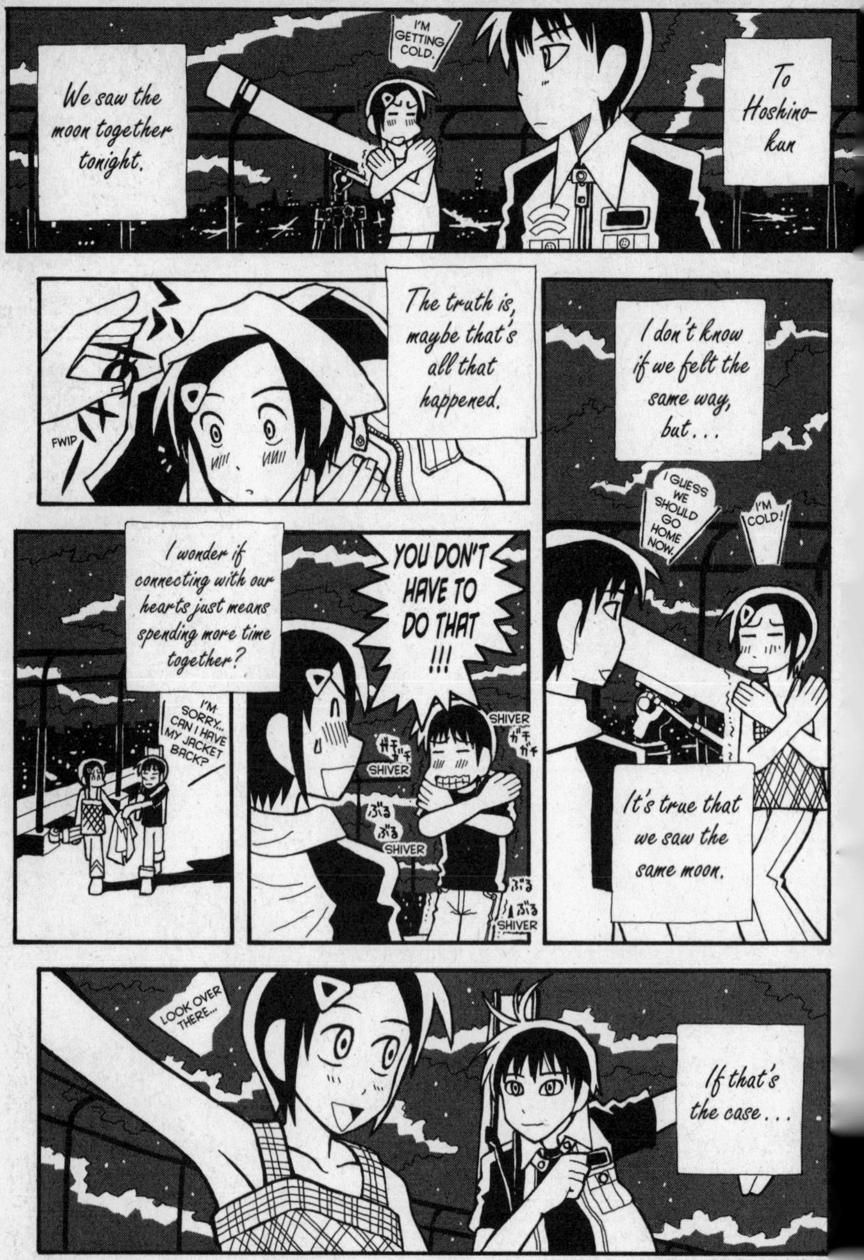
To Hoshino-kun
I'M GETTING COLD.
We saw the moon together tonight.
I don't know if we felt the same way, but...
I'M COLD!
I GUESS WE SHOULD GO HOME NOW.
It's true that we saw the same moon.
The truth is, maybe that's all that happened.
FWIP
YOU DON'T HAVE TO DO THAT !!!
SHIVER ガチガチ
ガチガチ SHIVER
ぶるぶる SHIVER
ぶるぶる SHIVER
I wonder if connecting with our hearts just means spending more time together?
I'M SORRY... CAN I HAVE MY JACKET BACK?
If that's the case...
LOOK OVER THERE...

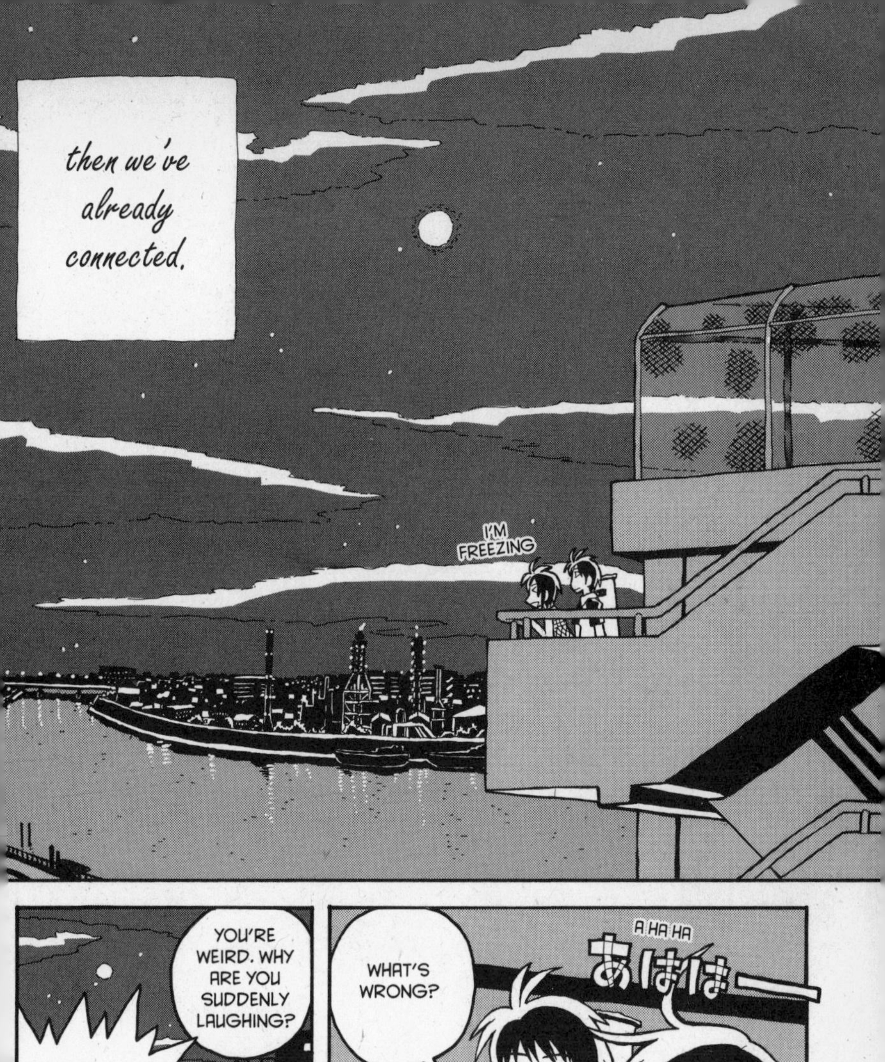
then we've already connected.
I'M FREEZING

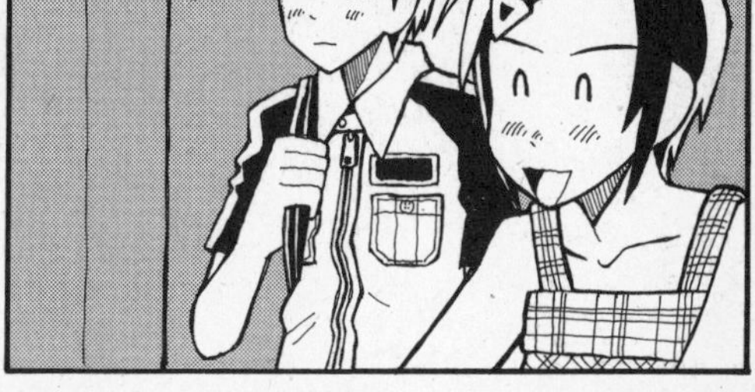
A HA HA
あははー
WHAT'S WRONG?

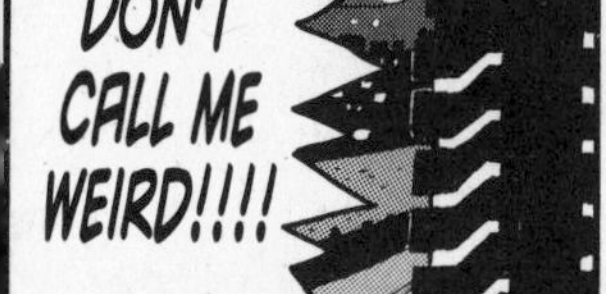
YOU'RE WEIRD. WHY ARE YOU SUDDENLY LAUGHING?
DON'T CALL ME WEIRD!!!!

TRACK 28

THE END.

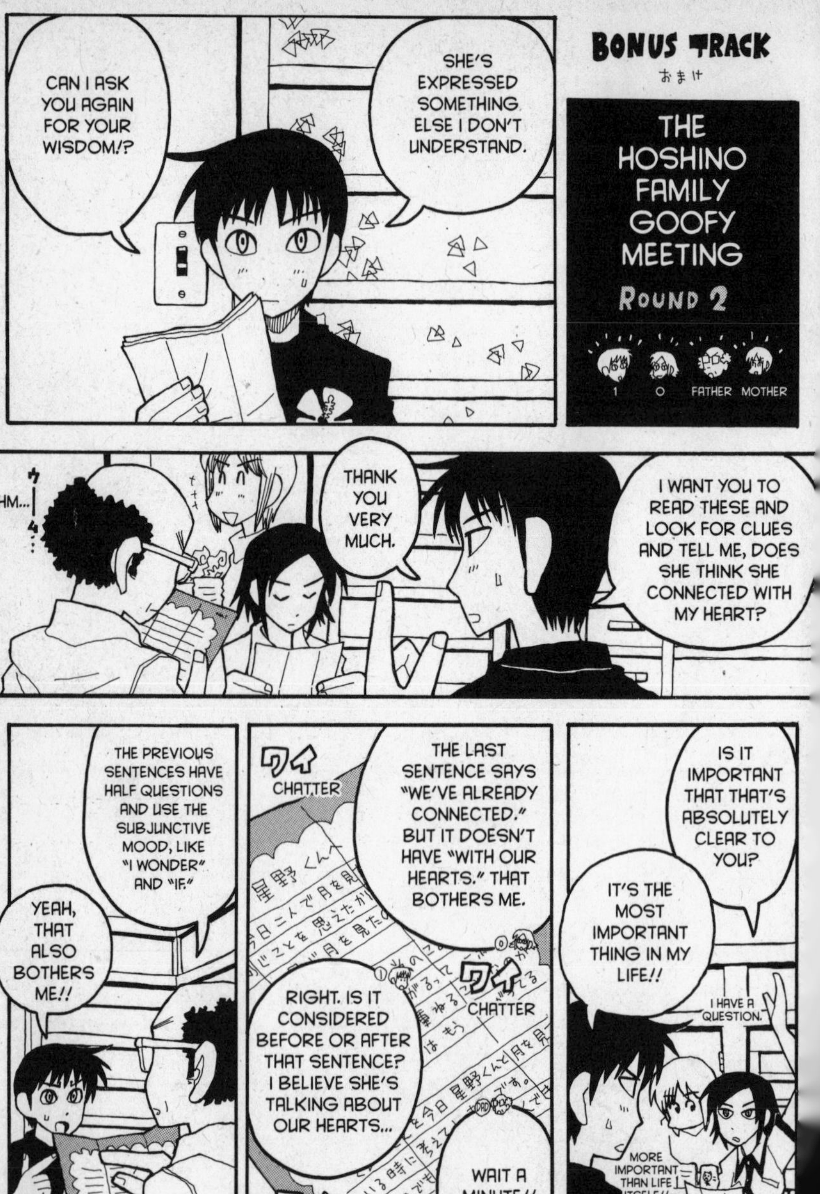
BONUS TRACK
おまけ
THE HOSHINO FAMILY GOOFY MEETING
ROUND 2
1 O FATHER MOTHER
SHE'S EXPRESSED SOMETHING ELSE I DON'T UNDERSTAND.
CAN I ASK YOU AGAIN FOR YOUR WISDOM!?
I WANT YOU TO READ THESE AND LOOK FOR CLUES AND TELL ME, DOES SHE THINK SHE CONNECTED WITH MY HEART?
THANK YOU VERY MUCH.
HM... ウーム…
IS IT IMPORTANT THAT THAT'S ABSOLUTELY CLEAR TO YOU?
IT'S THE MOST IMPORTANT THING IN MY LIFE!!
I HAVE A QUESTION.
MORE IMPORTANT THAN LIFE ITSELF!!
ワイ CHATTER
THE LAST SENTENCE SAYS "WE'VE ALREADY CONNECTED." BUT IT DOESN'T HAVE "WITH OUR HEARTS." THAT BOTHERS ME.
ワイ CHATTER
RIGHT. IS IT CONSIDERED BEFORE OR AFTER THAT SENTENCE? I BELIEVE SHE'S TALKING ABOUT OUR HEARTS...
WAIT A MINUTE!!
ワイ CHATTER
THE PREVIOUS SENTENCES HAVE HALF QUESTIONS AND USE THE SUBJUNCTIVE MOOD, LIKE "I WONDER" AND "IF."
YEAH, THAT ALSO BOTHERS ME!!

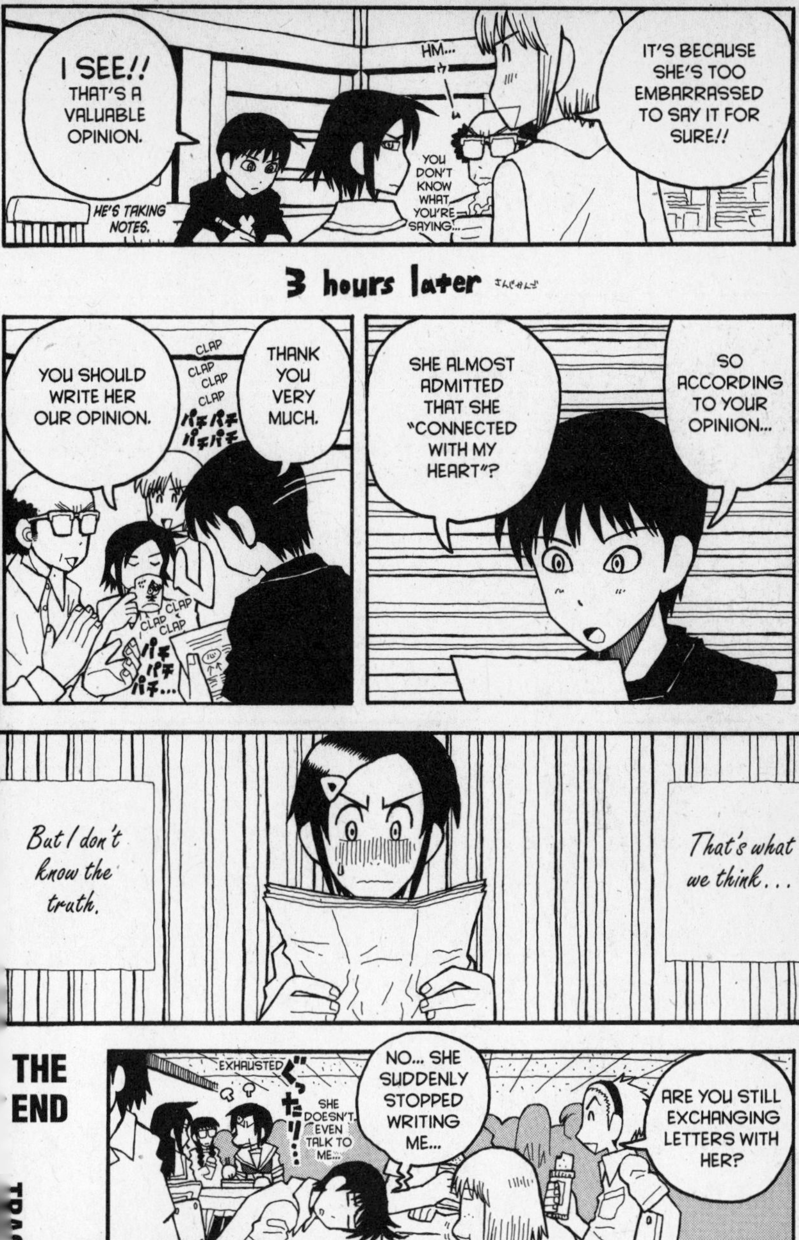
IT'S BECAUSE SHE'S TOO EMBARRASSED TO SAY IT FOR SURE!!
HM... ウ〜ム
YOU DON'T KNOW WHAT YOU'RE SAYING...
I SEE!! THAT'S A VALUABLE OPINION.
HE'S TAKING NOTES.
3 hours later
SO ACCORDING TO YOUR OPINION...
SHE ALMOST ADMITTED THAT SHE "CONNECTED WITH MY HEART"?
THANK YOU VERY MUCH.
CLAP CLAP CLAP CLAP
パチパチパチパチ
YOU SHOULD WRITE HER OUR OPINION.
CLAP CLAP CLAP
パチパチパチ...
That's what we think...
But I don't know the truth.
ARE YOU STILL EXCHANGING LETTERS WITH HER?
NO... SHE SUDDENLY STOPPED WRITING ME...
SHE DOESN'T EVEN TALK TO ME...
EXHAUSTED ぐったり…
THE END

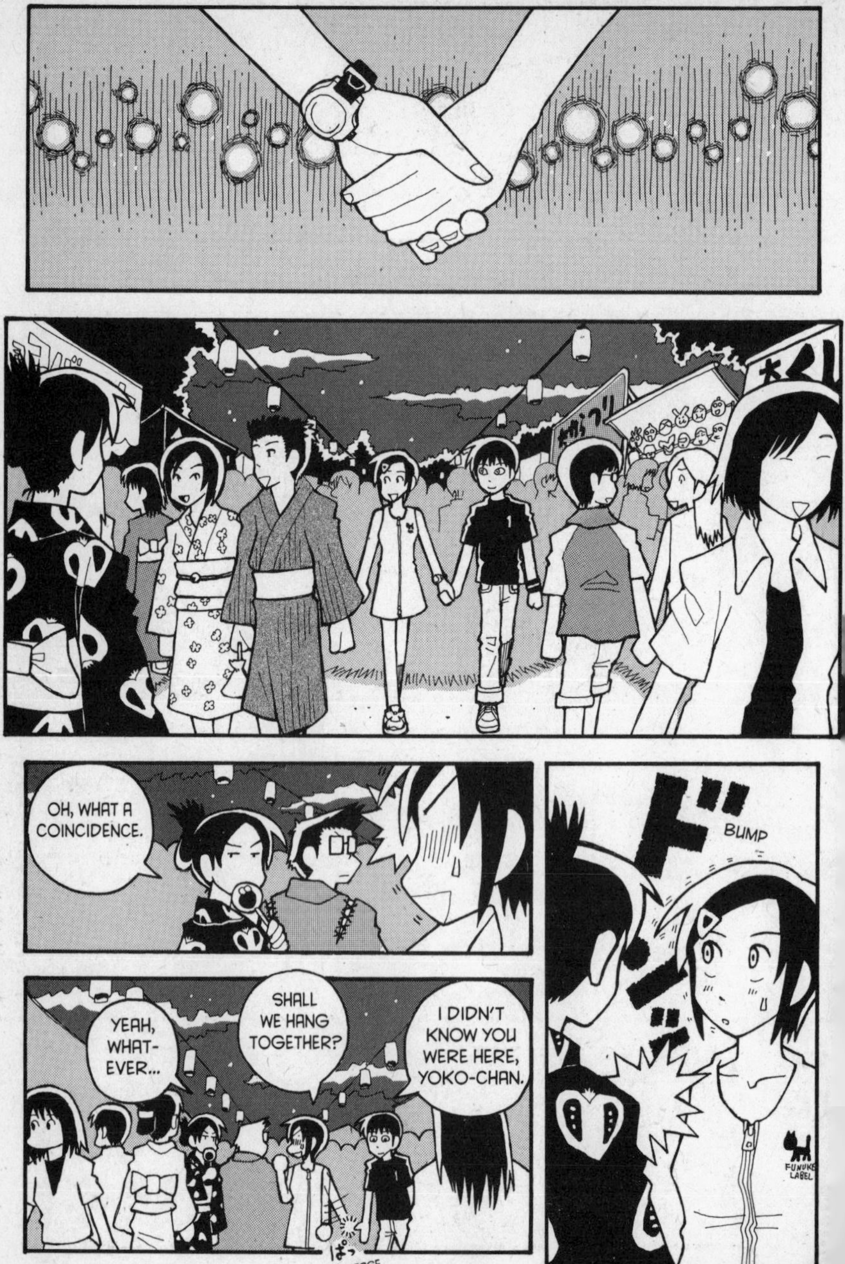

ド
BUMP
FUNUKE LABEL
OH, WHAT A COINCIDENCE.
I DIDN'T KNOW YOU WERE HERE, YOKO-CHAN.
SHALL WE HANG TOGETHER?
YEAH, WHAT-EVER...
ぱっ
RELEASE

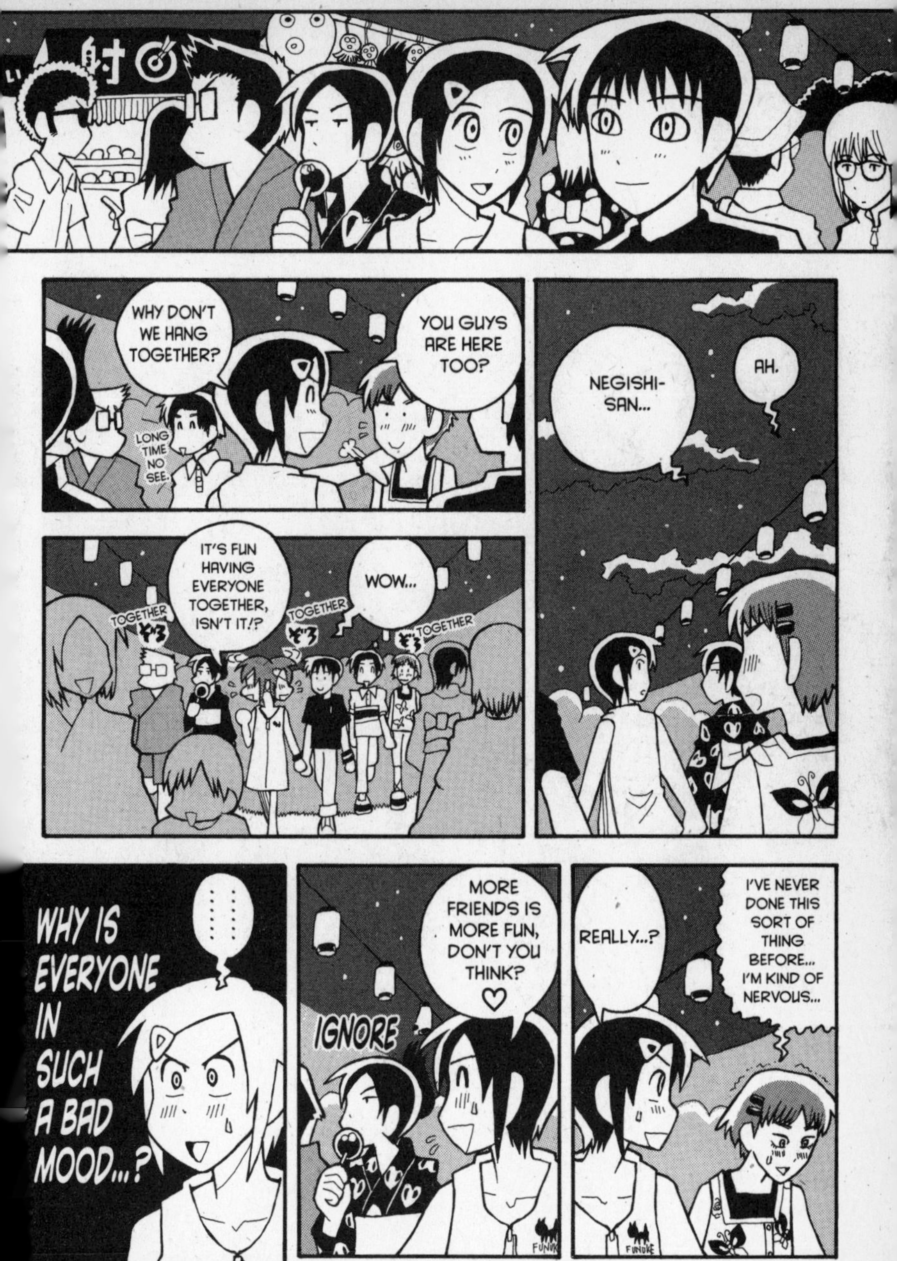

射
AH.
NEGISHI-SAN...
YOU GUYS ARE HERE TOO?
WHY DON'T WE HANG TOGETHER?
LONG TIME NO SEE.
WOW...
IT'S FUN HAVING EVERYONE TOGETHER, ISN'T IT!?
TOGETHER ぞろ
TOGETHER ぞろ
TOGETHER ぞろ
I'VE NEVER DONE THIS SORT OF THING BEFORE... I'M KIND OF NERVOUS...
REALLY...?
FUNUKE
MORE FRIENDS IS MORE FUN, DON'T YOU THINK? ♡
IGNORE
......
WHY IS EVERYONE IN SUCH A BAD MOOD...?

TRACK #29 DATING TOGETHER WITH FRIENDS

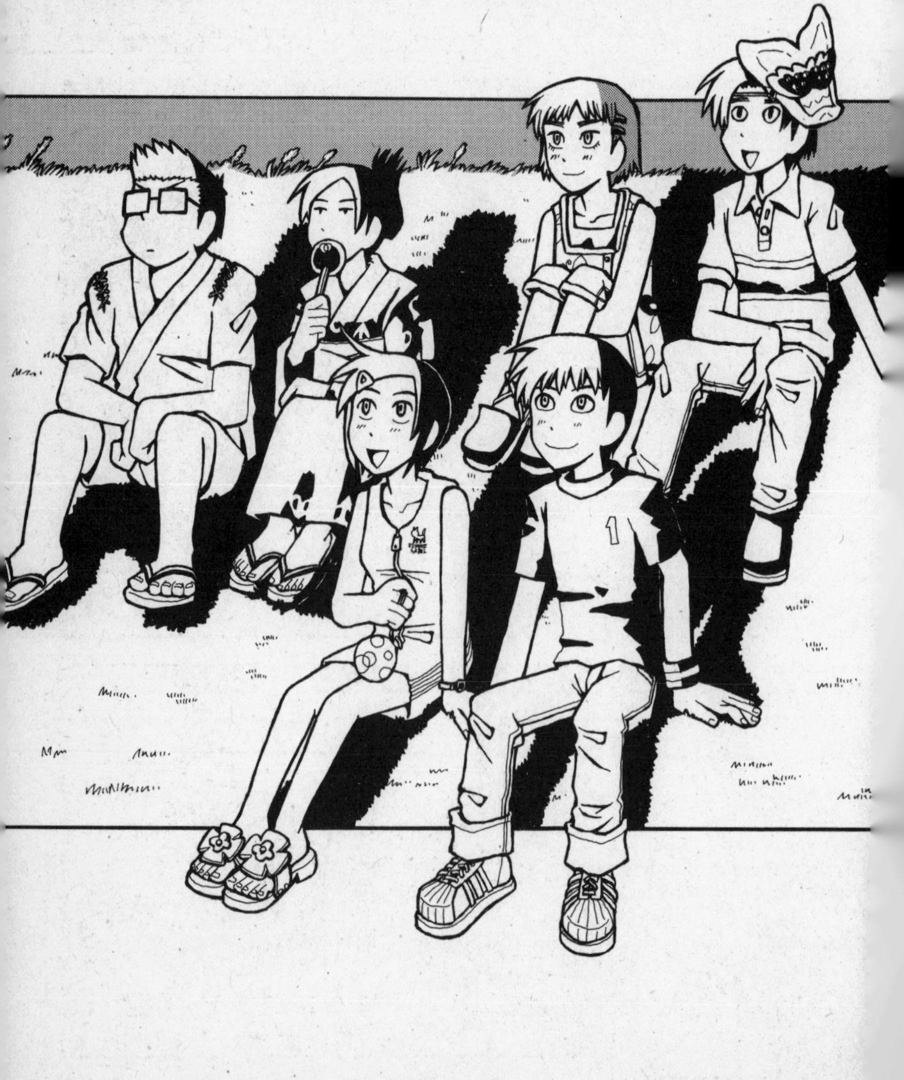

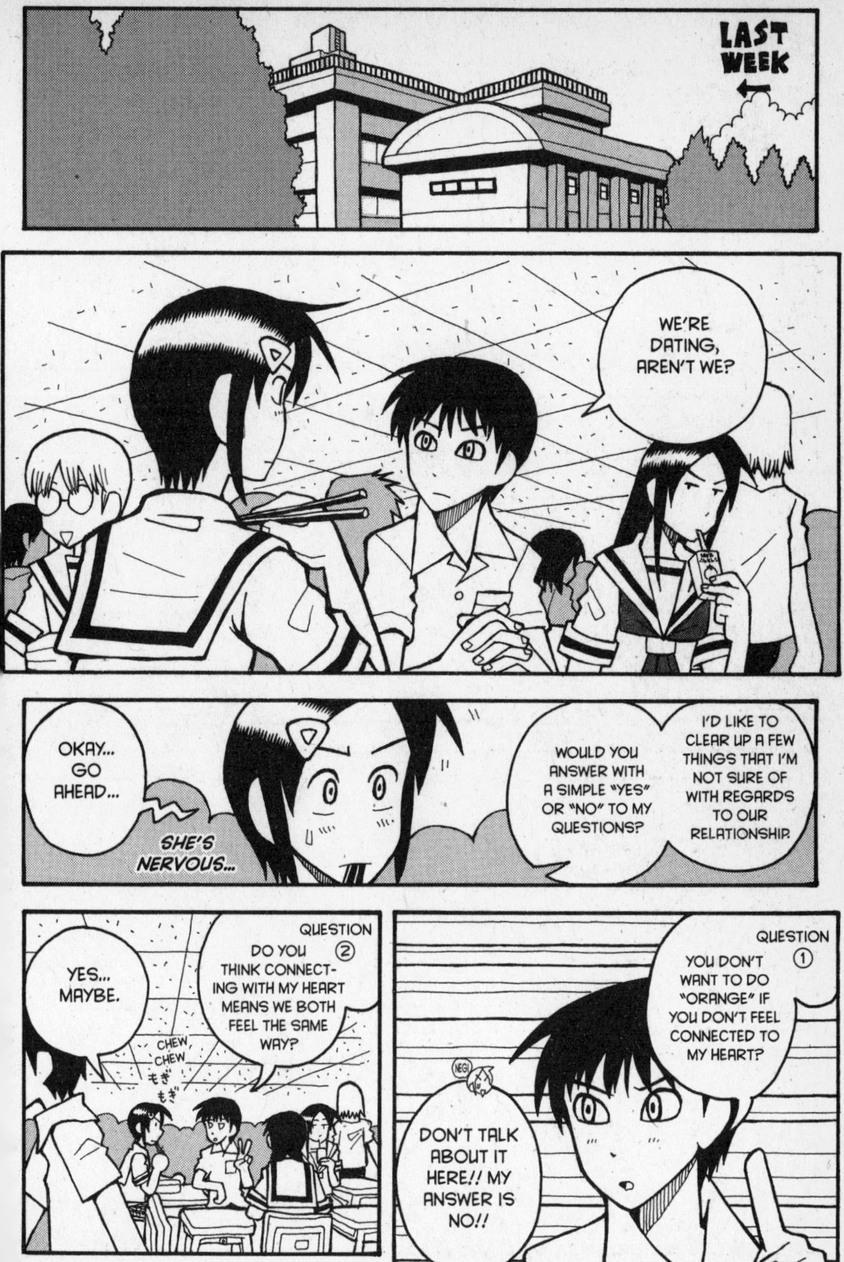
LAST WEEK
WE'RE DATING, AREN'T WE?
I'D LIKE TO CLEAR UP A FEW THINGS THAT I'M NOT SURE OF WITH REGARDS TO OUR RELATIONSHIP.
WOULD YOU ANSWER WITH A SIMPLE "YES" OR "NO" TO MY QUESTIONS?
OKAY... GO AHEAD...
SHE'S NERVOUS...
QUESTION ① YOU DON'T WANT TO DO "ORANGE" IF YOU DON'T FEEL CONNECTED TO MY HEART?
NEGI
DON'T TALK ABOUT IT HERE!! MY ANSWER IS NO!!
QUESTION ② DO YOU THINK CONNECTING WITH MY HEART MEANS WE BOTH FEEL THE SAME WAY?
YES... MAYBE.
CHEW, CHEW
もぎもぎ

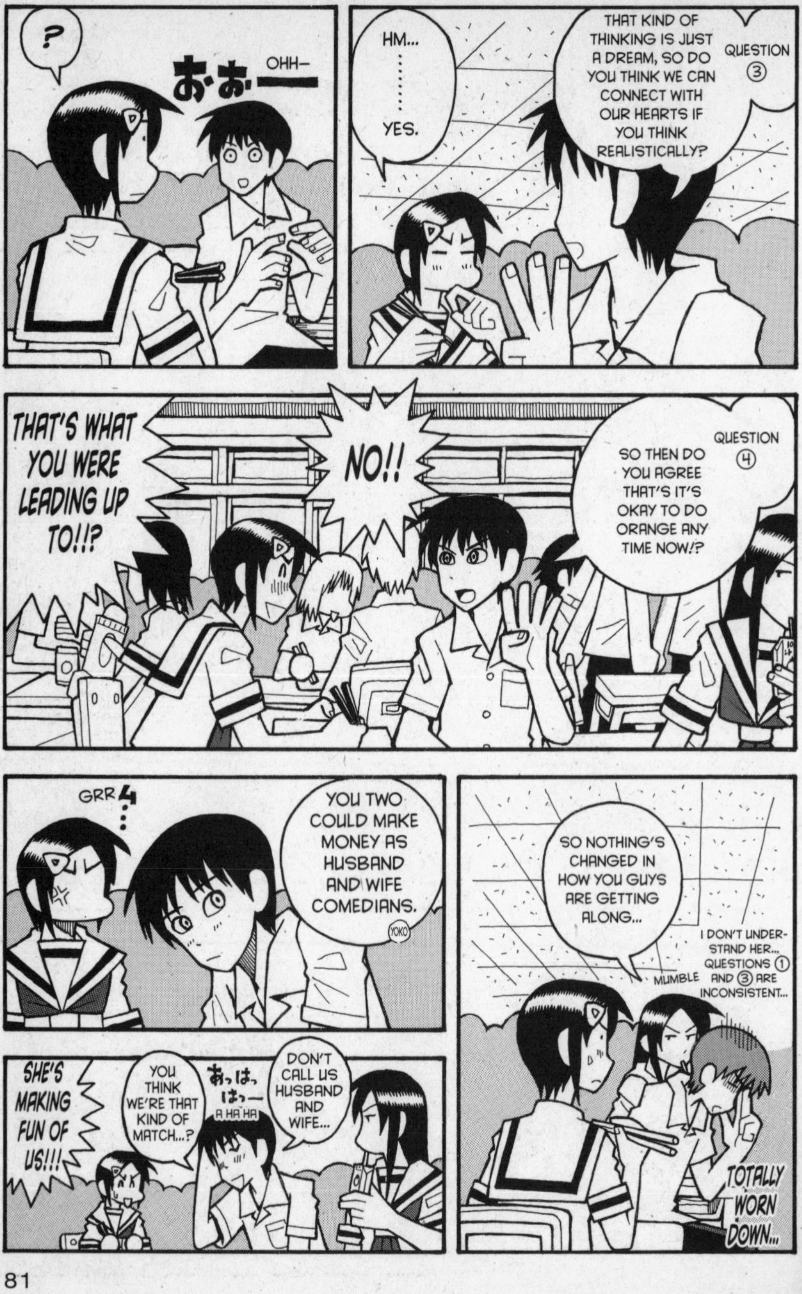
THAT KIND OF THINKING IS JUST A DREAM, SO DO YOU THINK WE CAN CONNECT WITH OUR HEARTS IF YOU THINK REALISTICALLY?
QUESTION ③
HM... ...... YES.
おおー
OHH—
?
QUESTION ④
SO THEN DO YOU AGREE THAT'S IT'S OKAY TO DO ORANGE ANY TIME NOW!?
NO!!
THAT'S WHAT YOU WERE LEADING UP TO!!?
SO NOTHING'S CHANGED IN HOW YOU GUYS ARE GETTING ALONG...
I DON'T UNDERSTAND HER... QUESTIONS ① AND ③ ARE INCONSISTENT...
MUMBLE
TOTALLY WORN DOWN...
YOU TWO COULD MAKE MONEY AS HUSBAND AND WIFE COMEDIANS.
YOKO
GRR
DON'T CALL US HUSBAND AND WIFE...
おっはっはっー
A HA HA
YOU THINK WE'RE THAT KIND OF MATCH...?
SHE'S MAKING FUN OF US!!!

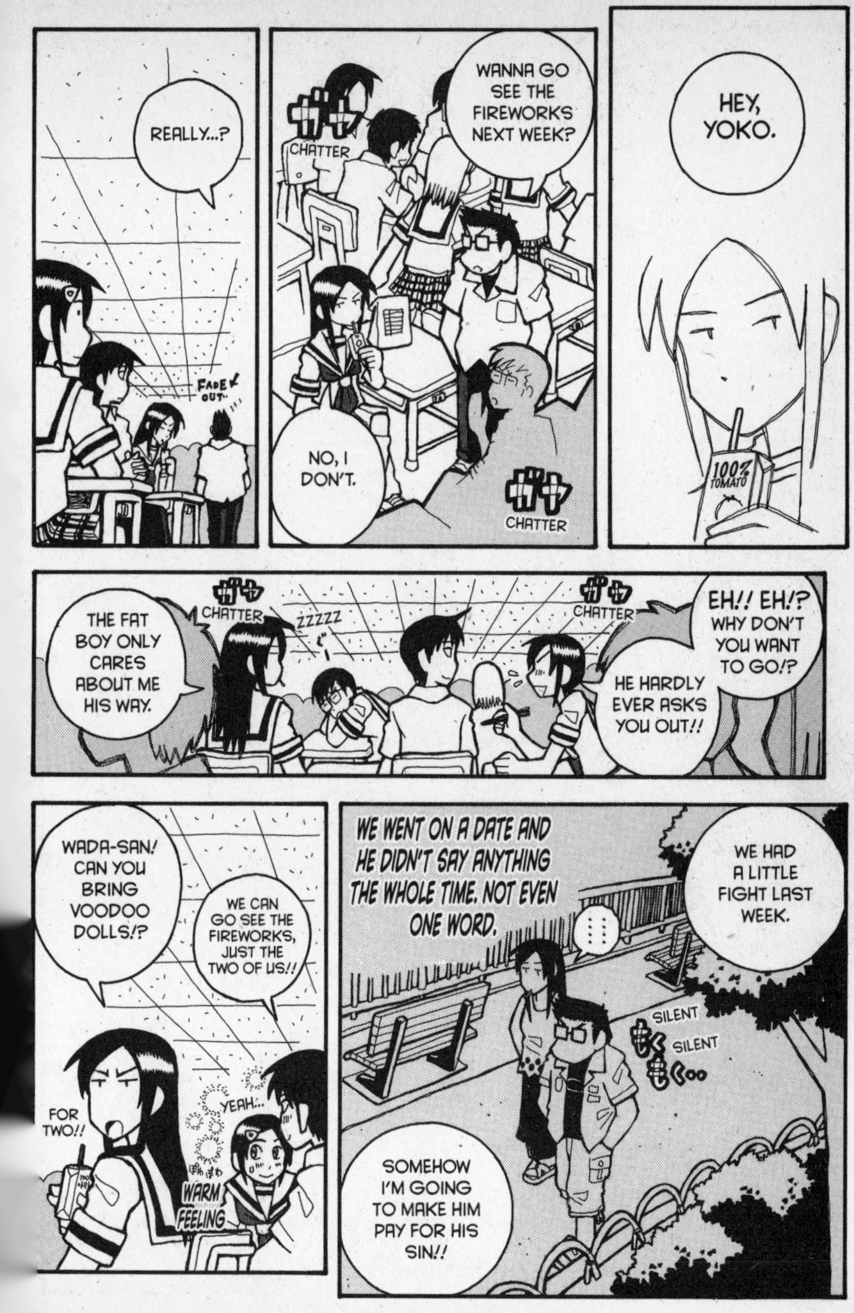
HEY, YOKO.
100% TOMATO
WANNA GO SEE THE FIREWORKS NEXT WEEK?
CHATTER
NO, I DON'T.
CHATTER
REALLY...?
FADE OUT
EH!! EH!? WHY DON'T YOU WANT TO GO!?
HE HARDLY EVER ASKS YOU OUT!!
CHATTER
ZZZZZ
CHATTER
THE FAT BOY ONLY CARES ABOUT ME HIS WAY.
WE HAD A LITTLE FIGHT LAST WEEK.
WE WENT ON A DATE AND HE DIDN'T SAY ANYTHING THE WHOLE TIME. NOT EVEN ONE WORD.
......
SILENT
SILENT
SOMEHOW I'M GOING TO MAKE HIM PAY FOR HIS SIN!!
WE CAN GO SEE THE FIREWORKS, JUST THE TWO OF US!!
WADA-SAN! CAN YOU BRING VOODOO DOLLS!?
YEAH...
FOR TWO!!
WARM FEELING

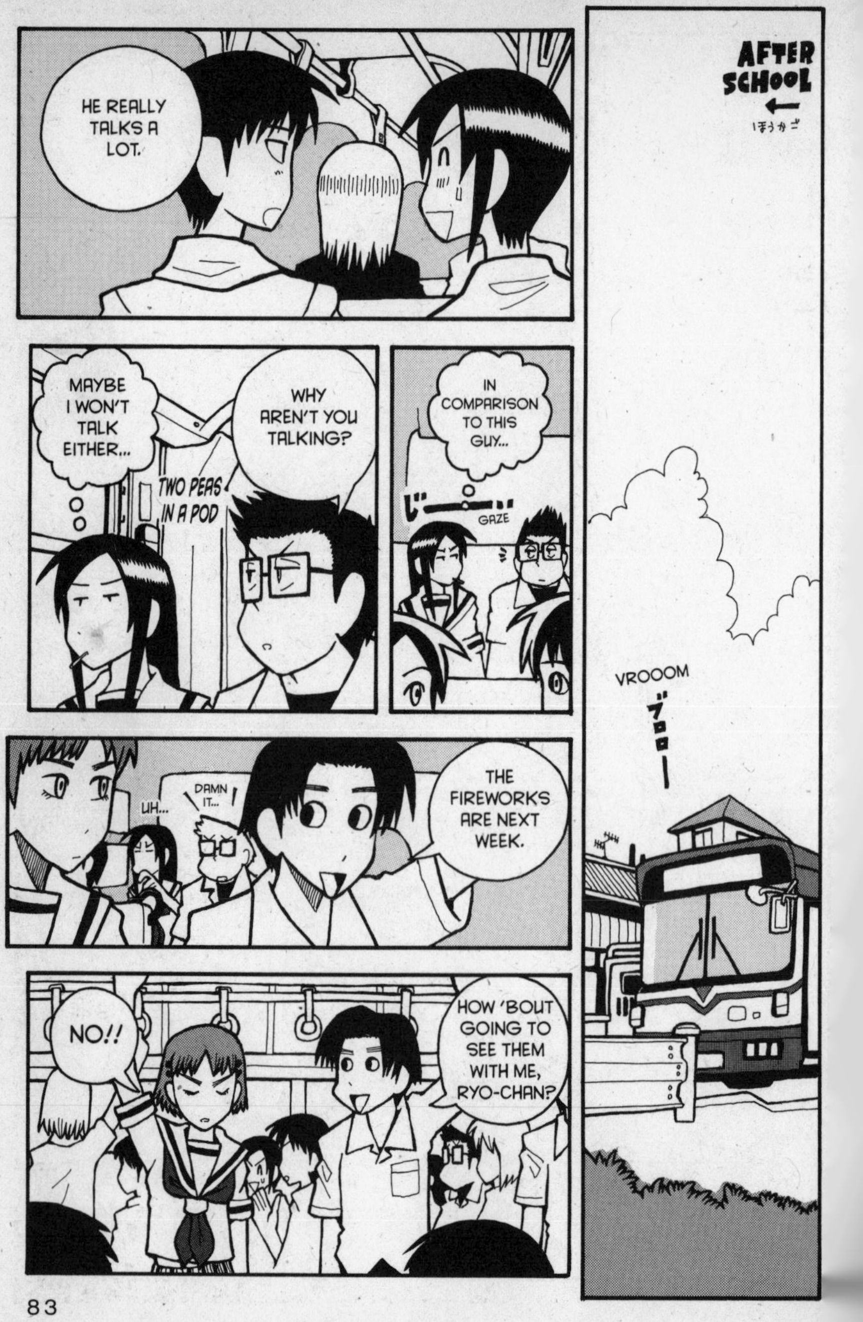
AFTER SCHOOL
ほうかご
VROOOM
ブロロー
HE REALLY TALKS A LOT.
IN COMPARISON TO THIS GUY...
じー
GAZE
WHY AREN'T YOU TALKING?
MAYBE I WON'T TALK EITHER...
TWO PEAS IN A POD
THE FIREWORKS ARE NEXT WEEK.
DAMN IT...
UH...
HOW 'BOUT GOING TO SEE THEM WITH ME, RYO-CHAN?
NO!!

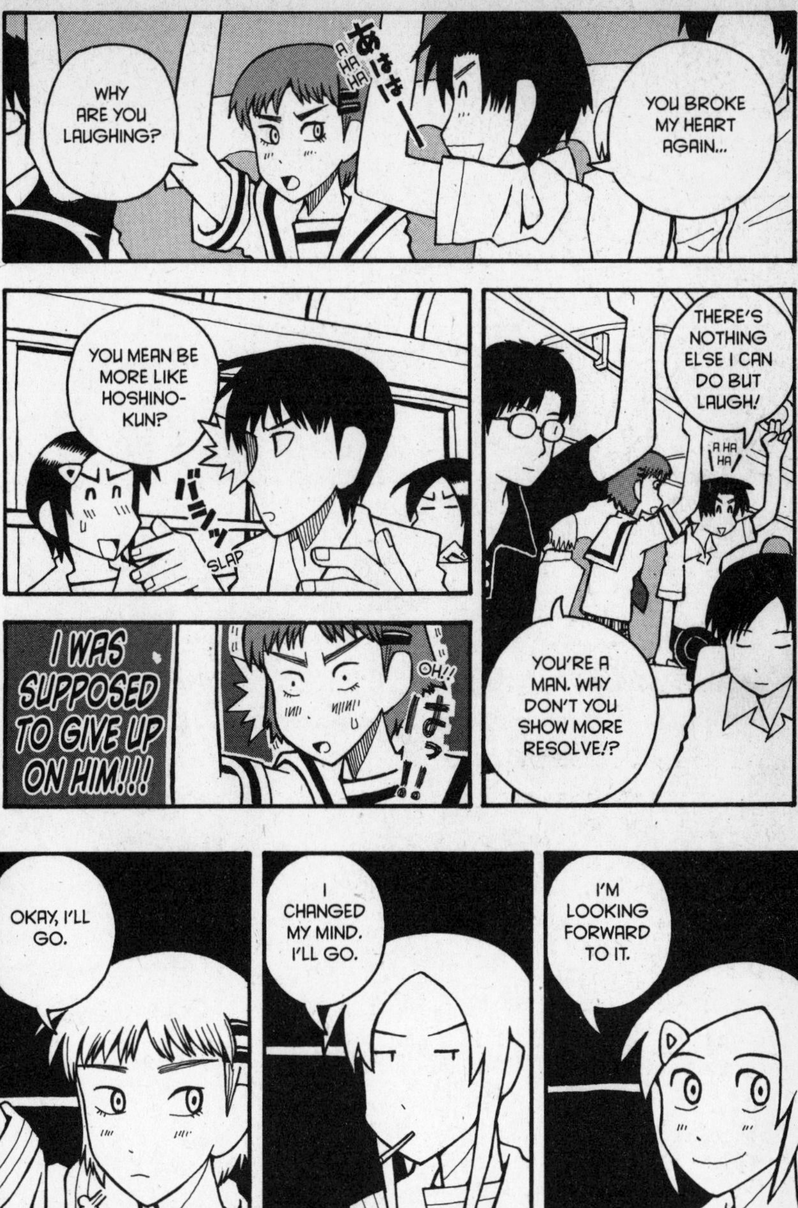
YOU BROKE MY HEART AGAIN...
あはは—
A HA HA
WHY ARE YOU LAUGHING?
THERE'S NOTHING ELSE I CAN DO BUT LAUGH!
A HA HA
YOU'RE A MAN. WHY DON'T YOU SHOW MORE RESOLVE!?
YOU MEAN BE MORE LIKE HOSHINO-KUN?
バシッ
SLAP
OH!!
はっ!!
I WAS SUPPOSED TO GIVE UP ON HIM!!!
I'M LOOKING FORWARD TO IT.
I CHANGED MY MIND. I'LL GO.
OKAY, I'LL GO.

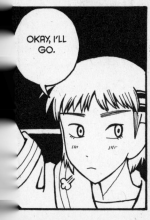

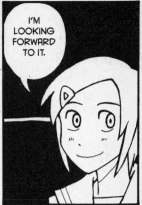

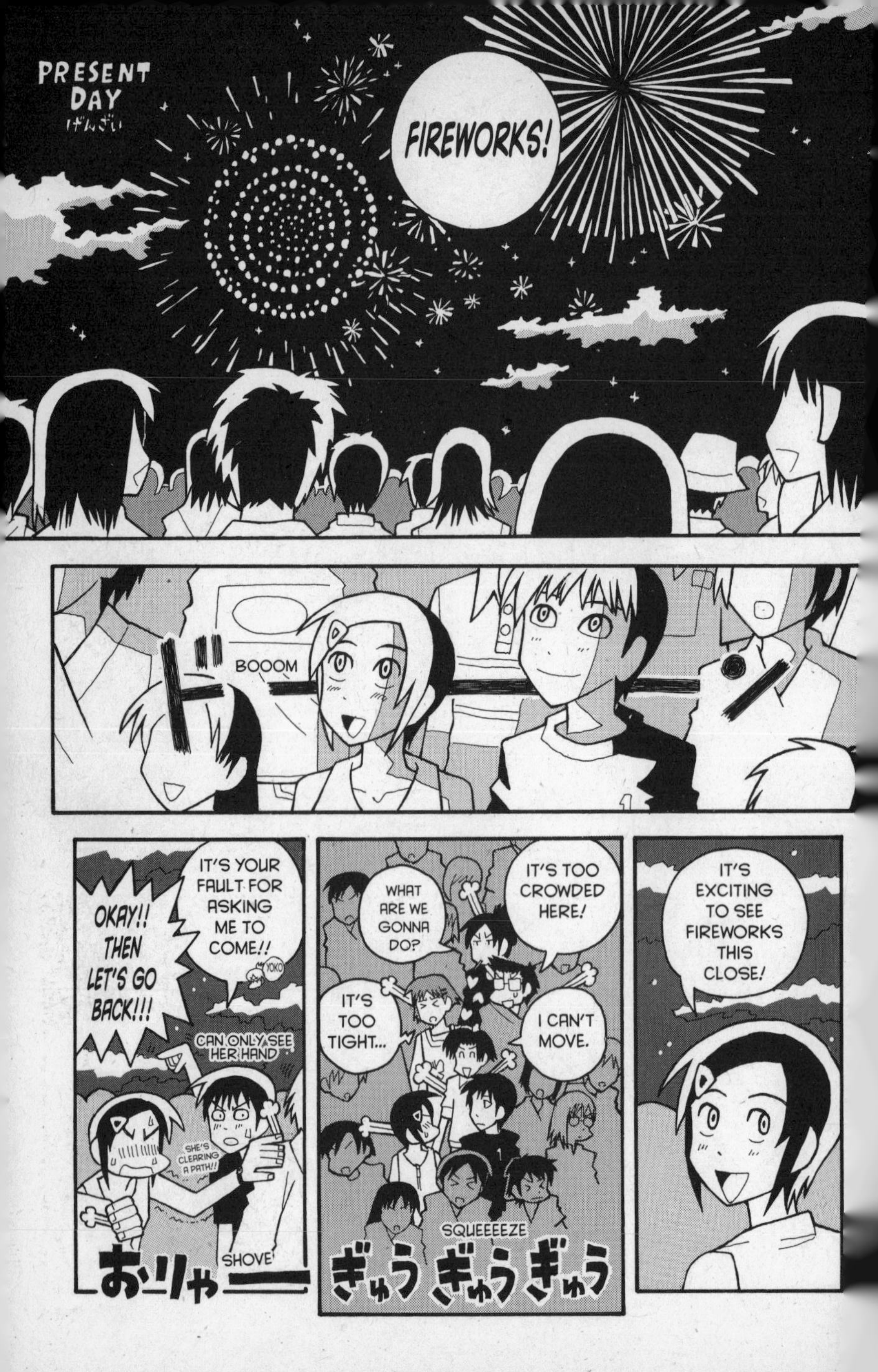
PRESENT DAY
げんざい
FIREWORKS!
BOOOM
IT'S EXCITING TO SEE FIREWORKS THIS CLOSE!
IT'S TOO CROWDED HERE!
WHAT ARE WE GONNA DO?
I CAN'T MOVE.
IT'S TOO TIGHT...
SQUEEEEZE
ぎゅうぎゅうぎゅう
IT'S YOUR FAULT FOR ASKING ME TO COME!!
YOKO
OKAY!! THEN LET'S GO BACK!!!
CAN ONLY SEE HER HAND
SHE'S CLEARING A PATH!!
SHOVE
おりゃーー

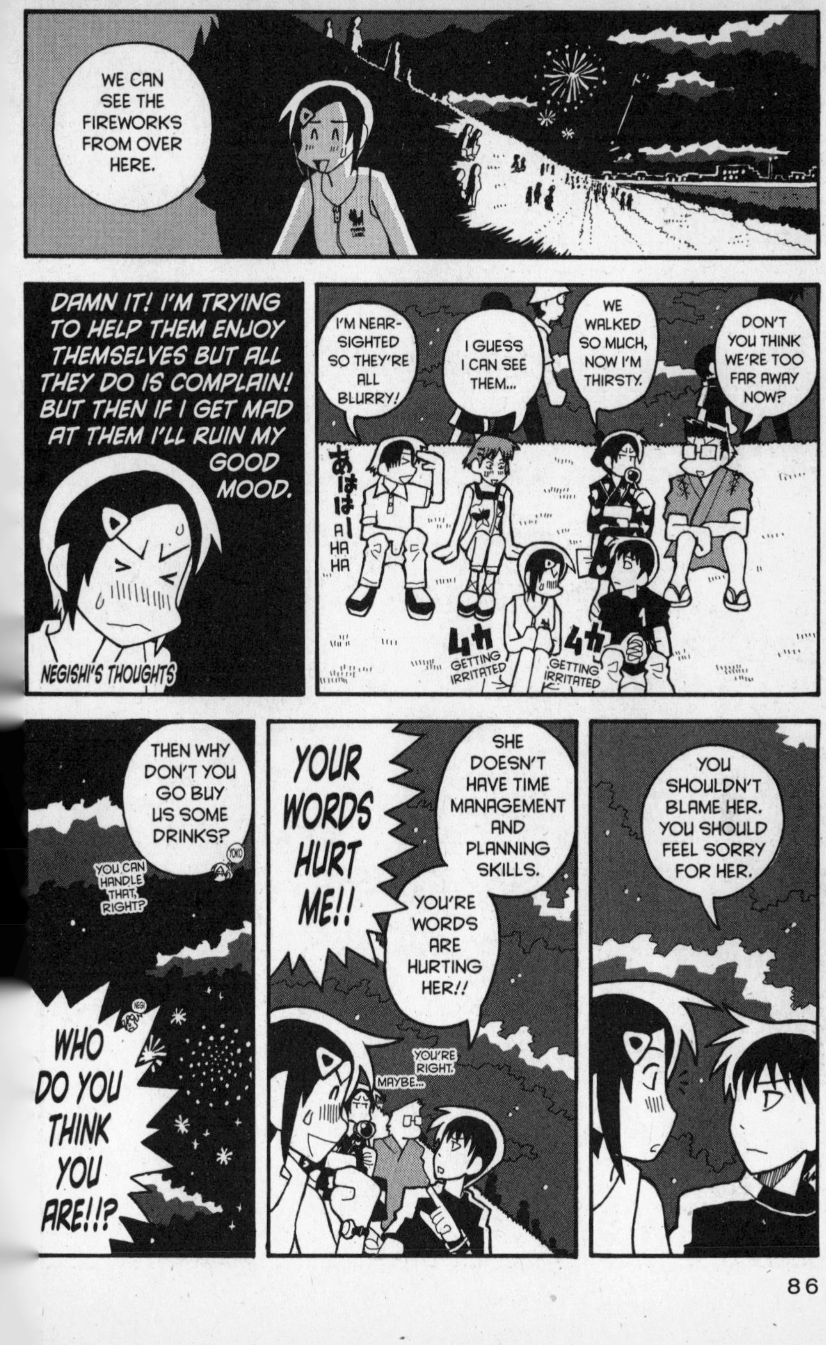
WE CAN SEE THE FIREWORKS FROM OVER HERE.
DON'T YOU THINK WE'RE TOO FAR AWAY NOW?
WE WALKED SO MUCH, NOW I'M THIRSTY.
I GUESS I CAN SEE THEM...
I'M NEAR-SIGHTED SO THEY'RE ALL BLURRY!
あははー
A HA HA
ムカ GETTING IRRITATED
ムカ GETTING IRRITATED
DAMN IT! I'M TRYING TO HELP THEM ENJOY THEMSELVES BUT ALL THEY DO IS COMPLAIN! BUT THEN IF I GET MAD AT THEM I'LL RUIN MY GOOD MOOD.
NEGISHI'S THOUGHTS
YOU SHOULDN'T BLAME HER. YOU SHOULD FEEL SORRY FOR HER.
SHE DOESN'T HAVE TIME MANAGEMENT AND PLANNING SKILLS.
YOUR WORDS HURT ME!!
YOU'RE WORDS ARE HURTING HER!!
YOU'RE RIGHT.
MAYBE...
THEN WHY DON'T YOU GO BUY US SOME DRINKS?
YOKO
YOU CAN HANDLE THAT, RIGHT?
NEGI
WHO DO YOU THINK YOU ARE!!?

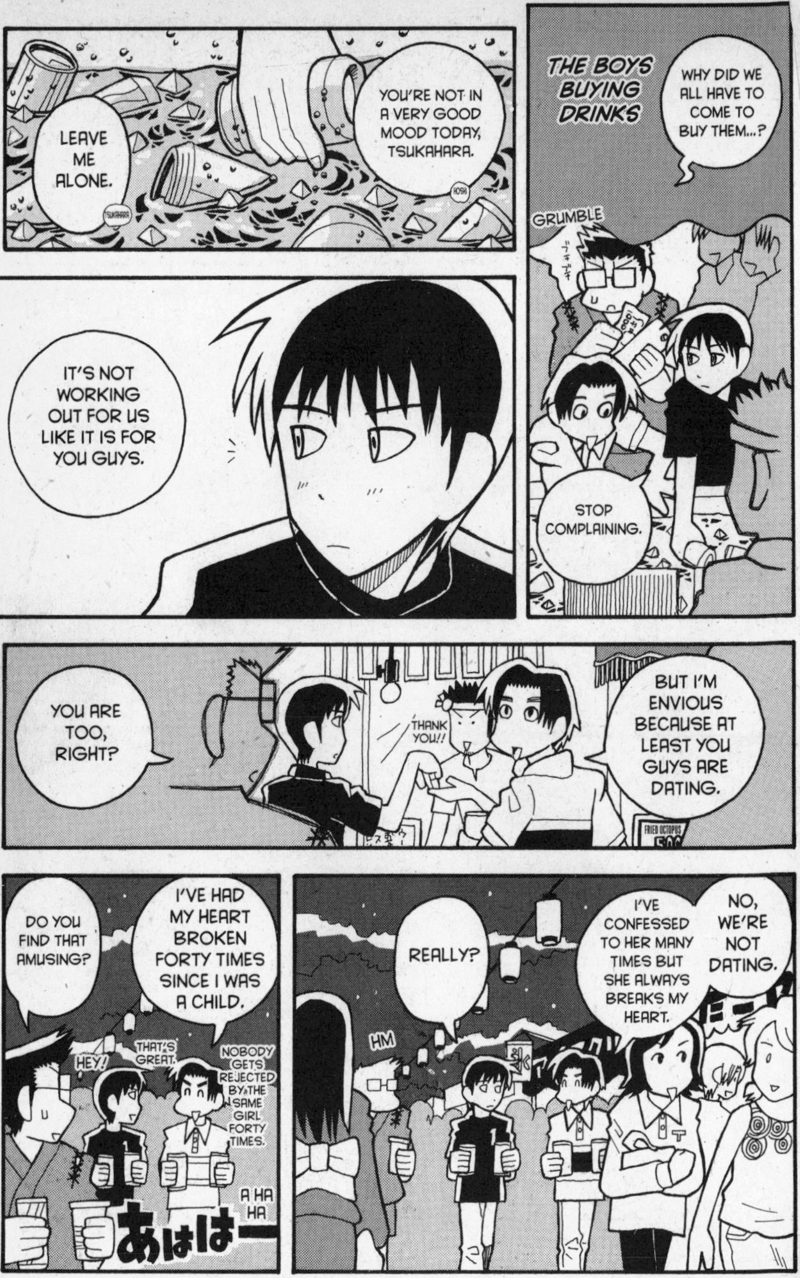
THE BOYS BUYING DRINKS
WHY DID WE ALL HAVE TO COME TO BUY THEM...?
GRUMBLE
STOP COMPLAINING.
YOU'RE NOT IN A VERY GOOD MOOD TODAY, TSUKAHARA.
LEAVE ME ALONE.
IT'S NOT WORKING OUT FOR US LIKE IT IS FOR YOU GUYS.
BUT I'M ENVIOUS BECAUSE AT LEAST YOU GUYS ARE DATING.
FRIED OCTOPUS
THANK YOU!!
YOU ARE TOO, RIGHT?
NO, WE'RE NOT DATING.
I'VE CONFESSED TO HER MANY TIMES BUT SHE ALWAYS BREAKS MY HEART.
REALLY?
HM
I'VE HAD MY HEART BROKEN FORTY TIMES SINCE I WAS A CHILD.
DO YOU FIND THAT AMUSING?
NOBODY GETS REJECTED BY THE SAME GIRL FORTY TIMES.
THAT'S GREAT.
HEY!
A HA HA
あははー

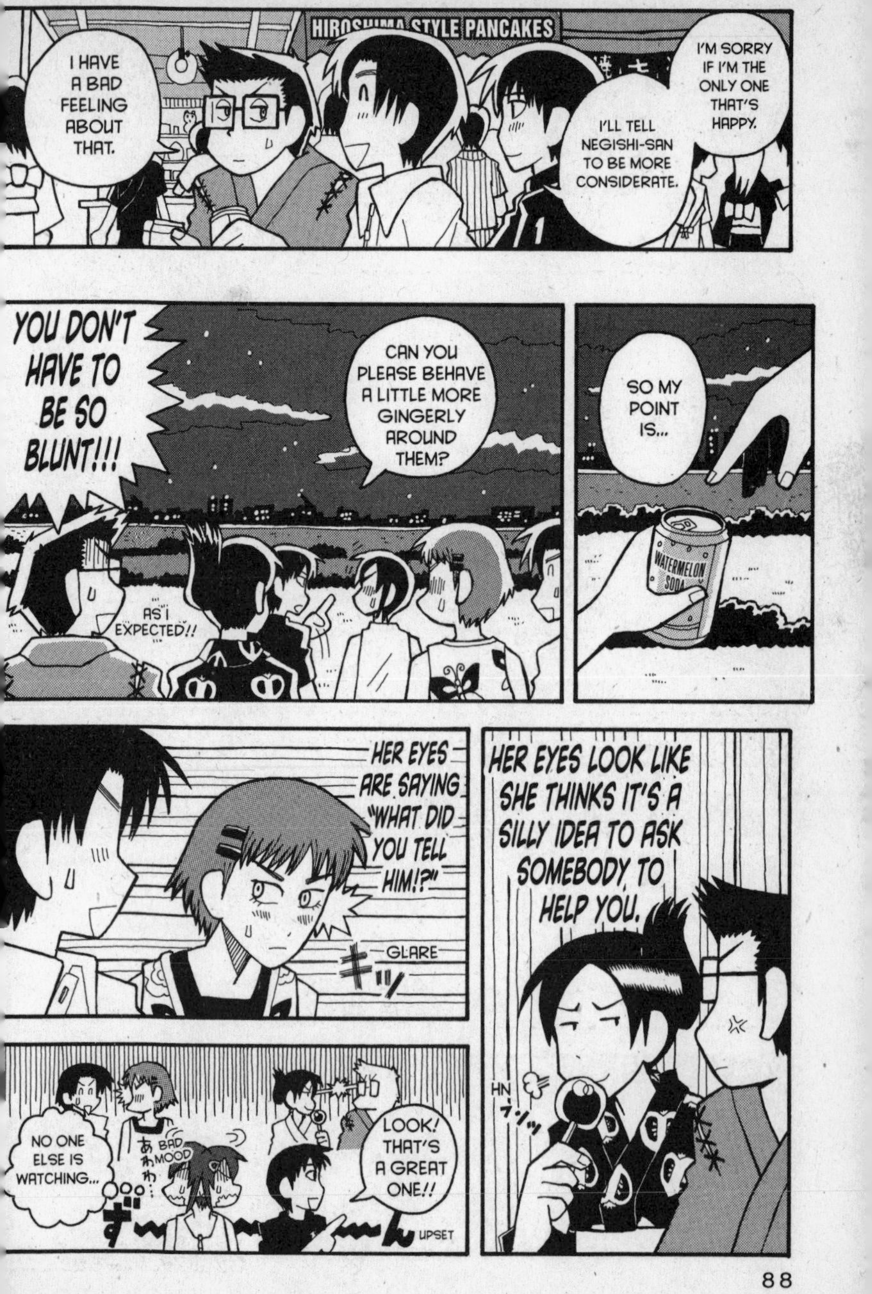
HIROSHIMA STYLE PANCAKES
I'M SORRY IF I'M THE ONLY ONE THAT'S HAPPY.
I'LL TELL NEGISHI-SAN TO BE MORE CONSIDERATE.
I HAVE A BAD FEELING ABOUT THAT.
SO MY POINT IS...
WATERMELON SODA
CAN YOU PLEASE BEHAVE A LITTLE MORE GINGERLY AROUND THEM?
YOU DON'T HAVE TO BE SO BLUNT!!!
AS I EXPECTED!!
HER EYES LOOK LIKE SHE THINKS IT'S A SILLY IDEA TO ASK SOMEBODY TO HELP YOU.
HN
HER EYES ARE SAYING "WHAT DID YOU TELL HIM!?"
GLARE
LOOK! THAT'S A GREAT ONE!!
BAD MOOD
NO ONE ELSE IS WATCHING...
UPSET

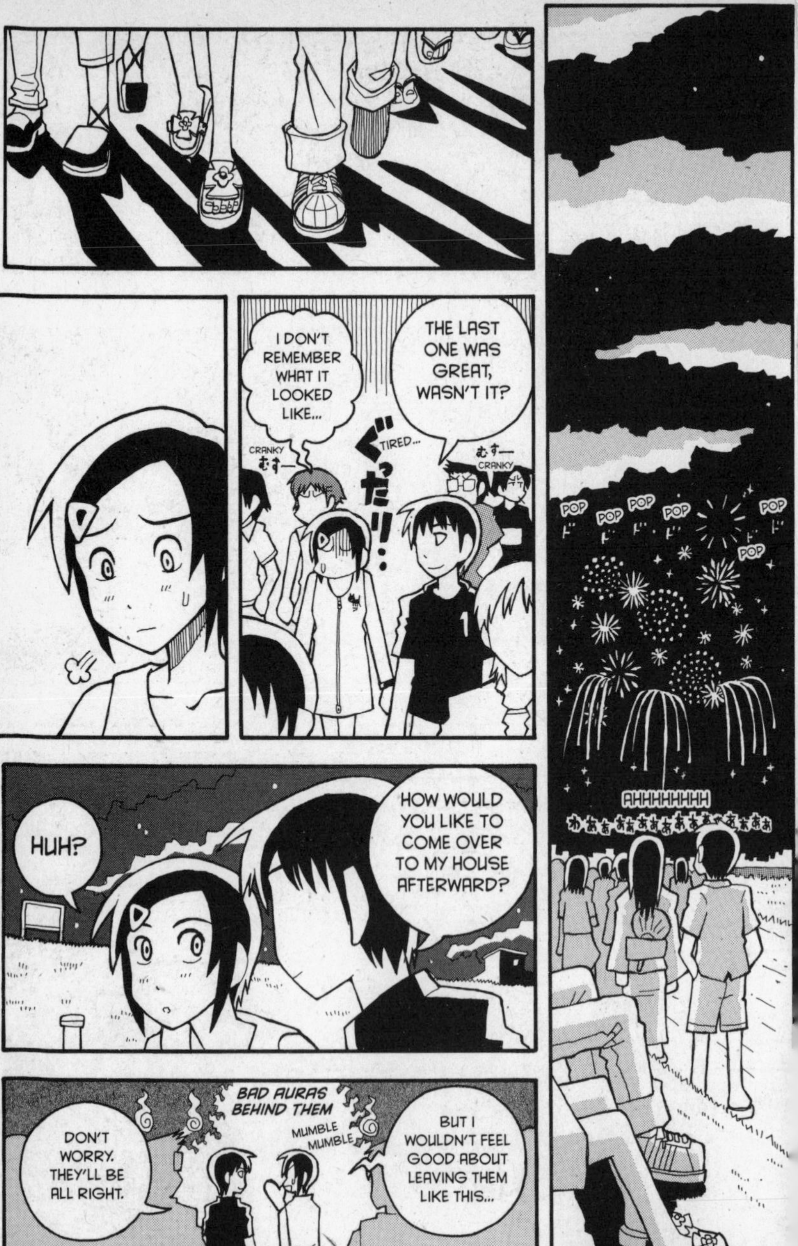

POP
POP
POP
POP
POP
POP
AHHHHHHHH
THE LAST ONE WAS GREAT, WASN'T IT?
I DON'T REMEMBER WHAT IT LOOKED LIKE...
むすー
CRANKY
ぐったり!!
TIRED...
CRANKY
むすー
HOW WOULD YOU LIKE TO COME OVER TO MY HOUSE AFTERWARD?
HUH?
BUT I WOULDN'T FEEL GOOD ABOUT LEAVING THEM LIKE THIS...
BAD AURAS BEHIND THEM
MUMBLE MUMBLE
DON'T WORRY. THEY'LL BE ALL RIGHT.

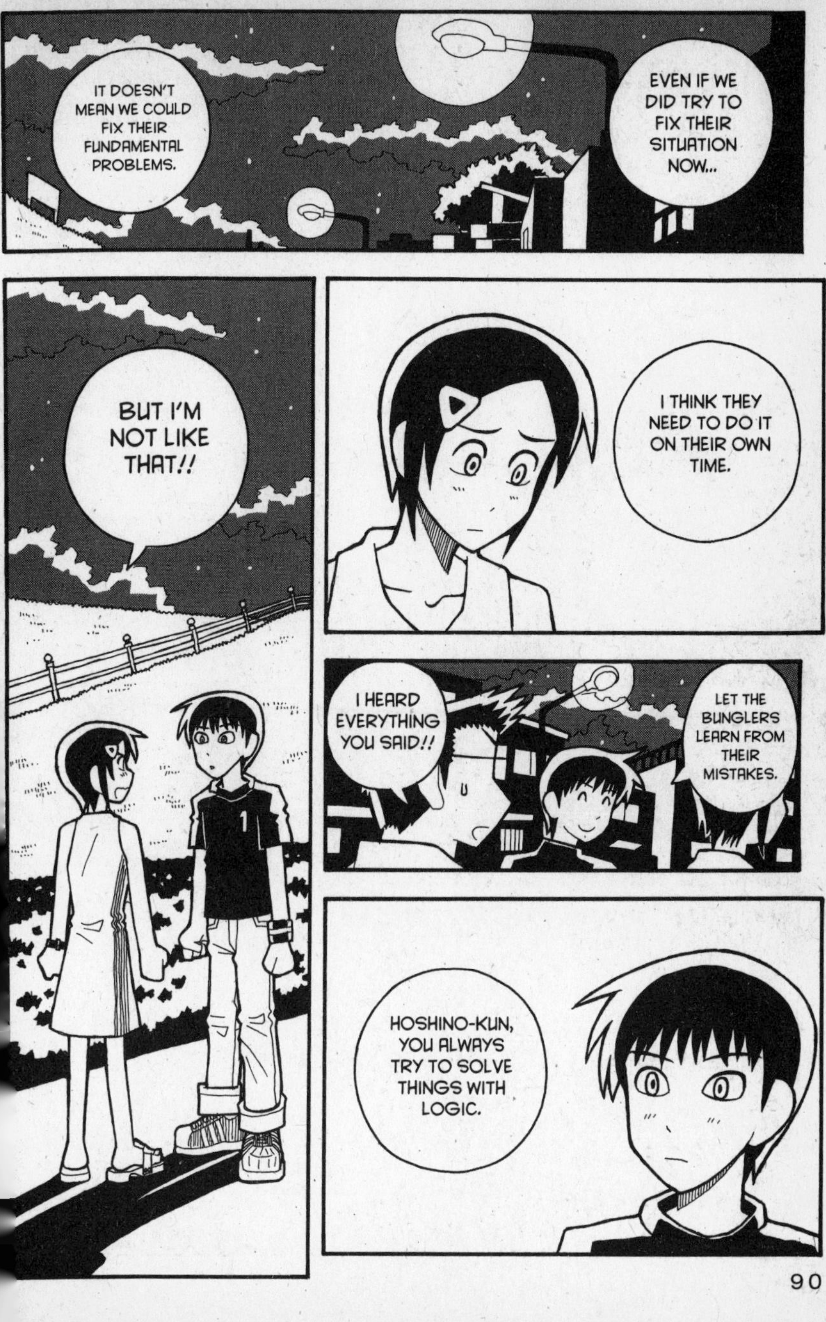
EVEN IF WE DID TRY TO FIX THEIR SITUATION NOW...
IT DOESN'T MEAN WE COULD FIX THEIR FUNDAMENTAL PROBLEMS.
I THINK THEY NEED TO DO IT ON THEIR OWN TIME.
LET THE BUNGLERS LEARN FROM THEIR MISTAKES.
I HEARD EVERYTHING YOU SAID!!
HOSHINO-KUN, YOU ALWAYS TRY TO SOLVE THINGS WITH LOGIC.
BUT I'M NOT LIKE THAT!!

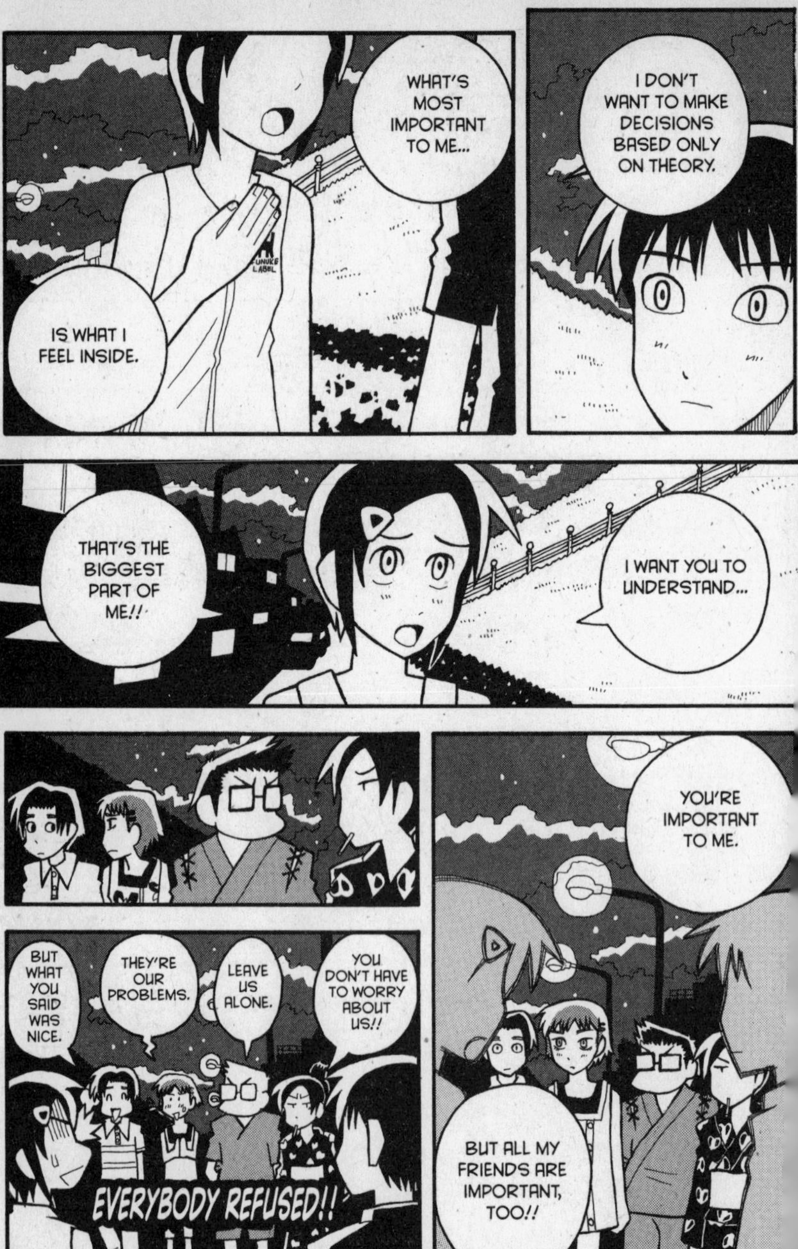
I DON'T WANT TO MAKE DECISIONS BASED ONLY ON THEORY.
WHAT'S MOST IMPORTANT TO ME...
FUNUKE LABEL
IS WHAT I FEEL INSIDE.
I WANT YOU TO UNDERSTAND...
THAT'S THE BIGGEST PART OF ME!!
YOU'RE IMPORTANT TO ME.
BUT ALL MY FRIENDS ARE IMPORTANT, TOO!!
YOU DON'T HAVE TO WORRY ABOUT US!!
LEAVE US ALONE.
THEY'RE OUR PROBLEMS.
BUT WHAT YOU SAID WAS NICE.
EVERYBODY REFUSED!!

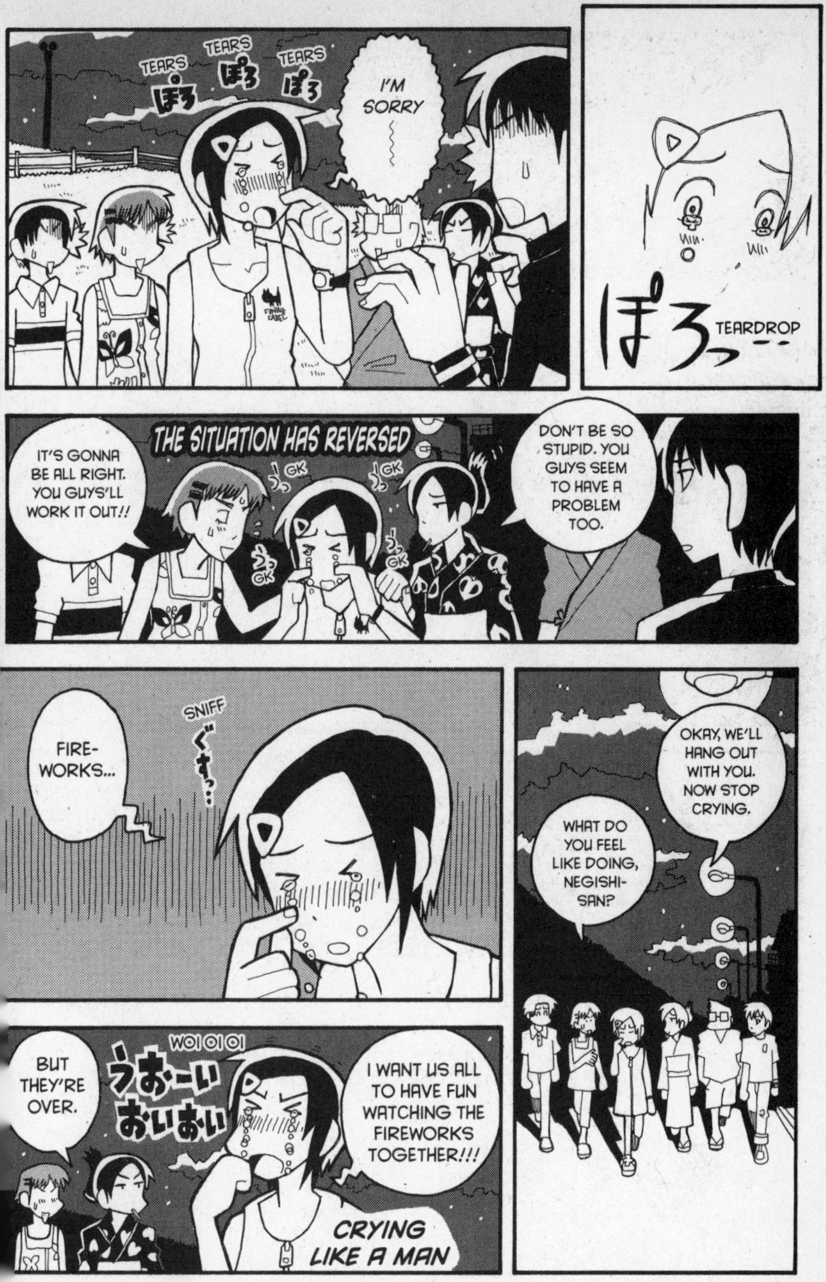

ぽろっ
TEARDROP
I'M SORRY
TEARS ぽろ
TEARS ぽろ
TEARS ぽろ
DON'T BE SO STUPID. YOU GUYS SEEM TO HAVE A PROBLEM TOO.
THE SITUATION HAS REVERSED
うっ GK
うっ GK
うっ GK
IT'S GONNA BE ALL RIGHT. YOU GUYS'LL WORK IT OUT!!
OKAY, WE'LL HANG OUT WITH YOU. NOW STOP CRYING.
WHAT DO YOU FEEL LIKE DOING, NEGISHI-SAN?
SNIFF ぐすっ…
FIRE-WORKS...
I WANT US ALL TO HAVE FUN WATCHING THE FIREWORKS TOGETHER!!!
WOI OI OI うおーい おいおい
BUT THEY'RE OVER.
CRYING LIKE A MAN

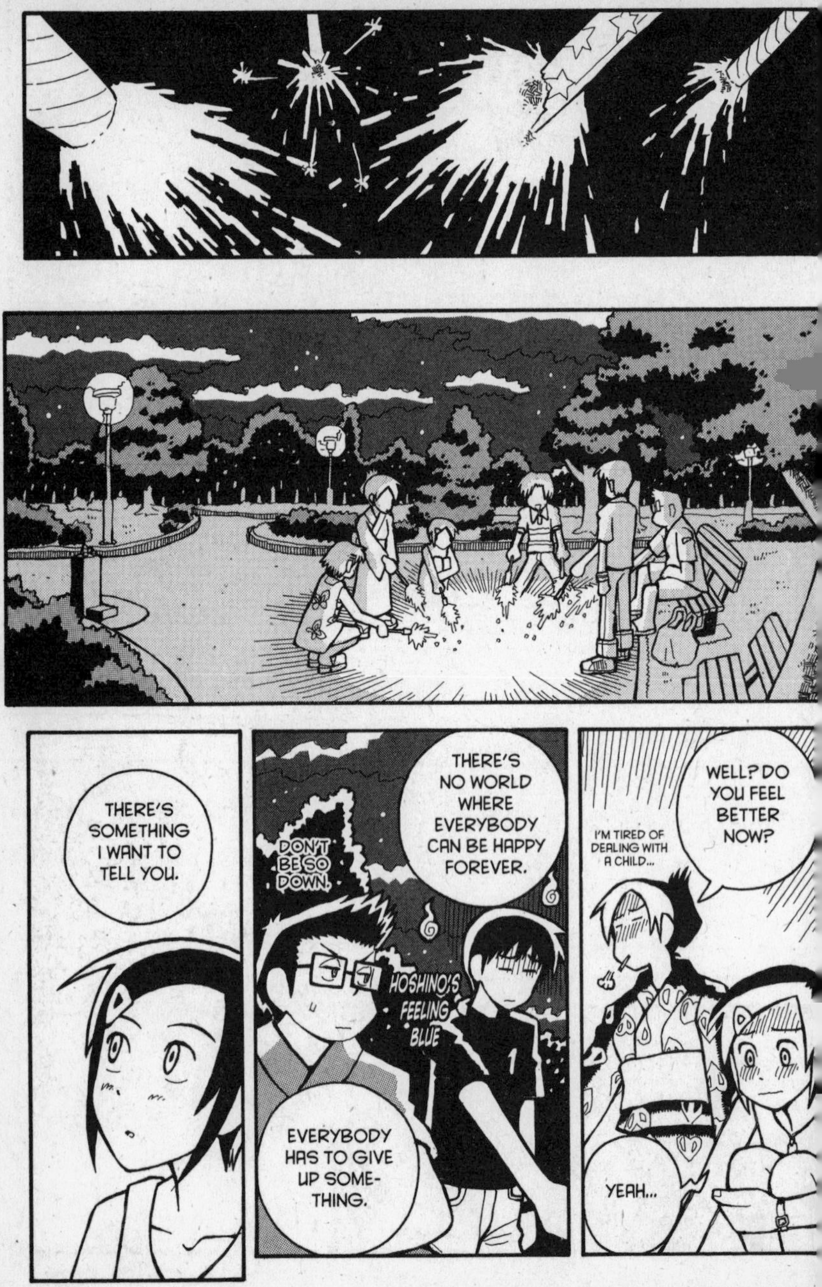
WELL? DO YOU FEEL BETTER NOW?
I'M TIRED OF DEALING WITH A CHILD...
YEAH...
THERE'S NO WORLD WHERE EVERYBODY CAN BE HAPPY FOREVER.
DON'T BE SO DOWN.
HOSHINO'S FEELING BLUE
EVERYBODY HAS TO GIVE UP SOME-THING.
THERE'S SOMETHING I WANT TO TELL YOU.

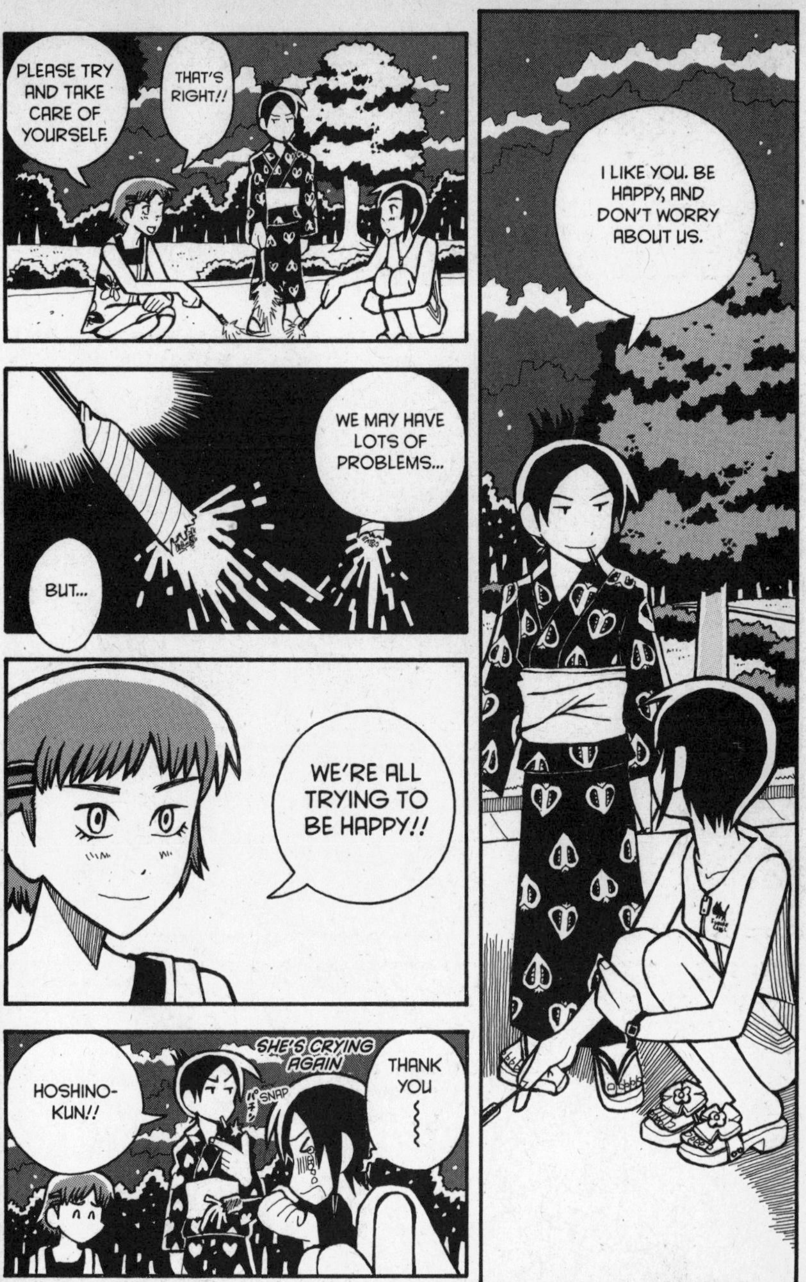
I LIKE YOU. BE HAPPY, AND DON'T WORRY ABOUT US.
THAT'S RIGHT!!
PLEASE TRY AND TAKE CARE OF YOURSELF.
WE MAY HAVE LOTS OF PROBLEMS...
BUT...
WE'RE ALL TRYING TO BE HAPPY!!
THANK YOU ~~~
SHE'S CRYING AGAIN
パチン SNAP
HOSHINO-KUN!!

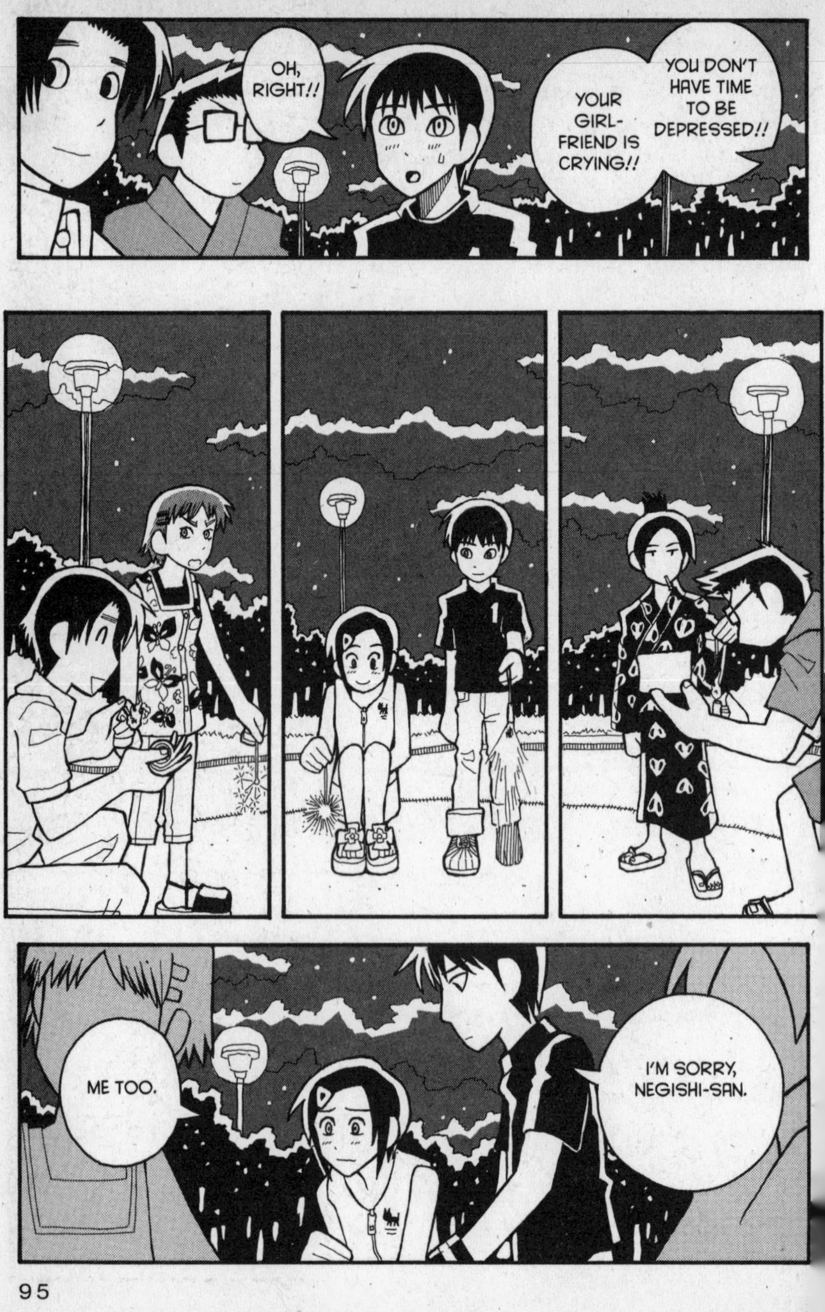
YOU DON'T HAVE TIME TO BE DEPRESSED!!
YOUR GIRL-FRIEND IS CRYING!!
OH, RIGHT!!
I'M SORRY, NEGISHI-SAN.
ME TOO.

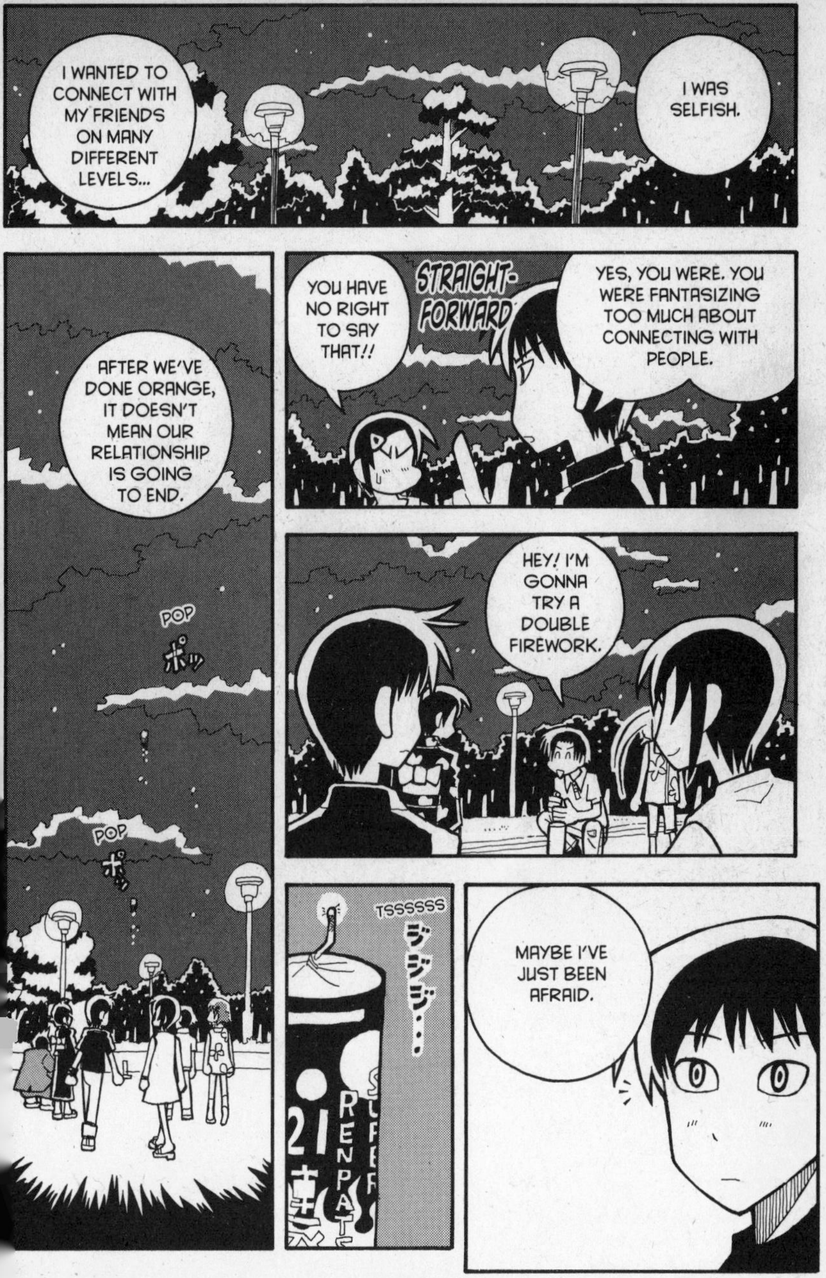
I WAS SELFISH.
I WANTED TO CONNECT WITH MY FRIENDS ON MANY DIFFERENT LEVELS...
YES, YOU WERE. YOU WERE FANTASIZING TOO MUCH ABOUT CONNECTING WITH PEOPLE.
STRAIGHT-FORWARD
YOU HAVE NO RIGHT TO SAY THAT!!
HEY! I'M GONNA TRY A DOUBLE FIREWORK.
MAYBE I'VE JUST BEEN AFRAID.
TSSSSSS
ジジジ・・・
SUPER
21
AFTER WE'VE DONE ORANGE, IT DOESN'T MEAN OUR RELATIONSHIP IS GOING TO END.
POP
ポッ
POP
ポッ

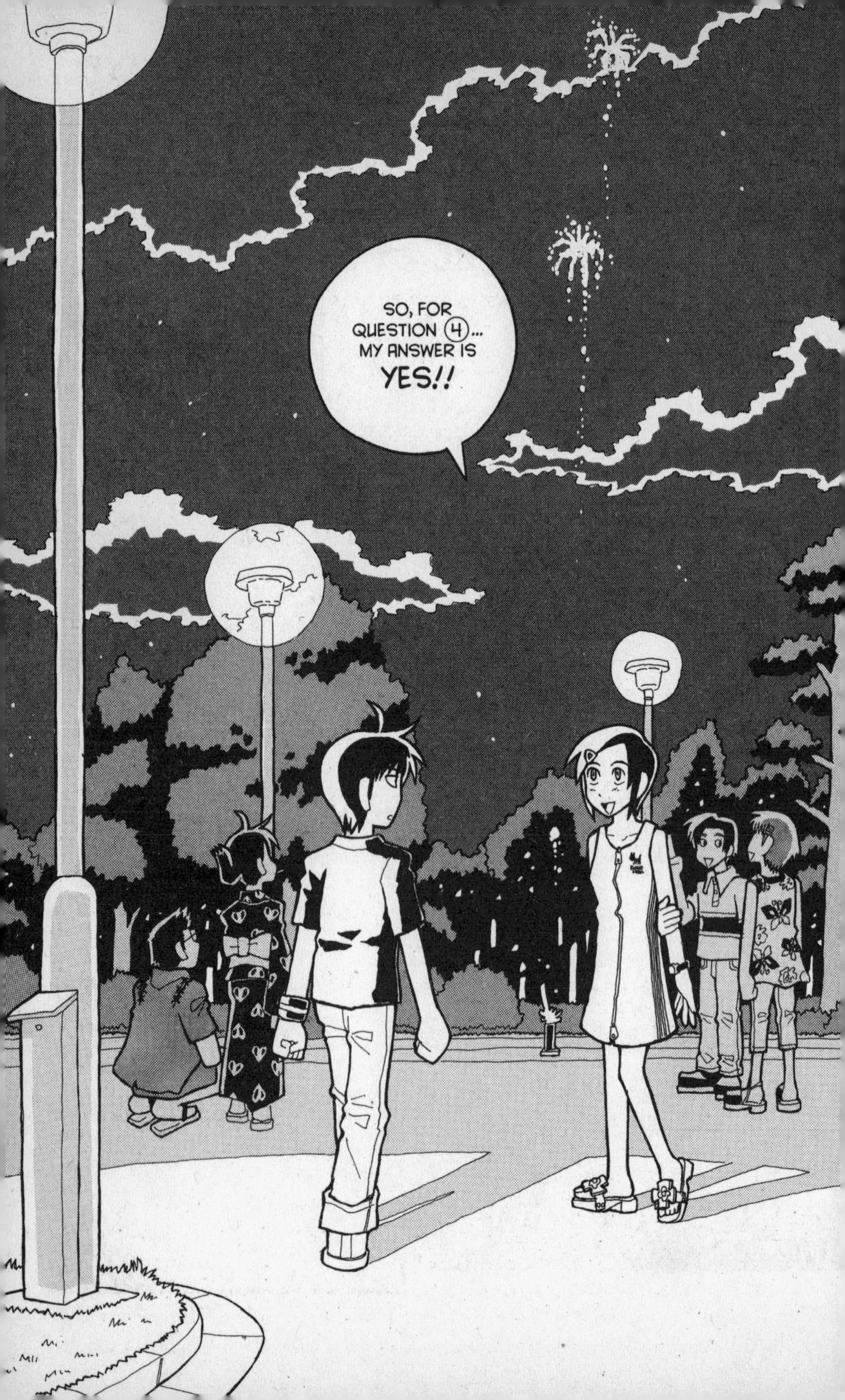
SO, FOR QUESTION ④... MY ANSWER IS YES!!

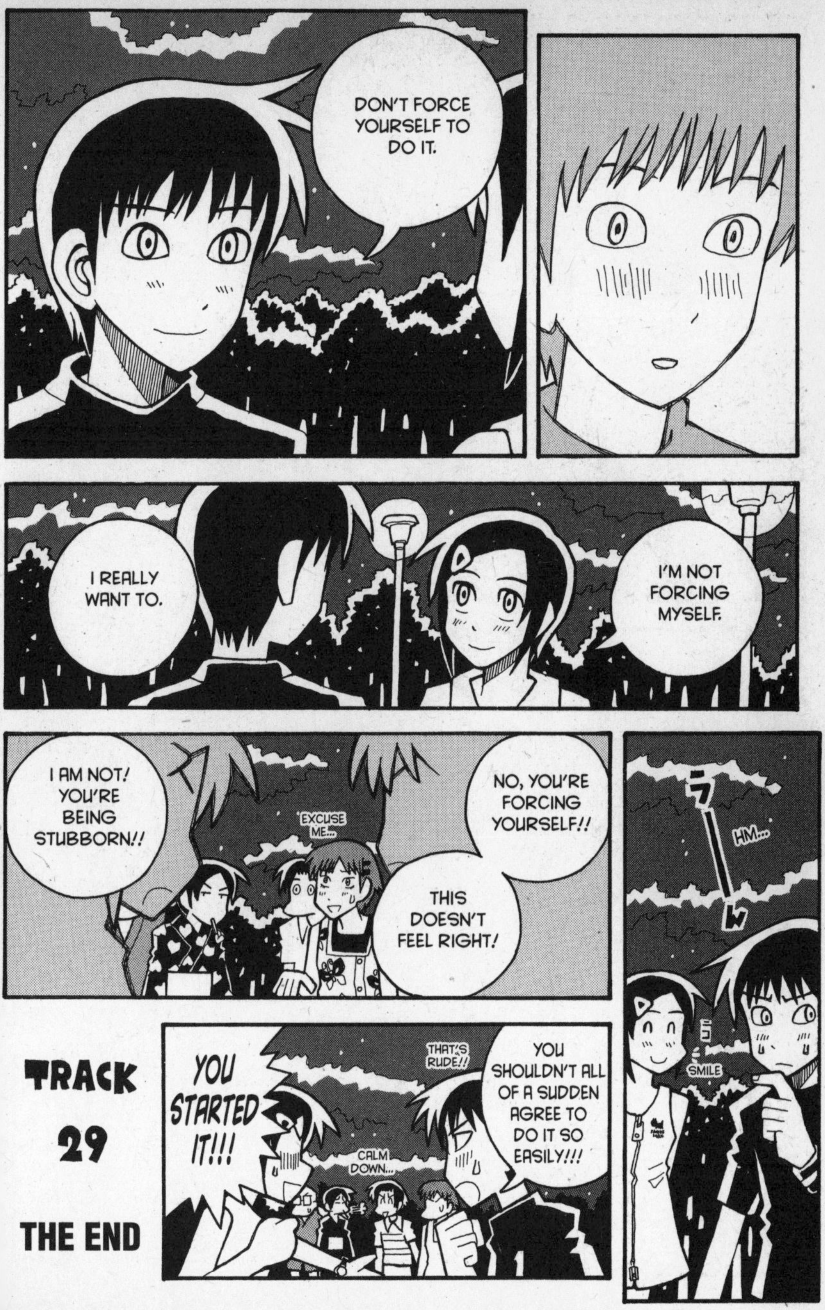
DON'T FORCE YOURSELF TO DO IT.
I'M NOT FORCING MYSELF.
I REALLY WANT TO.
うーん
HM...
ニコ
SMILE
NO, YOU'RE FORCING YOURSELF!!
THIS DOESN'T FEEL RIGHT!
EXCUSE ME...
I AM NOT! YOU'RE BEING STUBBORN!!
YOU SHOULDN'T ALL OF A SUDDEN AGREE TO DO IT SO EASILY!!!
THAT'S RUDE!!
CALM DOWN...
YOU STARTED IT!!!
TRACK 29
THE END

BONUS TRACK

おまけ

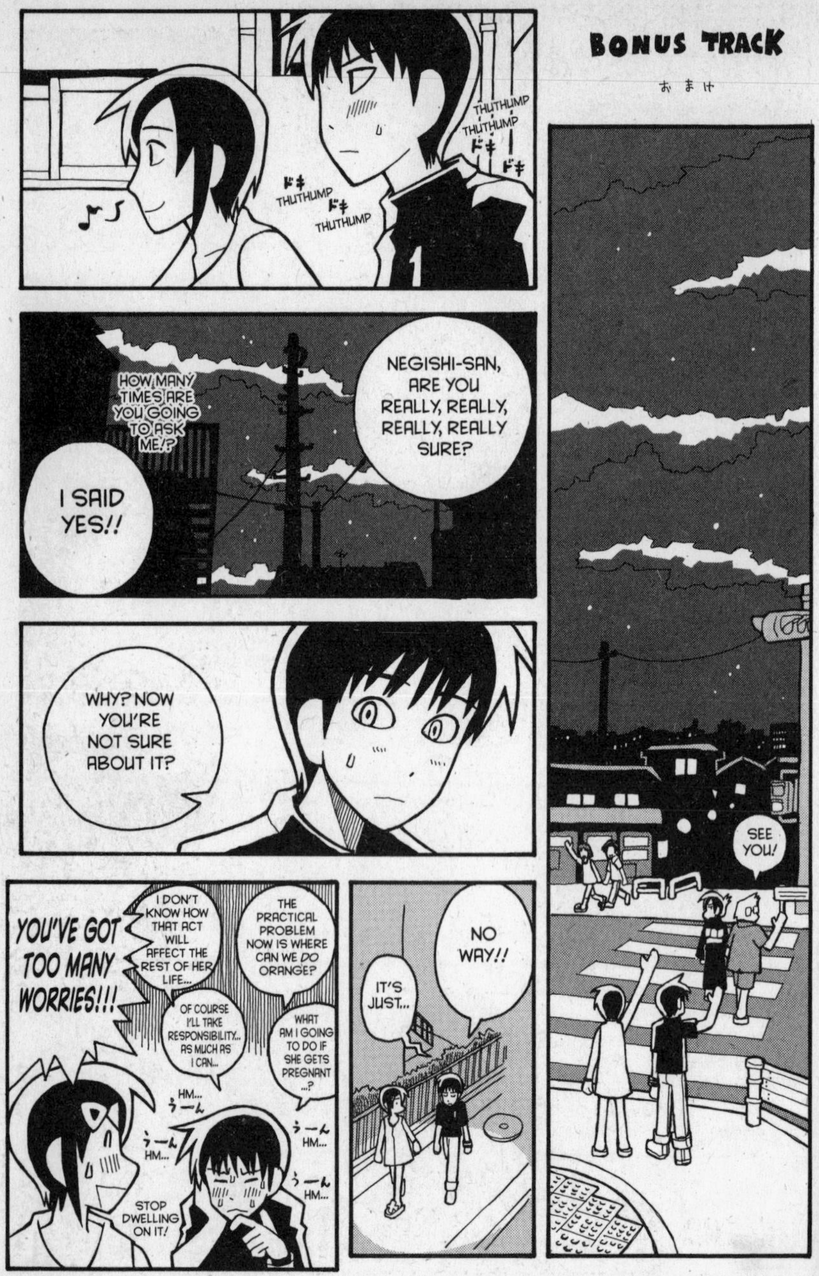

SEE YOU!
THUTHUMP
THUTHUMP
ドキ
ドキ
ドキ
THUTHUMP
ドキ
THUTHUMP
NEGISHI-SAN, ARE YOU REALLY, REALLY, REALLY, REALLY SURE?
HOW MANY TIMES ARE YOU GOING TO ASK ME!?
I SAID YES!!
WHY? NOW YOU'RE NOT SURE ABOUT IT?
NO WAY!!
IT'S JUST...
THE PRACTICAL PROBLEM NOW IS WHERE CAN WE DO ORANGE?
I DON'T KNOW HOW THAT ACT WILL AFFECT THE REST OF HER LIFE...
WHAT AM I GOING TO DO IF SHE GETS PREGNANT ...?
OF COURSE I'LL TAKE RESPONSIBILITY... AS MUCH AS I CAN...
HM... うーん
うーん HM...
うーん HM...
うーん HM...
YOU'VE GOT TOO MANY WORRIES!!!
STOP DWELLING ON IT!

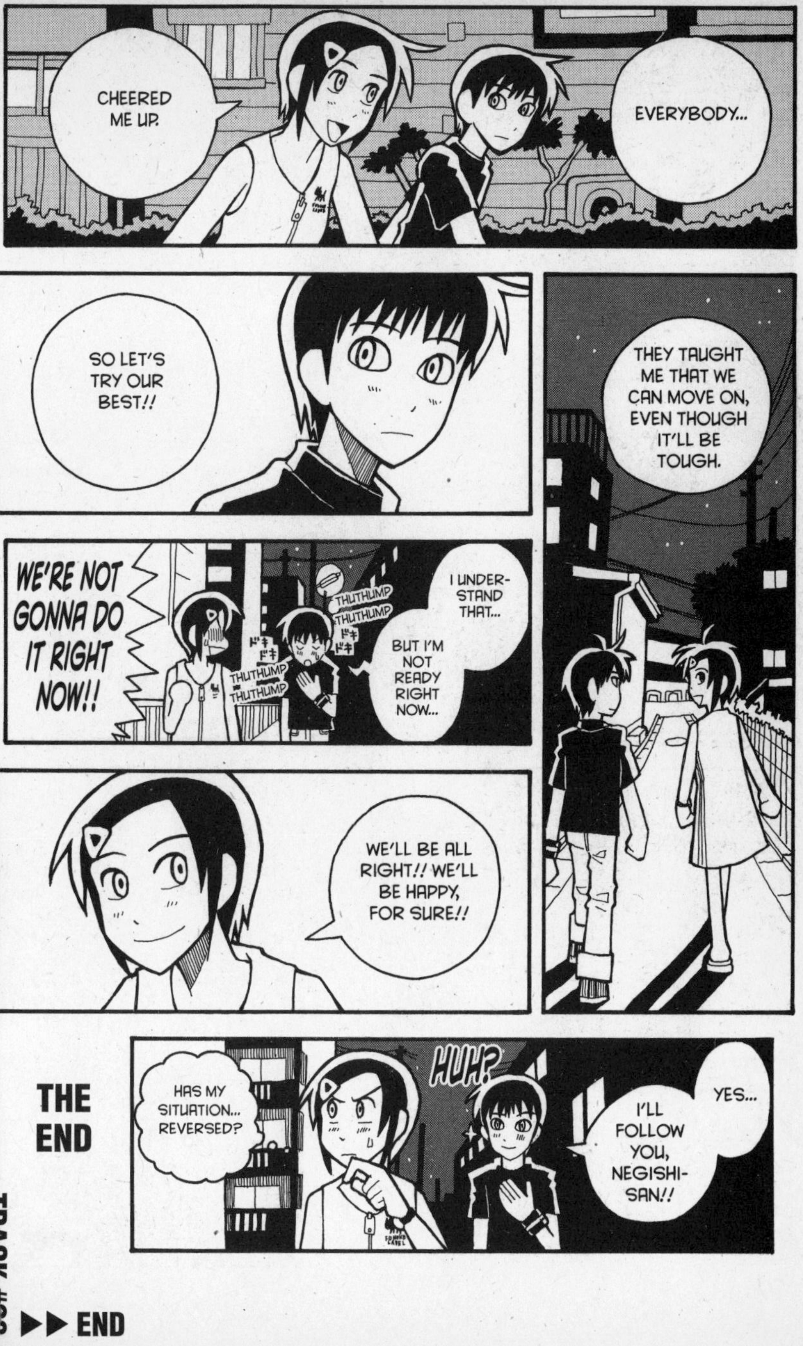
EVERYBODY...
CHEERED ME UP.
THEY TAUGHT ME THAT WE CAN MOVE ON, EVEN THOUGH IT'LL BE TOUGH.
SO LET'S TRY OUR BEST!!
I UNDER-STAND THAT...
BUT I'M NOT READY RIGHT NOW...
THUTHUMP THUTHUMP
ドキ ドキ
ドキ ドキ
THUTHUMP THUTHUMP
WE'RE NOT GONNA DO IT RIGHT NOW!!
WE'LL BE ALL RIGHT!! WE'LL BE HAPPY, FOR SURE!!
YES...
I'LL FOLLOW YOU, NEGISHI-SAN!!
HUH?
HAS MY SITUATION... REVERSED?

THE END

▶▶ END

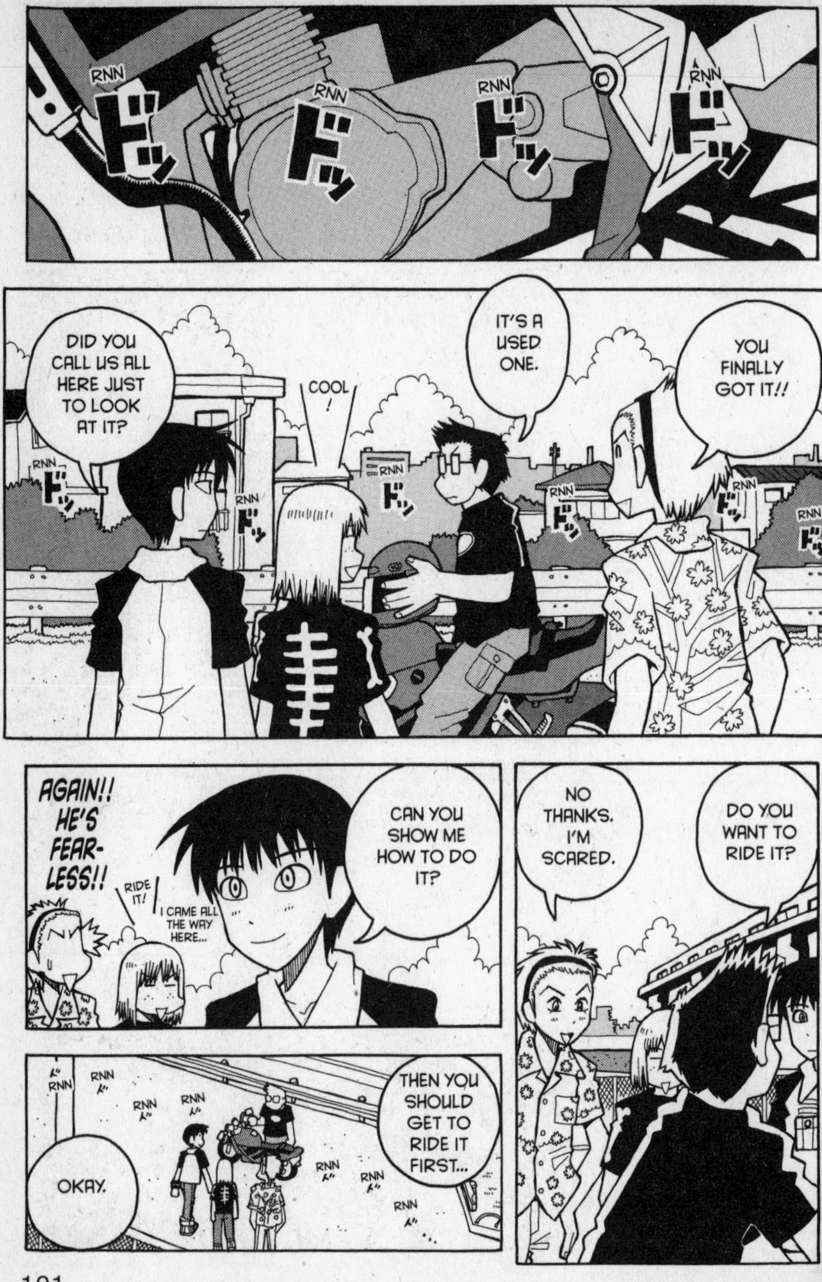
RNN ドッ
RNN ドッ
RNN ドッ
RNN ドッ
YOU FINALLY GOT IT!!
IT'S A USED ONE.
COOL!
DID YOU CALL US ALL HERE JUST TO LOOK AT IT?
RNN ドッ
RNN ドッ
RNN ドッ
RNN ドッ
RNN ドッ
RNN ドッ
DO YOU WANT TO RIDE IT?
NO THANKS. I'M SCARED.
CAN YOU SHOW ME HOW TO DO IT?
I CAME ALL THE WAY HERE...
RIDE IT!
AGAIN!! HE'S FEARLESS!!
THEN YOU SHOULD GET TO RIDE IT FIRST...
OKAY.
RNN
RNN
RNN
RNN

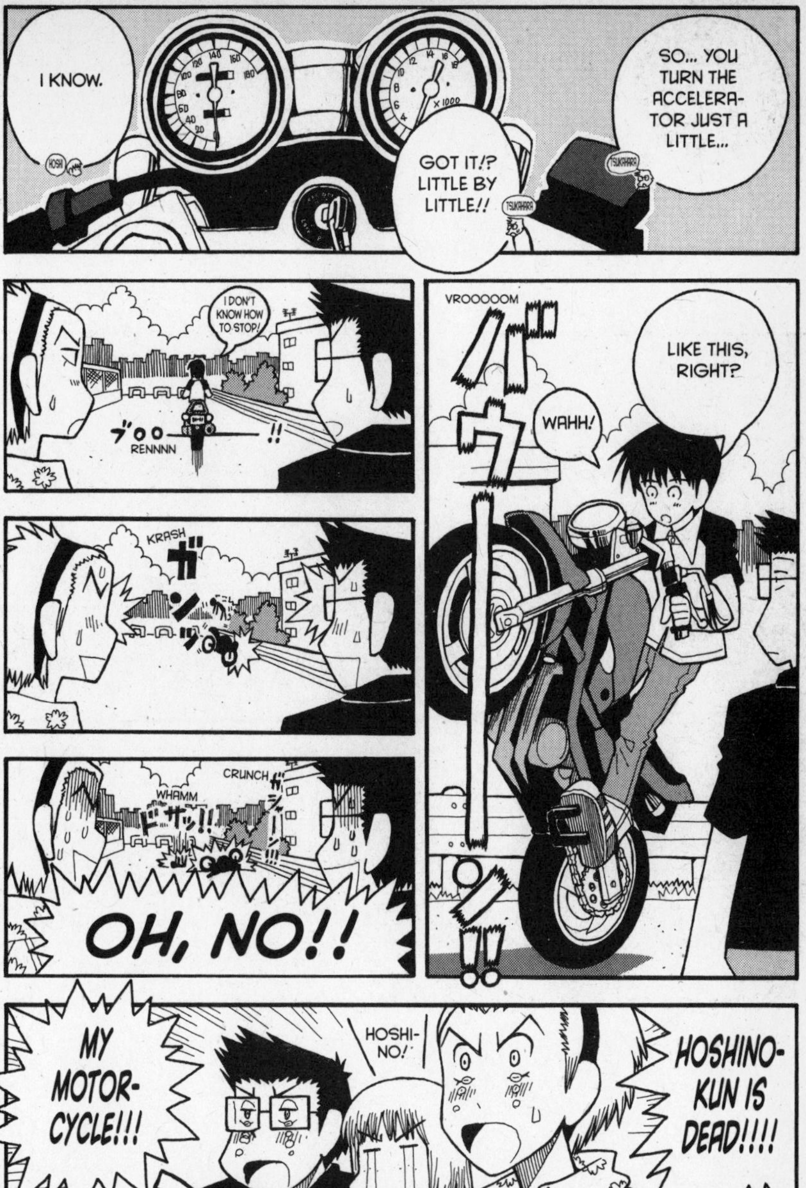
SO... YOU TURN THE ACCELERA-TOR JUST A LITTLE...
TSUKAHARA
GOT IT!? LITTLE BY LITTLE!!
TSUKAHARA
I KNOW.
HOSHI
VROOOOOM
LIKE THIS, RIGHT?
WAHH!
I DON'T KNOW HOW TO STOP!
RENNNN
KRASH
CRUNCH
WHAMM
OH, NO!!
HOSHINO-KUN IS DEAD!!!!
HOSHI-NO!
MY MOTOR-CYCLE!!!
WHOOOAH

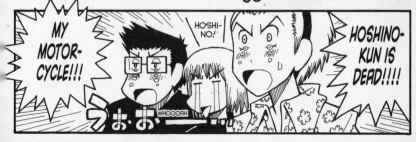

 **LET'S SPEND THE NIGHT TOGETHER**

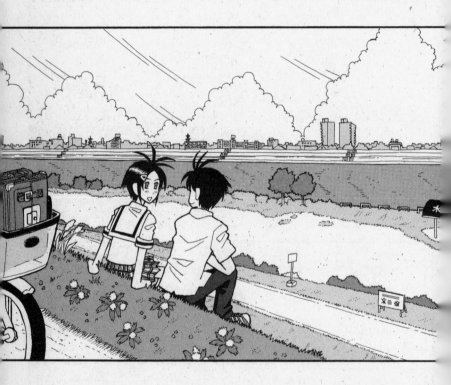

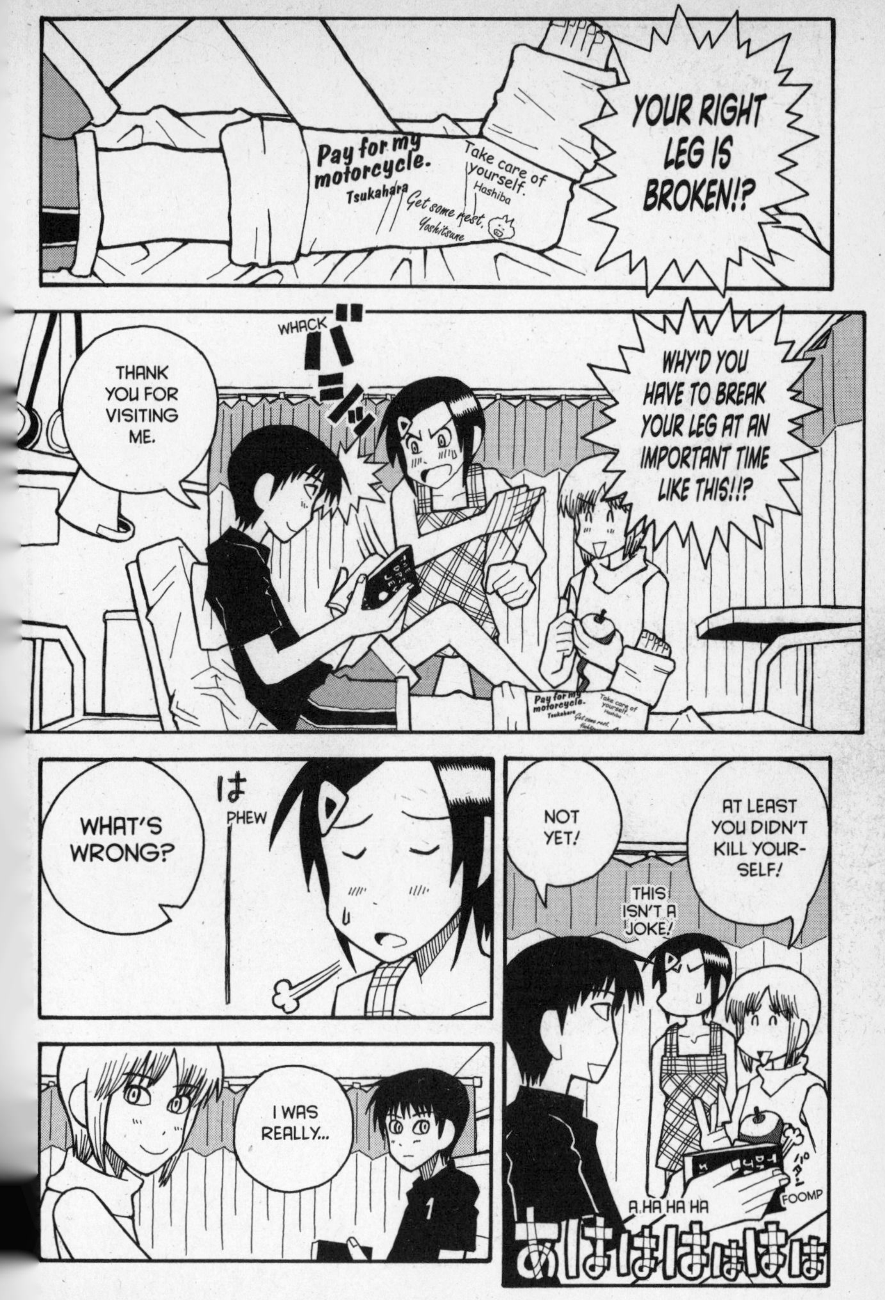
YOUR RIGHT LEG IS BROKEN!?
Take care of yourself.
Hashiba
Pay for my motorcycle.
Tsukahara
Get some rest.
Yoshitsune
WHY'D YOU HAVE TO BREAK YOUR LEG AT AN IMPORTANT TIME LIKE THIS!!?
バシッ
WHACK
THANK YOU FOR VISITING ME.
AT LEAST YOU DIDN'T KILL YOURSELF!
NOT YET!
THIS ISN'T A JOKE!
FOOMP
A HA HA HA
あはははははは
は
PHEW
WHAT'S WRONG?
I WAS REALLY...

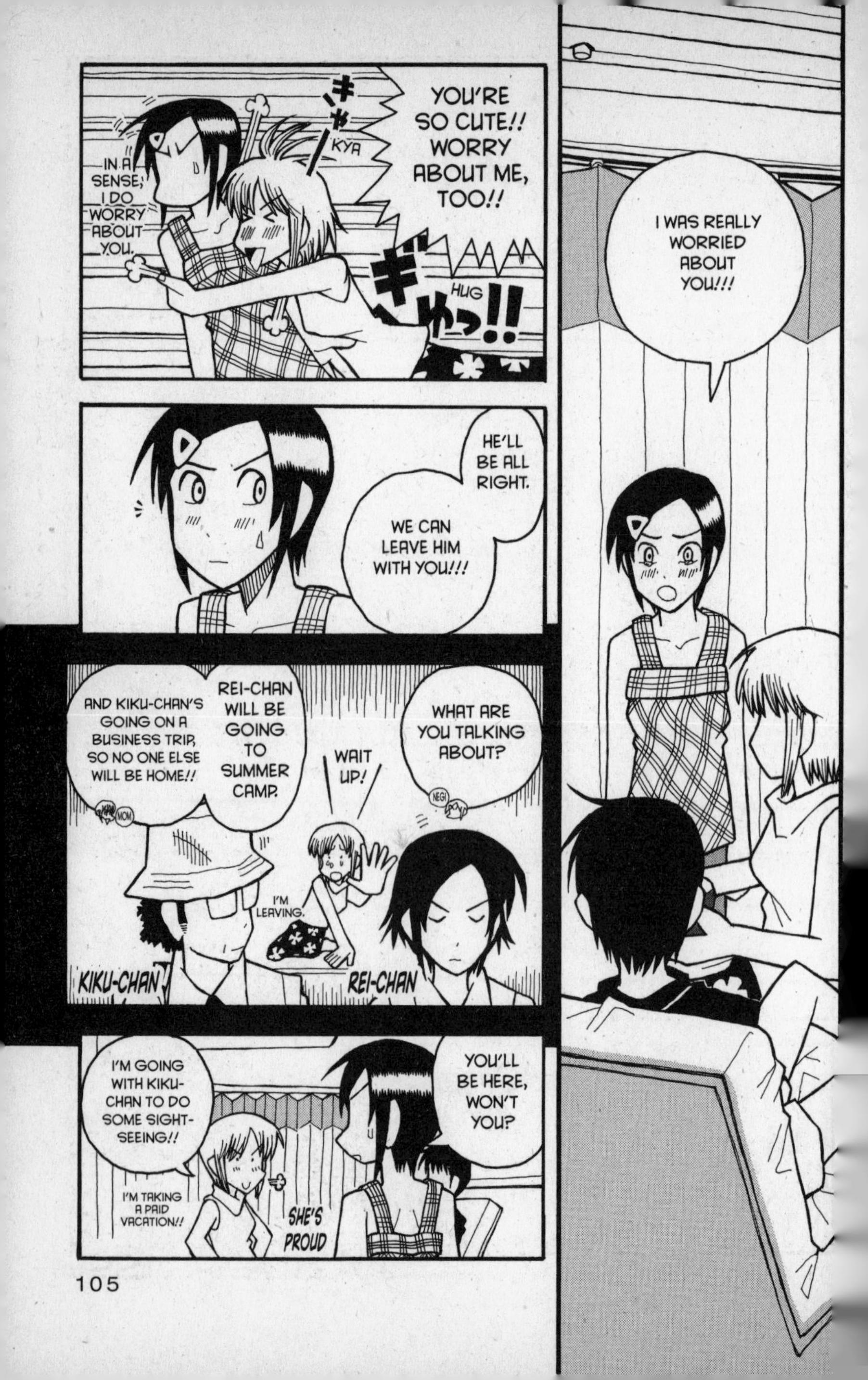
I WAS REALLY WORRIED ABOUT YOU!!!
YOU'RE SO CUTE!! WORRY ABOUT ME, TOO!!
KYA
HUG
IN A SENSE, I DO WORRY ABOUT YOU.
HE'LL BE ALL RIGHT.
WE CAN LEAVE HIM WITH YOU!!!
WHAT ARE YOU TALKING ABOUT?
NEGI
WAIT UP!
REI-CHAN WILL BE GOING TO SUMMER CAMP.
AND KIKU-CHAN'S GOING ON A BUSINESS TRIP, SO NO ONE ELSE WILL BE HOME!!
MOM
I'M LEAVING.
REI-CHAN
KIKU-CHAN
YOU'LL BE HERE, WON'T YOU?
SHE'S PROUD
I'M GOING WITH KIKU-CHAN TO DO SOME SIGHT-SEEING!!
I'M TAKING A PAID VACATION!!

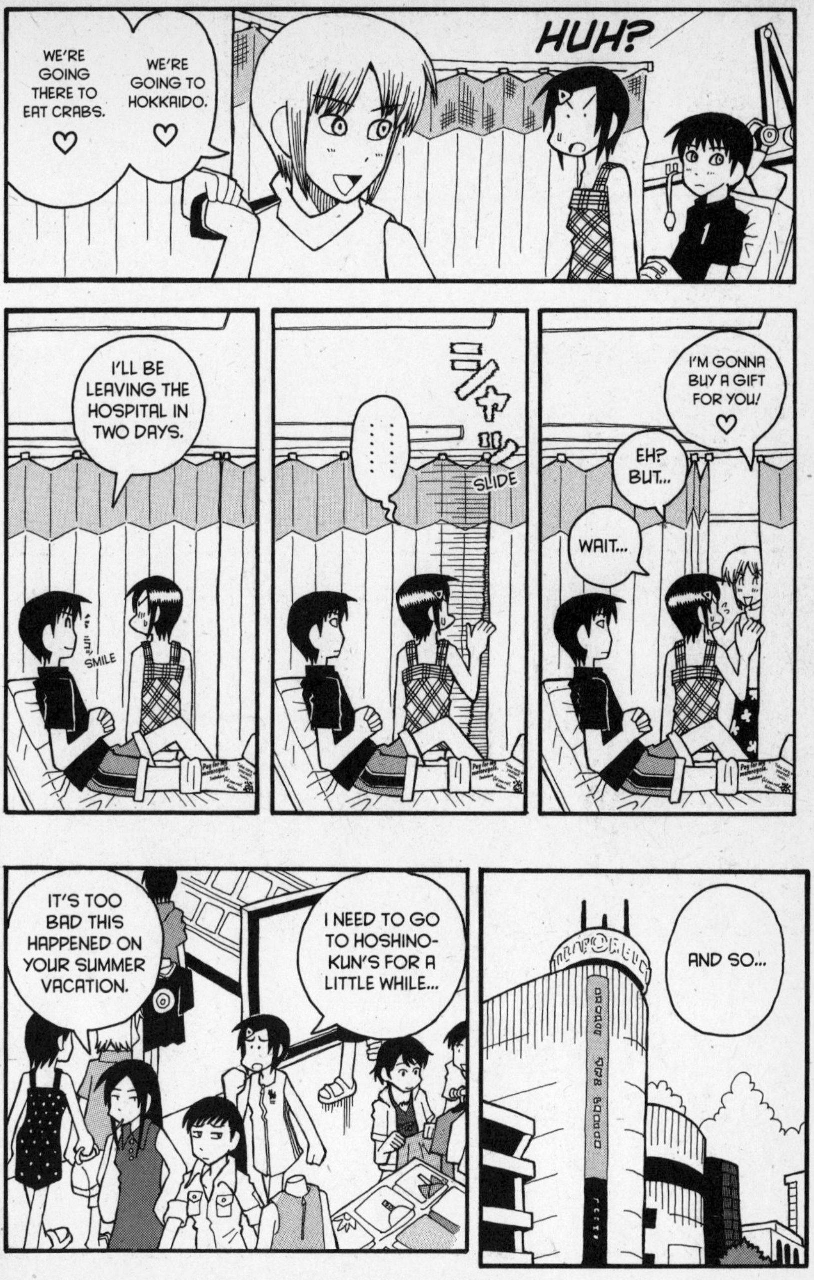
HUH?
WE'RE GOING TO HOKKAIDO. ♥
WE'RE GOING THERE TO EAT CRABS. ♥
I'M GONNA BUY A GIFT FOR YOU! ♥
EH? BUT...
WAIT...
SLIDE
......
I'LL BE LEAVING THE HOSPITAL IN TWO DAYS.
SMILE
AND SO...
I NEED TO GO TO HOSHINO-KUN'S FOR A LITTLE WHILE...
IT'S TOO BAD THIS HAPPENED ON YOUR SUMMER VACATION.

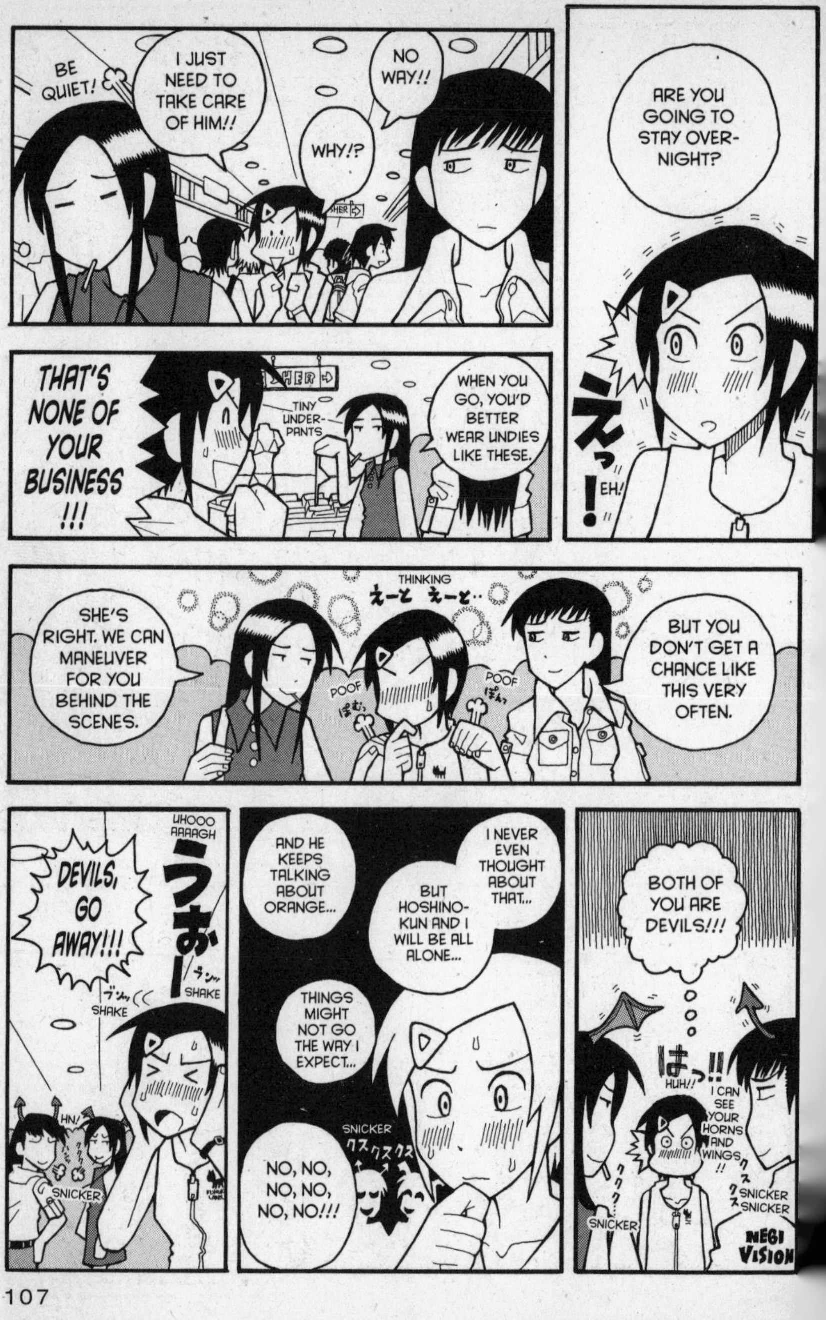
ARE YOU GOING TO STAY OVER-NIGHT?
えっ!
EH!
NO WAY!!
WHY!?
I JUST NEED TO TAKE CARE OF HIM!!
BE QUIET!
WHEN YOU GO, YOU'D BETTER WEAR UNDIES LIKE THESE.
TINY UNDER-PANTS
THAT'S NONE OF YOUR BUSINESS!!!
BUT YOU DON'T GET A CHANCE LIKE THIS VERY OFTEN.
POOF
THINKING
えーと えーと‥
POOF
ぽむっ
SHE'S RIGHT. WE CAN MANEUVER FOR YOU BEHIND THE SCENES.
BOTH OF YOU ARE DEVILS!!!
はっ!!
HUH!!
I CAN SEE YOUR HORNS AND WINGS!!
SNICKER SNICKER
ククク…
SNICKER
NEGI VISION
I NEVER EVEN THOUGHT ABOUT THAT...
BUT HOSHINO-KUN AND I WILL BE ALL ALONE...
AND HE KEEPS TALKING ABOUT ORANGE...
THINGS MIGHT NOT GO THE WAY I EXPECT...
SNICKER
クスクスクス
NO, NO, NO, NO, NO, NO!!!
UHOOO AAAAGH
うおー
DEVILS, GO AWAY!!!
SHAKE
SHAKE
HN!
SNICKER

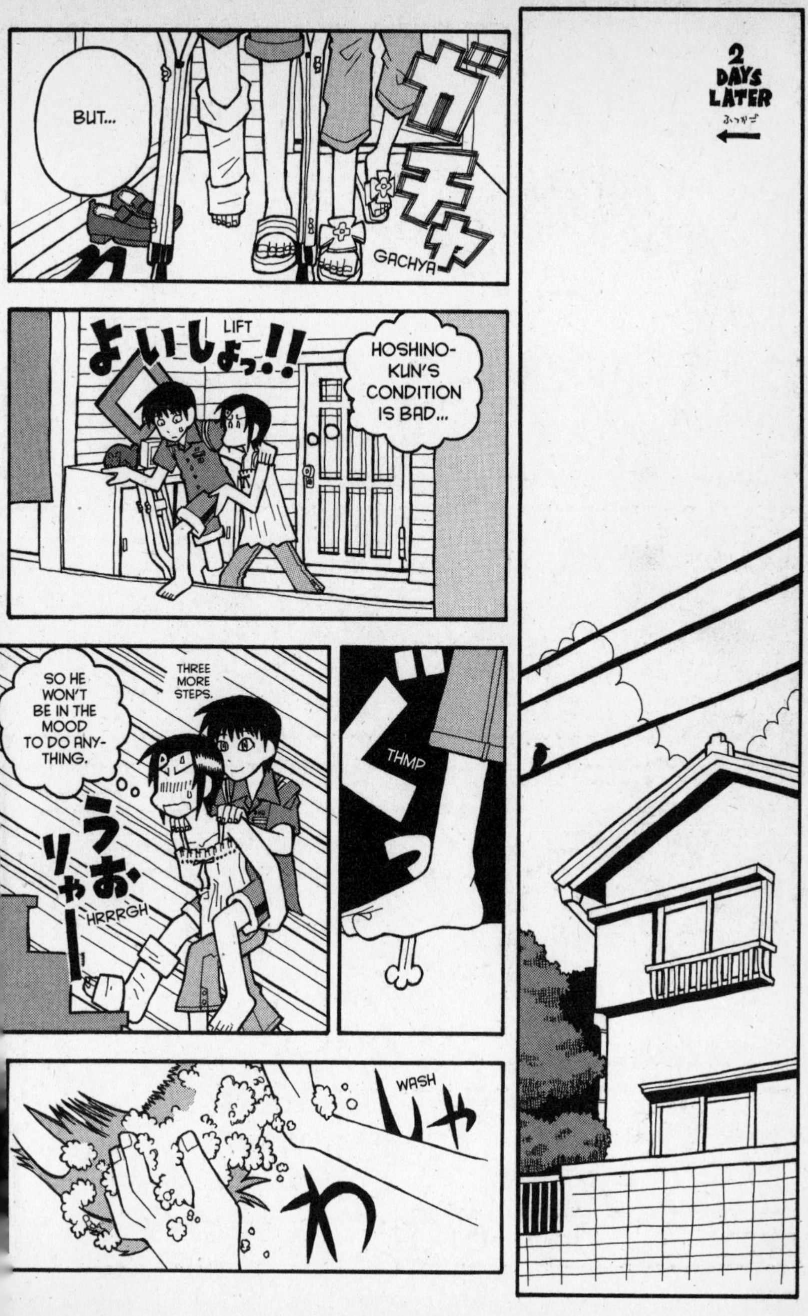
2 DAYS LATER
BUT...
GACHYA
LIFT
HOSHINO-KUN'S CONDITION IS BAD...
THMP
THREE MORE STEPS.
SO HE WON'T BE IN THE MOOD TO DO ANYTHING.
HRRRGH
WASH

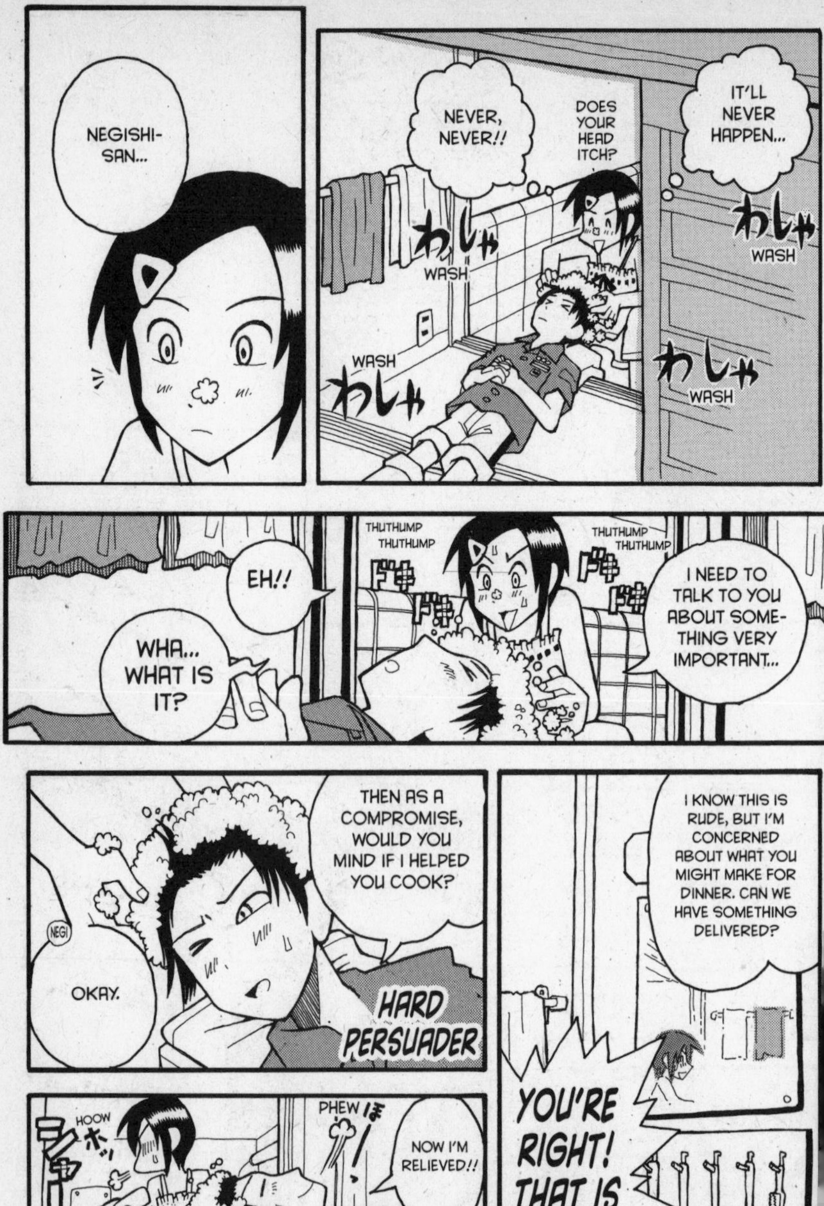
IT'LL NEVER HAPPEN...
わしゃ
WASH
DOES YOUR HEAD ITCH?
NEVER, NEVER!!
わしゃ
WASH
WASH
わしゃ
わしゃ
WASH
NEGISHI-SAN...
I NEED TO TALK TO YOU ABOUT SOMETHING VERY IMPORTANT...
THUTHUMP THUTHUMP
ドキ ドキ
THUTHUMP THUTHUMP
ドキ ドキ
EH!!
WHA... WHAT IS IT?
I KNOW THIS IS RUDE, BUT I'M CONCERNED ABOUT WHAT YOU MIGHT MAKE FOR DINNER. CAN WE HAVE SOMETHING DELIVERED?
YOU'RE RIGHT! THAT IS RUDE!!!
THEN AS A COMPROMISE, WOULD YOU MIND IF I HELPED YOU COOK?
HARD PERSUADER
NEGI
OKAY.
NOW I'M RELIEVED!!
PHEW ほっ
HOOW ホッ
KSHHH

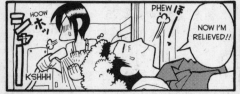

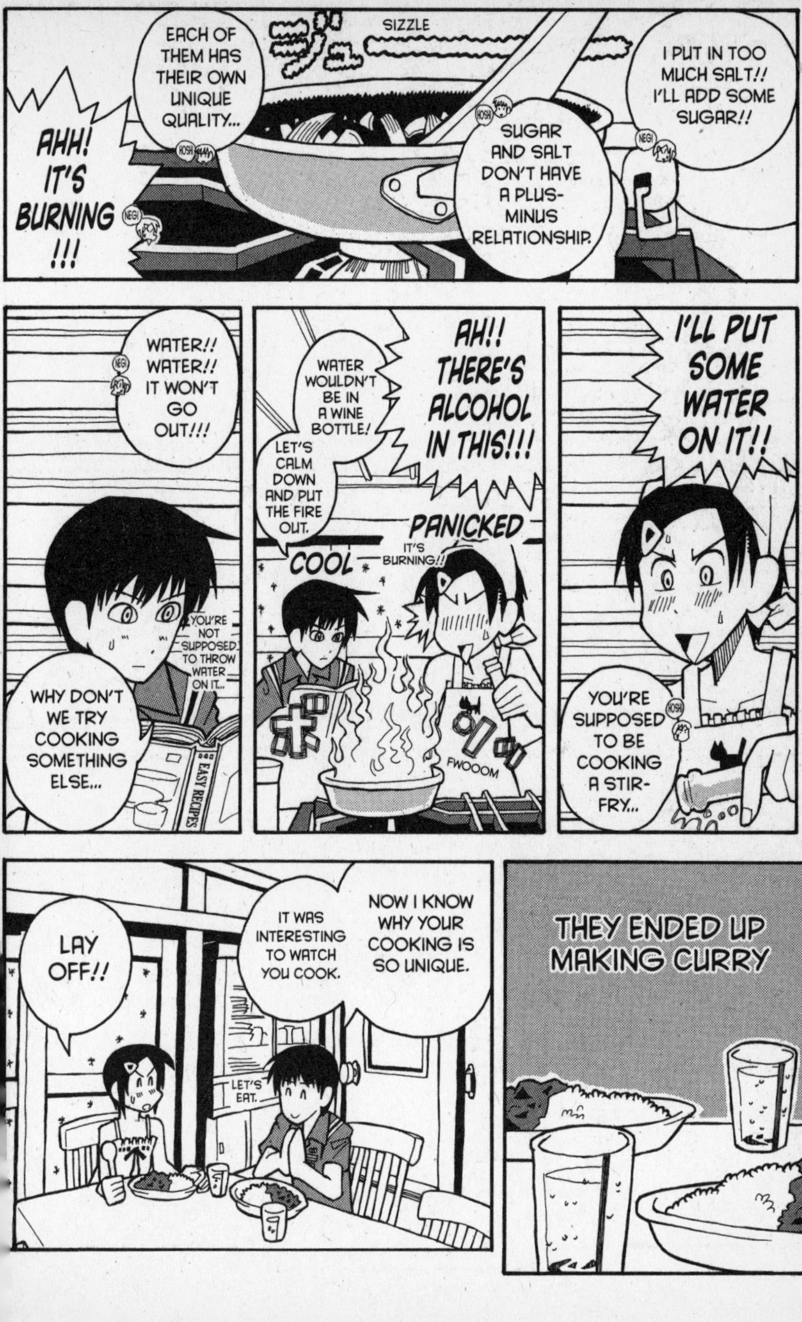
I PUT IN TOO MUCH SALT!! I'LL ADD SOME SUGAR!!
NEGI
SIZZLE
SUGAR AND SALT DON'T HAVE A PLUS-MINUS RELATIONSHIP.
HOSHI
EACH OF THEM HAS THEIR OWN UNIQUE QUALITY...
HOSHI
AHH! IT'S BURNING!!!
NEGI
I'LL PUT SOME WATER ON IT!!
HOSHI
YOU'RE SUPPOSED TO BE COOKING A STIR-FRY...
AH!! THERE'S ALCOHOL IN THIS!!!
WATER WOULDN'T BE IN A WINE BOTTLE!
LET'S CALM DOWN AND PUT THE FIRE OUT.
PANICKED
IT'S BURNING!!
COOL
FWOOOM
WATER!! WATER!! IT WON'T GO OUT!!!
NEGI
YOU'RE NOT SUPPOSED TO THROW WATER ON IT...
WHY DON'T WE TRY COOKING SOMETHING ELSE...
EASY RECIPES
THEY ENDED UP MAKING CURRY
NOW I KNOW WHY YOUR COOKING IS SO UNIQUE.
IT WAS INTERESTING TO WATCH YOU COOK.
LAY OFF!!
LET'S EAT.

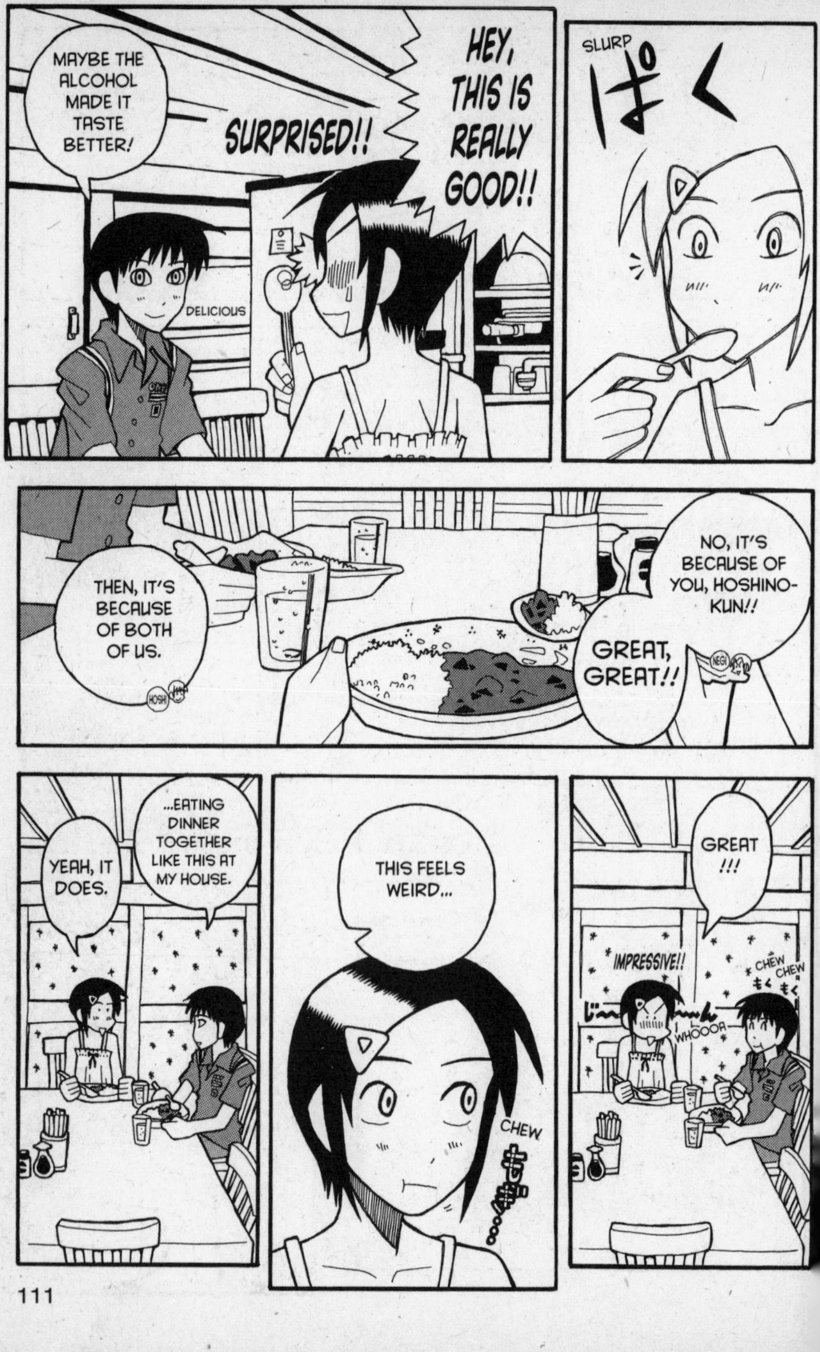
SLURP
ぱく
HEY, THIS IS REALLY GOOD!!
SURPRISED!!
MAYBE THE ALCOHOL MADE IT TASTE BETTER!
DELICIOUS
NO, IT'S BECAUSE OF YOU, HOSHINO-KUN!!
GREAT, GREAT!!
NEGI
THEN, IT'S BECAUSE OF BOTH OF US.
HOSHI
GREAT !!!
CHEW CHEW
もく もく
IMPRESSIVE!!
WHOOOA
THIS FEELS WEIRD...
CHEW
...EATING DINNER TOGETHER LIKE THIS AT MY HOUSE.
YEAH, IT DOES.

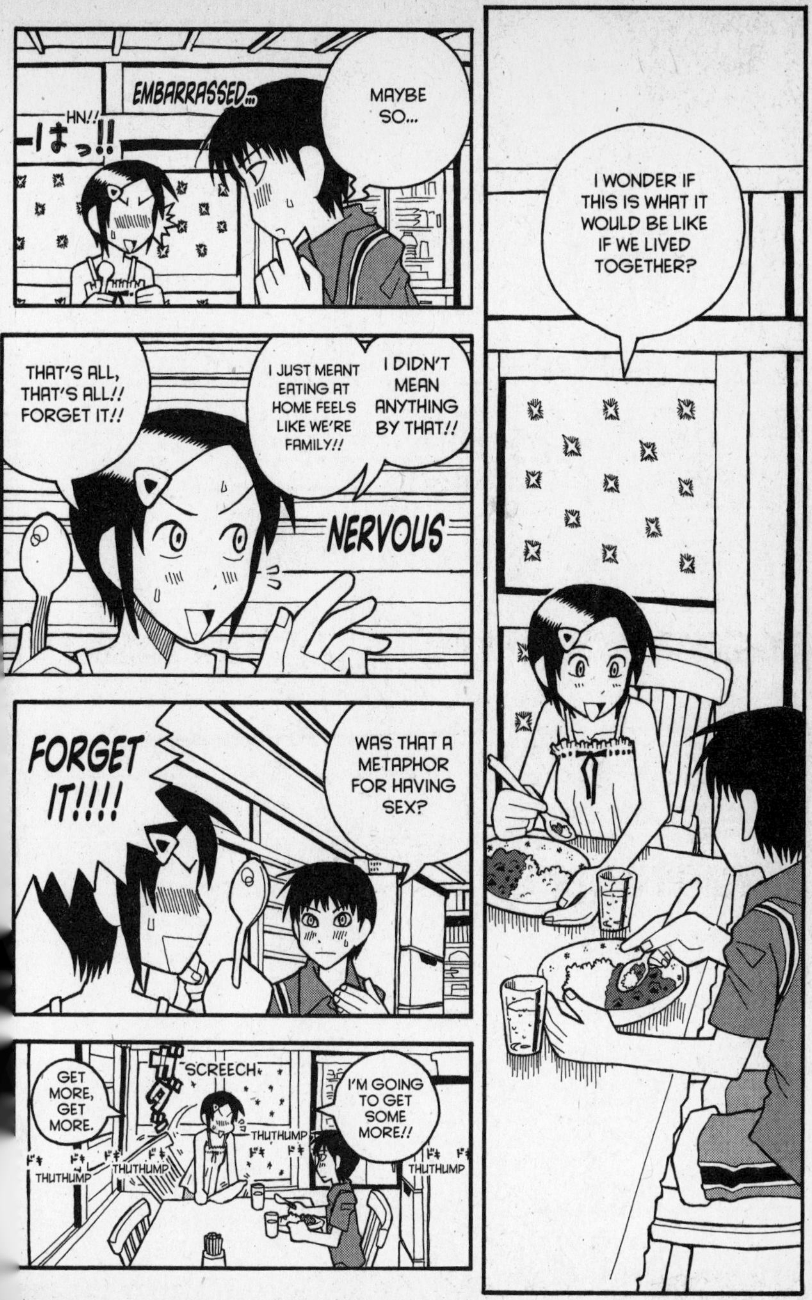
I WONDER IF THIS IS WHAT IT WOULD BE LIKE IF WE LIVED TOGETHER?
MAYBE SO...
EMBARRASSED...
HN!!
はっ!!
I DIDN'T MEAN ANYTHING BY THAT!!
I JUST MEANT EATING AT HOME FEELS LIKE WE'RE FAMILY!!
THAT'S ALL, THAT'S ALL!! FORGET IT!!
NERVOUS
WAS THAT A METAPHOR FOR HAVING SEX?
FORGET IT!!!!
I'M GOING TO GET SOME MORE!!
THUTHUMP
THUTHUMP
SCREECH
GET MORE, GET MORE.
THUTHUMP
THUTHUMP

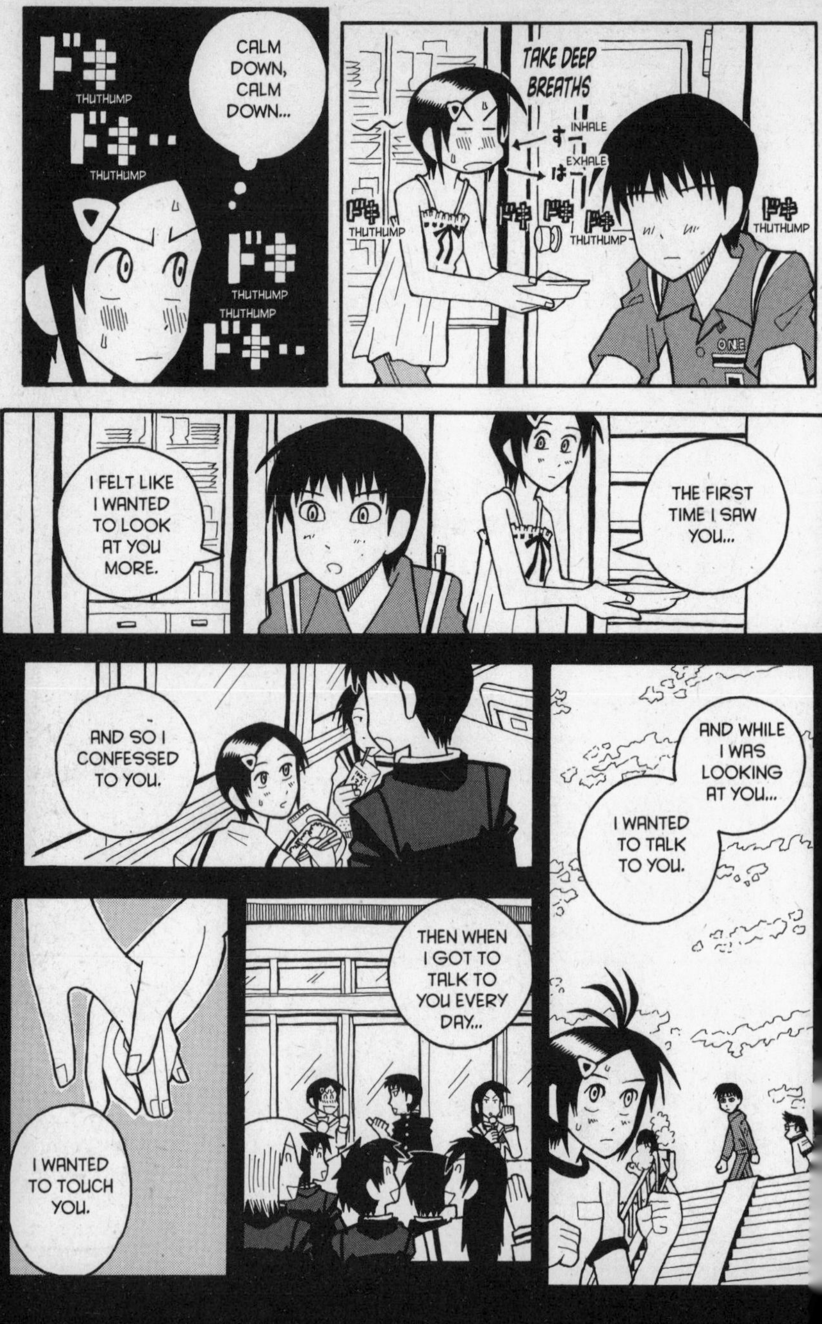
TAKE DEEP BREATHS
すー INHALE
はー EXHALE
ドキ THUTHUMP
ドキ
ドキ
ドキ THUTHUMP
ドキ THUTHUMP
CALM DOWN, CALM DOWN...
ドキ THUTHUMP
ドキ・・ THUTHUMP
ドキ THUTHUMP
THUTHUMP ドキ・・
THE FIRST TIME I SAW YOU...
I FELT LIKE I WANTED TO LOOK AT YOU MORE.
AND WHILE I WAS LOOKING AT YOU...
I WANTED TO TALK TO YOU.
AND SO I CONFESSED TO YOU.
THEN WHEN I GOT TO TALK TO YOU EVERY DAY...
I WANTED TO TOUCH YOU.

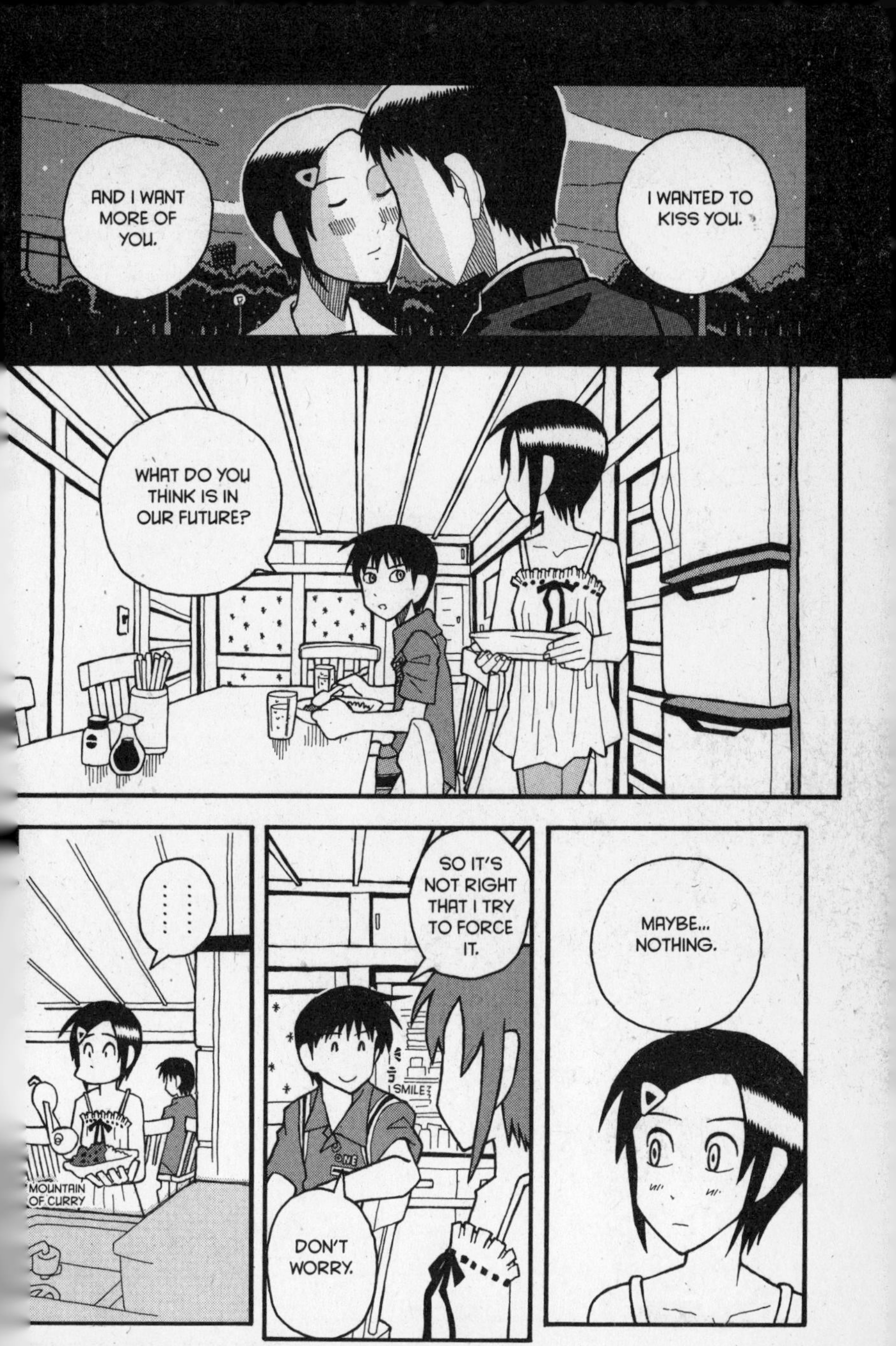
I WANTED TO KISS YOU.
AND I WANT MORE OF YOU.
WHAT DO YOU THINK IS IN OUR FUTURE?
MAYBE... NOTHING.
SO IT'S NOT RIGHT THAT I TRY TO FORCE IT.
SMILE
DON'T WORRY.
......
MOUNTAIN OF CURRY

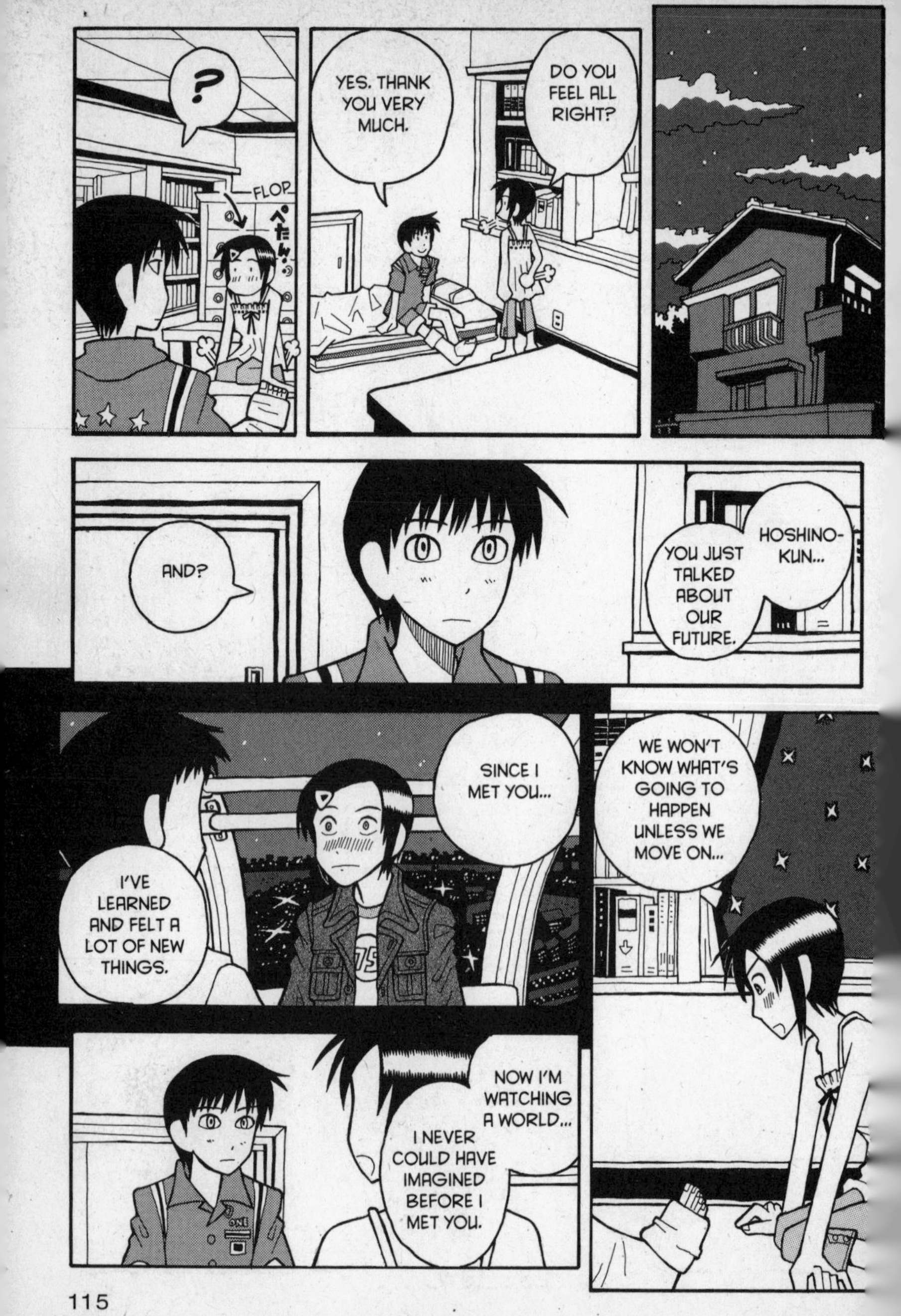
DO YOU FEEL ALL RIGHT?
YES. THANK YOU VERY MUCH.
?
FLOP
ぺたん
HOSHINO-KUN...
YOU JUST TALKED ABOUT OUR FUTURE.
AND?
WE WON'T KNOW WHAT'S GOING TO HAPPEN UNLESS WE MOVE ON...
SINCE I MET YOU...
I'VE LEARNED AND FELT A LOT OF NEW THINGS.
NOW I'M WATCHING A WORLD...
I NEVER COULD HAVE IMAGINED BEFORE I MET YOU.

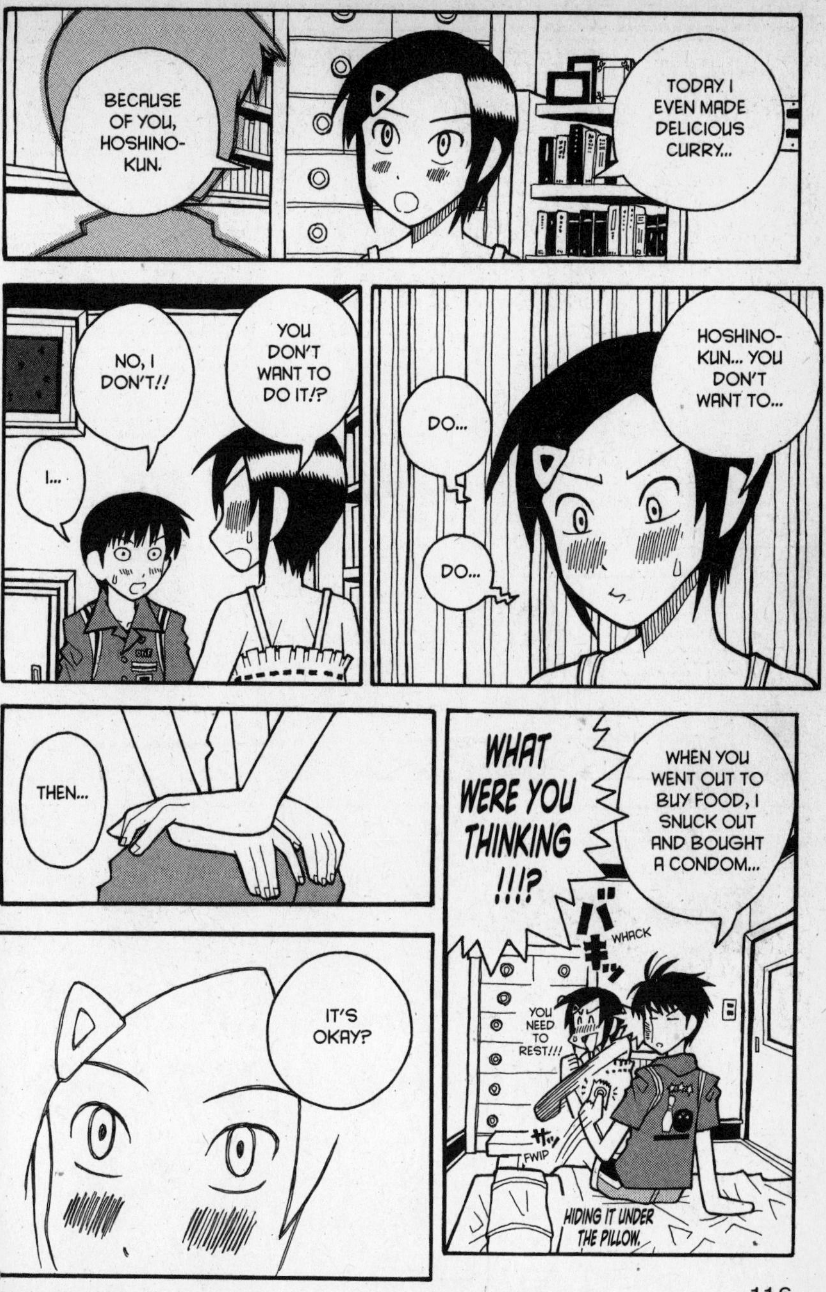
TODAY I EVEN MADE DELICIOUS CURRY...
BECAUSE OF YOU, HOSHINO-KUN.
HOSHINO-KUN... YOU DON'T WANT TO...
DO...
DO...
YOU DON'T WANT TO DO IT!?
NO, I DON'T!!
I...
WHEN YOU WENT OUT TO BUY FOOD, I SNUCK OUT AND BOUGHT A CONDOM...
WHAT WERE YOU THINKING!!!?
バキッ
WHACK
YOU NEED TO REST!!!
サッ
FWIP
HIDING IT UNDER THE PILLOW.
THEN...
IT'S OKAY?

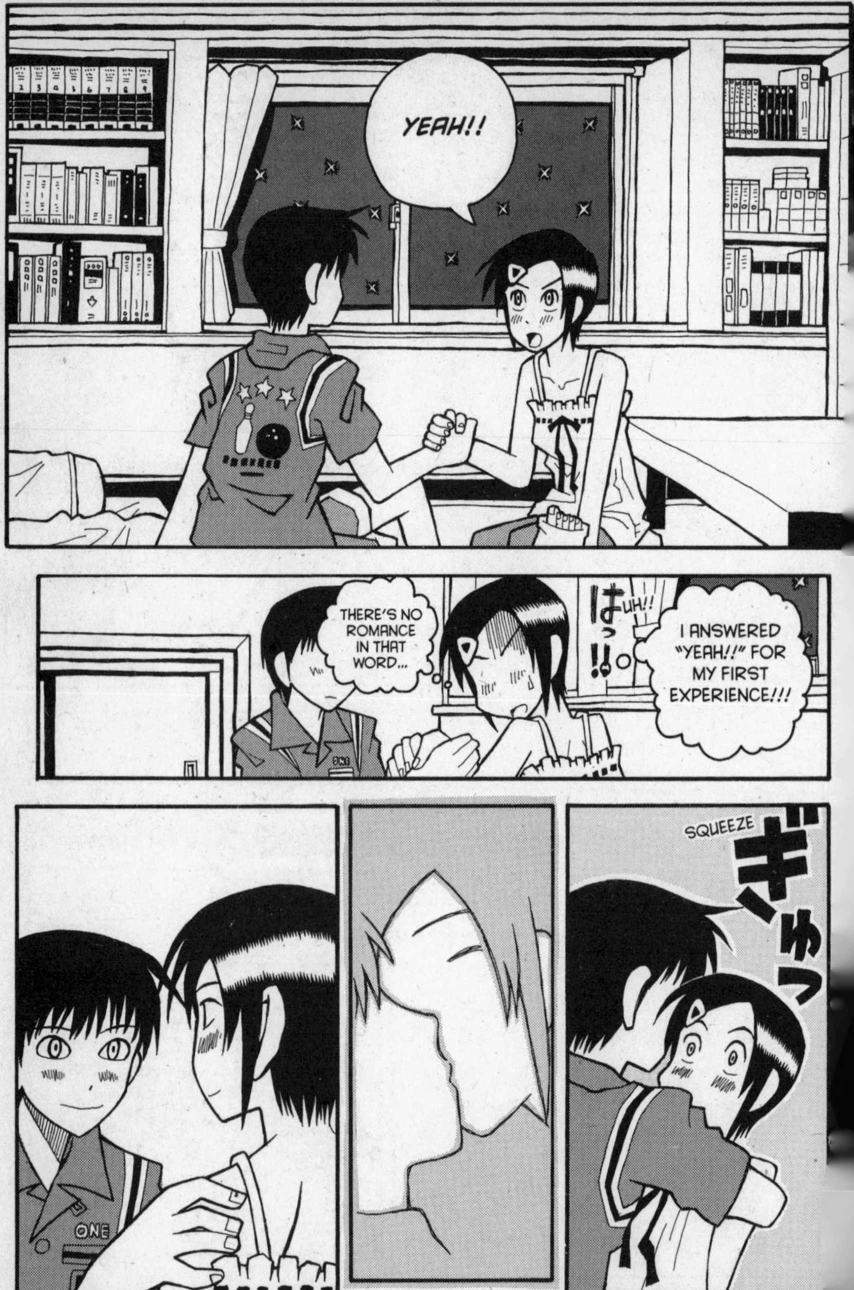
YEAH!!
I ANSWERED "YEAH!!" FOR MY FIRST EXPERIENCE!!!
はっ!! UH!!
THERE'S NO ROMANCE IN THAT WORD...
ぎゅっ SQUEEZE

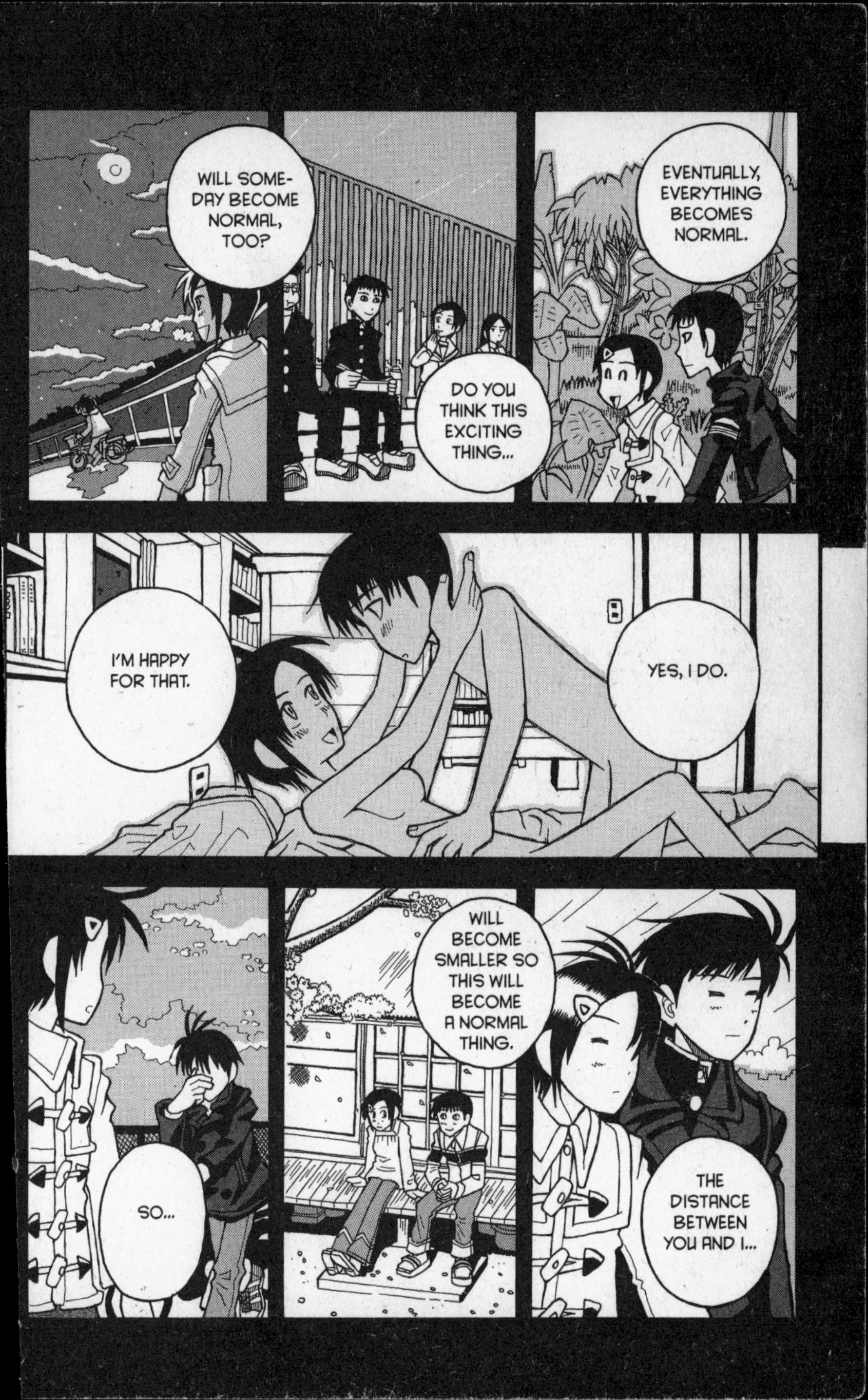
EVENTUALLY, EVERYTHING BECOMES NORMAL.
DO YOU THINK THIS EXCITING THING...
WILL SOME-DAY BECOME NORMAL, TOO?
YES, I DO.
I'M HAPPY FOR THAT.
THE DISTANCE BETWEEN YOU AND I...
WILL BECOME SMALLER SO THIS WILL BECOME A NORMAL THING.
SO...

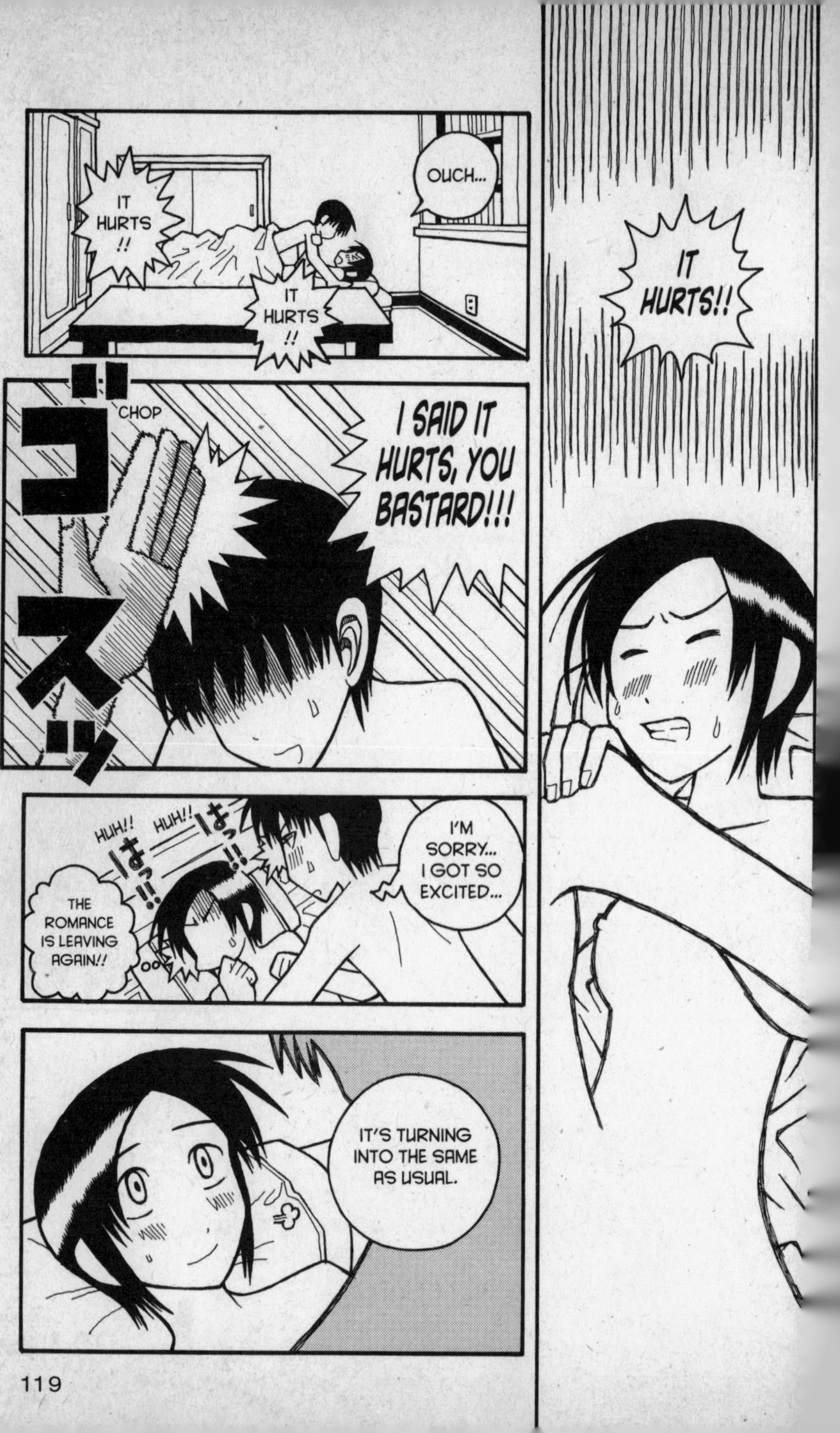
IT HURTS!!
OUCH...
IT HURTS !!
IT HURTS !!
I SAID IT HURTS, YOU BASTARD!!!
ゴスッ
CHOP
I'M SORRY... I GOT SO EXCITED...
HUH!!
はっ!!
HUH!!
はっ!!
THE ROMANCE IS LEAVING AGAIN!!
IT'S TURNING INTO THE SAME AS USUAL.

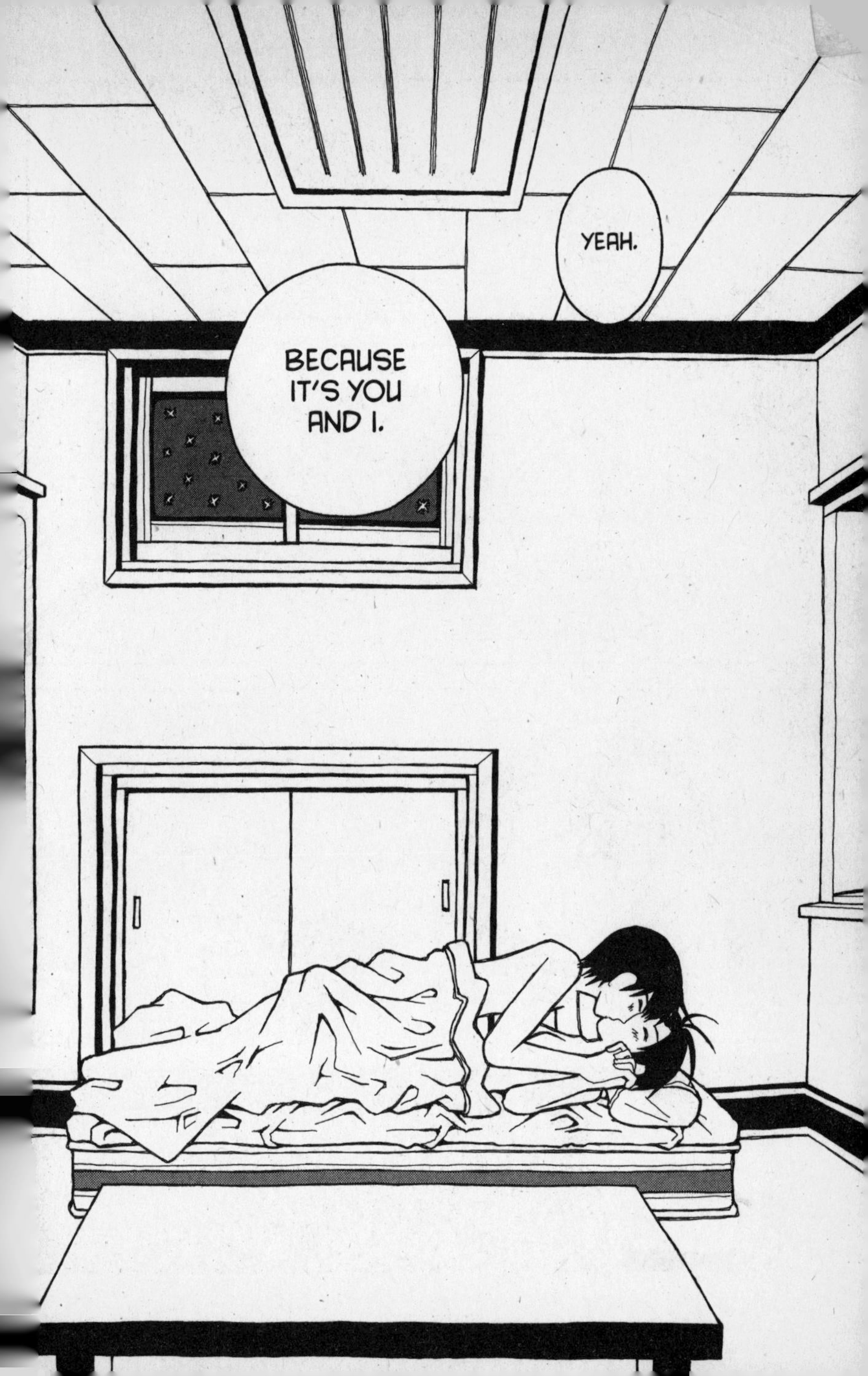
YEAH.
BECAUSE IT'S YOU AND I.

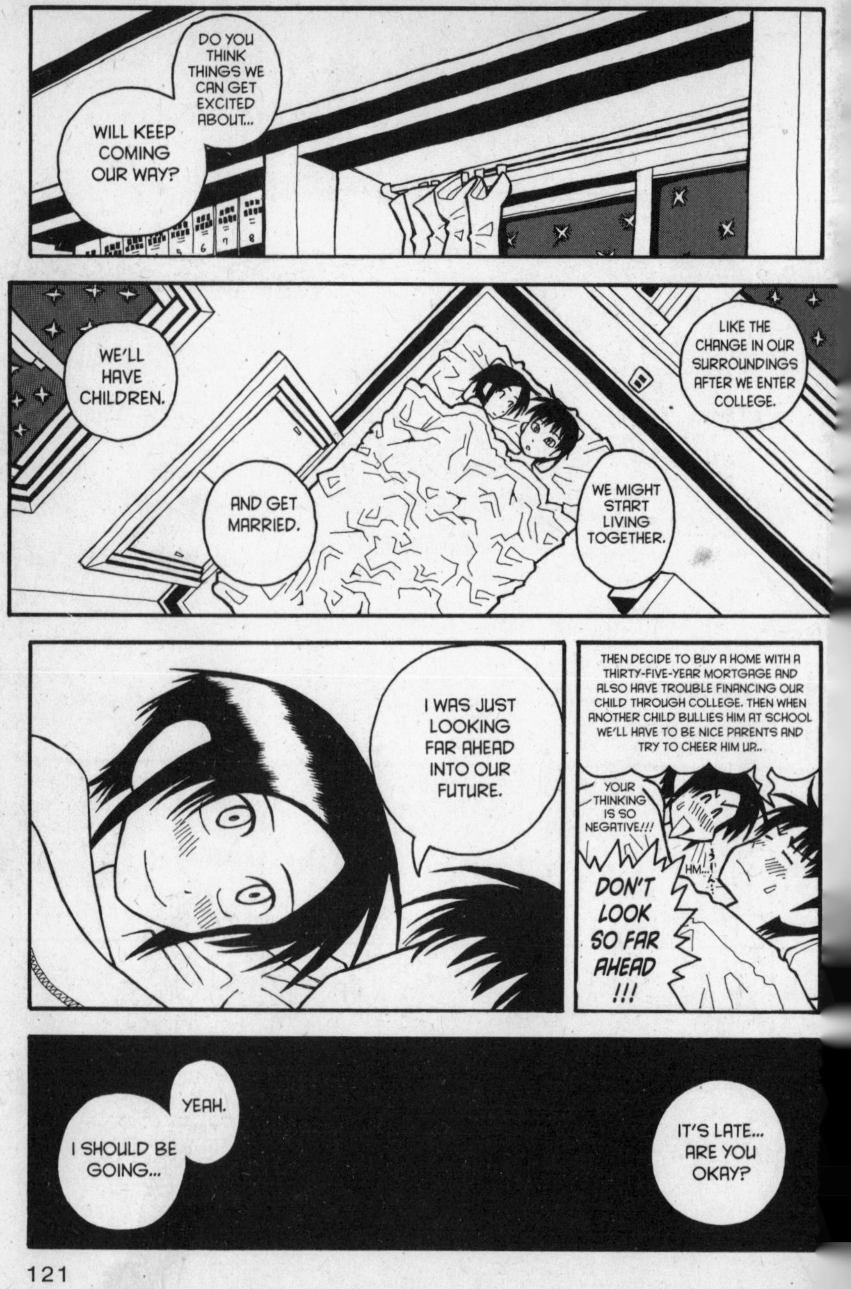
DO YOU THINK THINGS WE CAN GET EXCITED ABOUT...
WILL KEEP COMING OUR WAY?
LIKE THE CHANGE IN OUR SURROUNDINGS AFTER WE ENTER COLLEGE.
WE MIGHT START LIVING TOGETHER.
AND GET MARRIED.
WE'LL HAVE CHILDREN.
THEN DECIDE TO BUY A HOME WITH A THIRTY-FIVE-YEAR MORTGAGE AND ALSO HAVE TROUBLE FINANCING OUR CHILD THROUGH COLLEGE. THEN WHEN ANOTHER CHILD BULLIES HIM AT SCHOOL WE'LL HAVE TO BE NICE PARENTS AND TRY TO CHEER HIM UP...
YOUR THINKING IS SO NEGATIVE!!!
HM...
DON'T LOOK SO FAR AHEAD !!!
I WAS JUST LOOKING FAR AHEAD INTO OUR FUTURE.
IT'S LATE... ARE YOU OKAY?
YEAH.
I SHOULD BE GOING...

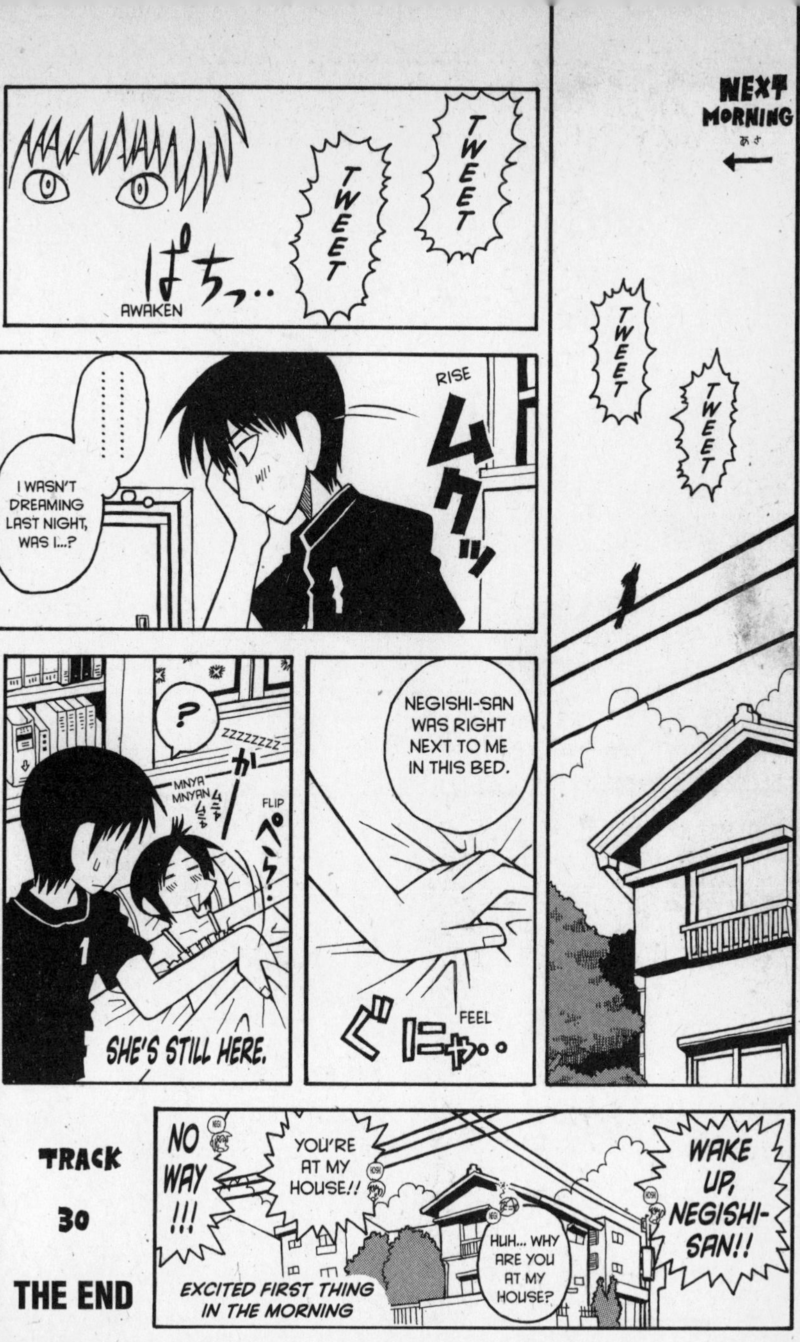
NEXT MORNING
あさ
TWEET
TWEET
TWEET
TWEET
ぱちっ..
AWAKEN
RISE
ムクッ
......
I WASN'T DREAMING LAST NIGHT, WAS I...?
NEGISHI-SAN WAS RIGHT NEXT TO ME IN THIS BED.
ぐにゃ。。
FEEL
?
ZZZZZZZZ
がー
MNYA MNYAN
ムニャムニャ
FLIP
ぺらっ
SHE'S STILL HERE.
WAKE UP, NEGISHI-SAN!!
HUH... WHY ARE YOU AT MY HOUSE?
YOU'RE AT MY HOUSE!!
NO WAY!!!
EXCITED FIRST THING IN THE MORNING

TRACK 30 THE END

BONUS TRACK

おまけ

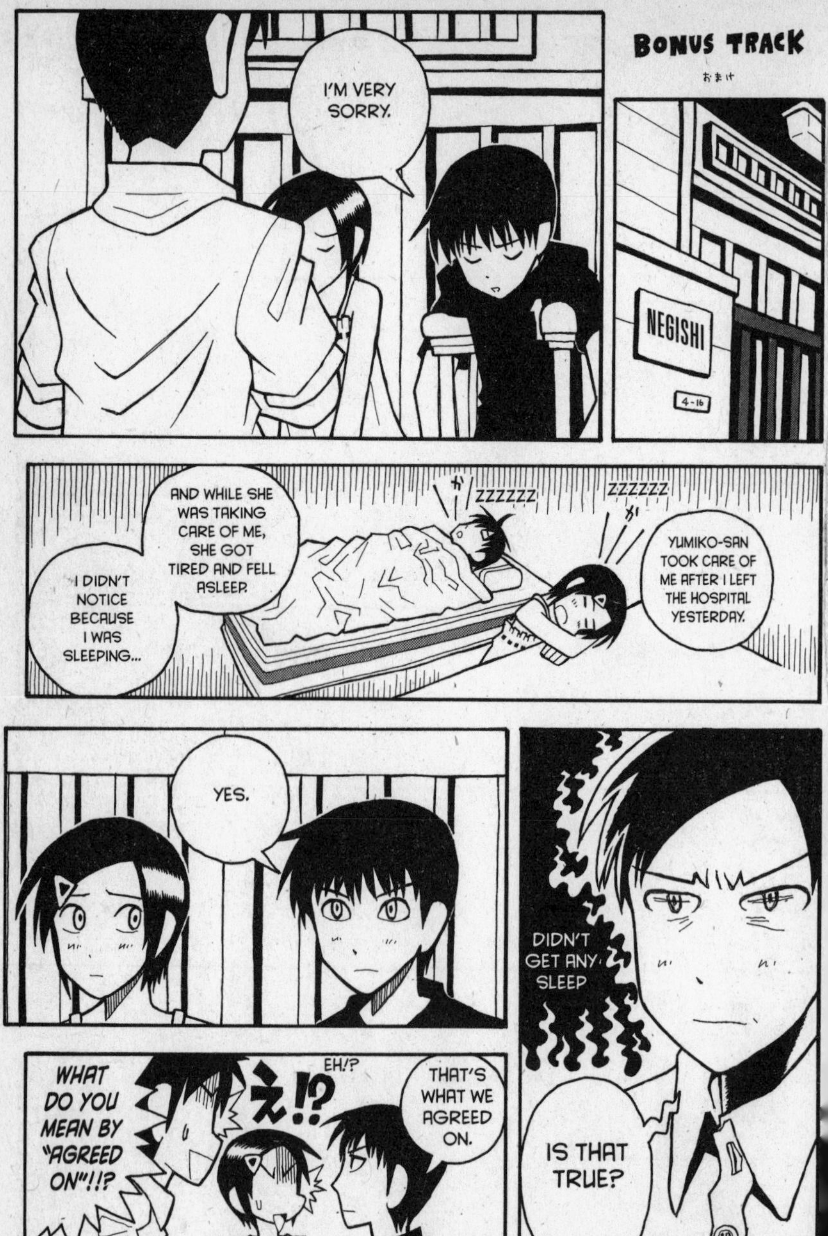
NEGISHI
4-16
I'M VERY SORRY.
YUMIKO-SAN TOOK CARE OF ME AFTER I LEFT THE HOSPITAL YESTERDAY.
ZZZZZZ
が
ZZZZZZ
が
AND WHILE SHE WAS TAKING CARE OF ME, SHE GOT TIRED AND FELL ASLEEP.
I DIDN'T NOTICE BECAUSE I WAS SLEEPING...
DIDN'T GET ANY SLEEP
IS THAT TRUE?
YES.
THAT'S WHAT WE AGREED ON.
え!?
EH!?
WHAT DO YOU MEAN BY "AGREED ON"!!?

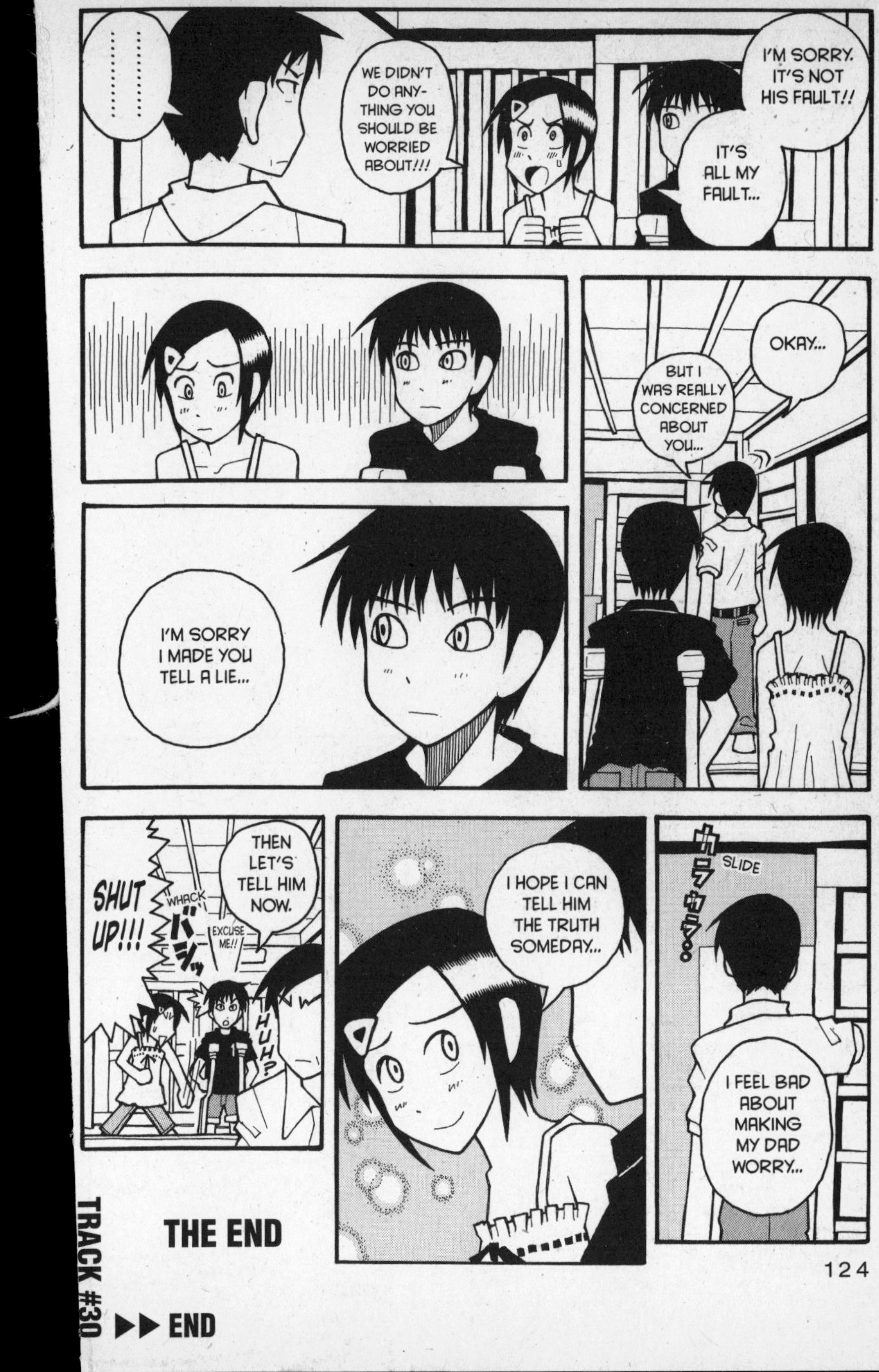
I'M SORRY. IT'S NOT HIS FAULT!!
IT'S ALL MY FAULT...
WE DIDN'T DO ANYTHING YOU SHOULD BE WORRIED ABOUT!!!
......
OKAY...
BUT I WAS REALLY CONCERNED ABOUT YOU...
I'M SORRY I MADE YOU TELL A LIE...
カラカラ
SLIDE
I FEEL BAD ABOUT MAKING MY DAD WORRY...
I HOPE I CAN TELL HIM THE TRUTH SOMEDAY...
THEN LET'S TELL HIM NOW.
SHUT UP!!!
WHACK
バシッ
EXCUSE ME!!
HUH?

THE END

TRACK #30 ▶▶ END

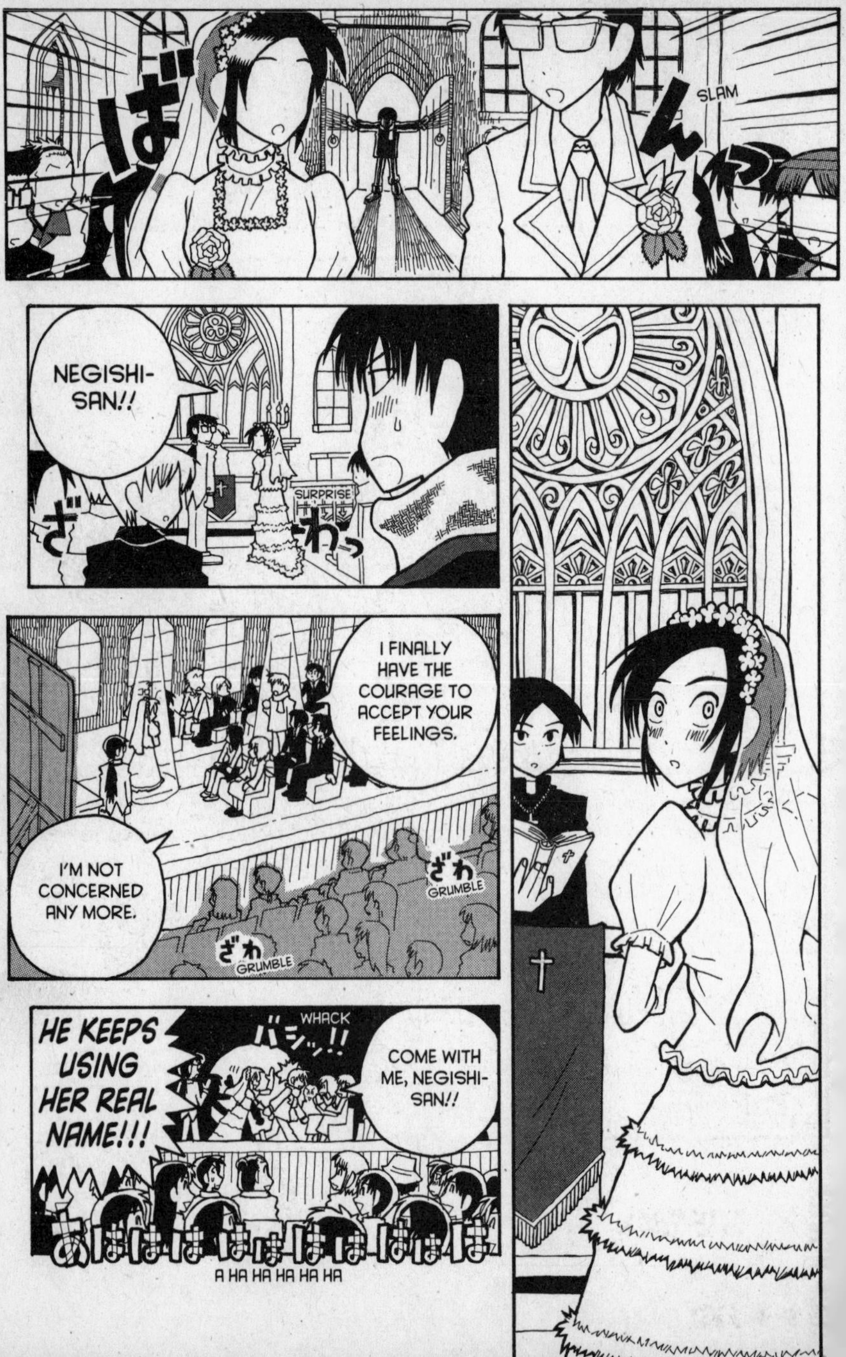
SLAM
ばんっ
NEGISHI-SAN!!
SURPRISE
わっ
ざ
I FINALLY HAVE THE COURAGE TO ACCEPT YOUR FEELINGS.
I'M NOT CONCERNED ANY MORE.
ざわ
GRUMBLE
ざわ
GRUMBLE
WHACK
バシッ!!
COME WITH ME, NEGISHI-SAN!!
HE KEEPS USING HER REAL NAME!!!
あははははははははは
A HA HA HA HA HA

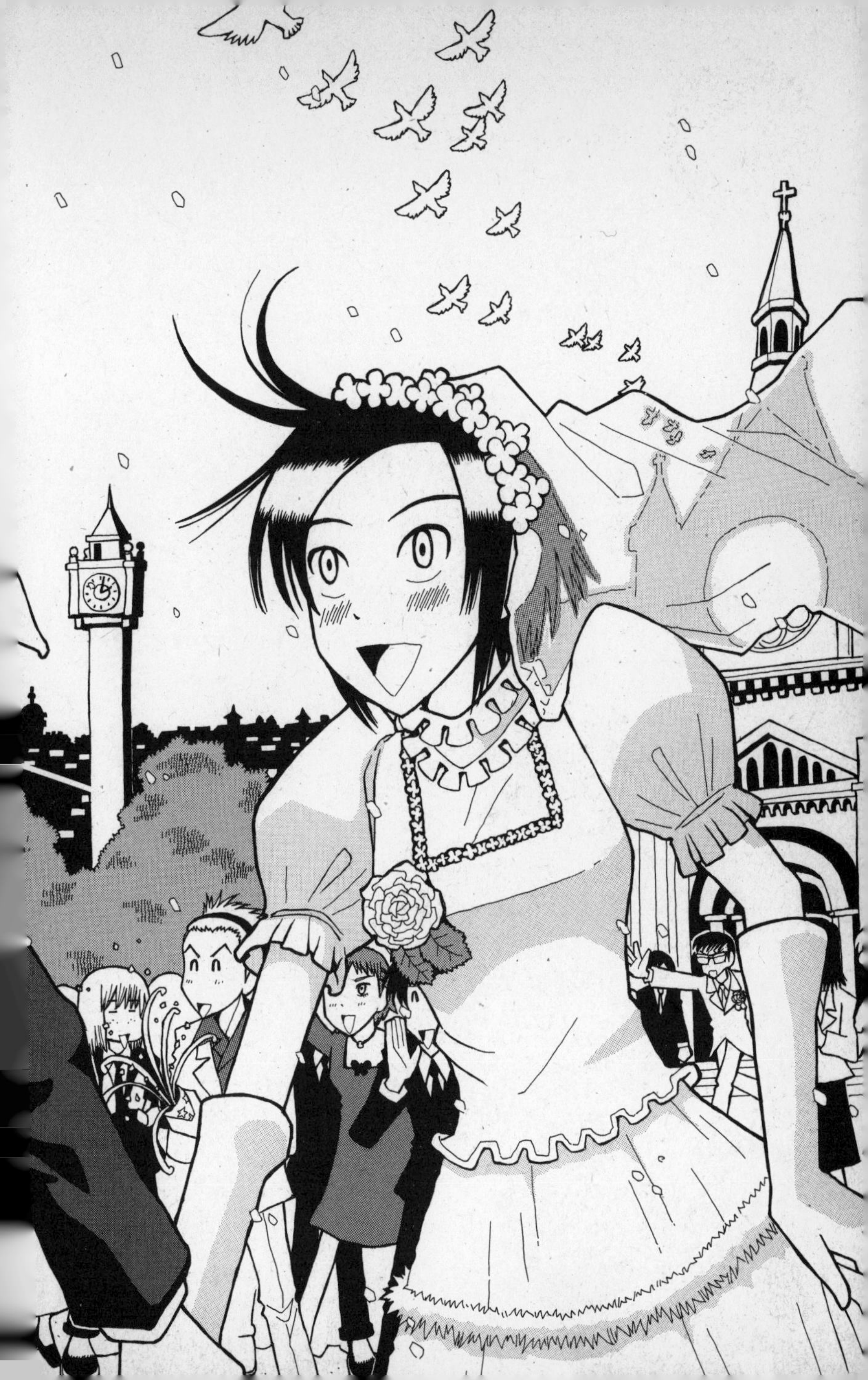

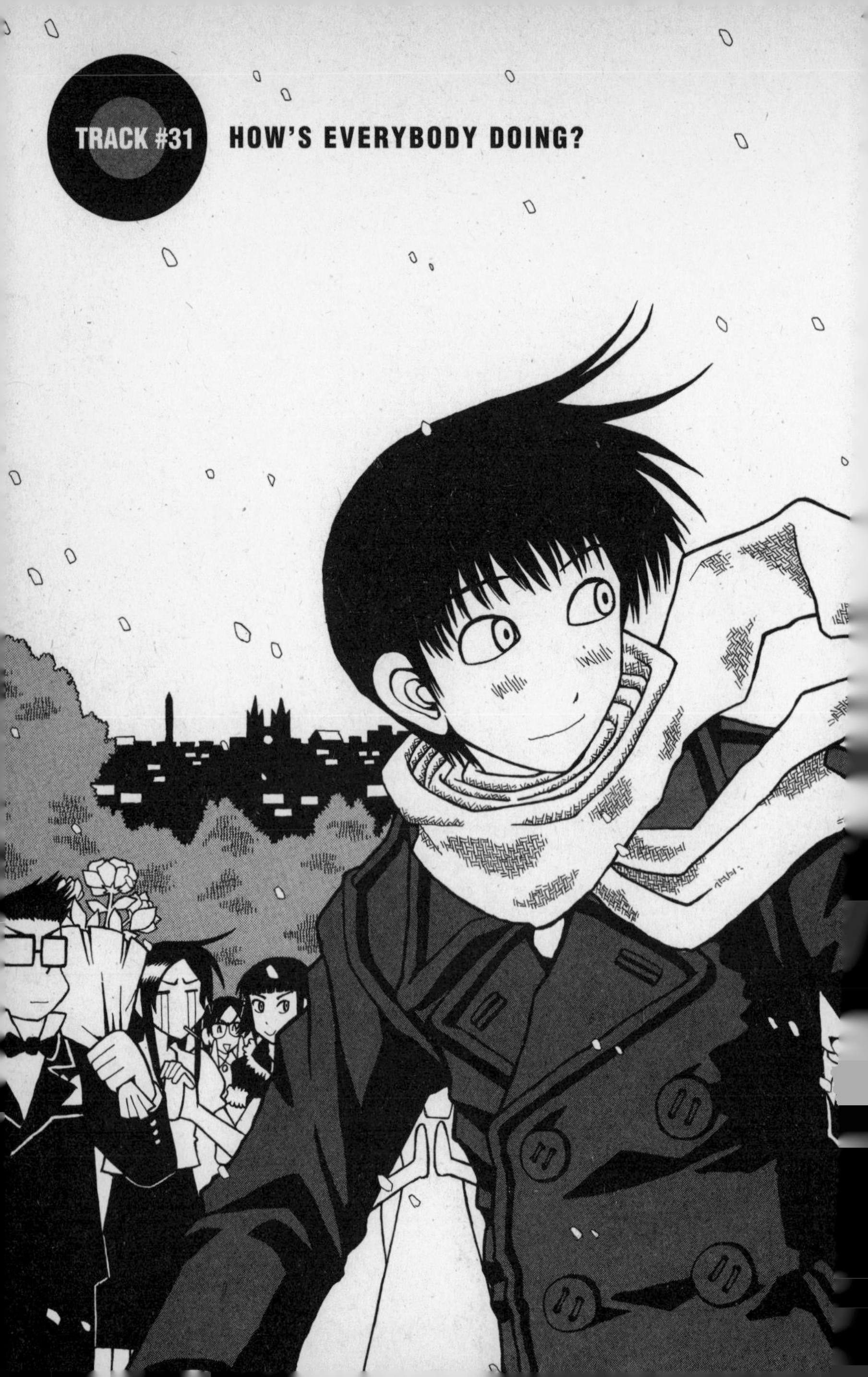
TRACK #31
HOW'S EVERYBODY DOING?

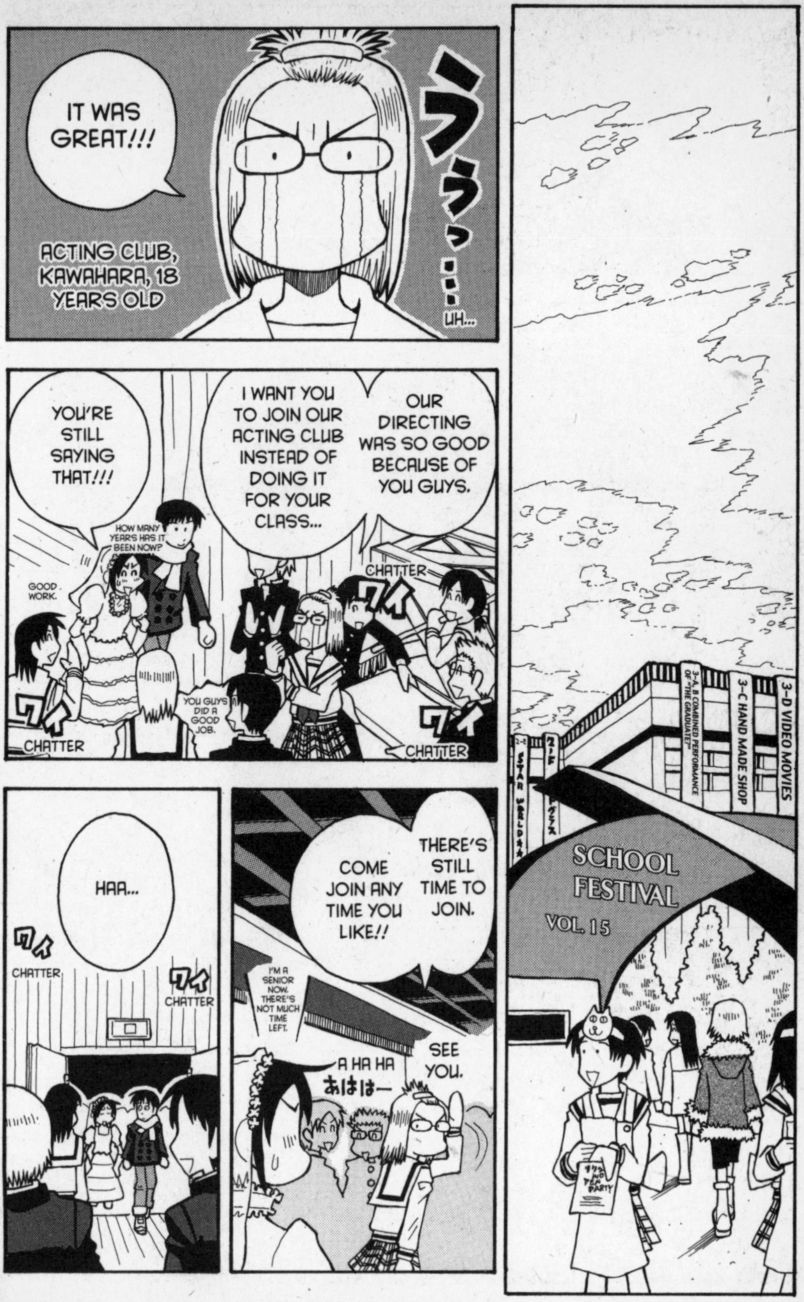
3-D VIDEO MOVIES
3-C HAND MADE SHOP
3-A, B COMBINED PERFORMANCE OF "THE GRADUATE"
STAR WORLD★
SCHOOL FESTIVAL
VOL. 15
うぅっ...
IT WAS GREAT!!!
UH...
ACTING CLUB, KAWAHARA, 18 YEARS OLD
OUR DIRECTING WAS SO GOOD BECAUSE OF YOU GUYS.
I WANT YOU TO JOIN OUR ACTING CLUB INSTEAD OF DOING IT FOR YOUR CLASS...
YOU'RE STILL SAYING THAT!!!
HOW MANY YEARS HAS IT BEEN NOW?
ワイ
CHATTER
GOOD WORK.
YOU GUYS DID A GOOD JOB.
ワイ
CHATTER
ワイ
CHATTER
THERE'S STILL TIME TO JOIN.
COME JOIN ANY TIME YOU LIKE!!
I'M A SENIOR NOW. THERE'S NOT MUCH TIME LEFT.
SEE YOU.
A HA HA
あはは—
HAA...
ワイ
CHATTER
ワイ
CHATTER

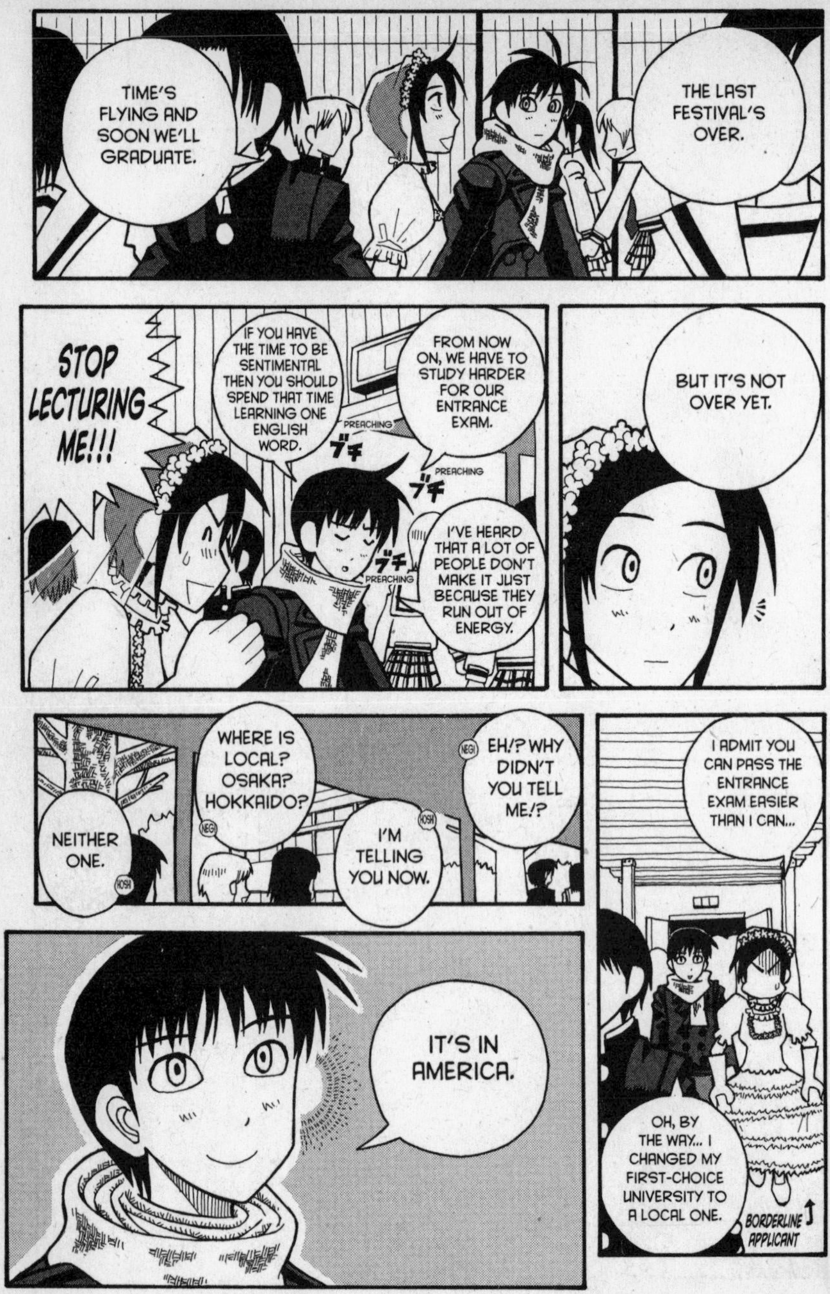
THE LAST FESTIVAL'S OVER.
TIME'S FLYING AND SOON WE'LL GRADUATE.
BUT IT'S NOT OVER YET.
FROM NOW ON, WE HAVE TO STUDY HARDER FOR OUR ENTRANCE EXAM.
IF YOU HAVE THE TIME TO BE SENTIMENTAL THEN YOU SHOULD SPEND THAT TIME LEARNING ONE ENGLISH WORD.
ブチ PREACHING
ブチ PREACHING
ブチ PREACHING
I'VE HEARD THAT A LOT OF PEOPLE DON'T MAKE IT JUST BECAUSE THEY RUN OUT OF ENERGY.
STOP LECTURING ME!!!
I ADMIT YOU CAN PASS THE ENTRANCE EXAM EASIER THAN I CAN...
OH, BY THE WAY... I CHANGED MY FIRST-CHOICE UNIVERSITY TO A LOCAL ONE.
BORDERLINE APPLICANT
NEGI
EH!? WHY DIDN'T YOU TELL ME!?
HOSHI
I'M TELLING YOU NOW.
NEGI
WHERE IS LOCAL? OSAKA? HOKKAIDO?
HOSHI
NEITHER ONE.
IT'S IN AMERICA.

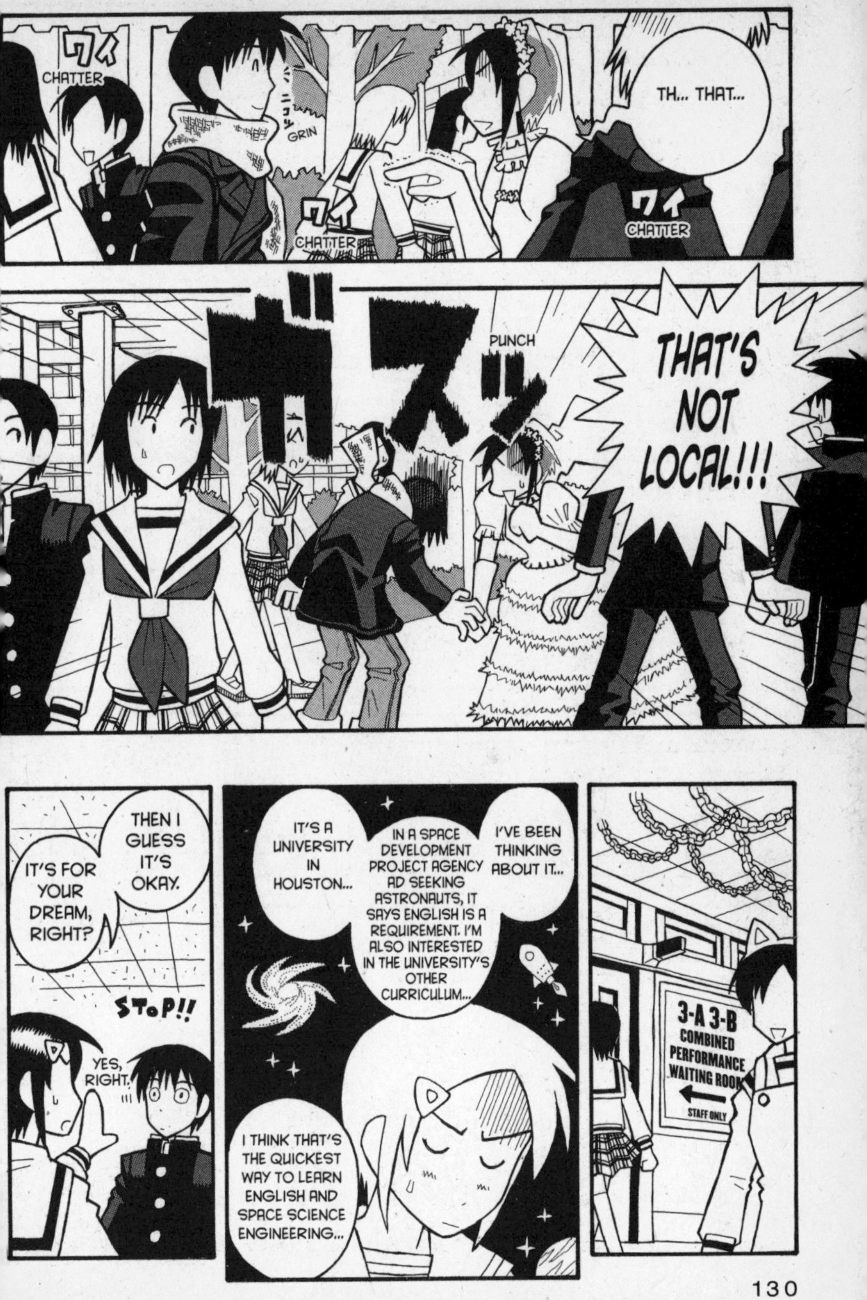
TH... THAT...
CHATTER
CHATTER
GRIN
CHATTER
THAT'S NOT LOCAL!!!
PUNCH
3-A 3-B COMBINED PERFORMANCE WAITING ROO
STAFF ONLY
I'VE BEEN THINKING ABOUT IT...
IN A SPACE DEVELOPMENT PROJECT AGENCY AD SEEKING ASTRONAUTS, IT SAYS ENGLISH IS A REQUIREMENT. I'M ALSO INTERESTED IN THE UNIVERSITY'S OTHER CURRICULUM...
IT'S A UNIVERSITY IN HOUSTON...
I THINK THAT'S THE QUICKEST WAY TO LEARN ENGLISH AND SPACE SCIENCE ENGINEERING...
THEN I GUESS IT'S OKAY.
IT'S FOR YOUR DREAM, RIGHT?
STOP!!
YES, RIGHT.

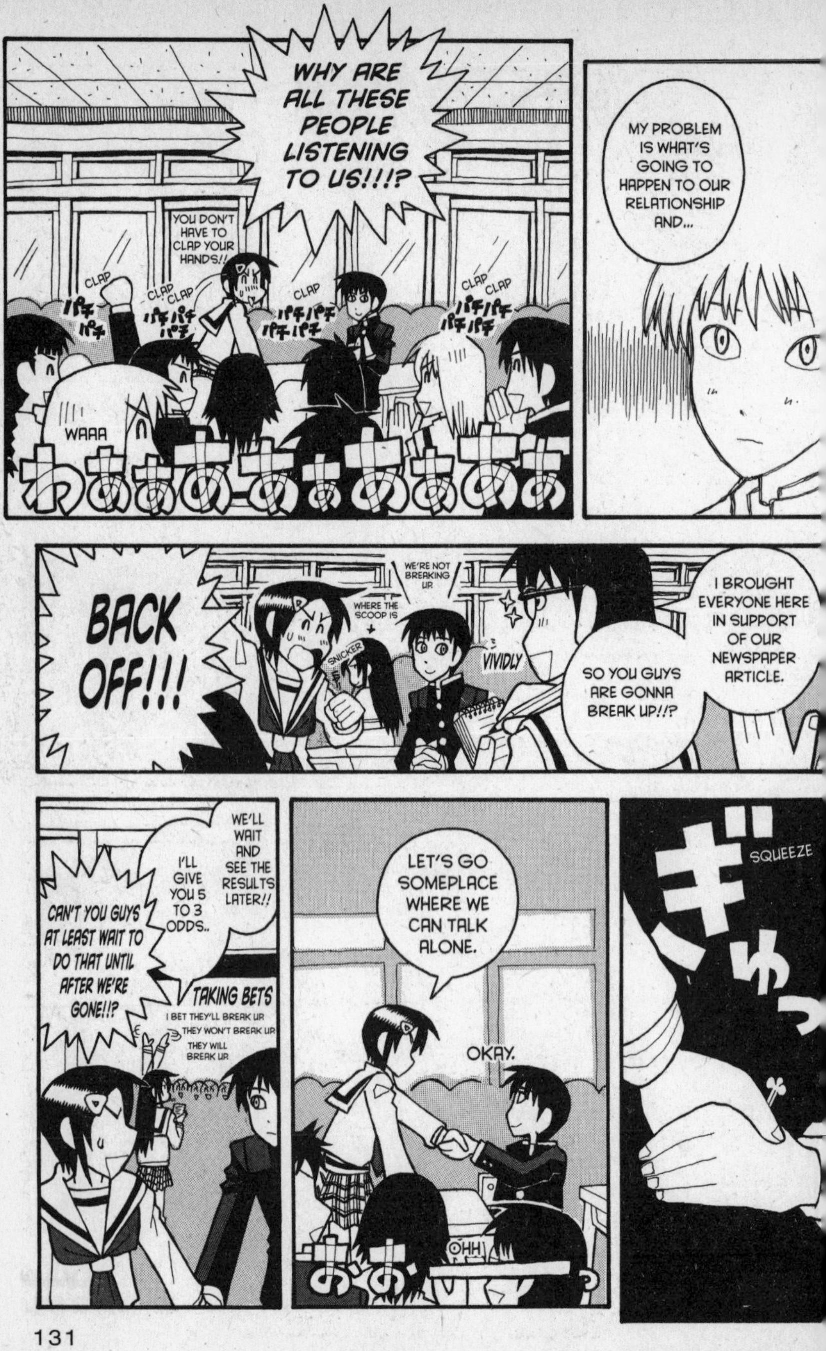
MY PROBLEM IS WHAT'S GOING TO HAPPEN TO OUR RELATIONSHIP AND...
WHY ARE ALL THESE PEOPLE LISTENING TO US!!!?
YOU DON'T HAVE TO CLAP YOUR HANDS!!
CLAP CLAP
CLAP
CLAP CLAP
CLAP
WAAA
I BROUGHT EVERYONE HERE IN SUPPORT OF OUR NEWSPAPER ARTICLE.
SO YOU GUYS ARE GONNA BREAK UP!!?
VIVIDLY
WE'RE NOT BREAKING UP.
WHERE THE SCOOP IS
SNICKER
BACK OFF!!!
SQUEEZE
LET'S GO SOMEPLACE WHERE WE CAN TALK ALONE.
OKAY.
OHH
WE'LL WAIT AND SEE THE RESULTS LATER!!
I'LL GIVE YOU 5 TO 3 ODDS..
CAN'T YOU GUYS AT LEAST WAIT TO DO THAT UNTIL AFTER WE'RE GONE!!?
TAKING BETS
I BET THEY'LL BREAK UP.
THEY WON'T BREAK UP.
THEY WILL BREAK UP.

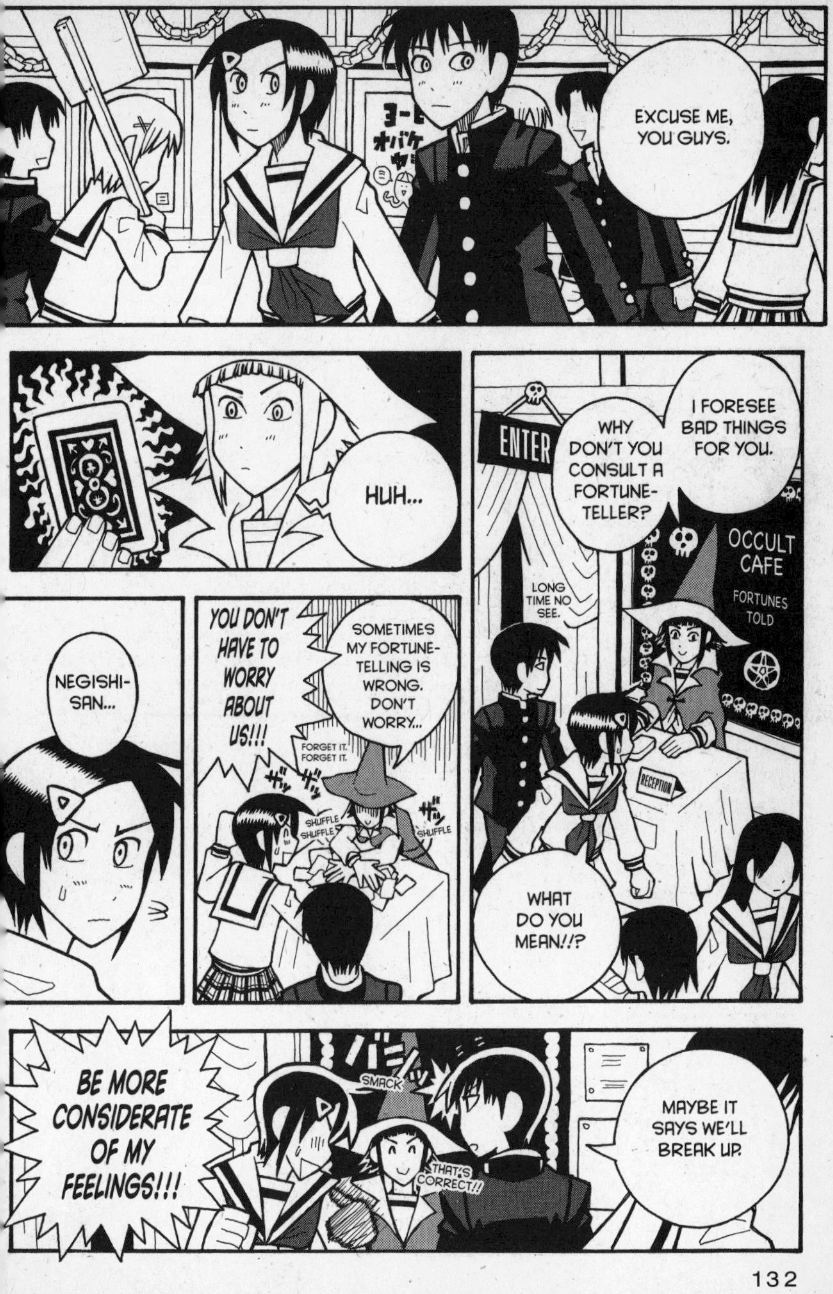
EXCUSE ME, YOU GUYS.
ENTER
I FORESEE BAD THINGS FOR YOU.
WHY DON'T YOU CONSULT A FORTUNE-TELLER?
OCCULT CAFE
FORTUNES TOLD
LONG TIME NO SEE.
RECEPTION
WHAT DO YOU MEAN!!?
HUH...
SOMETIMES MY FORTUNE-TELLING IS WRONG. DON'T WORRY...
YOU DON'T HAVE TO WORRY ABOUT US!!!
FORGET IT. FORGET IT.
SHUFFLE
SHUFFLE SHUFFLE
NEGISHI-SAN...
MAYBE IT SAYS WE'LL BREAK UP.
SMACK
THAT'S CORRECT!!
BE MORE CONSIDERATE OF MY FEELINGS!!!

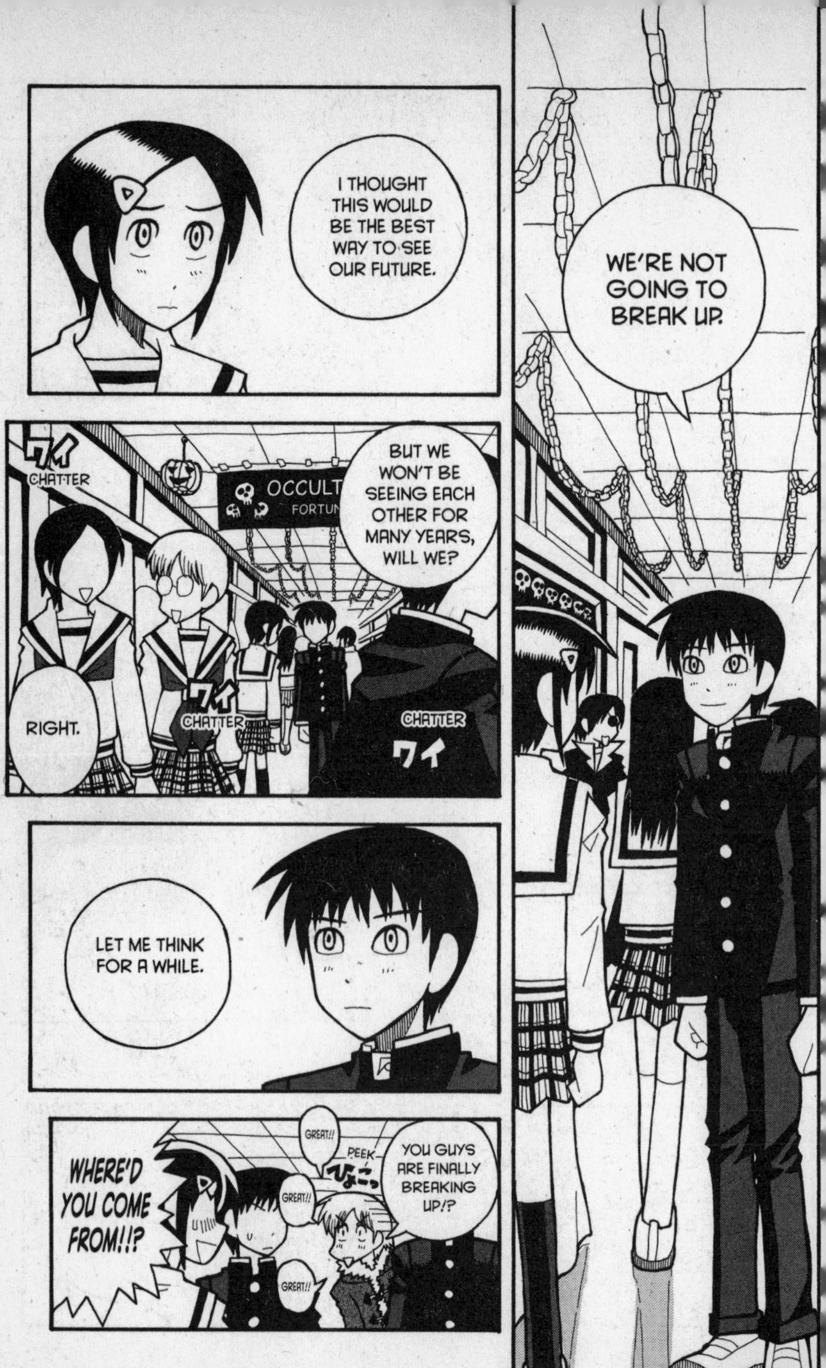
I THOUGHT THIS WOULD BE THE BEST WAY TO SEE OUR FUTURE.
BUT WE WON'T BE SEEING EACH OTHER FOR MANY YEARS, WILL WE?
OCCULT
CHATTER
CHATTER
CHATTER
RIGHT.
LET ME THINK FOR A WHILE.
YOU GUYS ARE FINALLY BREAKING UP!?
PEEK
GREAT!!
GREAT!!
GREAT!!
WHERE'D YOU COME FROM!!?
WE'RE NOT GOING TO BREAK UP.

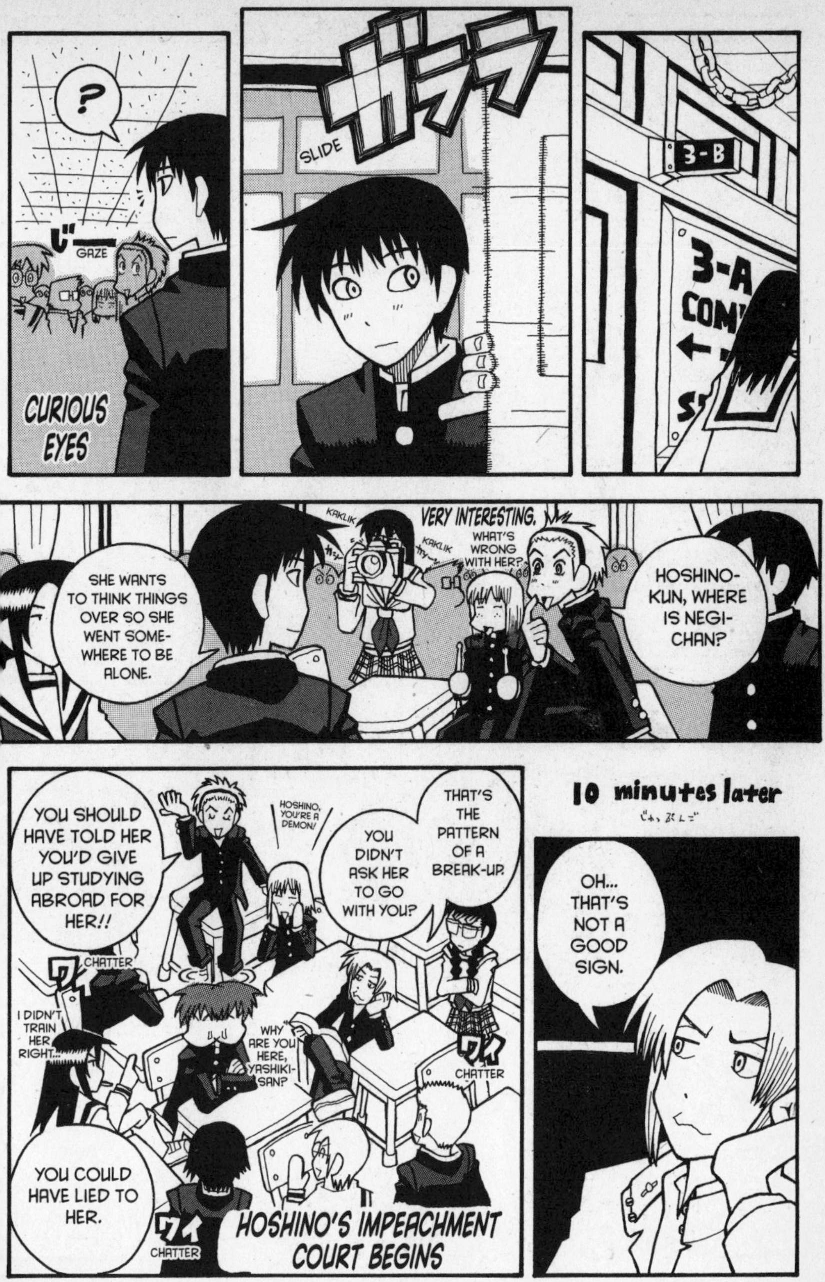
3-B
3-A
COM
SLIDE
?
GAZE
CURIOUS EYES
HOSHINO-KUN, WHERE IS NEGI-CHAN?
WHAT'S WRONG WITH HER?
VERY INTERESTING.
KAKLIK
KAKLIK
SHE WANTS TO THINK THINGS OVER SO SHE WENT SOME-WHERE TO BE ALONE.
10 minutes later
OH... THAT'S NOT A GOOD SIGN.
THAT'S THE PATTERN OF A BREAK-UP.
YOU DIDN'T ASK HER TO GO WITH YOU?
HOSHINO, YOU'RE A DEMON!
YOU SHOULD HAVE TOLD HER YOU'D GIVE UP STUDYING ABROAD FOR HER!!
CHATTER
CHATTER
WHY ARE YOU HERE, YASHIKI-SAN?
I DIDN'T TRAIN HER RIGHT...
YOU COULD HAVE LIED TO HER.
CHATTER
HOSHINO'S IMPEACHMENT COURT BEGINS

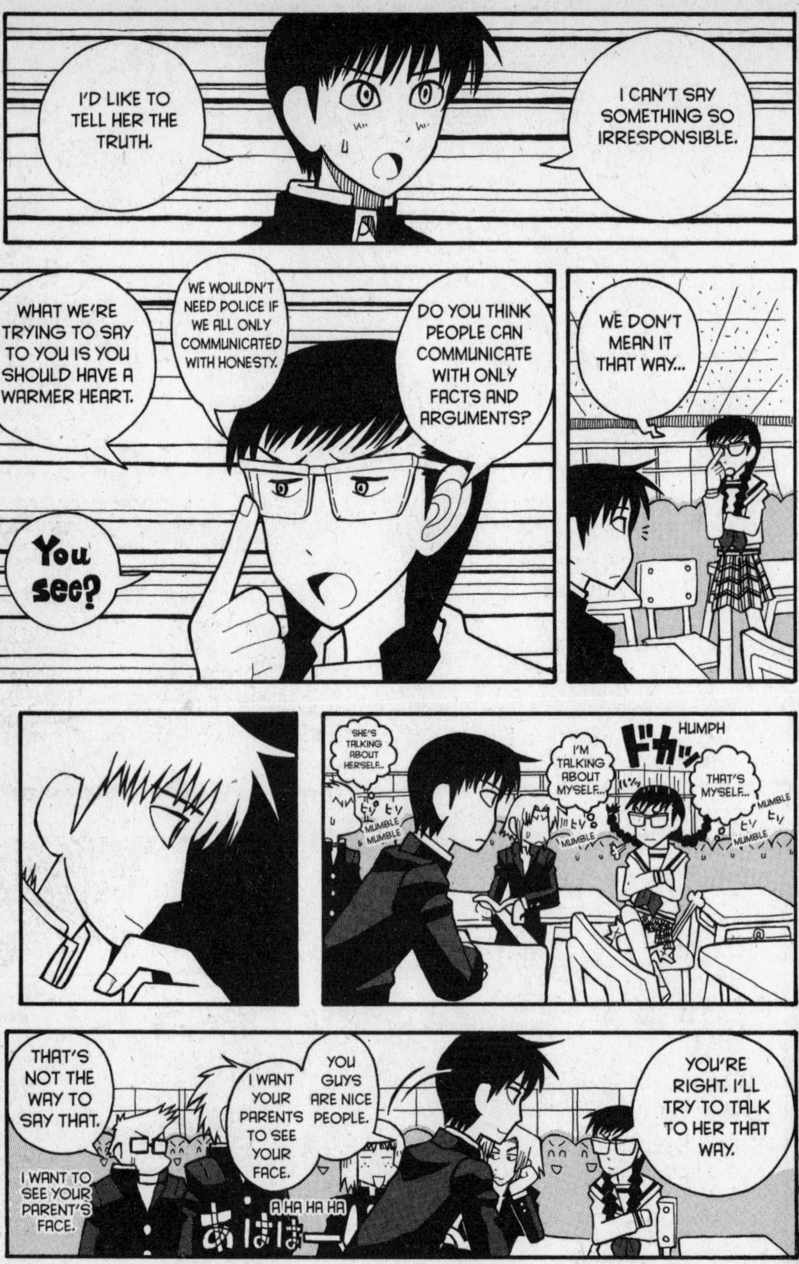
I CAN'T SAY SOMETHING SO IRRESPONSIBLE.
I'D LIKE TO TELL HER THE TRUTH.
WE DON'T MEAN IT THAT WAY...
DO YOU THINK PEOPLE CAN COMMUNICATE WITH ONLY FACTS AND ARGUMENTS?
WE WOULDN'T NEED POLICE IF WE ALL ONLY COMMUNICATED WITH HONESTY.
WHAT WE'RE TRYING TO SAY TO YOU IS YOU SHOULD HAVE A WARMER HEART.
You see?
HUMPH
ドカッ
THAT'S MYSELF...
MUMBLE
ヒソ
MUMBLE
I'M TALKING ABOUT MYSELF...
MUMBLE
SHE'S TALKING ABOUT HERSELF...
MUMBLE MUMBLE
YOU'RE RIGHT. I'LL TRY TO TALK TO HER THAT WAY.
YOU GUYS ARE NICE PEOPLE.
I WANT YOUR PARENTS TO SEE YOUR FACE.
A HA HA HA
あははー
THAT'S NOT THE WAY TO SAY THAT.
I WANT TO SEE YOUR PARENT'S FACE.

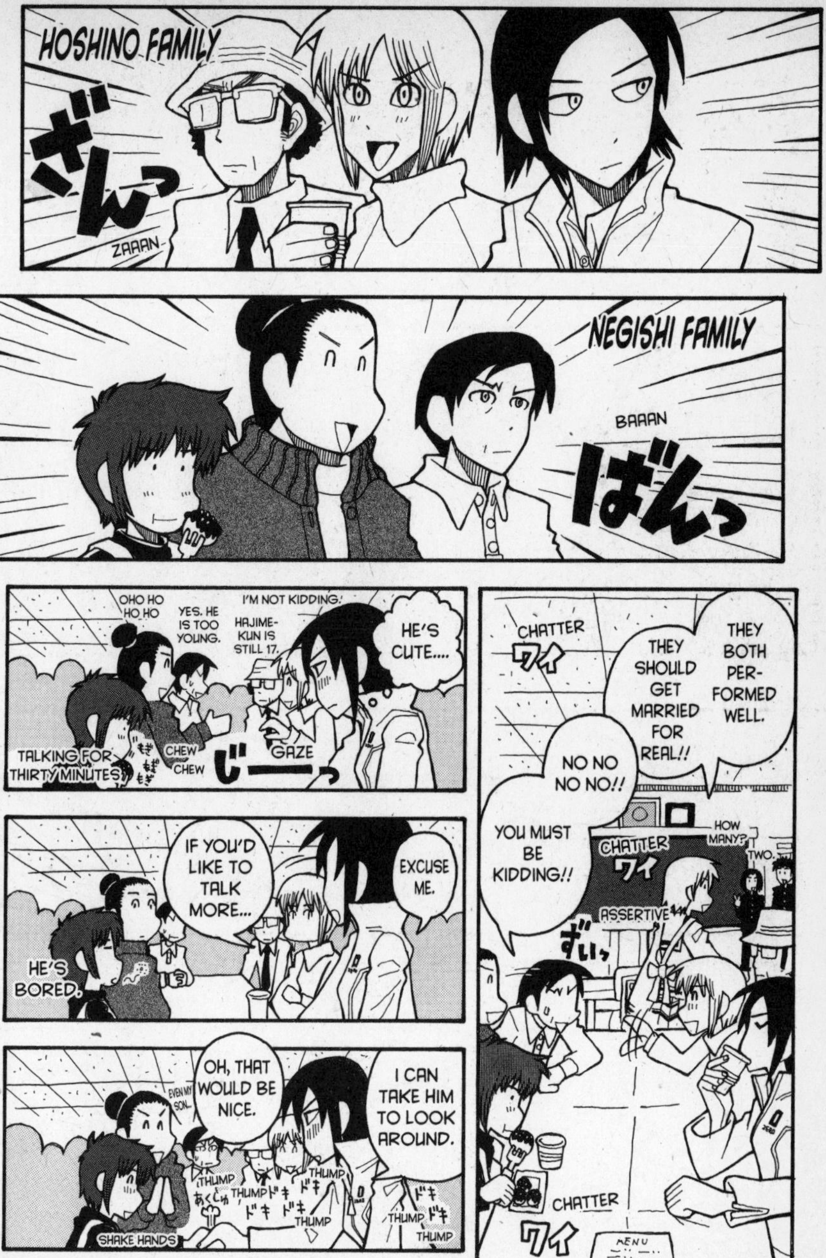
HOSHINO FAMILY
ざんっ
ZAAAN
NEGISHI FAMILY
BAAAN
ばんっ
HE'S CUTE....
I'M NOT KIDDING.
HAJIME-KUN IS STILL 17.
YES. HE IS TOO YOUNG.
OHO HO HO HO
GAZE
じーっ
CHEW CHEW
TALKING FOR THIRTY MINUTES
EXCUSE ME.
IF YOU'D LIKE TO TALK MORE...
HE'S BORED.
I CAN TAKE HIM TO LOOK AROUND.
OH, THAT WOULD BE NICE.
EVEN MY SON...
THUMP
ドキ
SHAKE HANDS
THEY BOTH PERFORMED WELL.
THEY SHOULD GET MARRIED FOR REAL!!
CHATTER
ワイ
NO NO NO NO!!
YOU MUST BE KIDDING!!
HOW MANY?
TWO.
CHATTER
ワイ
ASSERTIVE
ずいっ
CHATTER
ワイ
MENU

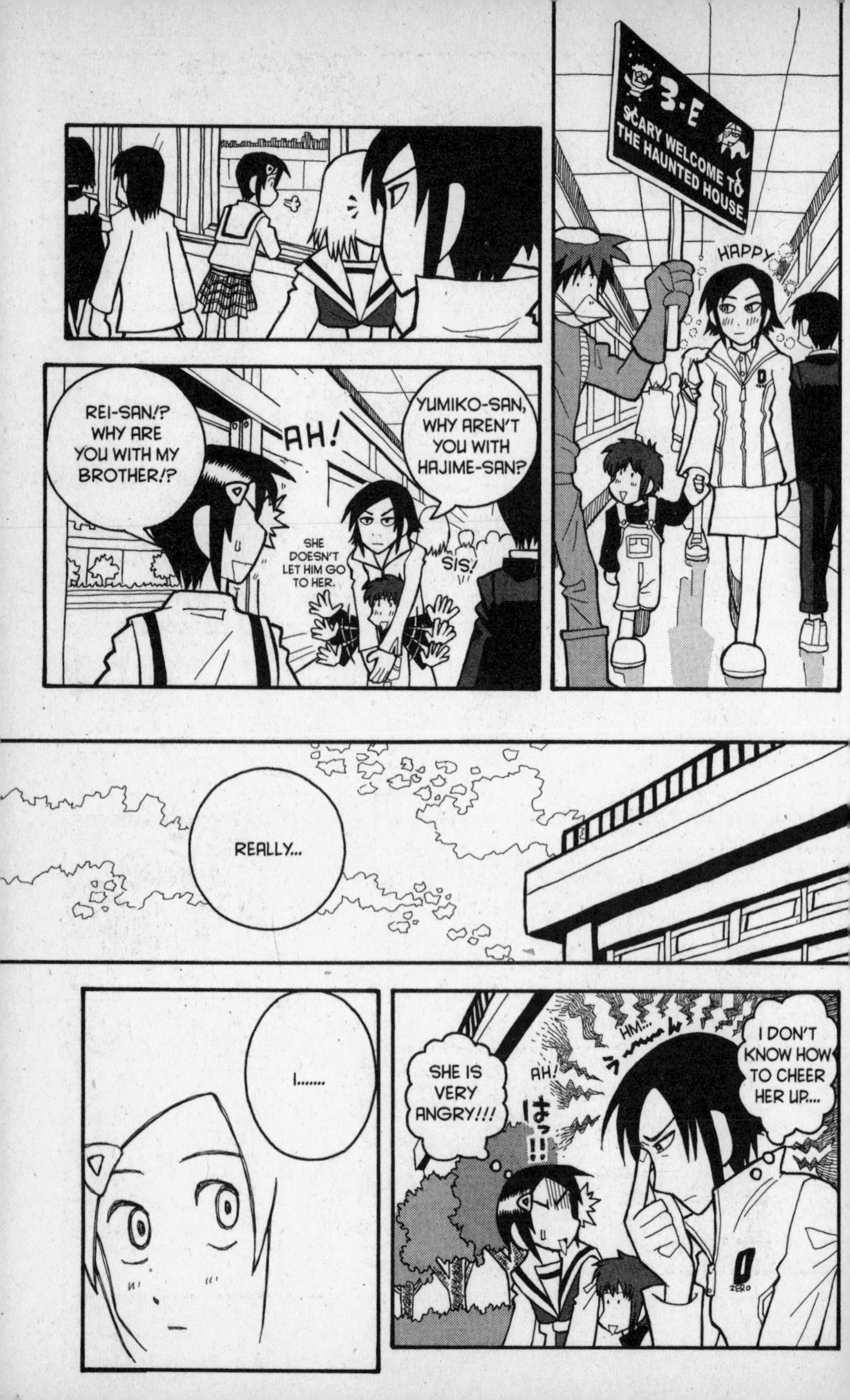
3·E
SCARY WELCOME TO THE HAUNTED HOUSE.
HAPPY
YUMIKO-SAN, WHY AREN'T YOU WITH HAJIME-SAN?
AH!
REI-SAN!? WHY ARE YOU WITH MY BROTHER!?
SIS!
SHE DOESN'T LET HIM GO TO HER.
REALLY...
I DON'T KNOW HOW TO CHEER HER UP....
HM...
AH!
はっ!!
SHE IS VERY ANGRY!!!
ZERO
I.......

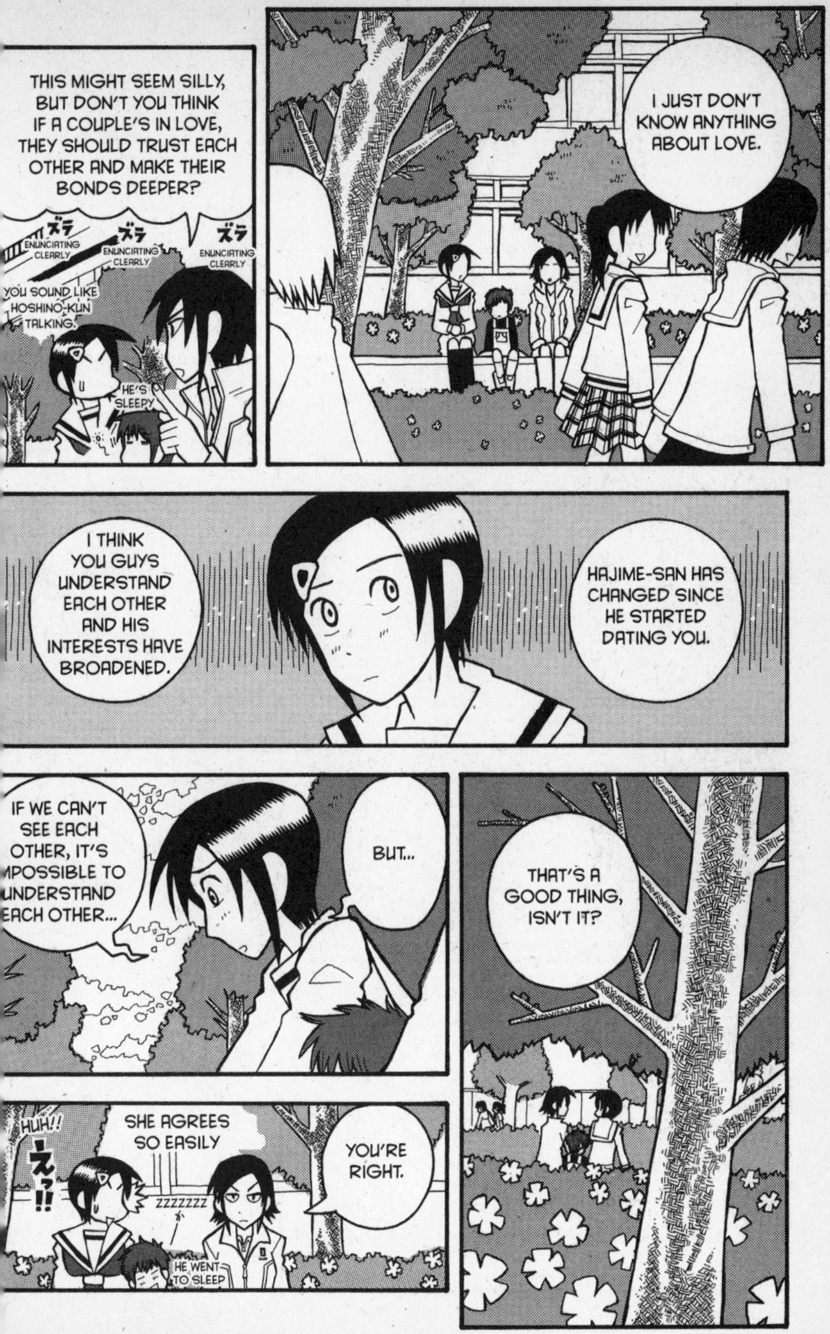
I JUST DON'T KNOW ANYTHING ABOUT LOVE.
THIS MIGHT SEEM SILLY, BUT DON'T YOU THINK IF A COUPLE'S IN LOVE, THEY SHOULD TRUST EACH OTHER AND MAKE THEIR BONDS DEEPER?
ズラ
ENUNCIATING CLEARLY
ズラ
ENUNCIATING CLEARLY
ズラ
ENUNCIATING CLEARLY
YOU SOUND LIKE HOSHINO-KUN TALKING.
HE'S SLEEPY
HAJIME-SAN HAS CHANGED SINCE HE STARTED DATING YOU.
I THINK YOU GUYS UNDERSTAND EACH OTHER AND HIS INTERESTS HAVE BROADENED.
THAT'S A GOOD THING, ISN'T IT?
BUT...
IF WE CAN'T SEE EACH OTHER, IT'S IMPOSSIBLE TO UNDERSTAND EACH OTHER...
YOU'RE RIGHT.
SHE AGREES SO EASILY
HUH!!
えっ!!
ZZZZZZZ
か
HE WENT TO SLEEP

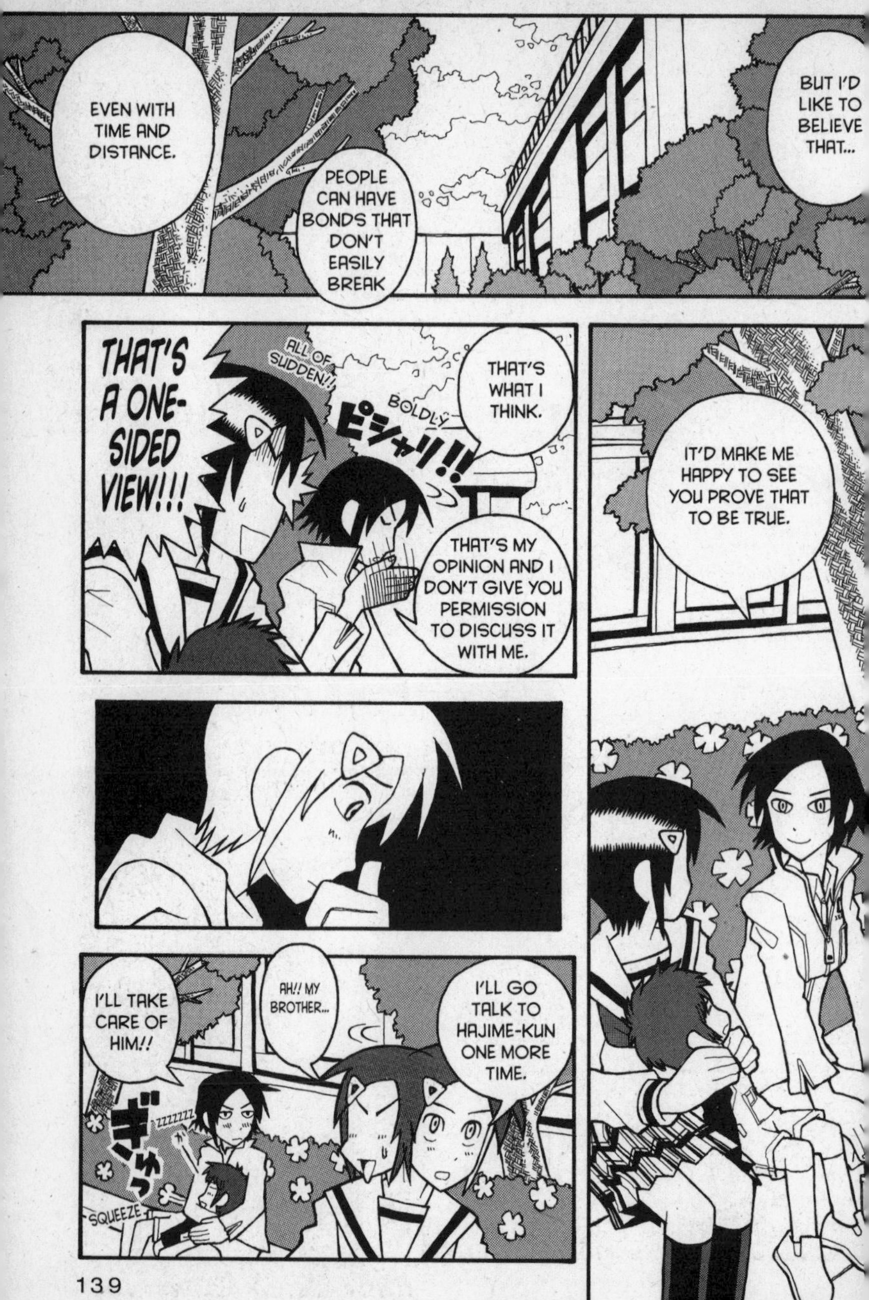
BUT I'D LIKE TO BELIEVE THAT...
PEOPLE CAN HAVE BONDS THAT DON'T EASILY BREAK
EVEN WITH TIME AND DISTANCE.
IT'D MAKE ME HAPPY TO SEE YOU PROVE THAT TO BE TRUE.
THAT'S WHAT I THINK.
BOLDLY
ピシャリ!!
ALL OF SUDDEN!!
THAT'S MY OPINION AND I DON'T GIVE YOU PERMISSION TO DISCUSS IT WITH ME.
THAT'S A ONE-SIDED VIEW!!!
I'LL GO TALK TO HAJIME-KUN ONE MORE TIME.
AH!! MY BROTHER...
I'LL TAKE CARE OF HIM!!
ZZZZZZZ
ぎゅっ
SQUEEZE

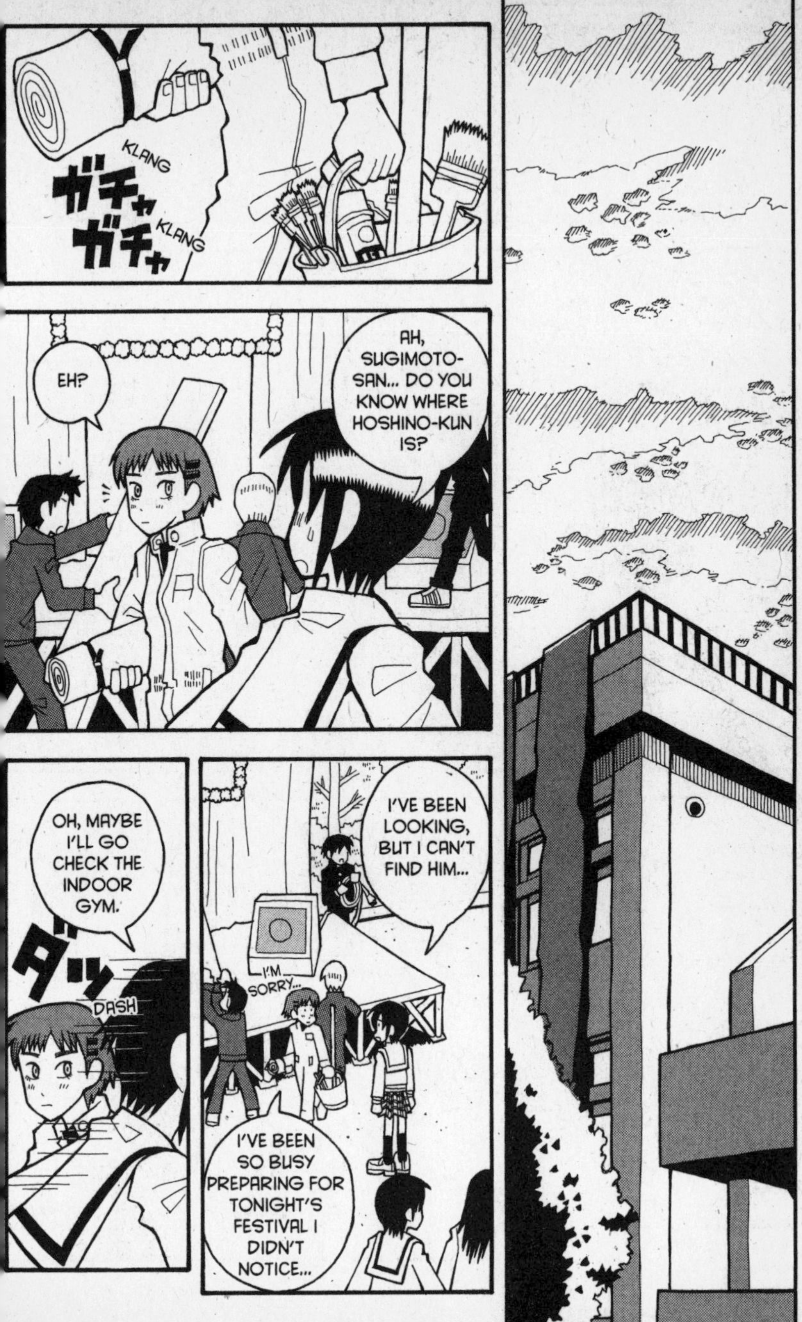
ガチャ
KLANG
ガチャ
KLANG
AH, SUGIMOTO-SAN... DO YOU KNOW WHERE HOSHINO-KUN IS?
EH?
I'VE BEEN LOOKING, BUT I CAN'T FIND HIM...
I'M SORRY...
I'VE BEEN SO BUSY PREPARING FOR TONIGHT'S FESTIVAL I DIDN'T NOTICE...
OH, MAYBE I'LL GO CHECK THE INDOOR GYM.
ダッ
DASH

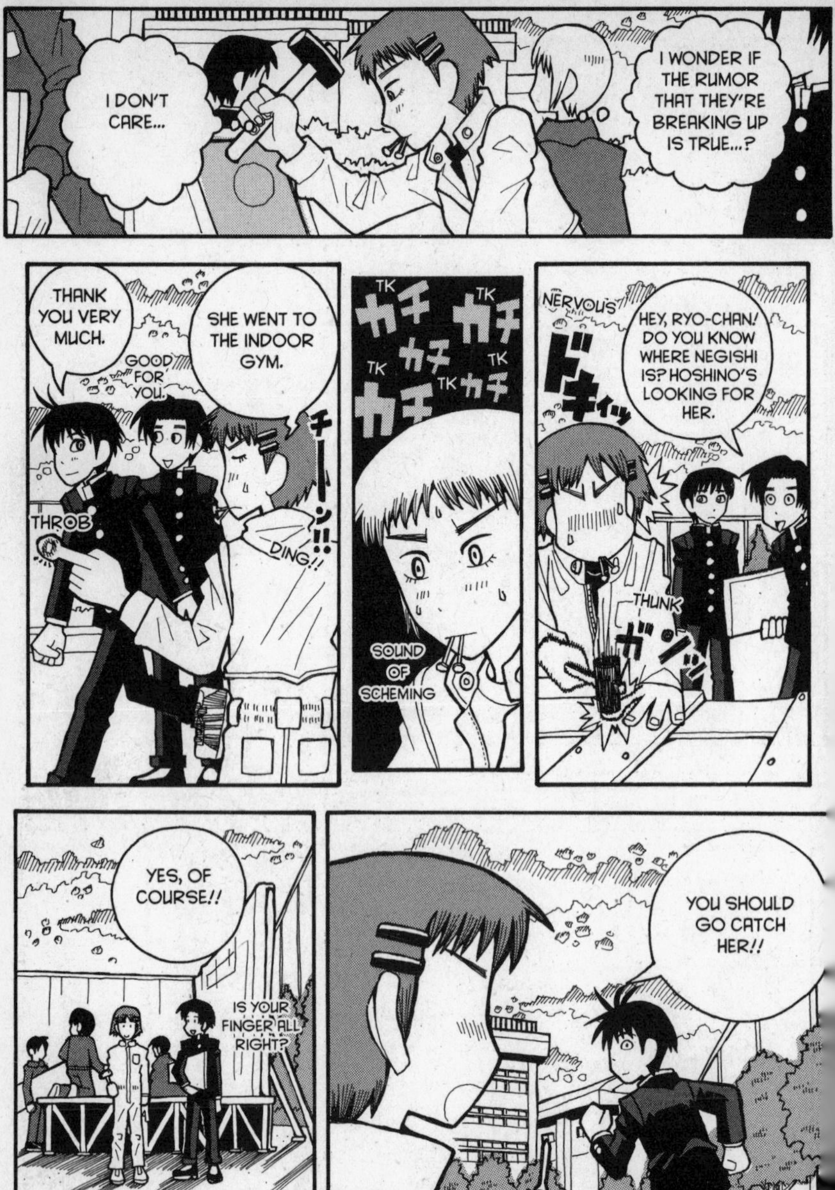
I WONDER IF THE RUMOR THAT THEY'RE BREAKING UP IS TRUE...?
I DON'T CARE...
NERVOUS
HEY, RYO-CHAN! DO YOU KNOW WHERE NEGISHI IS? HOSHINO'S LOOKING FOR HER.
THUNK
TK TK TK TK TK
SOUND OF SCHEMING
SHE WENT TO THE INDOOR GYM.
THANK YOU VERY MUCH.
GOOD FOR YOU.
THROB
DING!!
YOU SHOULD GO CATCH HER!!
YES, OF COURSE!!
IS YOUR FINGER ALL RIGHT?

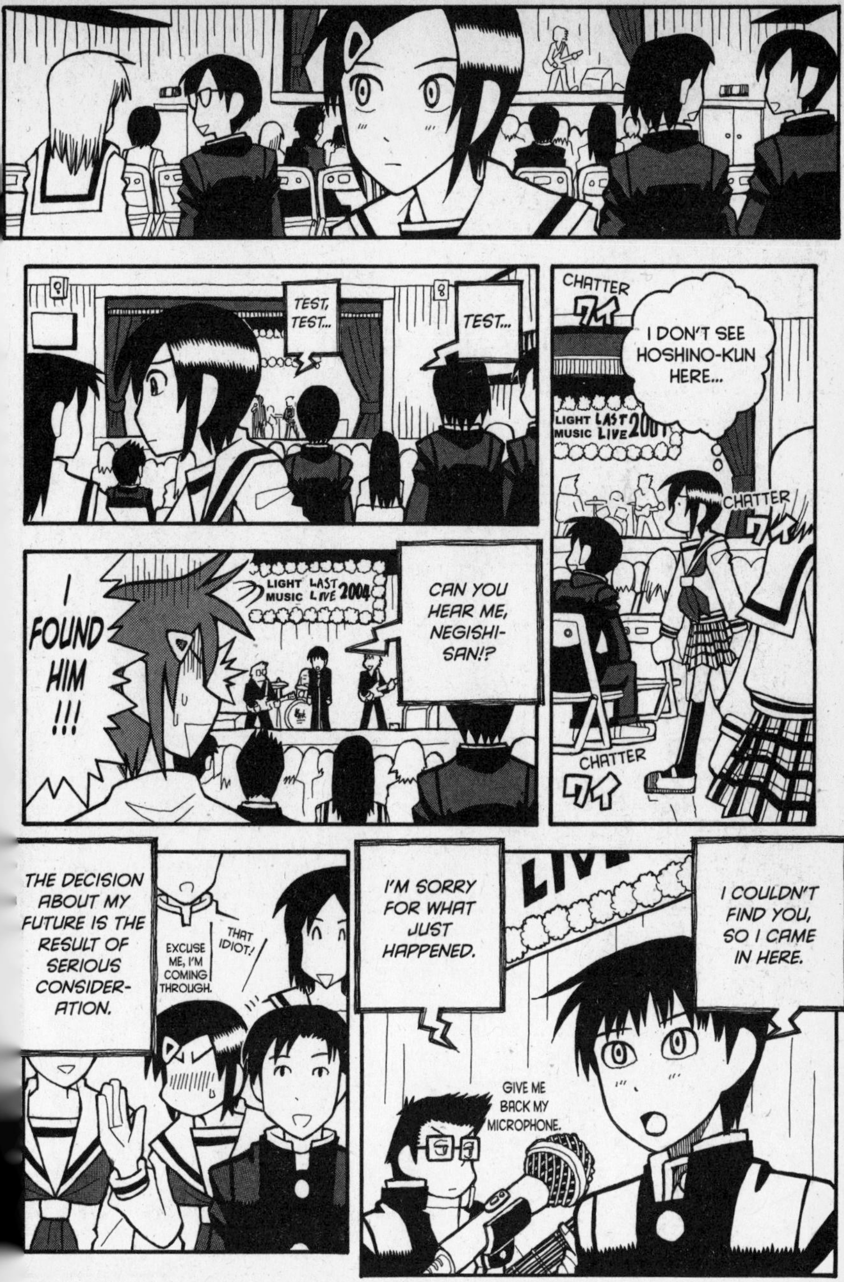
CHATTER
ワイ
I DON'T SEE HOSHINO-KUN HERE...
LIGHT MUSIC LAST LIVE
CHATTER
ワイ
CHATTER
ワイ
TEST...
TEST, TEST...
CAN YOU HEAR ME, NEGISHI-SAN!?
LIGHT MUSIC LAST LIVE 2004
I FOUND HIM!!!
I COULDN'T FIND YOU, SO I CAME IN HERE.
LIVE
GIVE ME BACK MY MICROPHONE.
I'M SORRY FOR WHAT JUST HAPPENED.
THE DECISION ABOUT MY FUTURE IS THE RESULT OF SERIOUS CONSIDERATION.
THAT IDIOT!
EXCUSE ME, I'M COMING THROUGH.

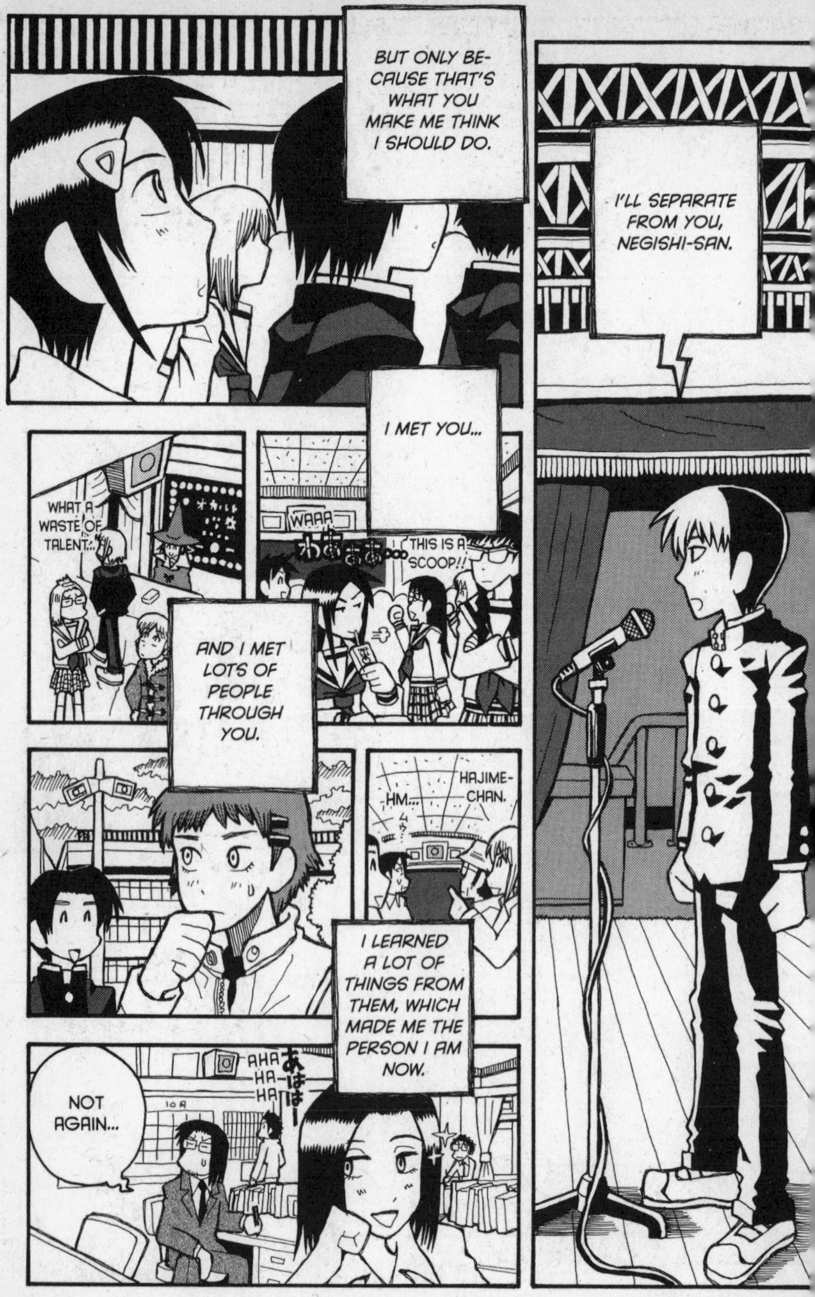
I'LL SEPARATE FROM YOU, NEGISHI-SAN.
BUT ONLY BE-CAUSE THAT'S WHAT YOU MAKE ME THINK I SHOULD DO.
I MET YOU...
WAAA
THIS IS A SCOOP!!
WHAT A WASTE OF TALENT...
AND I MET LOTS OF PEOPLE THROUGH YOU.
HAJIME-CHAN.
HM...
I LEARNED A LOT OF THINGS FROM THEM, WHICH MADE ME THE PERSON I AM NOW.
AHA HA HA
NOT AGAIN...

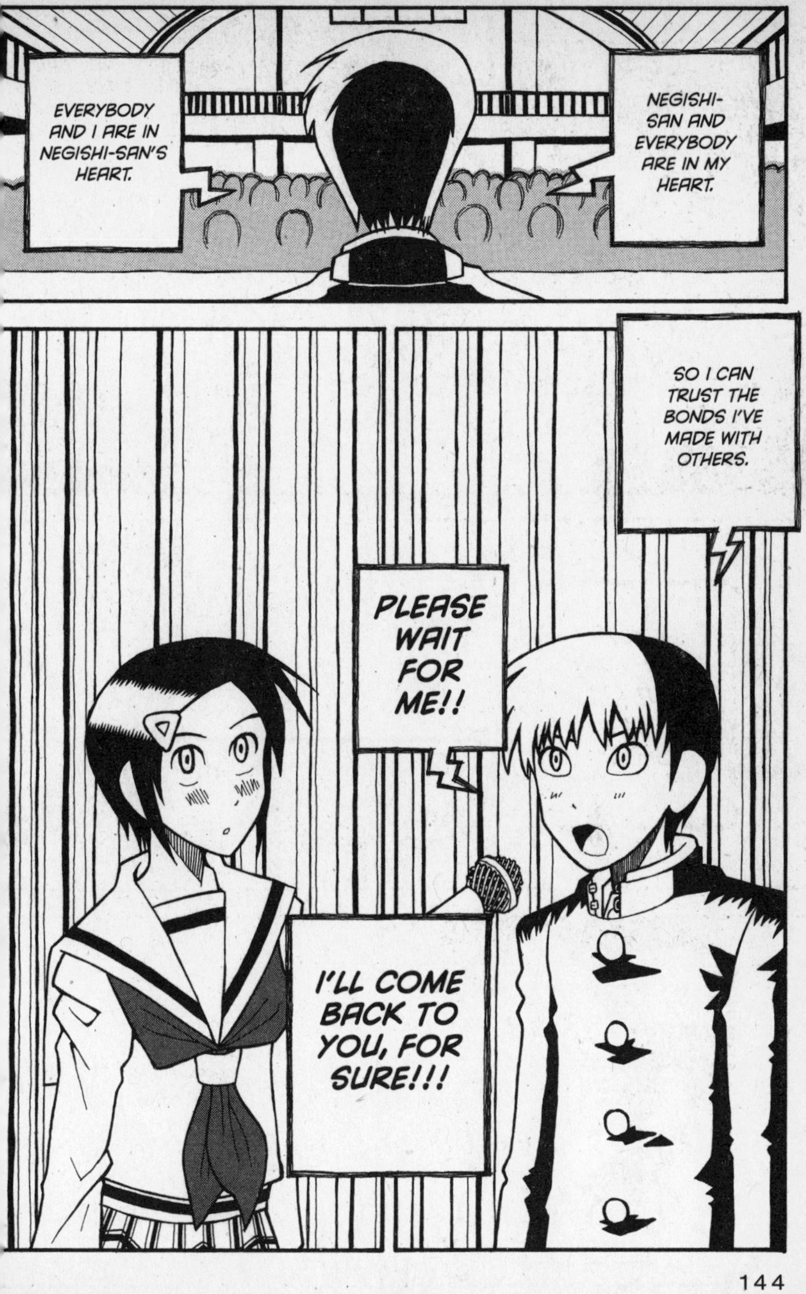
NEGISHI-SAN AND EVERYBODY ARE IN MY HEART.
EVERYBODY AND I ARE IN NEGISHI-SAN'S HEART.
SO I CAN TRUST THE BONDS I'VE MADE WITH OTHERS.
PLEASE WAIT FOR ME!!
I'LL COME BACK TO YOU, FOR SURE!!!

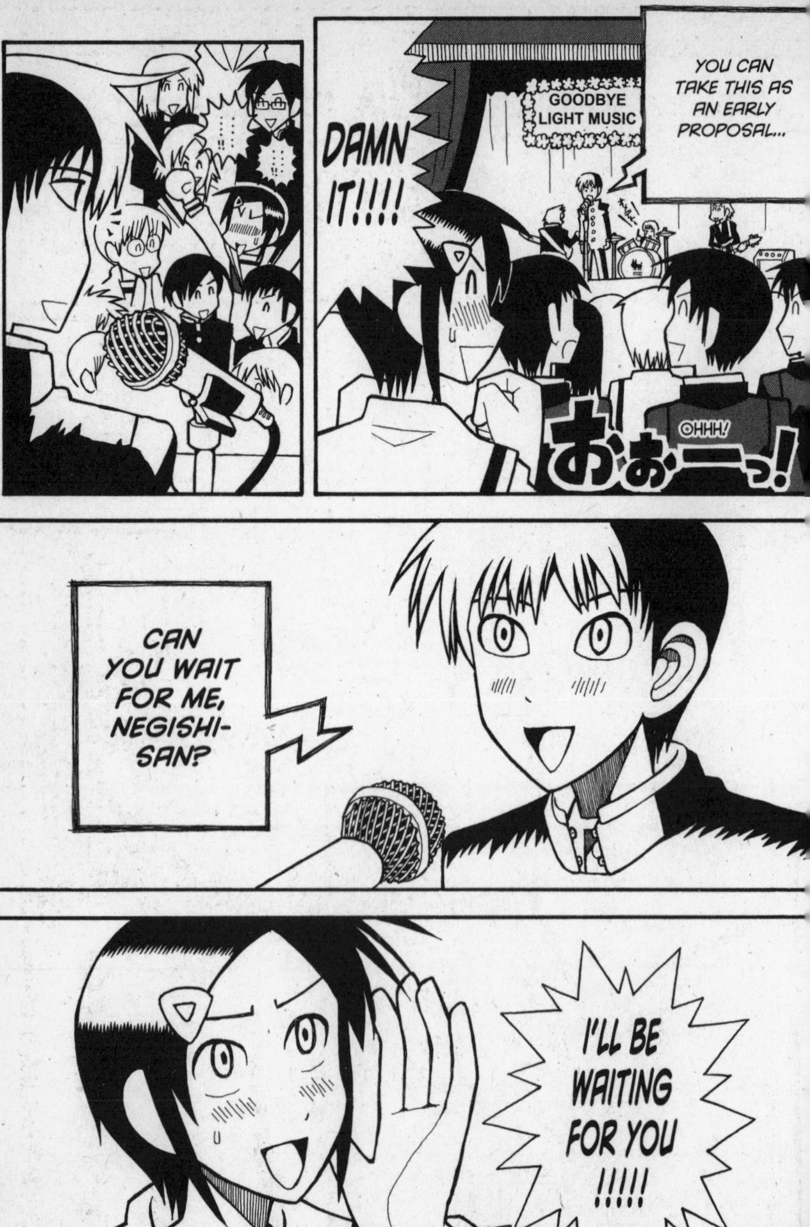
GOODBYE LIGHT MUSIC
YOU CAN TAKE THIS AS AN EARLY PROPOSAL...
DAMN IT!!!!!
おぉーっ!
OHHH!
CAN YOU WAIT FOR ME, NEGISHI-SAN?
I'LL BE WAITING FOR YOU !!!!!

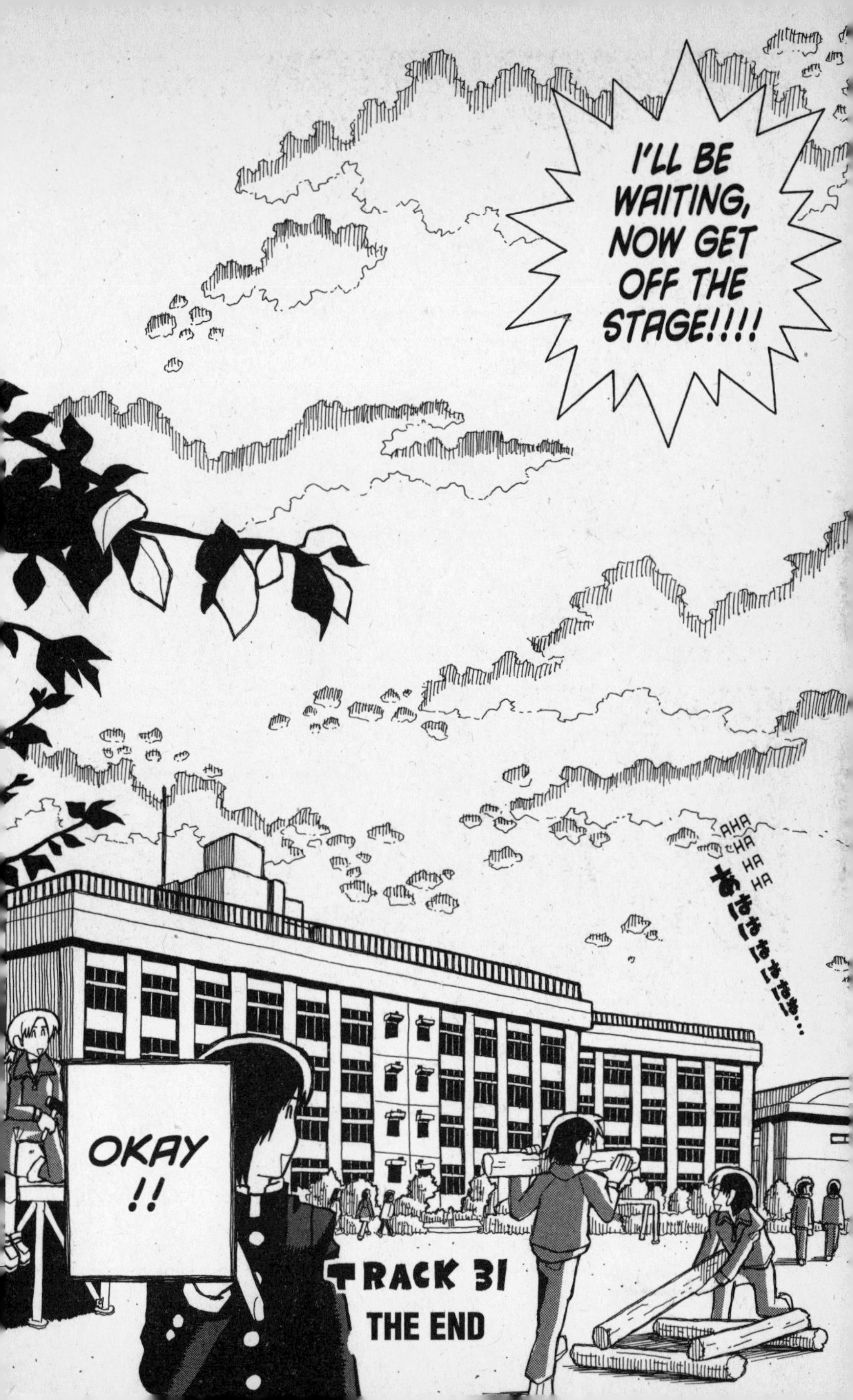
I'LL BE WAITING, NOW GET OFF THE STAGE!!!!
AHA HA HA HA
あははははは…
OKAY !!
TRACK 31
THE END

BONUS TRACK

おまけ

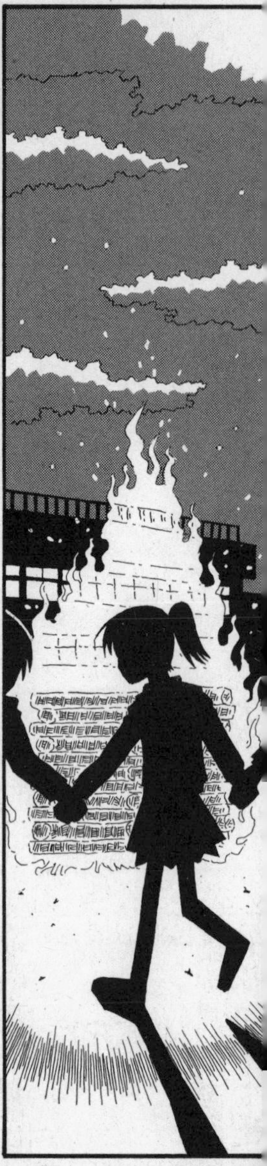

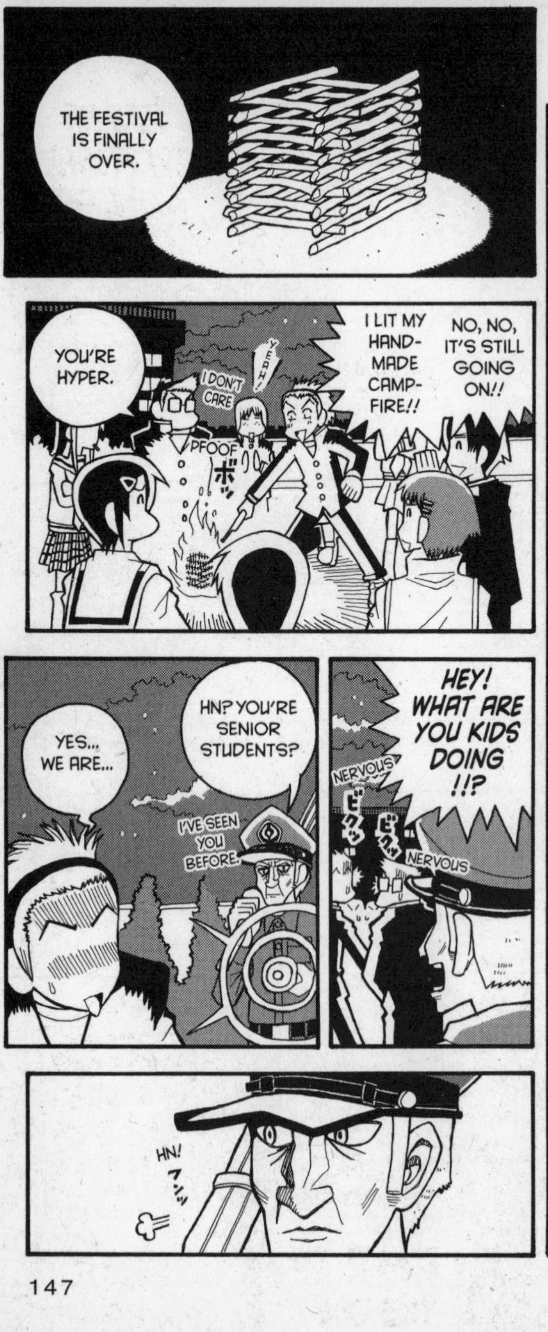
THE FESTIVAL IS FINALLY OVER.
NO, NO, IT'S STILL GOING ON!!
I LIT MY HAND-MADE CAMP-FIRE!!
YEAH!
I DON'T CARE
PFOOF
ボッ
YOU'RE HYPER.
HEY! WHAT ARE YOU KIDS DOING!!?
NERVOUS
ビクッ
ビクッ
NERVOUS
HN? YOU'RE SENIOR STUDENTS?
I'VE SEEN YOU BEFORE.
YES... WE ARE...
HN!
フンッ

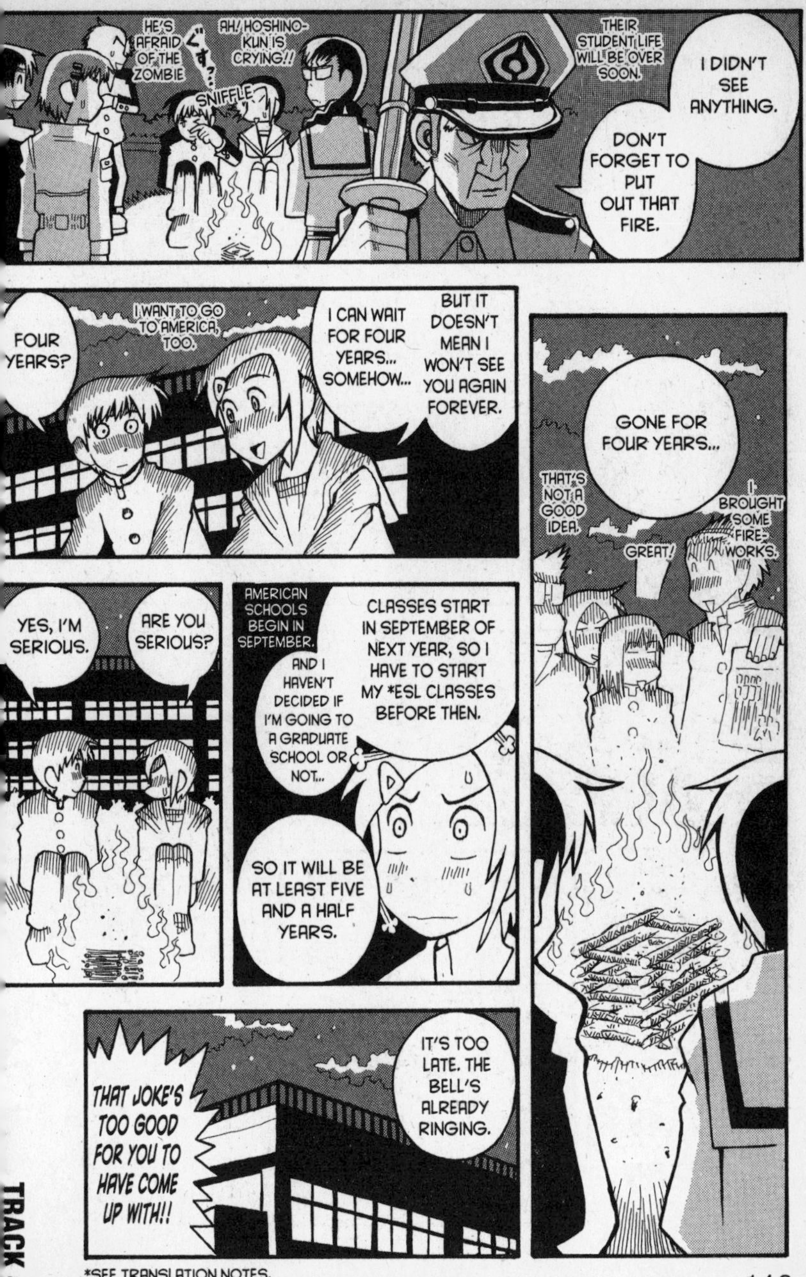
I DIDN'T SEE ANYTHING.
DON'T FORGET TO PUT OUT THAT FIRE.
THEIR STUDENT LIFE WILL BE OVER SOON.
AH! HOSHINO-KUN IS CRYING!!
ぐすっ
SNIFFLE
HE'S AFRAID OF THE ZOMBIE
GONE FOR FOUR YEARS...
I BROUGHT SOME FIRE-WORKS.
GREAT!
THAT'S NOT A GOOD IDEA.
BUT IT DOESN'T MEAN I WON'T SEE YOU AGAIN FOREVER.
I CAN WAIT FOR FOUR YEARS... SOMEHOW...
I WANT TO GO TO AMERICA, TOO.
FOUR YEARS?
CLASSES START IN SEPTEMBER OF NEXT YEAR, SO I HAVE TO START MY *ESL CLASSES BEFORE THEN.
AMERICAN SCHOOLS BEGIN IN SEPTEMBER.
AND I HAVEN'T DECIDED IF I'M GOING TO A GRADUATE SCHOOL OR NOT...
SO IT WILL BE AT LEAST FIVE AND A HALF YEARS.
ARE YOU SERIOUS?
YES, I'M SERIOUS.
IT'S TOO LATE. THE BELL'S ALREADY RINGING.
THAT JOKE'S TOO GOOD FOR YOU TO HAVE COME UP WITH!!

*SEE TRANSLATION NOTES.

TRACK #31 ▶▶ END

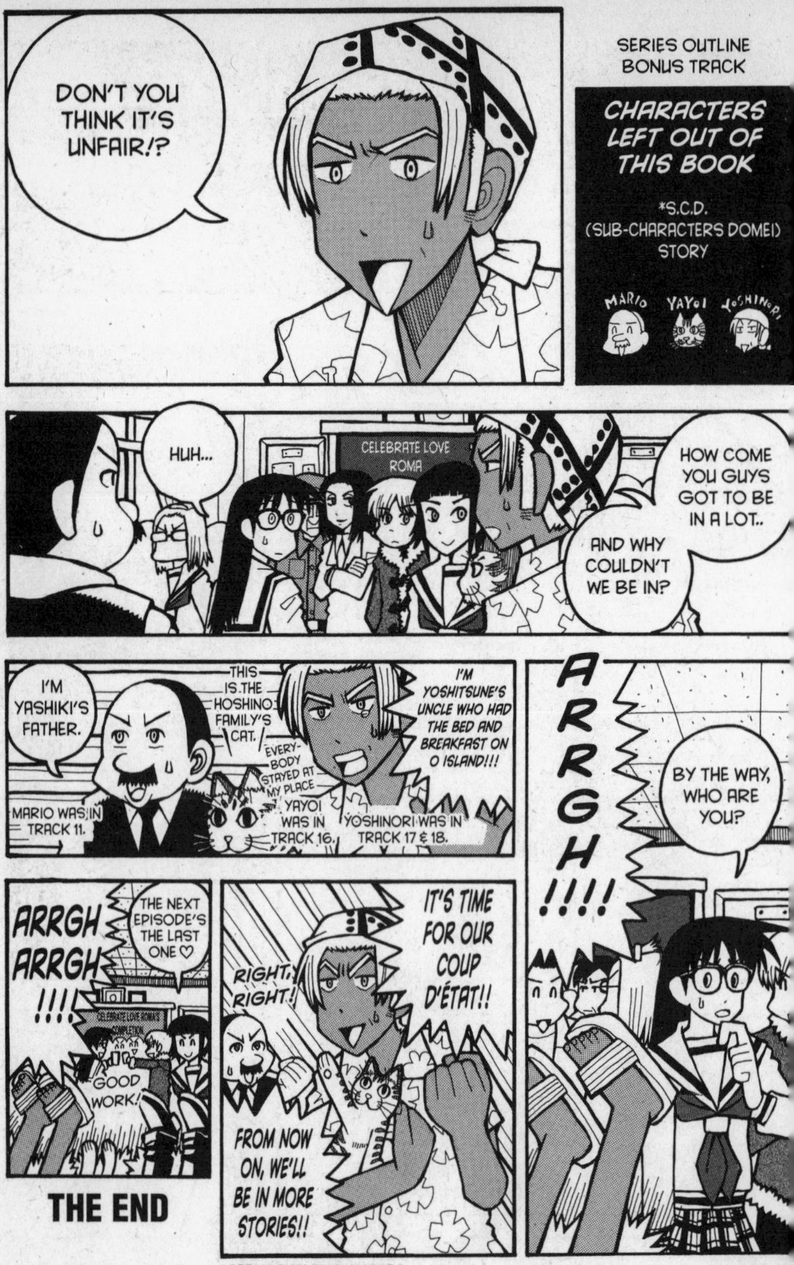
SERIES OUTLINE BONUS TRACK
CHARACTERS LEFT OUT OF THIS BOOK
*S.C.D. (SUB-CHARACTERS DOMEI) STORY
MARIO
YAYOI
YOSHINORI
DON'T YOU THINK IT'S UNFAIR!?
HOW COME YOU GUYS GOT TO BE IN A LOT..
AND WHY COULDN'T WE BE IN?
CELEBRATE LOVE ROMA
HUH...
ARRGH!!!!
BY THE WAY, WHO ARE YOU?
I'M YOSHITSUNE'S UNCLE WHO HAD THE BED AND BREAKFAST ON O ISLAND!!!
THIS IS THE HOSHINO FAMILY'S CAT.
EVERYBODY STAYED AT MY PLACE
I'M YASHIKI'S FATHER.
YOSHINORI WAS IN TRACK 17 & 18.
YAYOI WAS IN TRACK 16.
MARIO WAS IN TRACK 11.
IT'S TIME FOR OUR COUP D'ÉTAT!!
RIGHT, RIGHT!
FROM NOW ON, WE'LL BE IN MORE STORIES!!
THE NEXT EPISODE'S THE LAST ONE ♡
ARRGH ARRGH !!!!
CELEBRATE LOVE ROMA'S COMPLETION
GOOD WORK!

THE END

*SEE TRANSLATION NOTES.

LINER NOTES 2

THESE WERE AN EXTRA ILLUSTRATION SERIES FROM AFTERNOON MAGAZINE. AND THEN THERE'S A MANGA REPORT ABOUT MY TRIP TO TAIWAN. IT WAS REALLY HOT THERE.

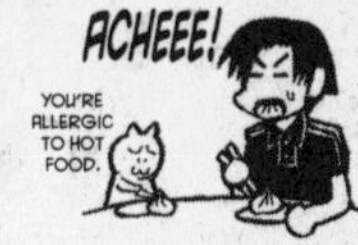
ACHEEE!
YOU'RE ALLERGIC TO HOT FOOD.

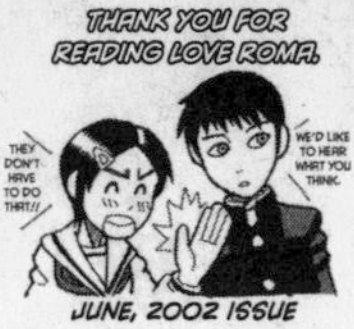
THANK YOU FOR READING LOVE ROMA.
WE'D LIKE TO HEAR WHAT YOU THINK.
THEY DON'T HAVE TO DO THAT!!

JUNE, 2002 ISSUE

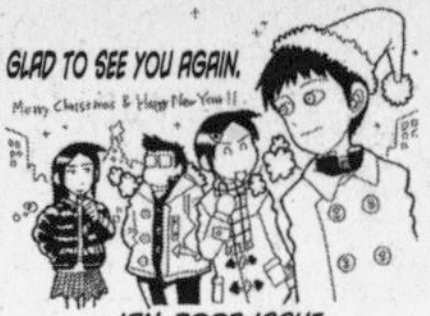
GLAD TO SEE YOU AGAIN.
Merry Christmas & Happy New Year!!

JAN. 2003 ISSUE

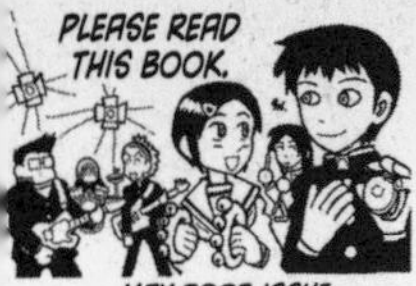
PLEASE READ THIS BOOK.

MAY 2003 ISSUE

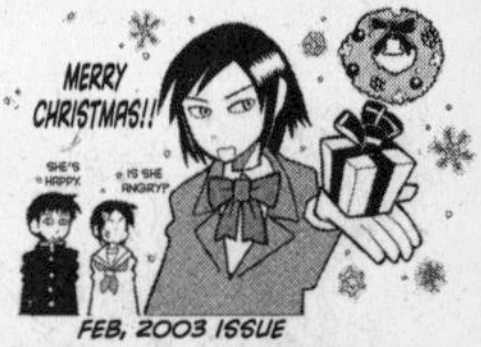
MERRY CHRISTMAS!!
IS SHE ANGRY?
SHE'S HAPPY.

FEB, 2003 ISSUE

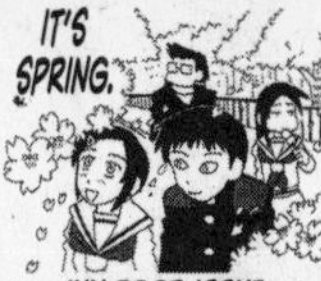
IT'S SPRING.

JUN 2003 ISSUE

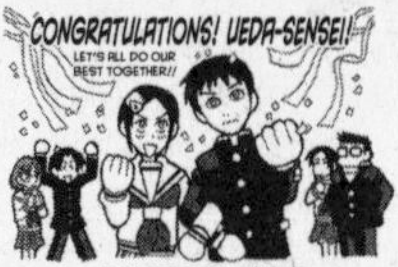
CONGRATULATIONS! UEDA-SENSEI!
LET'S ALL DO OUR BEST TOGETHER!!

JULY 2003 ISSUE

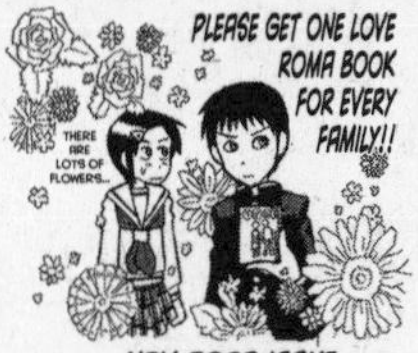
PLEASE GET ONE LOVE ROMA BOOK FOR EVERY FAMILY!!
THERE ARE LOTS OF FLOWERS...

NOV. 2003 ISSUE

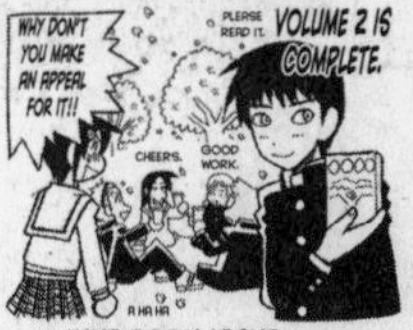
PLEASE READ IT.
VOLUME 2 IS COMPLETE.
WHY DON'T YOU MAKE AN APPEAL FOR IT!!
GOOD WORK.
CHEERS.
A HA HA

JUNE 2004 ISSUE

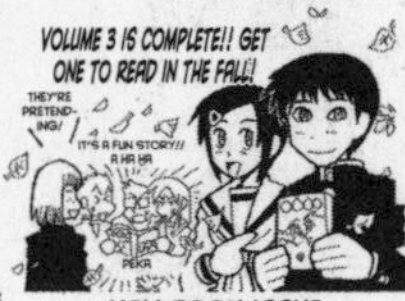
VOLUME 3 IS COMPLETE!! GET ONE TO READ IN THE FALL!
THEY'RE PRETENDING!
IT'S A FUN STORY!! A HA HA
PEKA

NOV. 2004 ISSUE

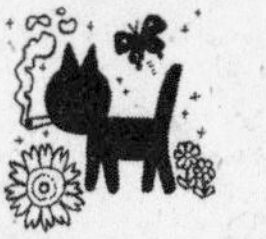

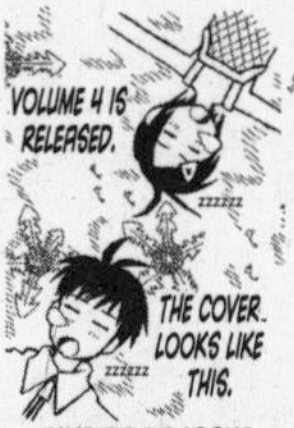
VOLUME 4 IS RELEASED.
ZZZZZZ
THE COVER LOOKS LIKE THIS.
ZZZZZZ

JUNE 2005 ISSUE

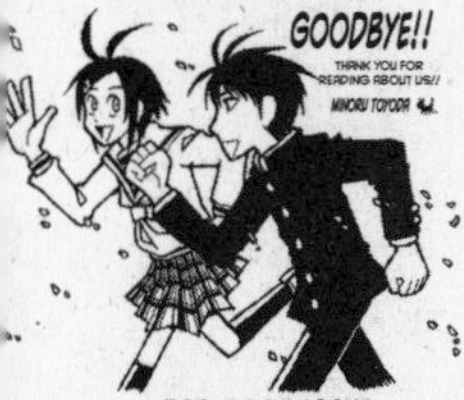
GOODBYE!!
THANK YOU FOR READING ABOUT US!!
MINORU TOYODA

DEC. 2005 ISSUE

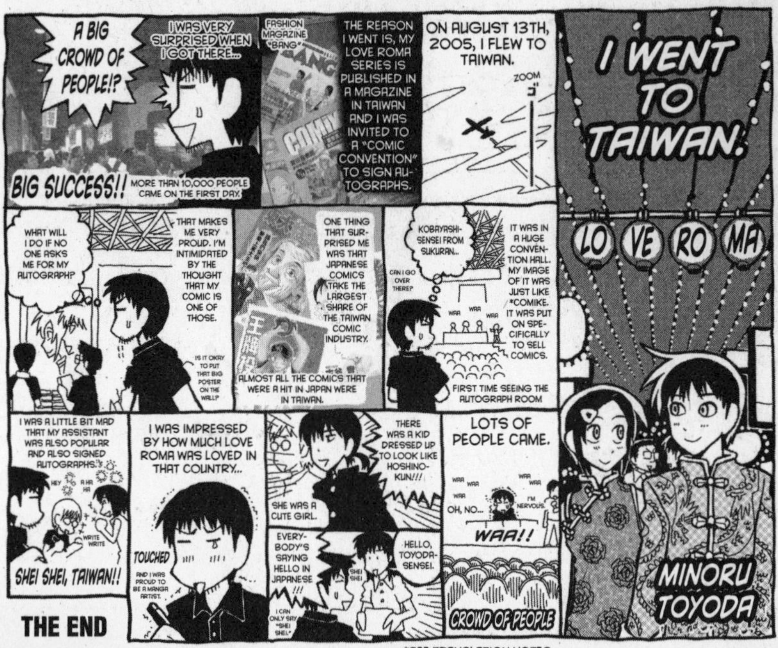
I WENT TO TAIWAN.
LO VE RO MA
MINORU TOYODA
ON AUGUST 13TH, 2005, I FLEW TO TAIWAN.
ZOOM
THE REASON I WENT IS, MY LOVE ROMA SERIES IS PUBLISHED IN A MAGAZINE IN TAIWAN AND I WAS INVITED TO A "COMIC CONVENTION" TO SIGN AUTOGRAPHS.
FASHION MAGAZINE "BANG"
A BIG CROWD OF PEOPLE!?
I WAS VERY SURPRISED WHEN I GOT THERE...
BIG SUCCESS!!
MORE THAN 10,000 PEOPLE CAME ON THE FIRST DAY.
IT WAS IN A HUGE CONVENTION HALL. MY IMAGE OF IT WAS JUST LIKE *COMIKE. IT WAS PUT ON SPECIFICALLY TO SELL COMICS.
KOBAYASHI-SENSEI FROM SUKURAN...
CAN I GO OVER THERE?
WAA
WAA
WAA
FIRST TIME SEEING THE AUTOGRAPH ROOM
ONE THING THAT SURPRISED ME WAS THAT JAPANESE COMICS TAKE THE LARGEST SHARE OF THE TAIWAN COMIC INDUSTRY.
ALMOST ALL THE COMICS THAT WERE A HIT IN JAPAN WERE IN TAIWAN.
THAT MAKES ME VERY PROUD. I'M INTIMIDATED BY THE THOUGHT THAT MY COMIC IS ONE OF THOSE.
WHAT WILL I DO IF NO ONE ASKS ME FOR MY AUTOGRAPH?
IS IT OKAY TO PUT THAT BIG POSTER ON THE WALL?
LOTS OF PEOPLE CAME.
WAA WAA
WAA WAA
WAA
I'M NERVOUS.
OH, NO...
WAA!!
CROWD OF PEOPLE
THERE WAS A KID DRESSED UP TO LOOK LIKE HOSHINO-KUN!!!
SHE WAS A CUTE GIRL.
EVERYBODY'S SAYING HELLO IN JAPANESE!!!
HELLO, TOYODA-SENSEI.
SHEI SHEI
I CAN ONLY SAY "SHEI SHEI."
I WAS IMPRESSED BY HOW MUCH LOVE ROMA WAS LOVED IN THAT COUNTRY...
TOUCHED
AND I WAS PROUD TO BE A MANGA ARTIST.
I WAS A LITTLE BIT MAD THAT MY ASSISTANT WAS ALSO POPULAR AND ALSO SIGNED AUTOGRAPHS.
HEY
A HA HA
WRITE WRITE
SHEI SHEI, TAIWAN!!
THE END

*SEE TRANSLATION NOTES.

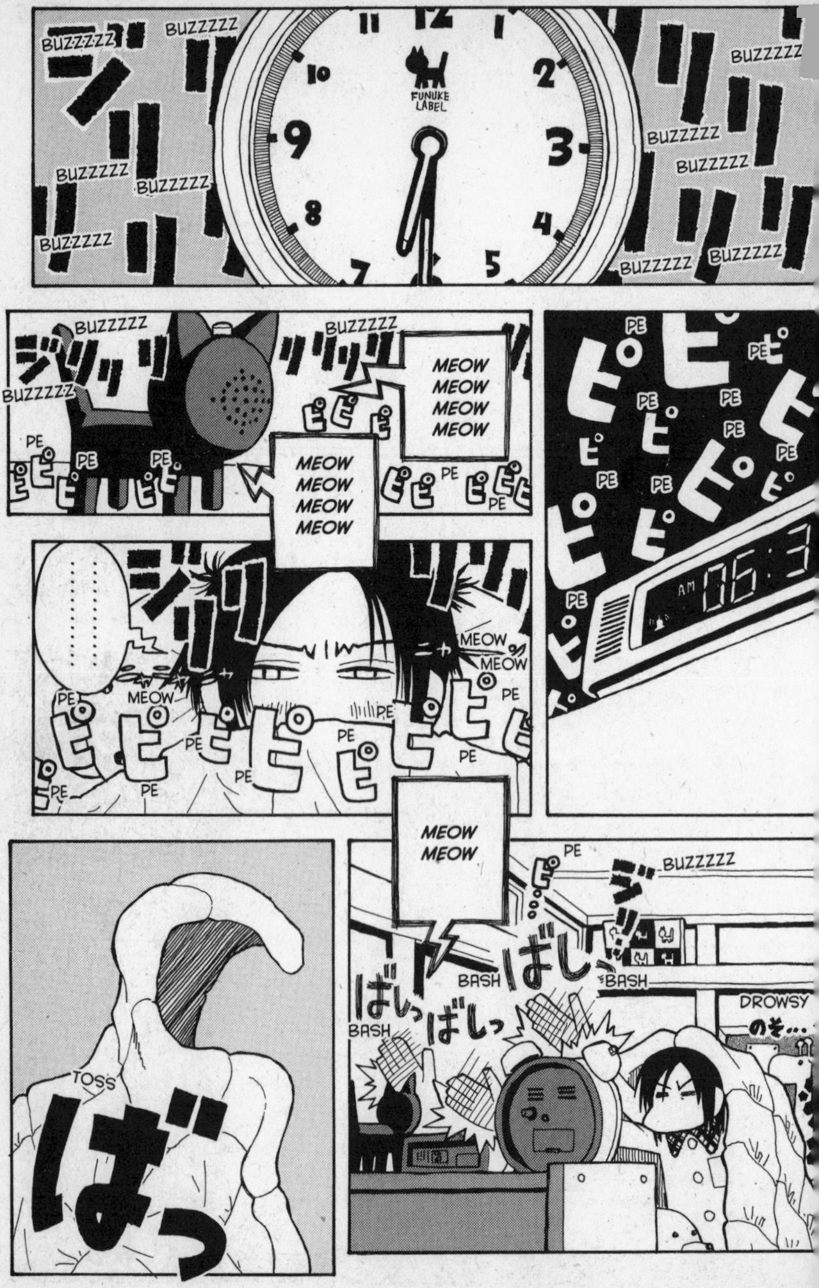
BUZZZZZ
BUZZZZZ
BUZZZZZ
BUZZZZZ
BUZZZZZ
FUNUKE LABEL
BUZZZZZ
BUZZZZZ
BUZZZZZ
BUZZZZZ
ジリリリ
PE
PE
PE
PE
PE
PE
PE
PE
PE
ピピピピ
AM 06:3
BUZZZZZ
BUZZZZZ
BUZZZZZ
ジリリリ
MEOW MEOW MEOW MEOW
MEOW MEOW MEOW MEOW
PE
PE
PE
PE
PE
ピピピピ
MEOW MEOW
MEOW
PE
PE
PE
PE
PE
PE
PE
......
MEOW MEOW
ピピピピ
PE
BUZZZZZ
ジリ
ばしっ
BASH
BASH
ばしっ ばしっ
BASH
DROWSY
のそ...
TOSS
ばっ

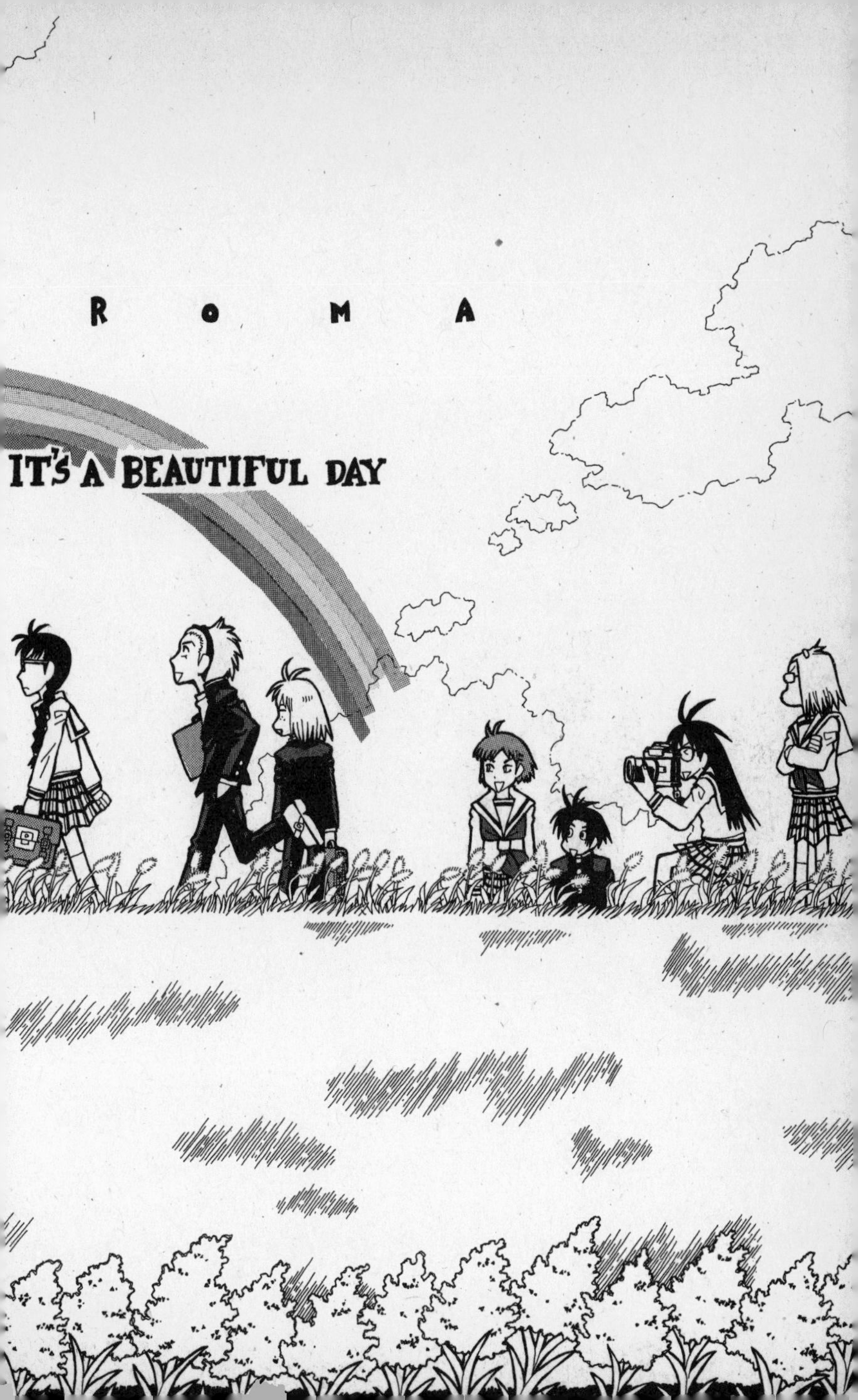
R O M A
IT'S A BEAUTIFUL DAY

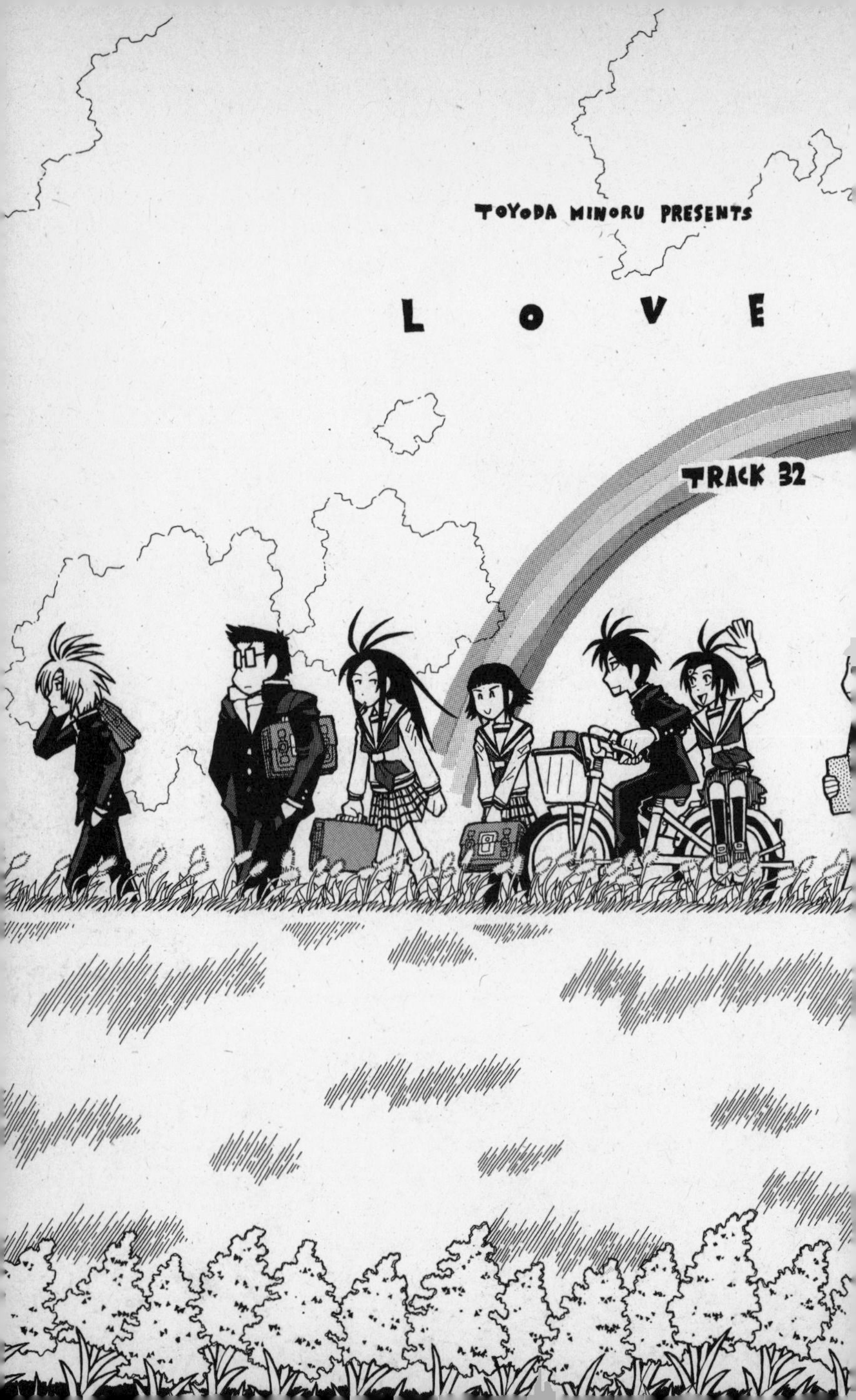
TOYODA MINORU PRESENTS
LOVE
TRACK 32

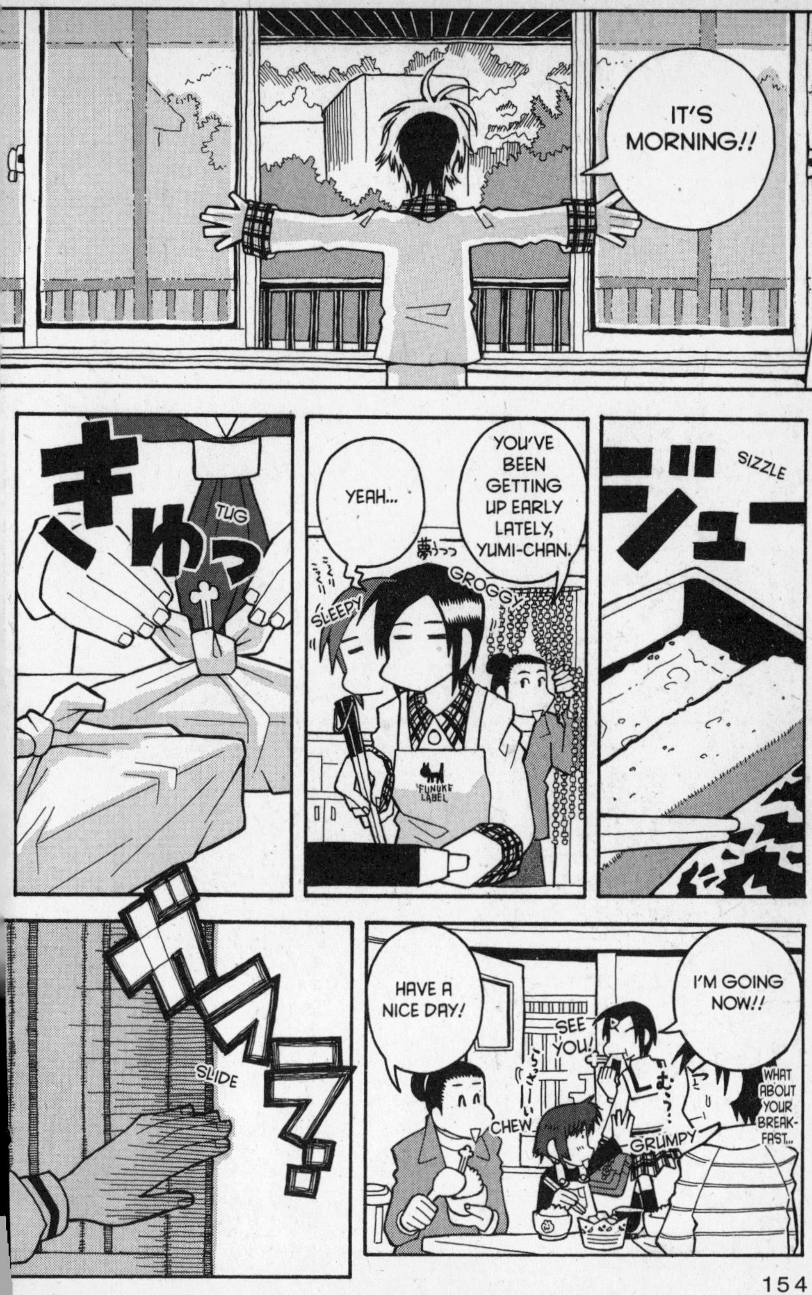
IT'S MORNING!!
ジュー
SIZZLE
YOU'VE BEEN GETTING UP EARLY LATELY, YUMI-CHAN.
YEAH...
GROGGY
SLEEPY
きゅっ
TUG
I'M GOING NOW!!
HAVE A NICE DAY!
SEE YOU!
WHAT ABOUT YOUR BREAKFAST...
GRUMPY
CHEW
SLIDE

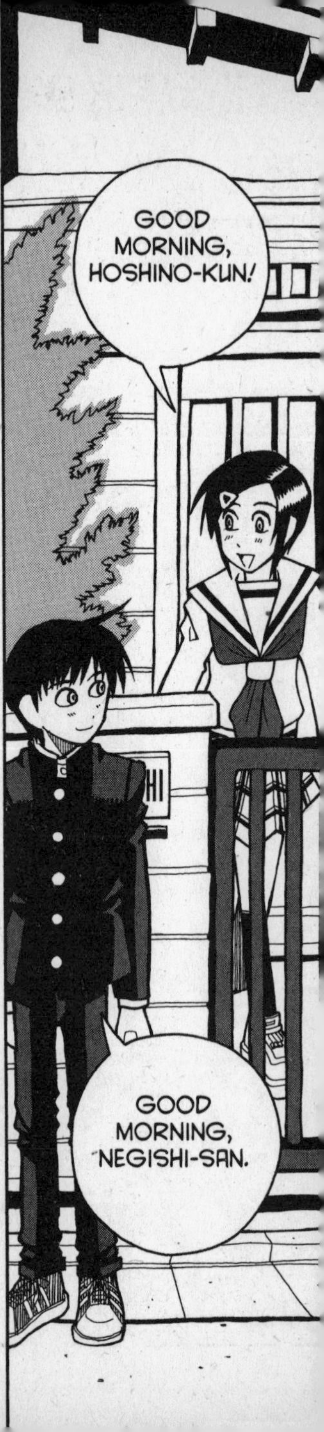
GOOD MORNING, HOSHINO-KUN!
GOOD MORNING, NEGISHI-SAN.

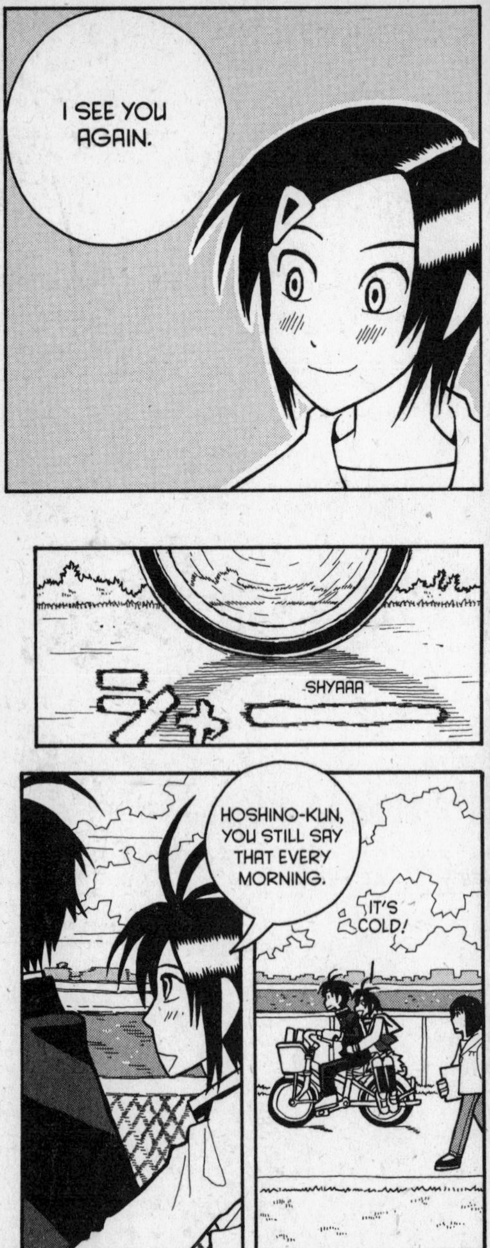
I SEE YOU AGAIN.
SHYAAA
HOSHINO-KUN, YOU STILL SAY THAT EVERY MORNING.
IT'S COLD!

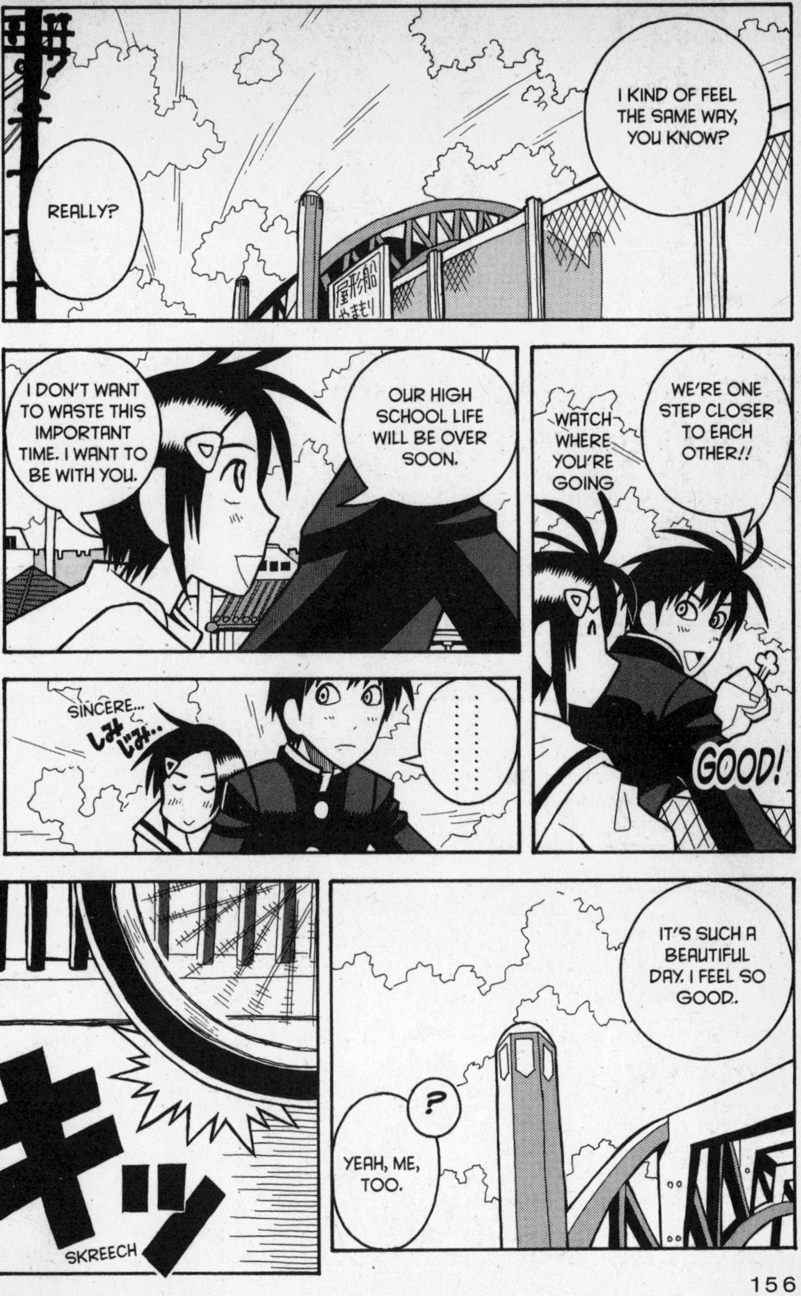
I KIND OF FEEL THE SAME WAY, YOU KNOW?
REALLY?
屋形船 やまもり
WE'RE ONE STEP CLOSER TO EACH OTHER!!
WATCH WHERE YOU'RE GOING
GOOD!
OUR HIGH SCHOOL LIFE WILL BE OVER SOON.
I DON'T WANT TO WASTE THIS IMPORTANT TIME. I WANT TO BE WITH YOU.
......
SINCERE...
しみじみ..
IT'S SUCH A BEAUTIFUL DAY. I FEEL SO GOOD.
?
YEAH, ME, TOO.
キッ
SKREECH

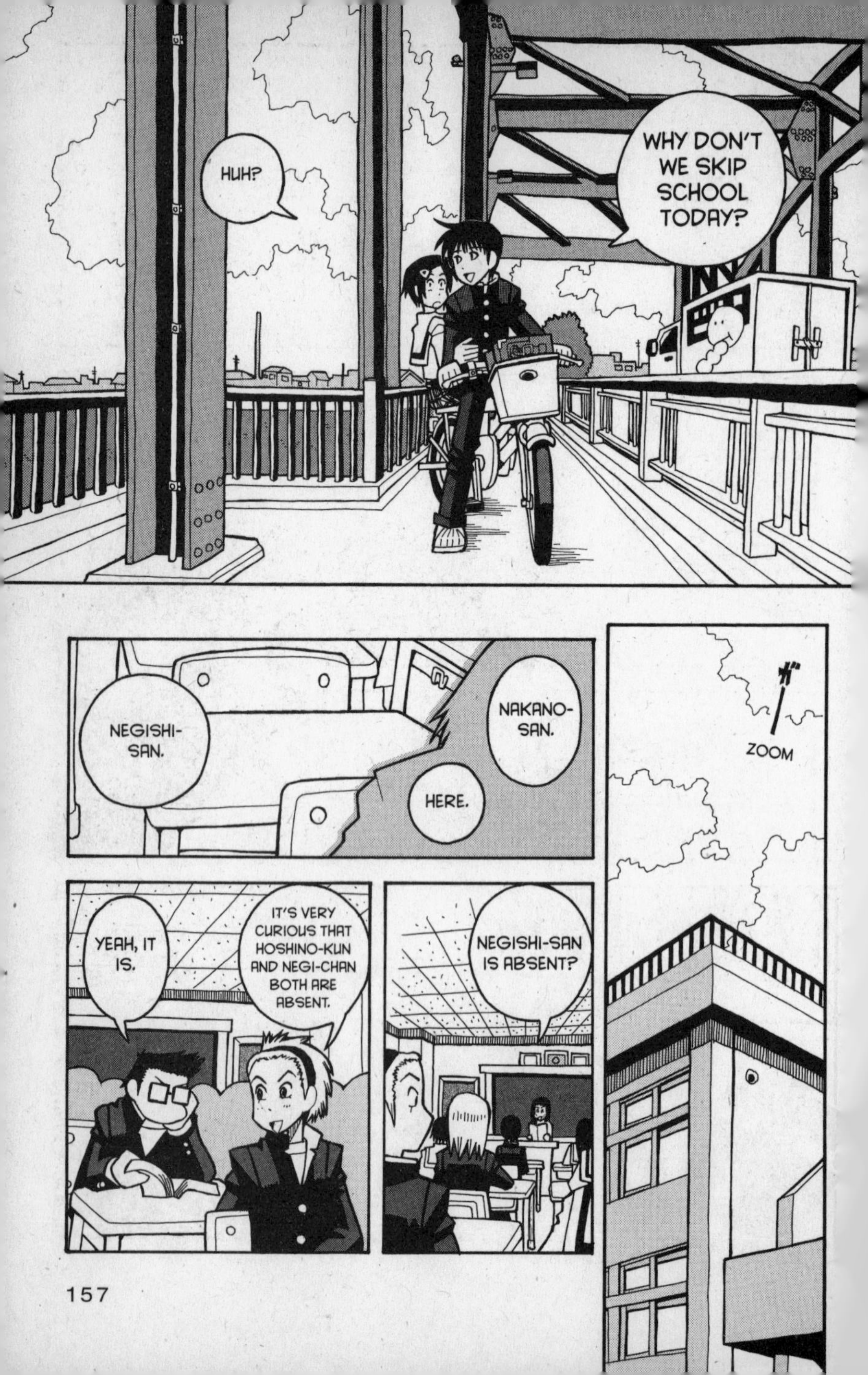
WHY DON'T WE SKIP SCHOOL TODAY?
HUH?
ガ
ZOOM
NAKANO-SAN.
HERE.
NEGISHI-SAN.
NEGISHI-SAN IS ABSENT?
IT'S VERY CURIOUS THAT HOSHINO-KUN AND NEGI-CHAN BOTH ARE ABSENT.
YEAH, IT IS.

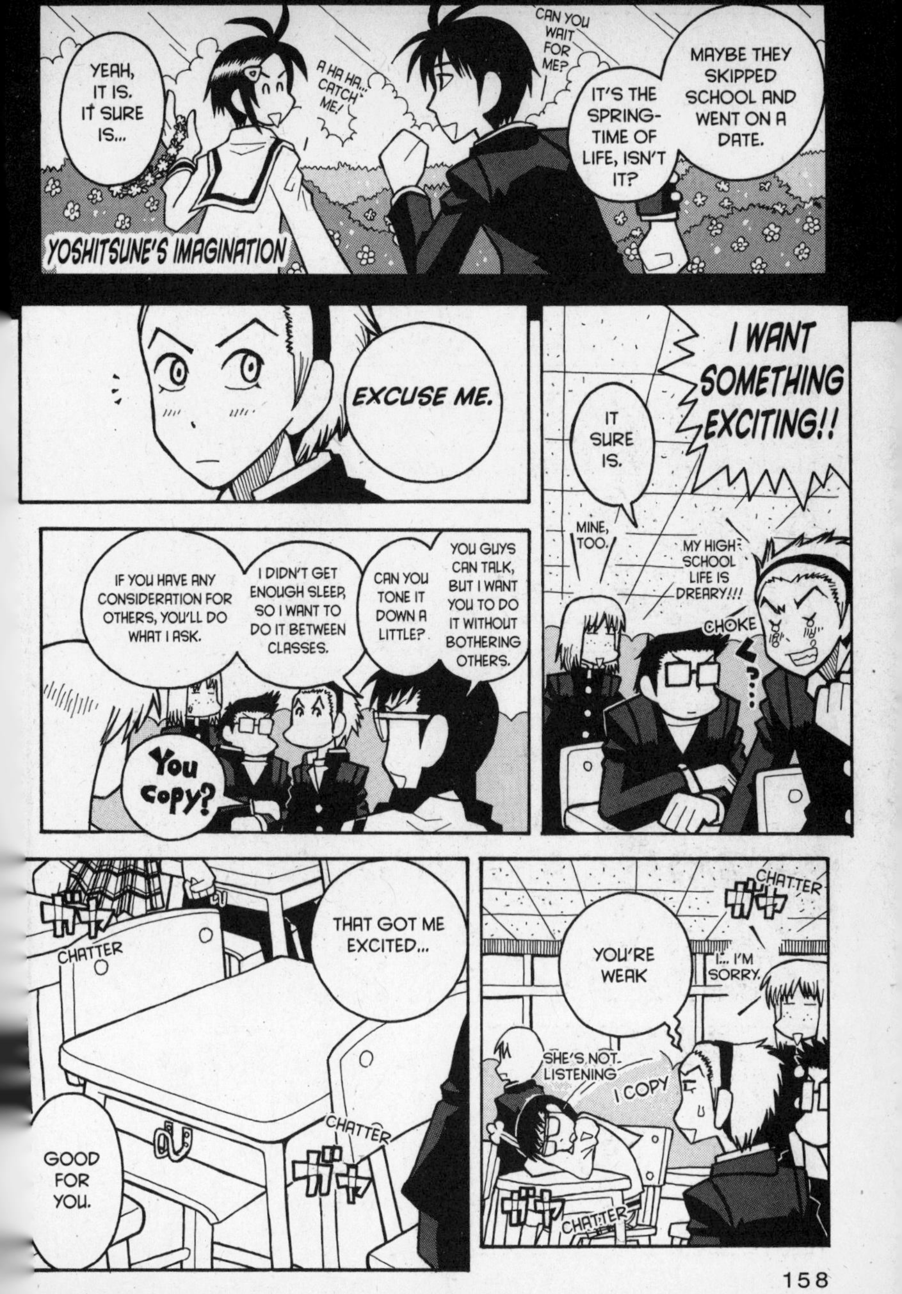
MAYBE THEY SKIPPED SCHOOL AND WENT ON A DATE.
IT'S THE SPRING-TIME OF LIFE, ISN'T IT?
CAN YOU WAIT FOR ME?
A HA HA... CATCH ME!
YEAH, IT IS. IT SURE IS...
YOSHITSUNE'S IMAGINATION
I WANT SOMETHING EXCITING!!
IT SURE IS.
MY HIGH SCHOOL LIFE IS DREARY!!!
CHOKE
MINE, TOO.
EXCUSE ME.
YOU GUYS CAN TALK, BUT I WANT YOU TO DO IT WITHOUT BOTHERING OTHERS.
CAN YOU TONE IT DOWN A LITTLE?
I DIDN'T GET ENOUGH SLEEP, SO I WANT TO DO IT BETWEEN CLASSES.
IF YOU HAVE ANY CONSIDERATION FOR OTHERS, YOU'LL DO WHAT I ASK.
You copy?
CHATTER
I... I'M SORRY.
YOU'RE WEAK
I COPY
SHE'S NOT LISTENING
CHATTER
THAT GOT ME EXCITED...
CHATTER
CHATTER
GOOD FOR YOU.

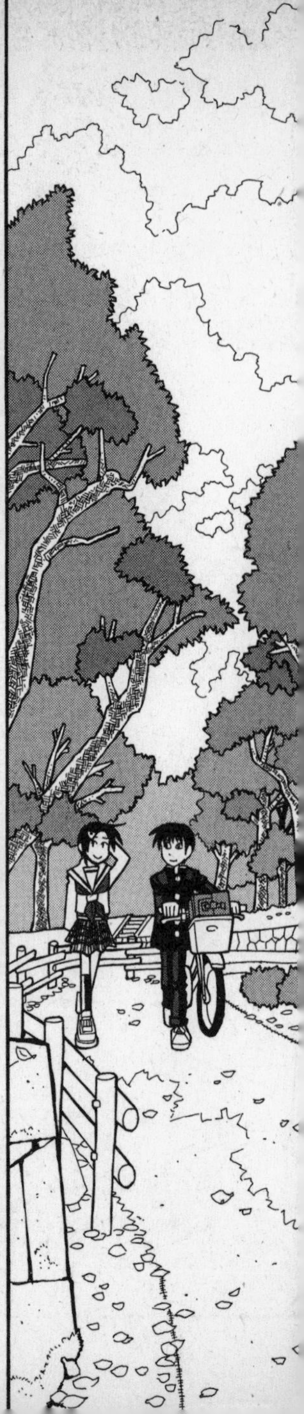

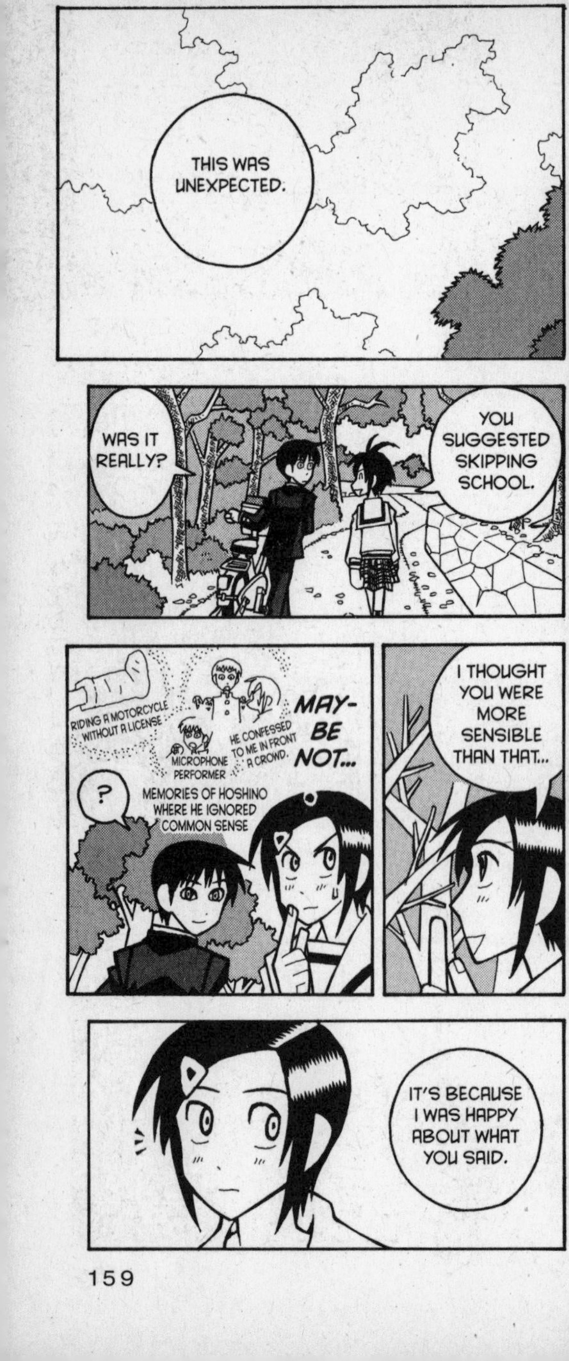

THIS WAS UNEXPECTED.
YOU SUGGESTED SKIPPING SCHOOL.
WAS IT REALLY?
I THOUGHT YOU WERE MORE SENSIBLE THAN THAT...
MAY-BE NOT...
RIDING A MOTORCYCLE WITHOUT A LICENSE
HE CONFESSED TO ME IN FRONT A CROWD.
MICROPHONE PERFORMER
MEMORIES OF HOSHINO WHERE HE IGNORED COMMON SENSE
?
IT'S BECAUSE I WAS HAPPY ABOUT WHAT YOU SAID.

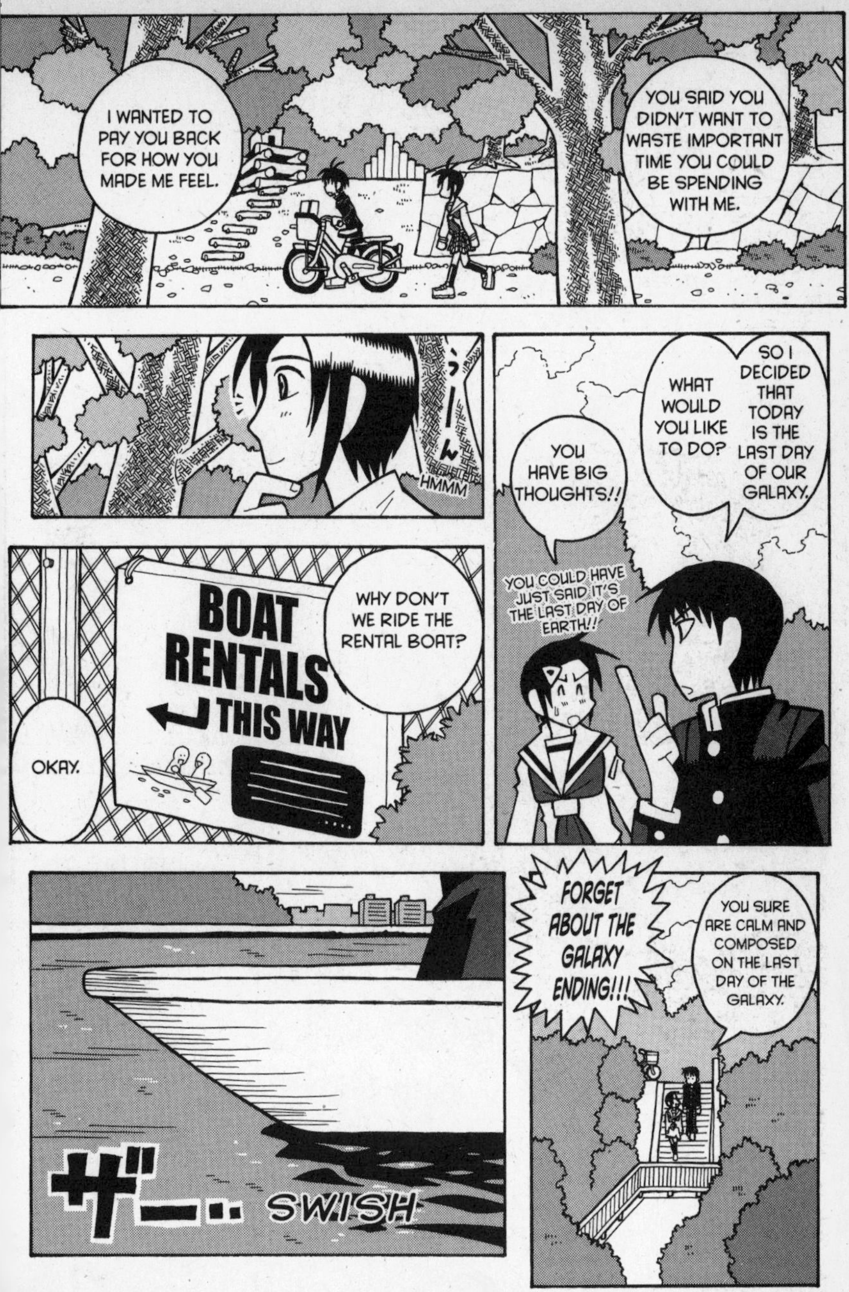
YOU SAID YOU DIDN'T WANT TO WASTE IMPORTANT TIME YOU COULD BE SPENDING WITH ME.
I WANTED TO PAY YOU BACK FOR HOW YOU MADE ME FEEL.
SO I DECIDED THAT TODAY IS THE LAST DAY OF OUR GALAXY.
WHAT WOULD YOU LIKE TO DO?
YOU HAVE BIG THOUGHTS!!
YOU COULD HAVE JUST SAID IT'S THE LAST DAY OF EARTH!!
うーん
HMMM
BOAT RENTALS
THIS WAY
WHY DON'T WE RIDE THE RENTAL BOAT?
OKAY.
YOU SURE ARE CALM AND COMPOSED ON THE LAST DAY OF THE GALAXY.
FORGET ABOUT THE GALAXY ENDING!!!
ザー..
SWISH

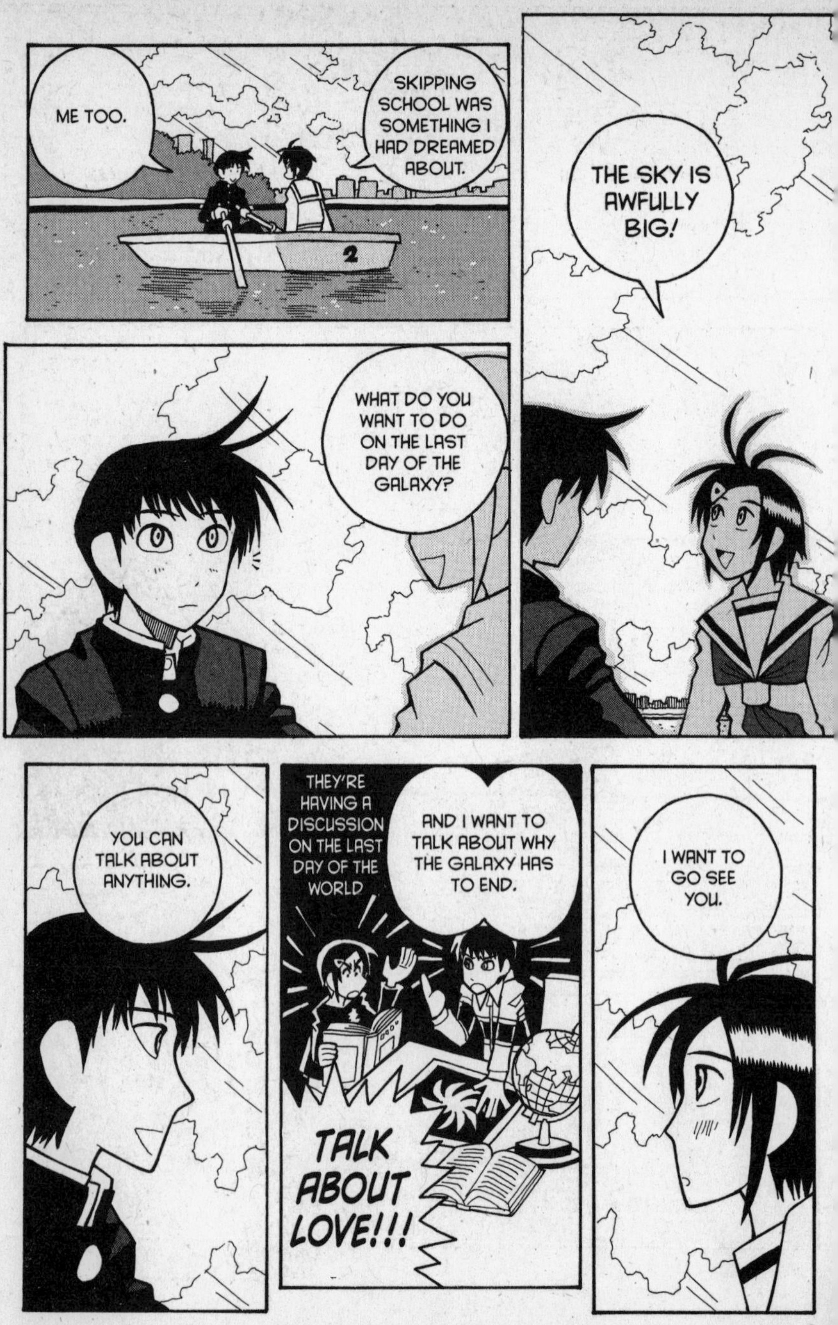
THE SKY IS AWFULLY BIG!
SKIPPING SCHOOL WAS SOMETHING I HAD DREAMED ABOUT.
ME TOO.
WHAT DO YOU WANT TO DO ON THE LAST DAY OF THE GALAXY?
I WANT TO GO SEE YOU.
AND I WANT TO TALK ABOUT WHY THE GALAXY HAS TO END.
THEY'RE HAVING A DISCUSSION ON THE LAST DAY OF THE WORLD
TALK ABOUT LOVE!!!
YOU CAN TALK ABOUT ANYTHING.

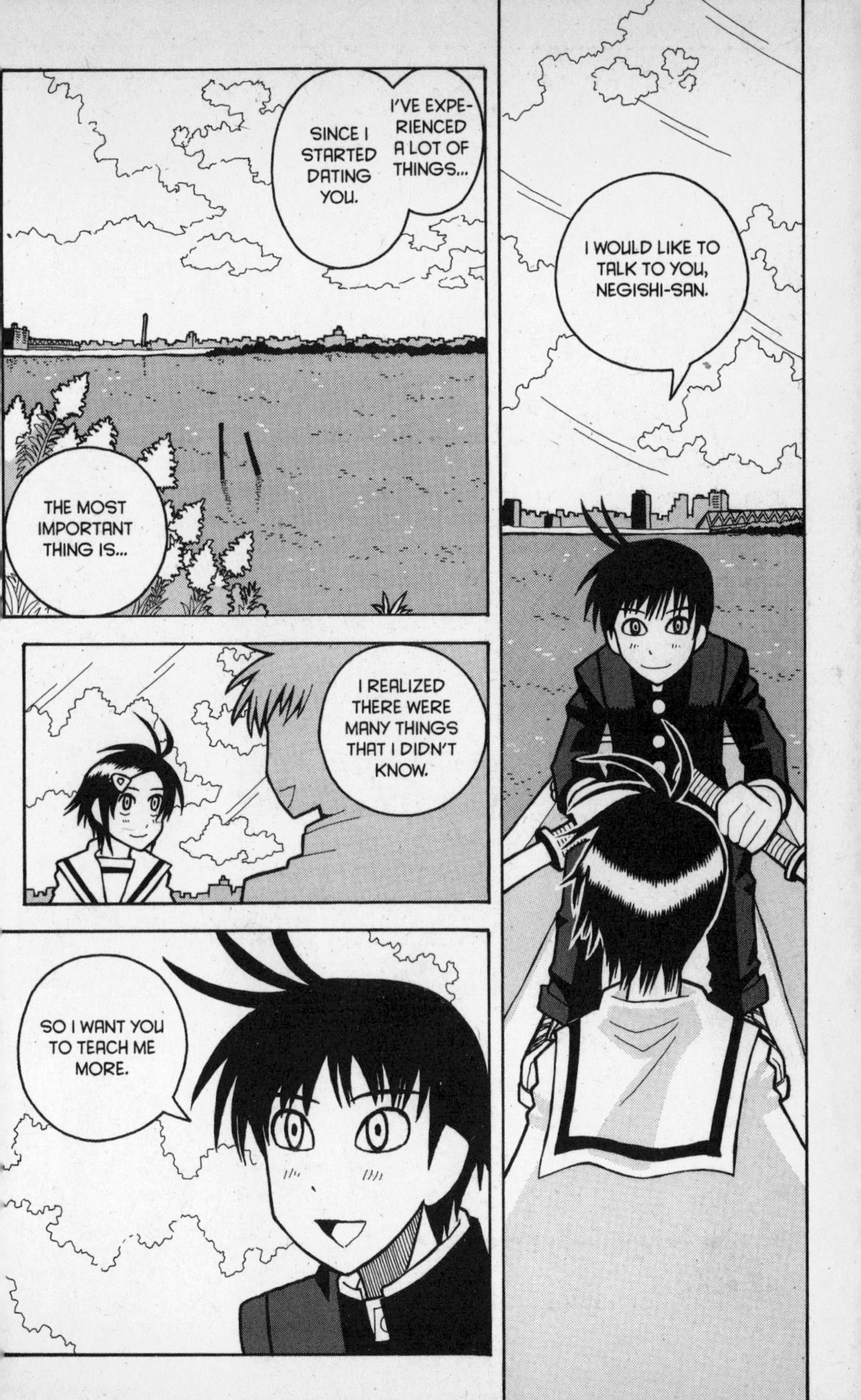
I WOULD LIKE TO TALK TO YOU, NEGISHI-SAN.
I'VE EXPE-RIENCED A LOT OF THINGS... SINCE I STARTED DATING YOU.
THE MOST IMPORTANT THING IS...
I REALIZED THERE WERE MANY THINGS THAT I DIDN'T KNOW.
SO I WANT YOU TO TEACH ME MORE.

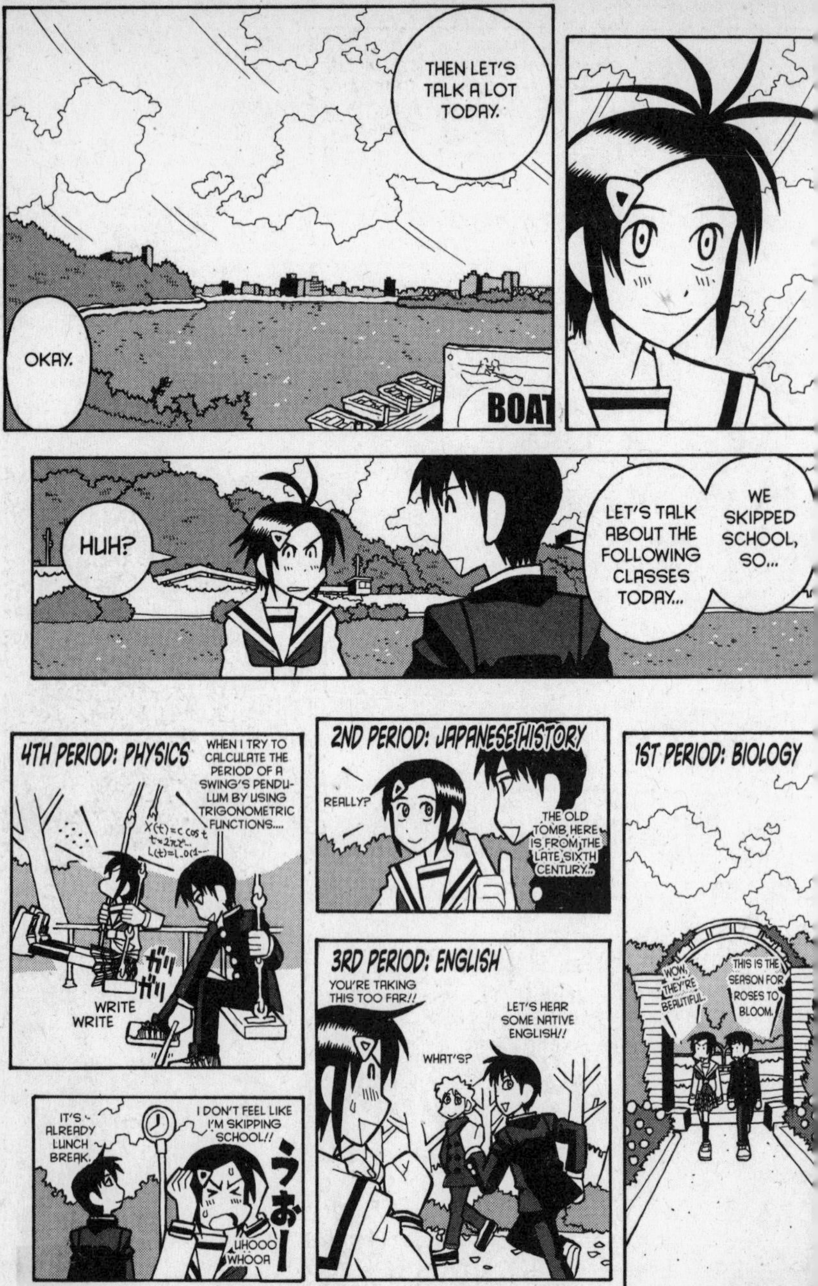
THEN LET'S TALK A LOT TODAY.
OKAY.
BOAT
WE SKIPPED SCHOOL, SO...
LET'S TALK ABOUT THE FOLLOWING CLASSES TODAY...
HUH?
1ST PERIOD: BIOLOGY
THIS IS THE SEASON FOR ROSES TO BLOOM.
WOW, THEY'RE BEAUTIFUL.
2ND PERIOD: JAPANESE HISTORY
THE OLD TOMB HERE IS FROM THE LATE SIXTH CENTURY...
REALLY?
3RD PERIOD: ENGLISH
LET'S HEAR SOME NATIVE ENGLISH!!
WHAT'S?
YOU'RE TAKING THIS TOO FAR!!
4TH PERIOD: PHYSICS
WHEN I TRY TO CALCULATE THE PERIOD OF A SWING'S PENDULUM BY USING TRIGONOMETRIC FUNCTIONS....
X(t)=c cos t
WRITE WRITE
I DON'T FEEL LIKE I'M SKIPPING SCHOOL!!
IT'S ALREADY LUNCH BREAK.
うぉー
WHOOO WHOOA

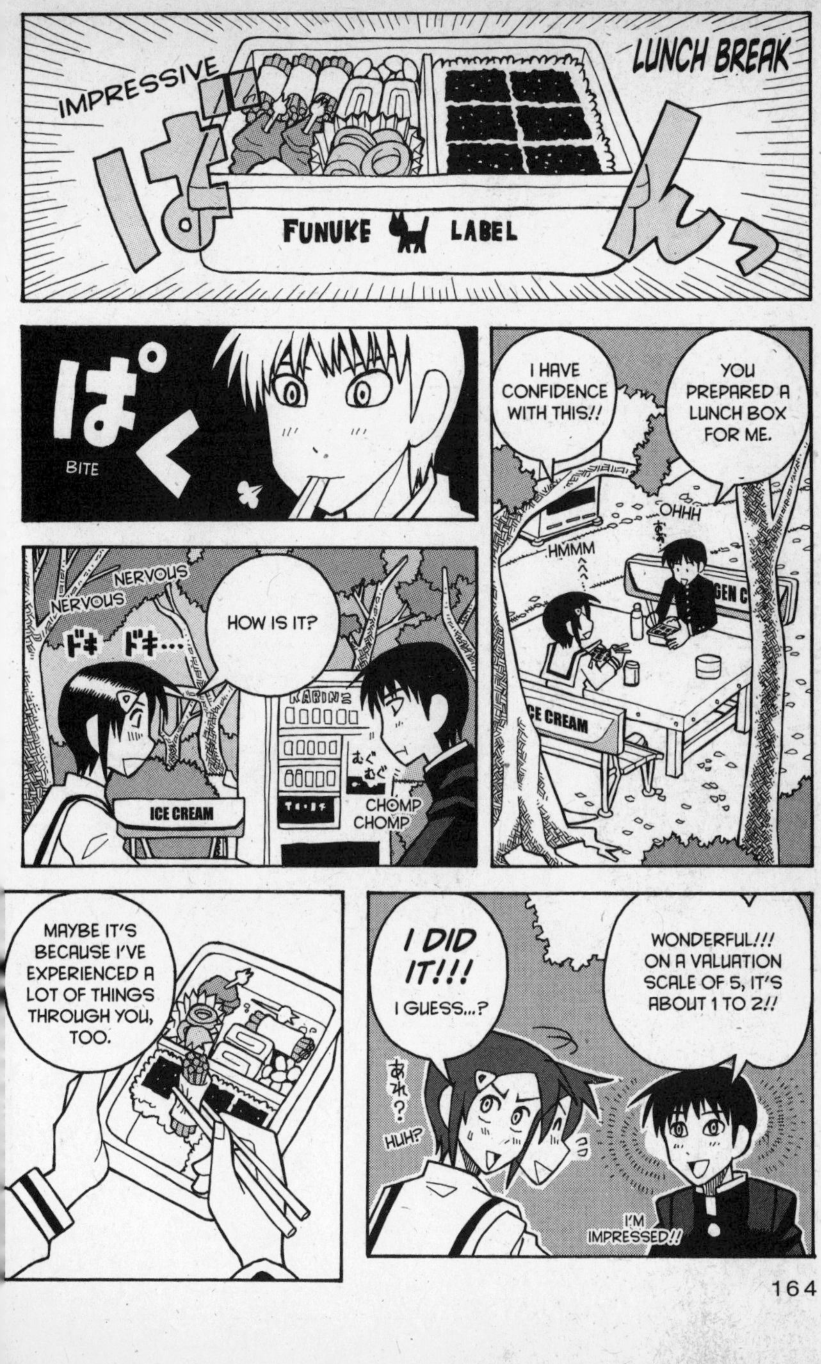
LUNCH BREAK
ぱんっ
IMPRESSIVE
FUNUKE LABEL
YOU PREPARED A LUNCH BOX FOR ME.
I HAVE CONFIDENCE WITH THIS!!
OHHH
HMMM
GEN C
ICE CREAM
ぱく
BITE
HOW IS IT?
ドキ ドキ…
NERVOUS NERVOUS
KARIN
むぐ むぐ
CHOMP CHOMP
ICE CREAM
WONDERFUL!!! ON A VALUATION SCALE OF 5, IT'S ABOUT 1 TO 2!!
I'M IMPRESSED!!
I DID IT!!! I GUESS...?
あれ？
HUH?
MAYBE IT'S BECAUSE I'VE EXPERIENCED A LOT OF THINGS THROUGH YOU, TOO.

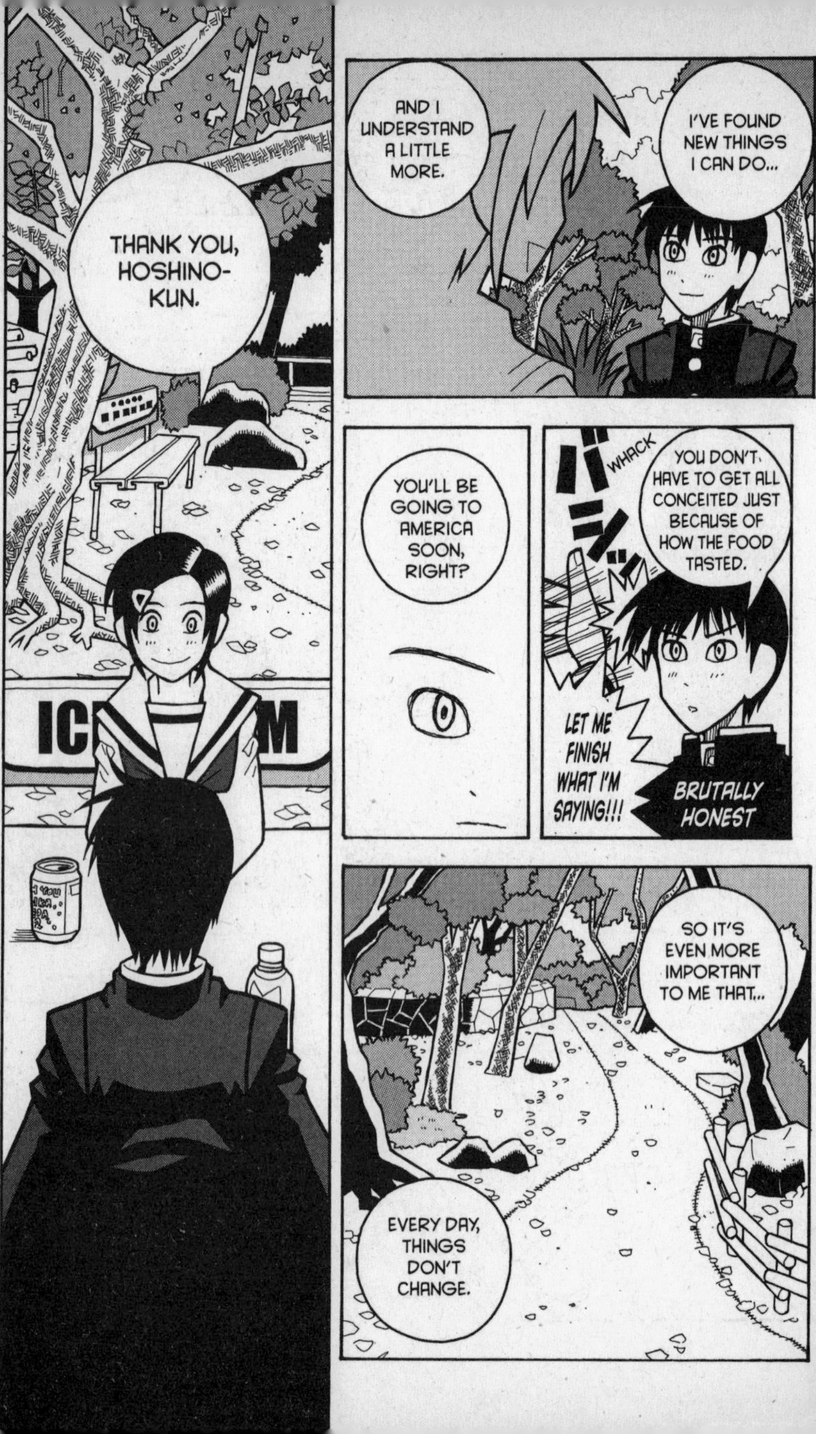
I'VE FOUND NEW THINGS I CAN DO...
AND I UNDERSTAND A LITTLE MORE.
WHACK
YOU DON'T HAVE TO GET ALL CONCEITED JUST BECAUSE OF HOW THE FOOD TASTED.
LET ME FINISH WHAT I'M SAYING!!!
BRUTALLY HONEST
YOU'LL BE GOING TO AMERICA SOON, RIGHT?
SO IT'S EVEN MORE IMPORTANT TO ME THAT...
EVERY DAY, THINGS DON'T CHANGE.
THANK YOU, HOSHINO-KUN.

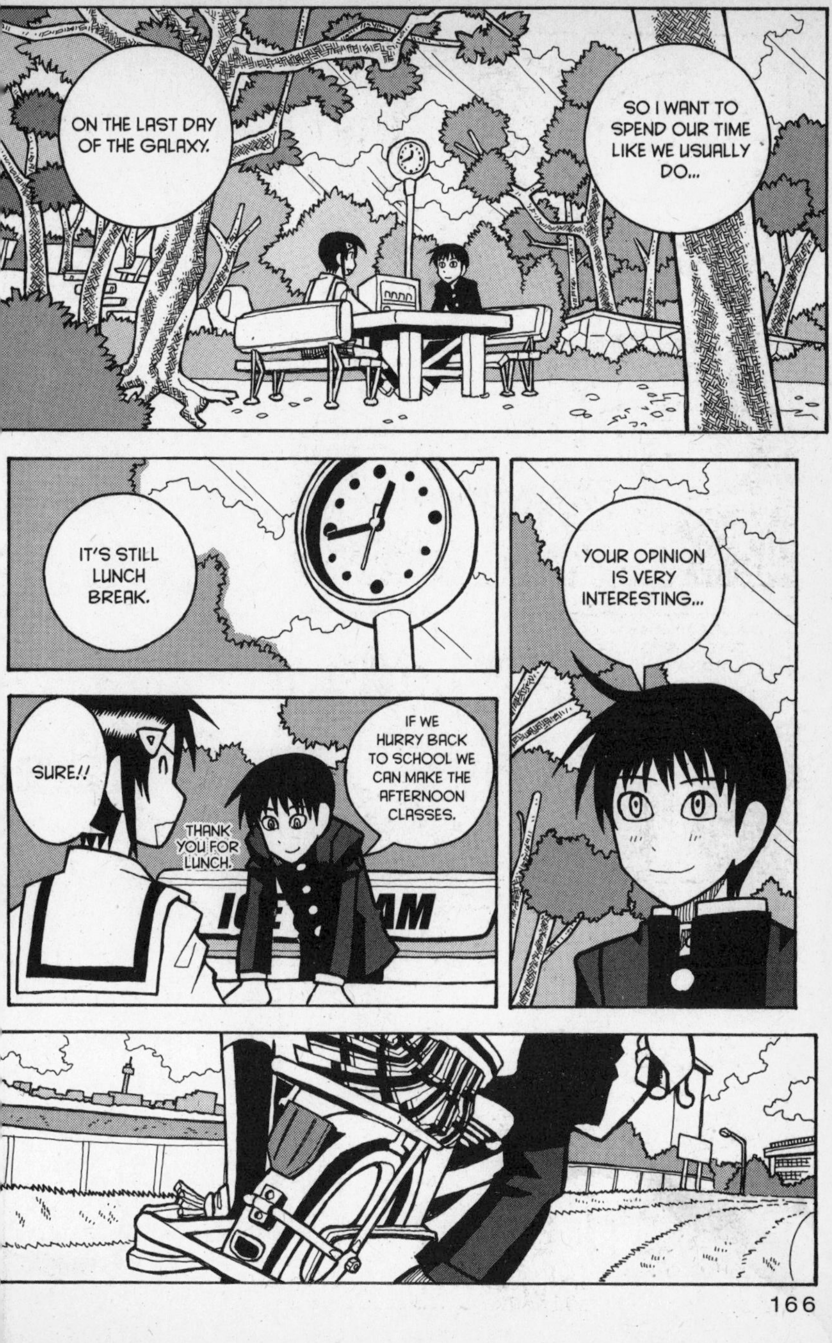
SO I WANT TO SPEND OUR TIME LIKE WE USUALLY DO...
ON THE LAST DAY OF THE GALAXY.
YOUR OPINION IS VERY INTERESTING...
IT'S STILL LUNCH BREAK.
IF WE HURRY BACK TO SCHOOL WE CAN MAKE THE AFTERNOON CLASSES.
SURE!!
THANK YOU FOR LUNCH.

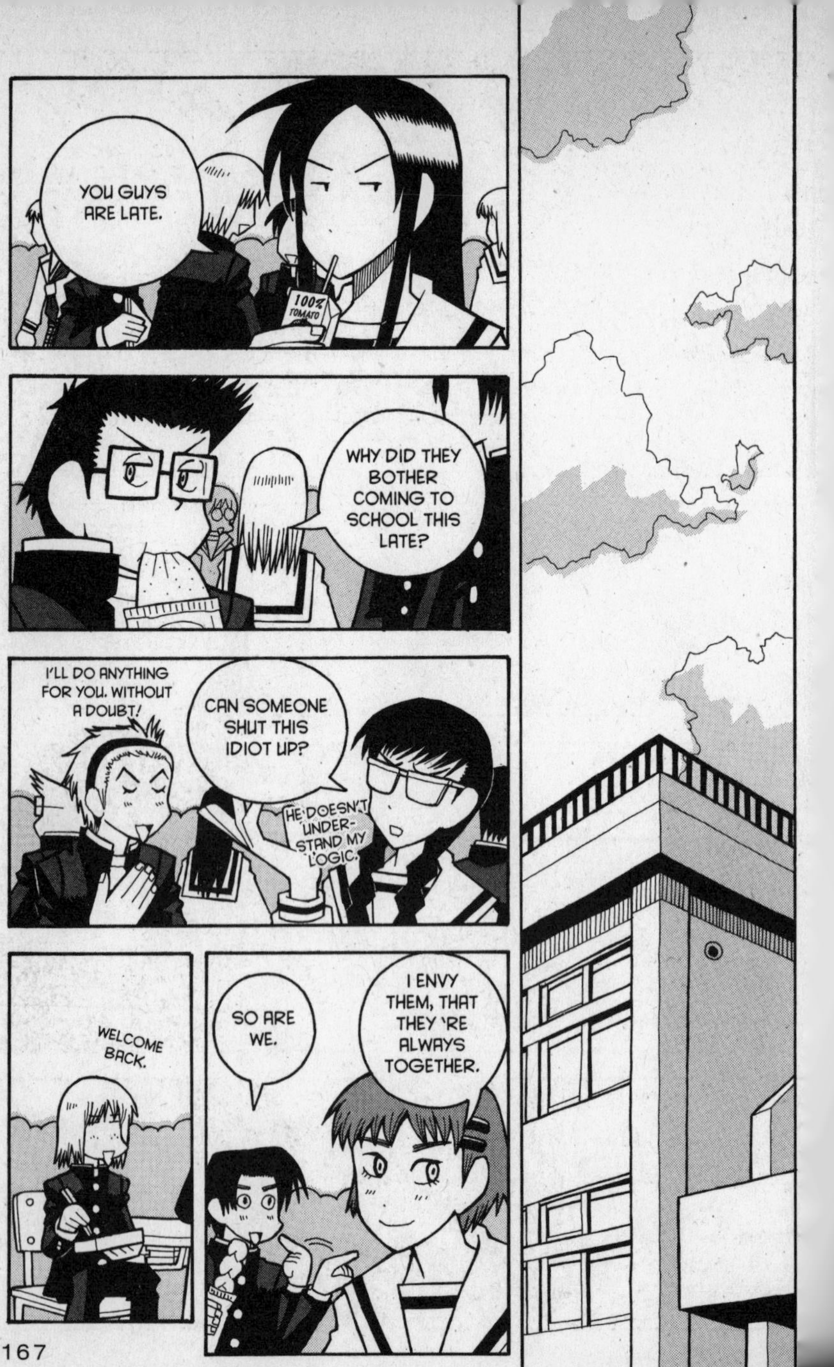
YOU GUYS ARE LATE.
100% TOMATO
WHY DID THEY BOTHER COMING TO SCHOOL THIS LATE?
CAN SOMEONE SHUT THIS IDIOT UP?
HE DOESN'T UNDER-STAND MY LOGIC.
I'LL DO ANYTHING FOR YOU. WITHOUT A DOUBT!
I ENVY THEM, THAT THEY 'RE ALWAYS TOGETHER.
SO ARE WE.
WELCOME BACK.

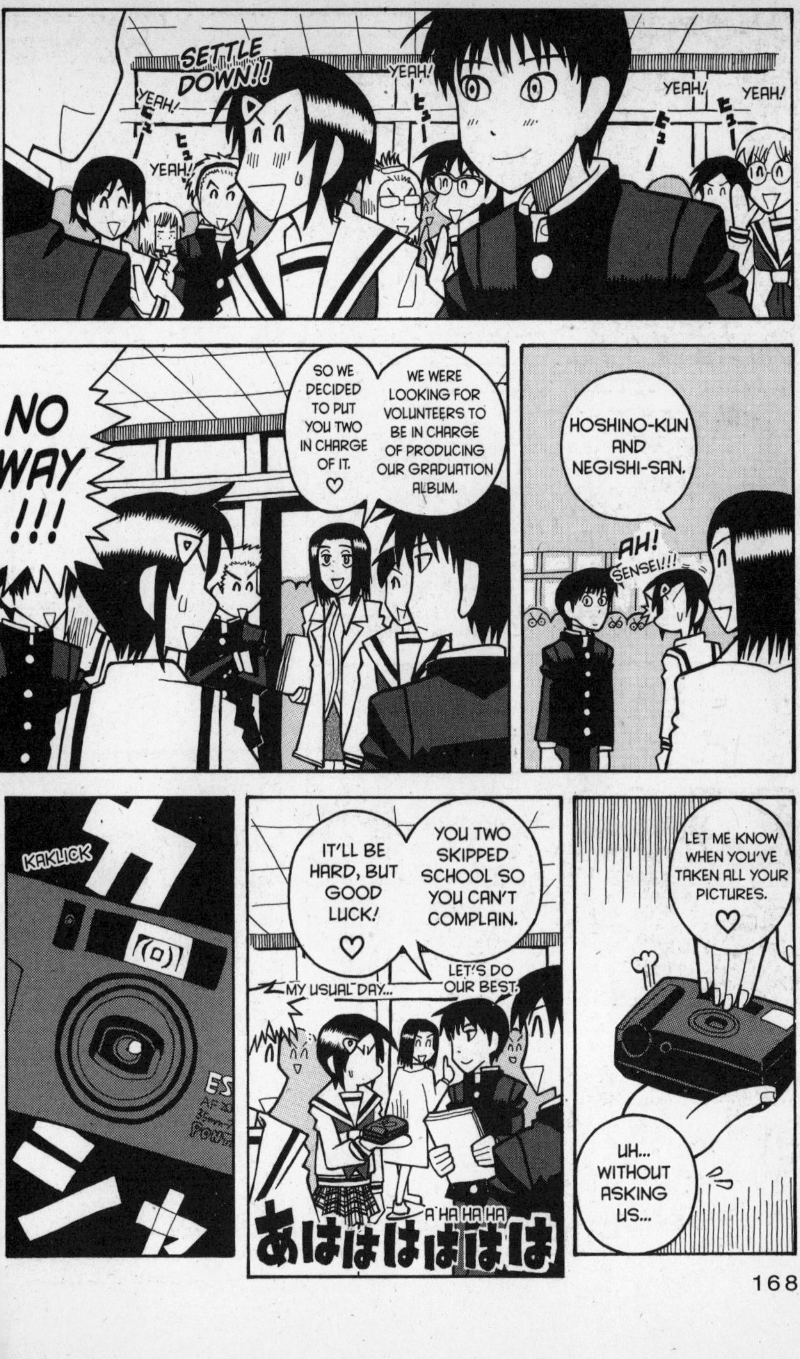
YEAH!
YEAH!
YEAH!
SETTLE DOWN!!
YEAH!
YEAH!
HOSHINO-KUN AND NEGISHI-SAN.
AH! SENSEI!!!
WE WERE LOOKING FOR VOLUNTEERS TO BE IN CHARGE OF PRODUCING OUR GRADUATION ALBUM.
SO WE DECIDED TO PUT YOU TWO IN CHARGE OF IT. ♡
NO WAY!!!
LET ME KNOW WHEN YOU'VE TAKEN ALL YOUR PICTURES. ♡
UH... WITHOUT ASKING US...
YOU TWO SKIPPED SCHOOL SO YOU CAN'T COMPLAIN.
IT'LL BE HARD, BUT GOOD LUCK! ♡
LET'S DO OUR BEST.
MY USUAL DAY...
A HA HA HA
あはははははは
KAKLICK

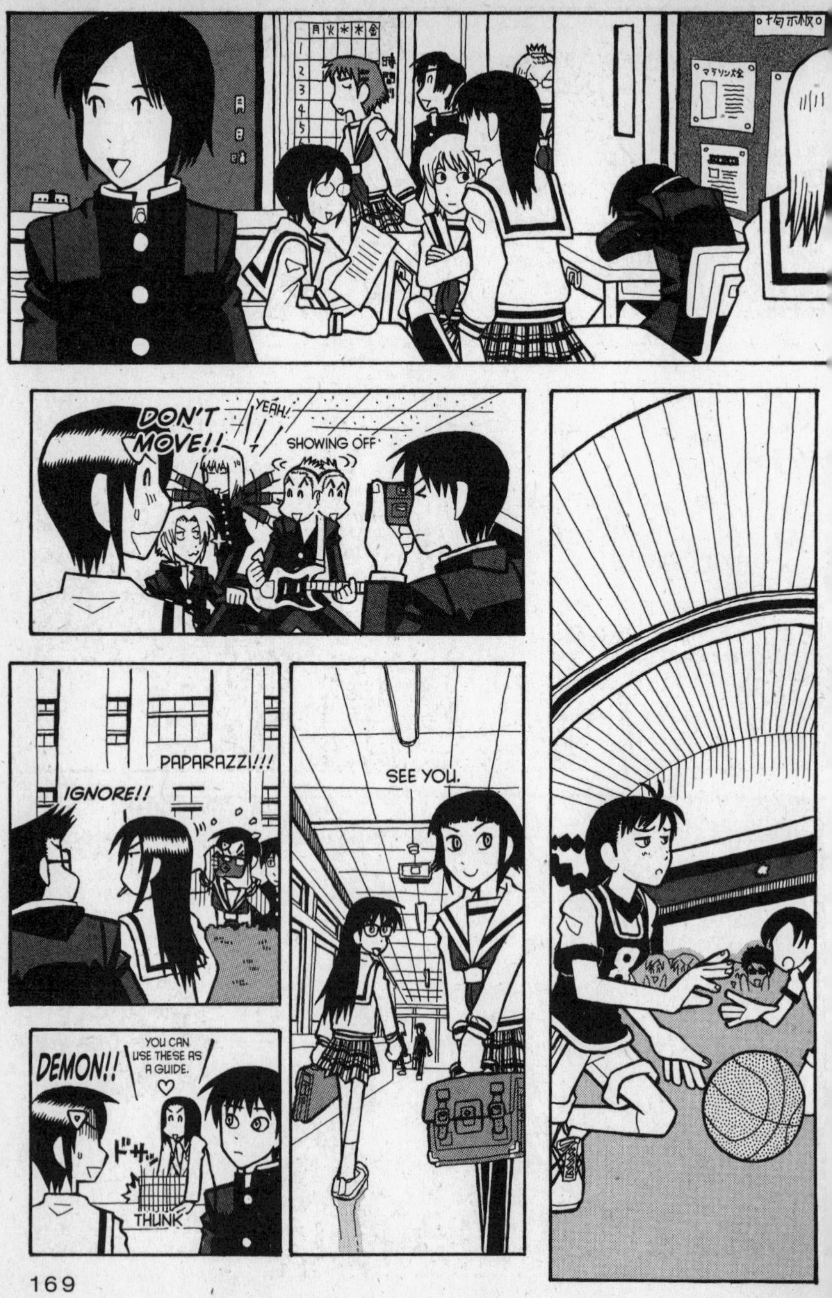
YEAH!
DON'T MOVE!!
SHOWING OFF
SEE YOU.
PAPARAZZI!!!
IGNORE!!
YOU CAN USE THESE AS A GUIDE.
DEMON!!
ドサッ
THUNK

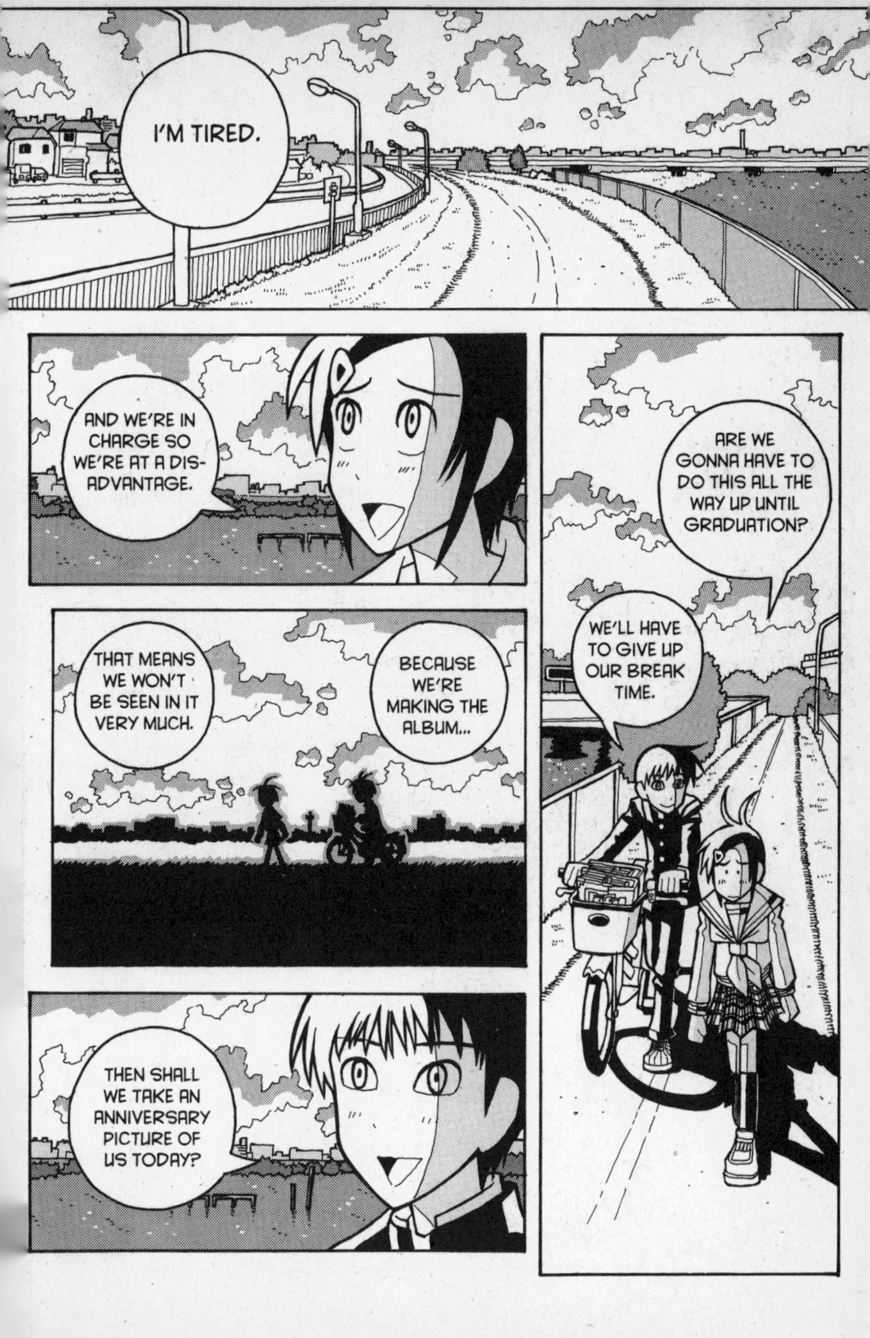
I'M TIRED.
ARE WE GONNA HAVE TO DO THIS ALL THE WAY UP UNTIL GRADUATION?
WE'LL HAVE TO GIVE UP OUR BREAK TIME.
AND WE'RE IN CHARGE SO WE'RE AT A DIS-ADVANTAGE.
BECAUSE WE'RE MAKING THE ALBUM...
THAT MEANS WE WON'T BE SEEN IN IT VERY MUCH.
THEN SHALL WE TAKE AN ANNIVERSARY PICTURE OF US TODAY?

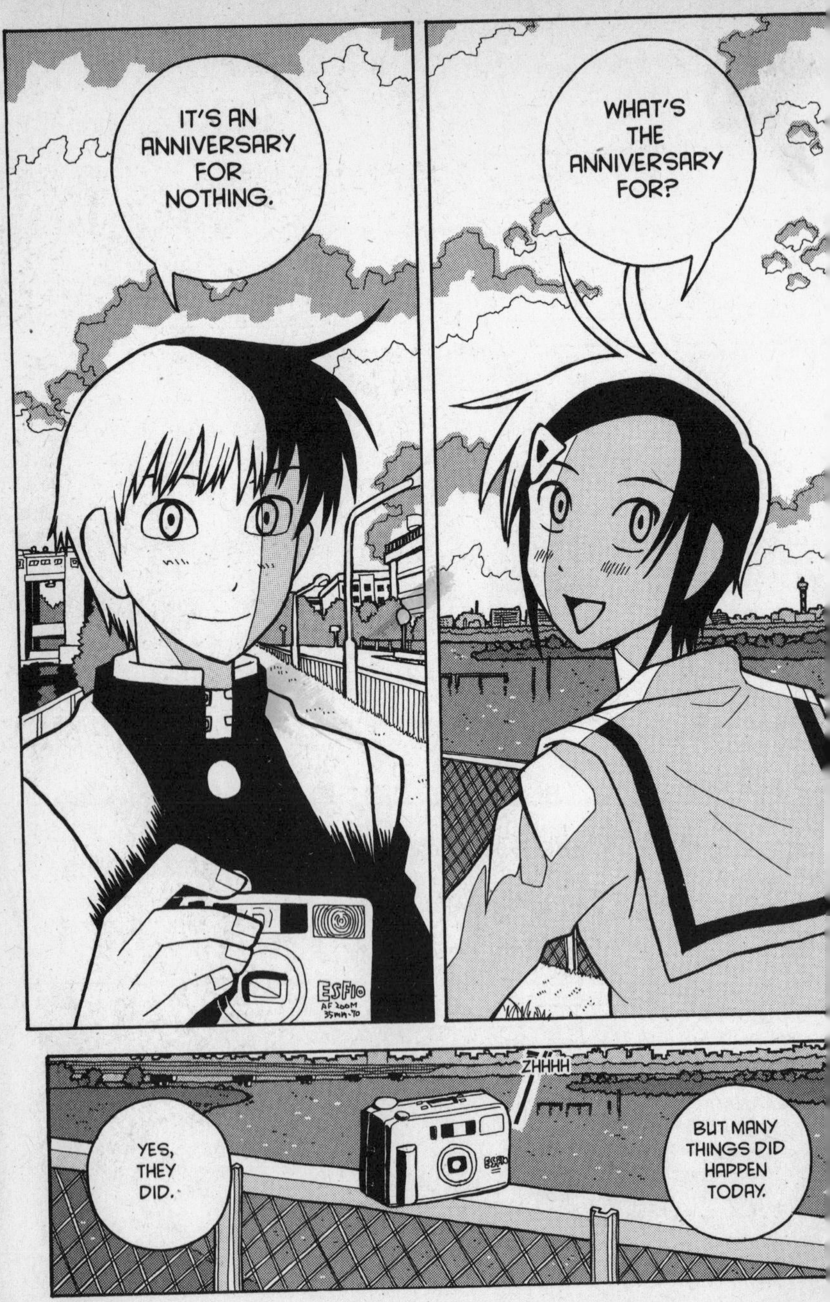
WHAT'S THE ANNIVERSARY FOR?
IT'S AN ANNIVERSARY FOR NOTHING.
BUT MANY THINGS DID HAPPEN TODAY.
ZHHHH
YES, THEY DID.

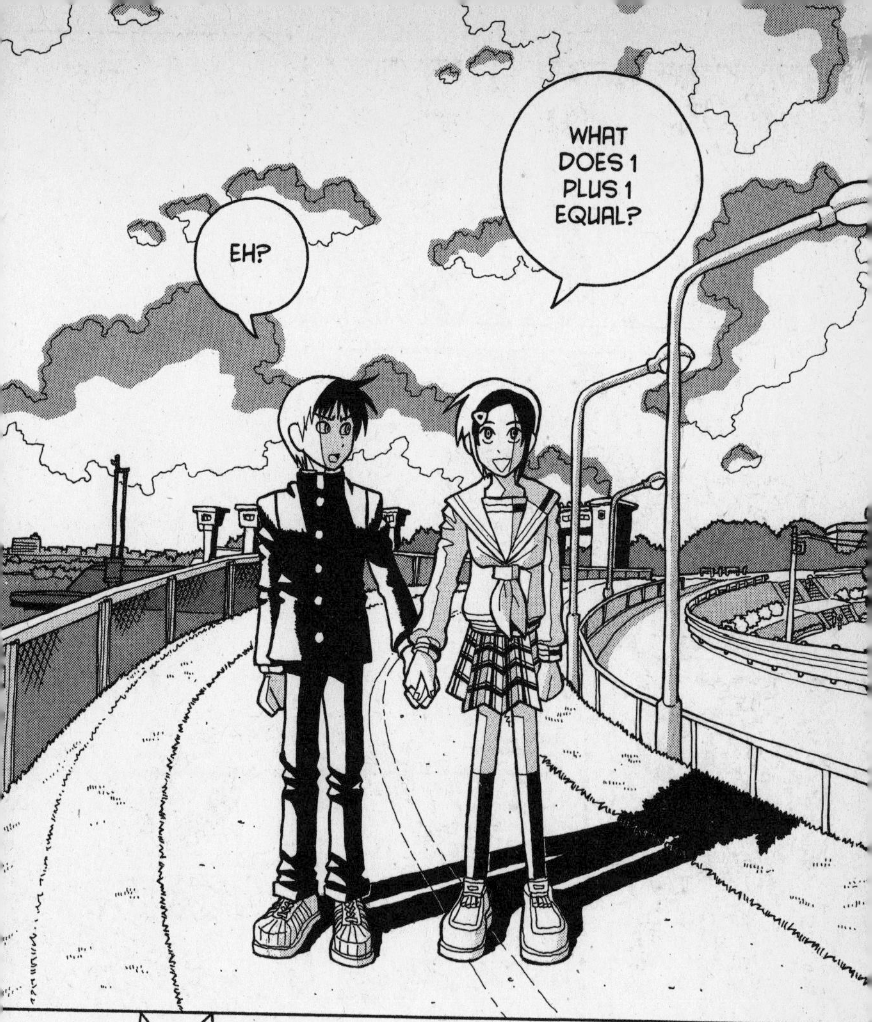
WHAT DOES 1 PLUS 1 EQUAL?
EH?

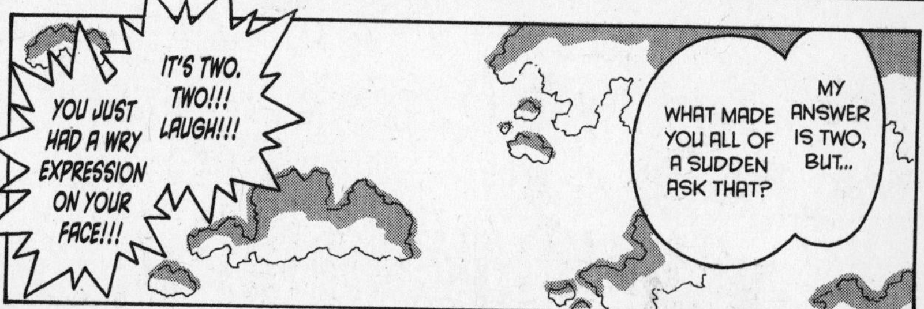
MY ANSWER IS TWO, BUT...
WHAT MADE YOU ALL OF A SUDDEN ASK THAT?
IT'S TWO. TWO!!! LAUGH!!!
YOU JUST HAD A WRY EXPRESSION ON YOUR FACE!!!

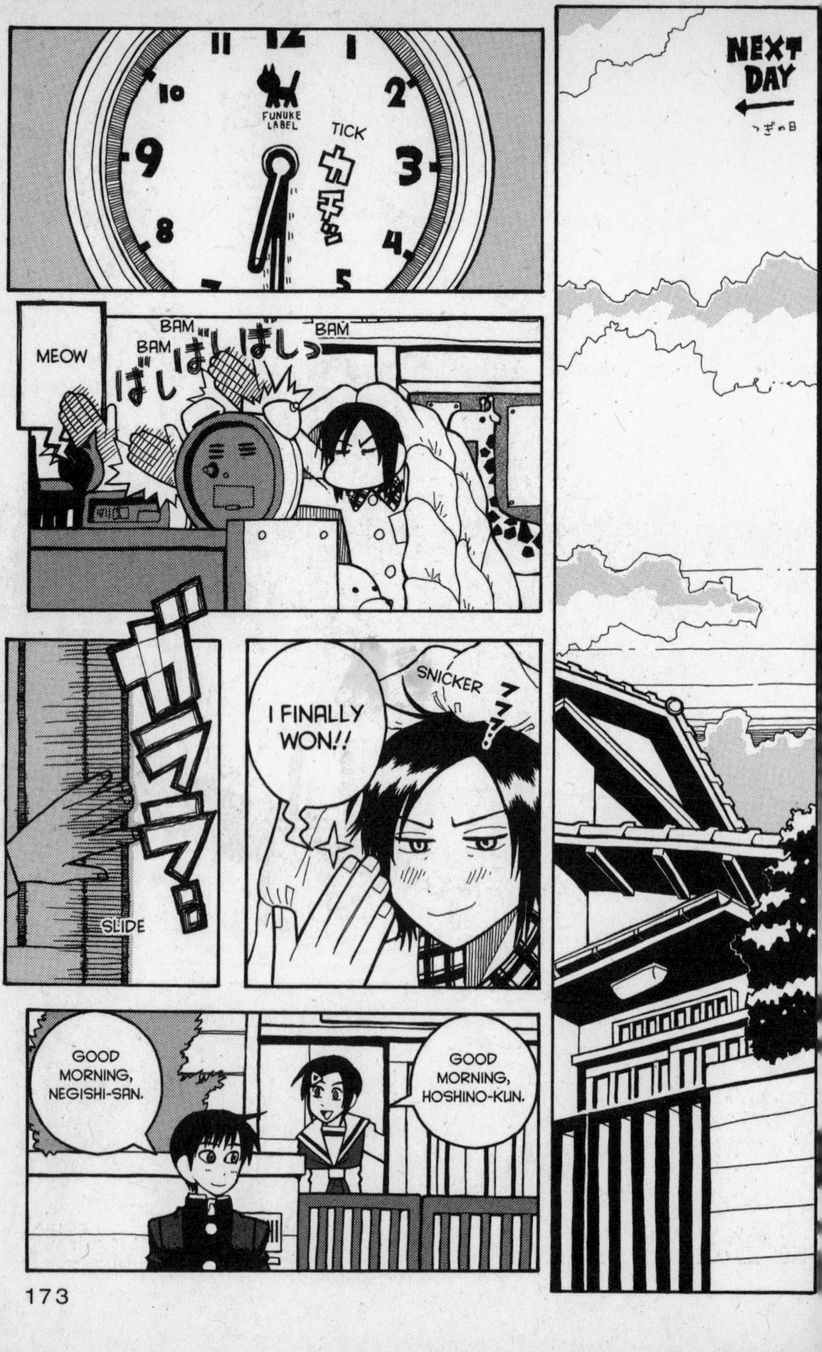
NEXT DAY
つぎの日
FUNUKE LABEL
TICK
BAM
BAM
ばしばしばしっ
BAM
MEOW
SNICKER
I FINALLY WON!!
SLIDE
GOOD MORNING, HOSHINO-KUN.
GOOD MORNING, NEGISHI-SAN.

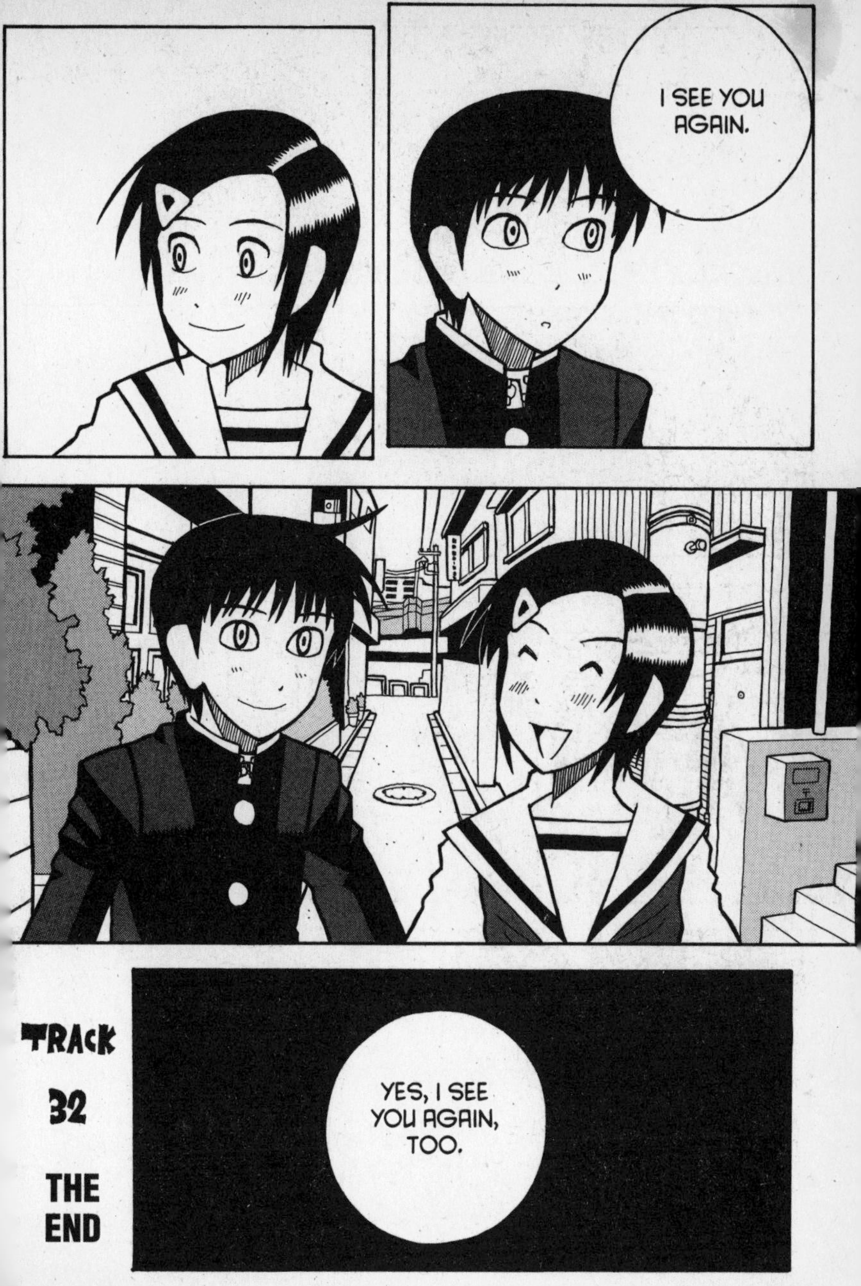
I SEE YOU AGAIN.
YES, I SEE YOU AGAIN, TOO.
TRACK 32 THE END

BONUS TRACK

おまけ

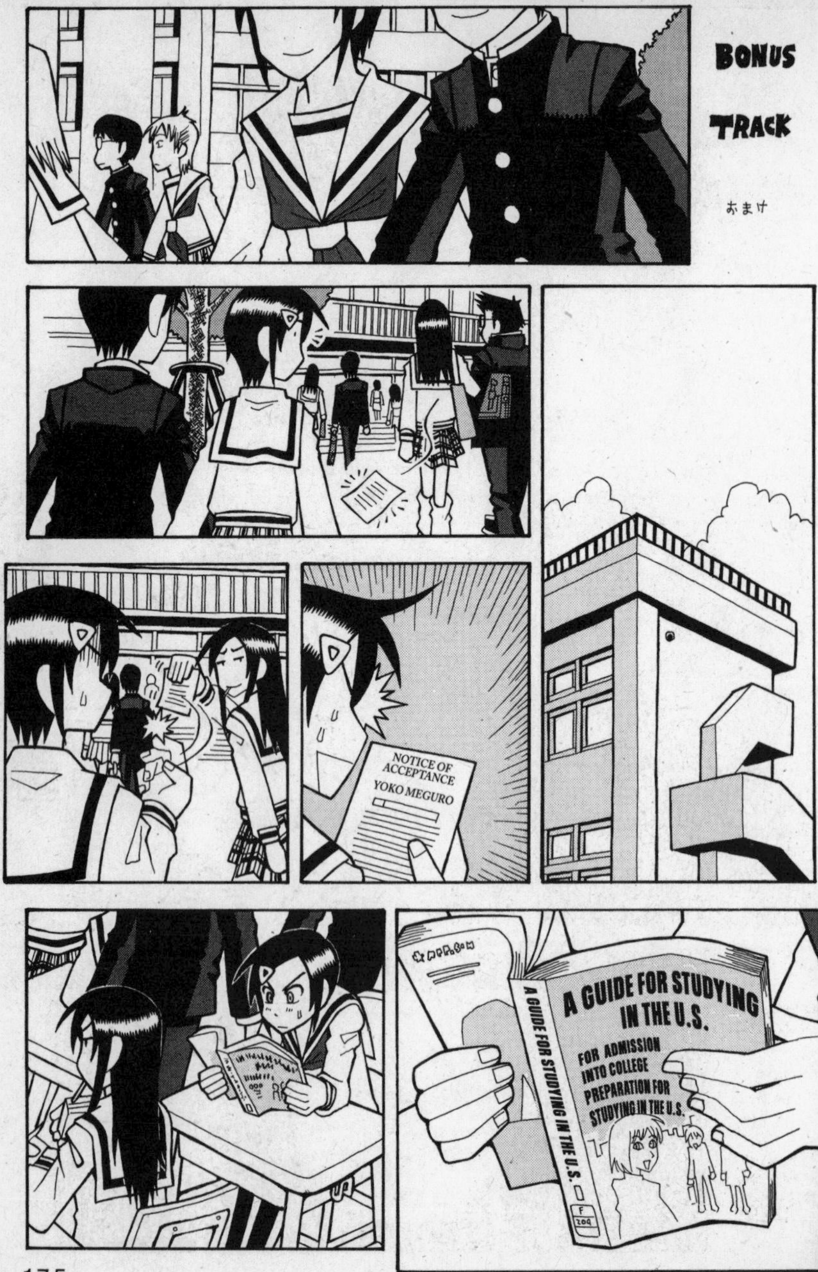
NOTICE OF ACCEPTANCE
YOKO MEGURO
A GUIDE FOR STUDYING IN THE U.S.
FOR ADMISSION INTO COLLEGE PREPARATION FOR STUDYING IN THE U.S.
A GUIDE FOR STUDYING IN THE U.S.

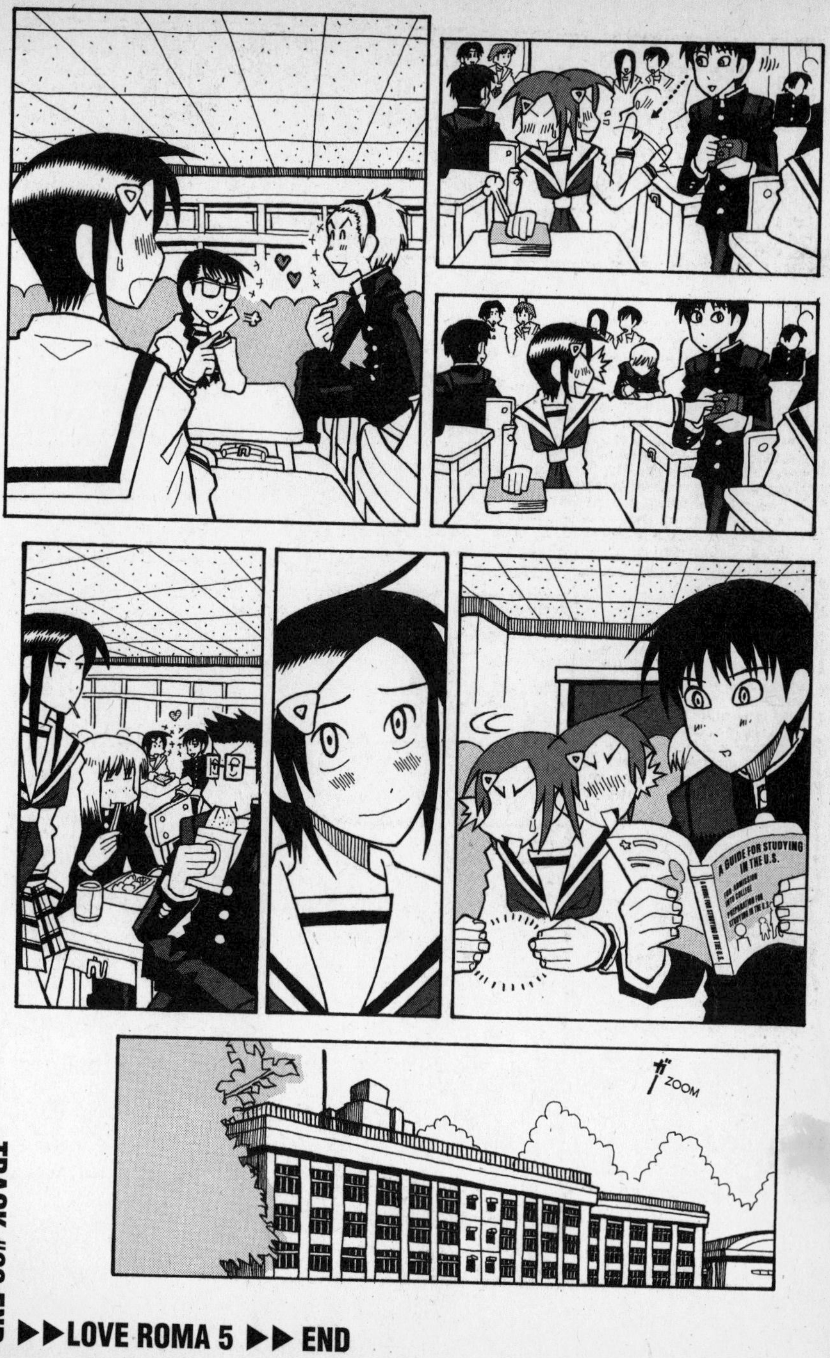
A GUIDE FOR STUDYING IN THE U.S.
ガ ZOOM

TRACK #32 END

▶▶LOVE ROMA 5 ▶▶ END

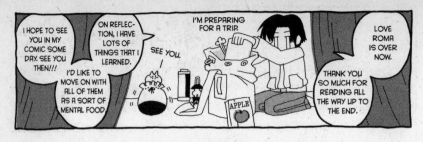

LOVE ROMA IS OVER NOW.
THANK YOU SO MUCH FOR READING ALL THE WAY UP TO THE END.
I'M PREPARING FOR A TRIP.
APPLE
SEE YOU.
ON REFLECTION, I HAVE LOTS OF THINGS THAT I LEARNED.
I'D LIKE TO MOVE ON WITH ALL OF THEM AS A SORT OF MENTAL FOOD.
I HOPE TO SEE YOU IN MY COMIC SOME DAY. SEE YOU THEN!!!

EXPLANATIONS

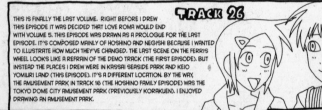

TRACK 26
THIS IS FINALLY THE LAST VOLUME. RIGHT BEFORE I DREW THIS EPISODE IT WAS DECIDED THAT LOVE ROMA WOULD END WITH VOLUME 5. THIS EPISODE WAS DRAWN AS A PROLOGUE FOR THE LAST EPISODE. IT'S COMPOSED MAINLY OF HOSHINO AND NEGISHI BECAUSE I WANTED TO ILLUSTRATE HOW MUCH THEY'VE CHANGED. THE LAST SCENE ON THE FERRIS WHEEL LOOKS LIKE A REFRAIN OF THE DEMO TRACK (THE FIRST EPISODE). BUT INSTEAD THE PLACES I DREW WERE IN KASSAI SEASIDE PARK AND KEIO YOMIURI LAND (THIS EPISODE). IT'S A DIFFERENT LOCATION. BY THE WAY, THE AMUSEMENT PARK IN TRACK 16 (THE HOSHINO FAMILY EPISODE) WAS THE TOKYO DOME CITY AMUSEMENT PARK (PREVIOUSLY KORAKUEN). I ENJOYED DRAWING AN AMUSEMENT PARK.
TRACK 27
I LIKE DRAWING DUMB BOYS. I DREW THE FOUR BOYS ON THE TITLE PAGE WHILE LOOKING AT THE RESERVOIR DOGS VIDEO BOX. IT'S A PICTURE OF THEM GOING TO RENT AN ADULT VIDEO.
TRACK 28
I WANTED TO TEST MYSELF BY WRITING A STORY ABOUT WRITING LETTERS. THE LAST SCENE ON THE ROOFTOP WAS THE TWELVE-FLOOR APARTMENT BUILDING I USED TO GO UP ON WHEN I WAS A KID, BUT NOW IT HAS A "KEEP OUT" SIGN ON IT. I LIKE IT UP ON THE ROOFTOP BECAUSE I FEEL FREE.
TRACK 29
I LOVE FIREWORKS. BEFORE I STARTED THIS JOB, I WENT TO SEE FIREWORKS AT LEAST THREE DIFFERENT PLACES EVERY SUMMER. THE LAST EPISODE WAS GETTING CLOSER SO I WANTED TO DRAW ALL THE LOVE ROMA CHARACTERS AND SHOW HOW THEY'VE GROWN.
TRACK 30
I WAS VERY NERVOUS BECAUSE I'D NEVER DRAWN A SEX SCENE BEFORE. SO IT WAS VERY EXCITING TO DRAW IT AS WELL AS THEM HAVING THEIR FIRST EXPERIENCE.
TRACK 31
ALL THE SUB-CHARACTERS RETURN!! AT LEAST THAT'S WHAT I WAS GOING TO DRAW, BUT I FORGOT YOSHITSUNE'S UNCLE FROM O ISLAND AND HOSHINO'S CAT. I ALSO FORGOT YASHIKI'S DAD. I APOLOGIZE TO THE TWO UNCLES AND CAT. IT WAS ALSO SATISFYING TO DRAW NEGISHI-SAN IN A WEDDING DRESS. BE HAPPY, EVERYBODY!
TRACK 32
I TRIED TO DRAW TRACK 30, 31, AND 32 ALL WITH DIFFERENT STORIES FOR THE LAST EPISODES. ONE OF THEM WAS WHEN THEIR RELATIONSHIP GOT CLOSER. ANOTHER ONE IS WHERE I BROUGHT ALL THE CHARACTERS BACK. AND THE STORY OF THIS TRACK IS "ON THE DAY OF THE LAST EPISODE, NOTHING CHANGES FROM THE USUAL." I THINK WHAT I DREW IN LOVE ROMA WERE SMALL THINGS FOR EACH PERSON BUT THEY WERE IMPORTANT TO THEM ON A DAILY BASIS. THANK YOU FOR READING FOR TWO AND A HALF YEARS. SEE YOU!!

I'M REALLY APPRECIATIVE OF EVERYBODY THAT BOUGHT AND READ THE BOOKS. LOVE.
HP "NET TOKIWASOU TEMPORARY" HTTP://MEMBERS.EDOGAWA.HOME.NE.JP/POO1007/
FUNUKE LABEL

FUNUKE LABEL

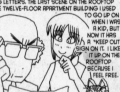

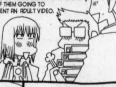

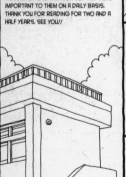

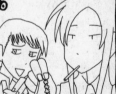

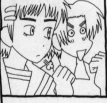

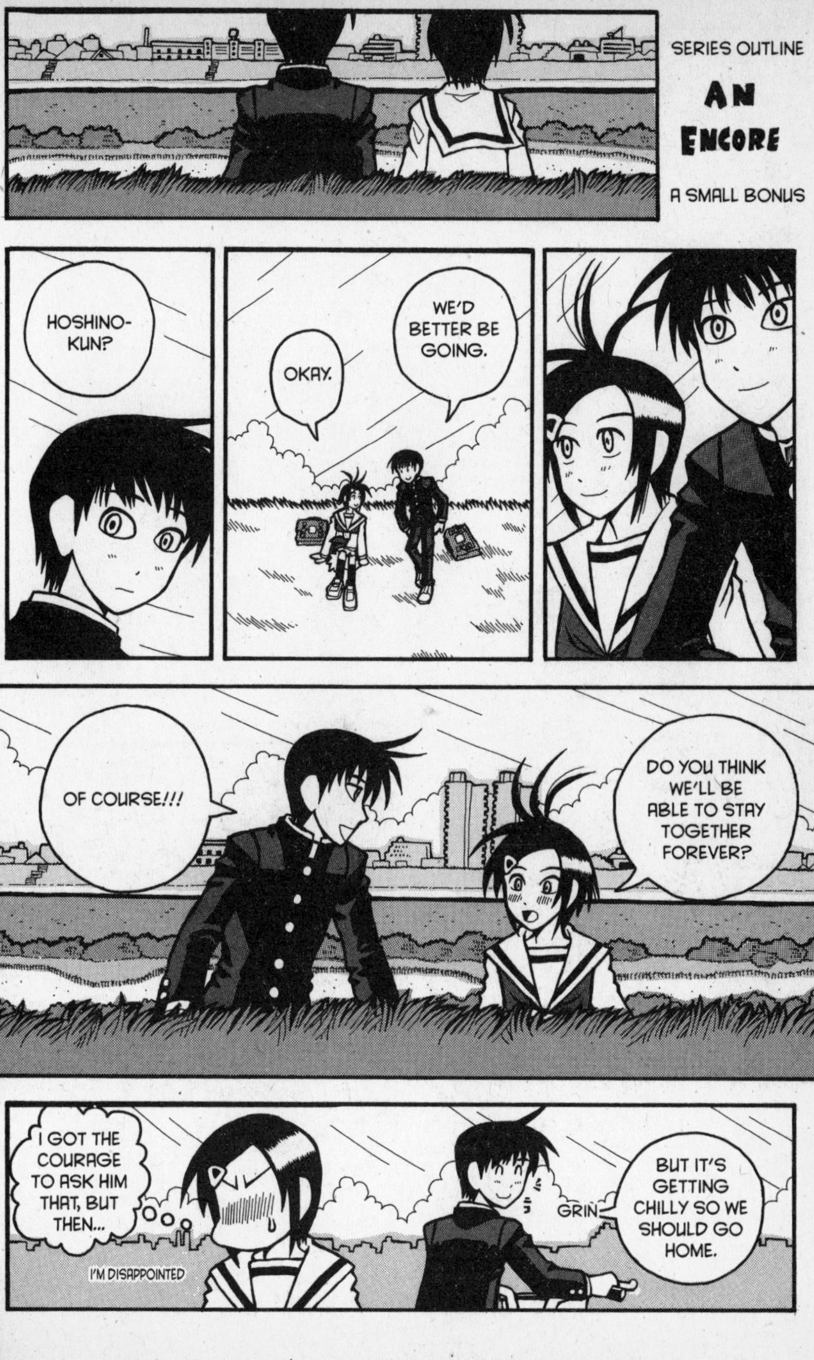
SERIES OUTLINE
AN ENCORE
A SMALL BONUS
WE'D BETTER BE GOING.
OKAY.
HOSHINO-KUN?
DO YOU THINK WE'LL BE ABLE TO STAY TOGETHER FOREVER?
OF COURSE!!!
BUT IT'S GETTING CHILLY SO WE SHOULD GO HOME.
GRIN
I GOT THE COURAGE TO ASK HIM THAT, BUT THEN...
I'M DISAPPOINTED

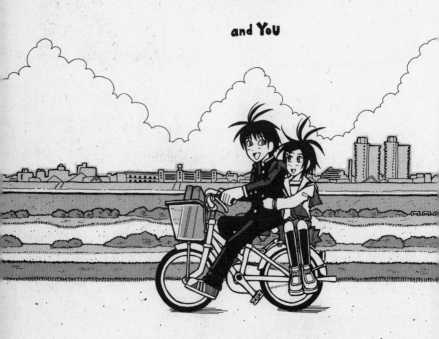

SPECIAL
THANKS

¥

MIWAKO
ITOU
SIMAD
nakaG
MissT
NAKA
Qko
ASHIBI
KOHI
NAKASHIMA

and YOU

THE END.

AUTHOR PROFILE

MINORU TOYODA

MANGA DEBUT

The first episode of *Love Roma* in Kodansha's *Afternoon* magazine.

AWARDS

Toyoda won a prize for *Reonizumu* in 2000, but he won first place for *Love Roma* in 2002. The award was the "Afternoon Shiki Prize," which is awarded to new cartoonists.

DATE OF BIRTH

Oct. 7, 1971

STATUS

Living with his parents.

FAVORITE THING

Nothing but comics.

LEAST FAVORITE THING

The occult.

ASPIRATIONS

Minoru hopes that his comics will overcome differences in language or culture and will be enjoyed by a large number of people.

HIDDEN TRACK

In Japan, virtually all manga are printed with a dust jacket. In the original *tankoban* (the Japanese term for a trade paperback) for *Love Roma*, the "hidden tracks" are hidden under the dust jacket, printed on the physical cover of the book itself. While this does happen in Japan from time to time, it remains uncommon; most covers are either black-and-white versions of the color cover on the dust jacket, or just the logo of the magazine in which the story was serialized. In this hidden track, the entire cast of Love Roma bids farewell to their devoted readers.

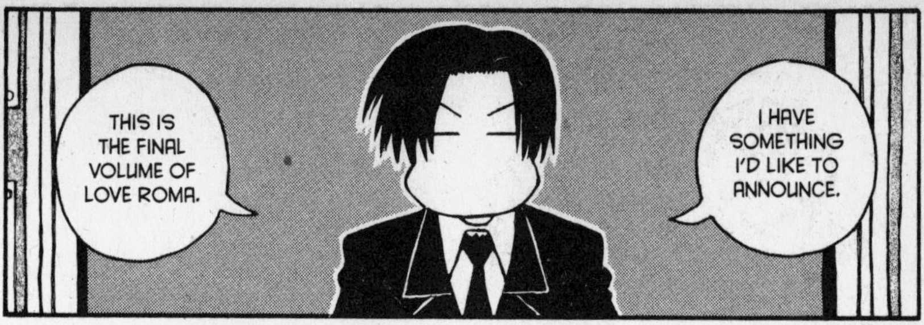
I HAVE SOMETHING I'D LIKE TO ANNOUNCE.
THIS IS THE FINAL VOLUME OF LOVE ROMA.

LOVE ROMA **HIDDEN TRACK** GOODBYE DOESN'T MEAN IT'S FOREVER.

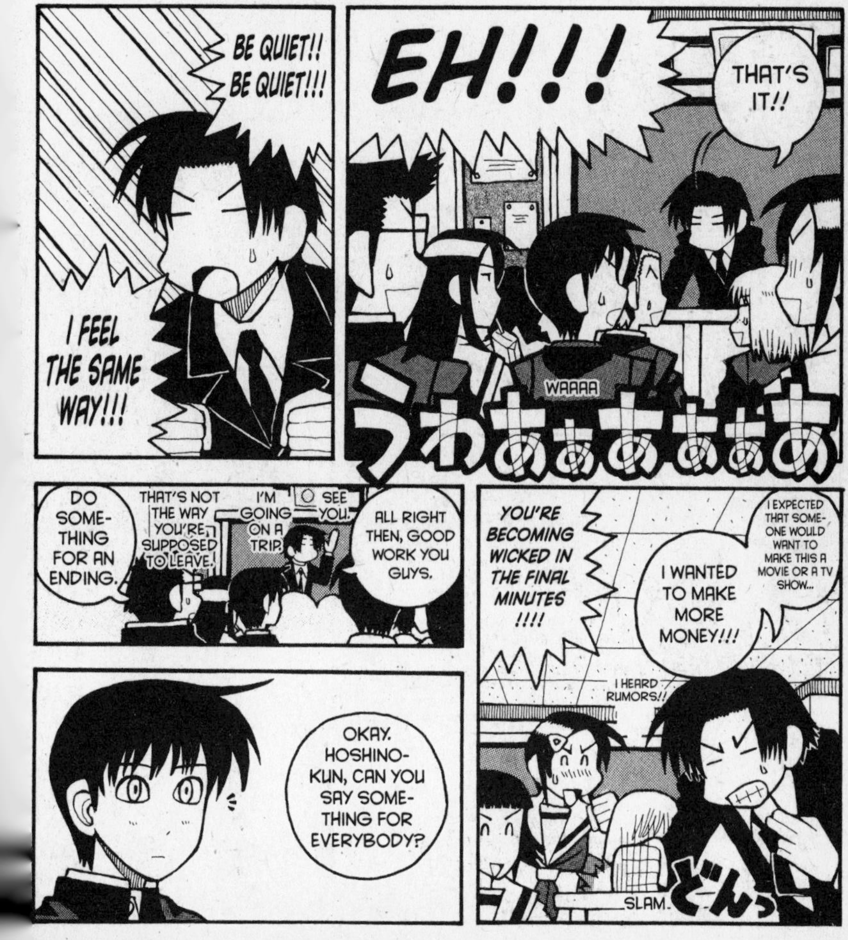
EH!!!
THAT'S IT!!
うわぁぁぁぁぁぁぁ
WAAAA
BE QUIET!! BE QUIET!!!
I FEEL THE SAME WAY!!!
I EXPECTED THAT SOMEONE WOULD WANT TO MAKE THIS A MOVIE OR A TV SHOW...
I WANTED TO MAKE MORE MONEY!!!
YOU'RE BECOMING WICKED IN THE FINAL MINUTES!!!!
I HEARD RUMORS!!
どんっ
SLAM
ALL RIGHT THEN, GOOD WORK YOU GUYS.
SEE YOU.
I'M GOING ON A TRIP.
THAT'S NOT THE WAY YOU'RE SUPPOSED TO LEAVE.
DO SOMETHING FOR AN ENDING.
OKAY. HOSHINO-KUN, CAN YOU SAY SOMETHING FOR EVERYBODY?

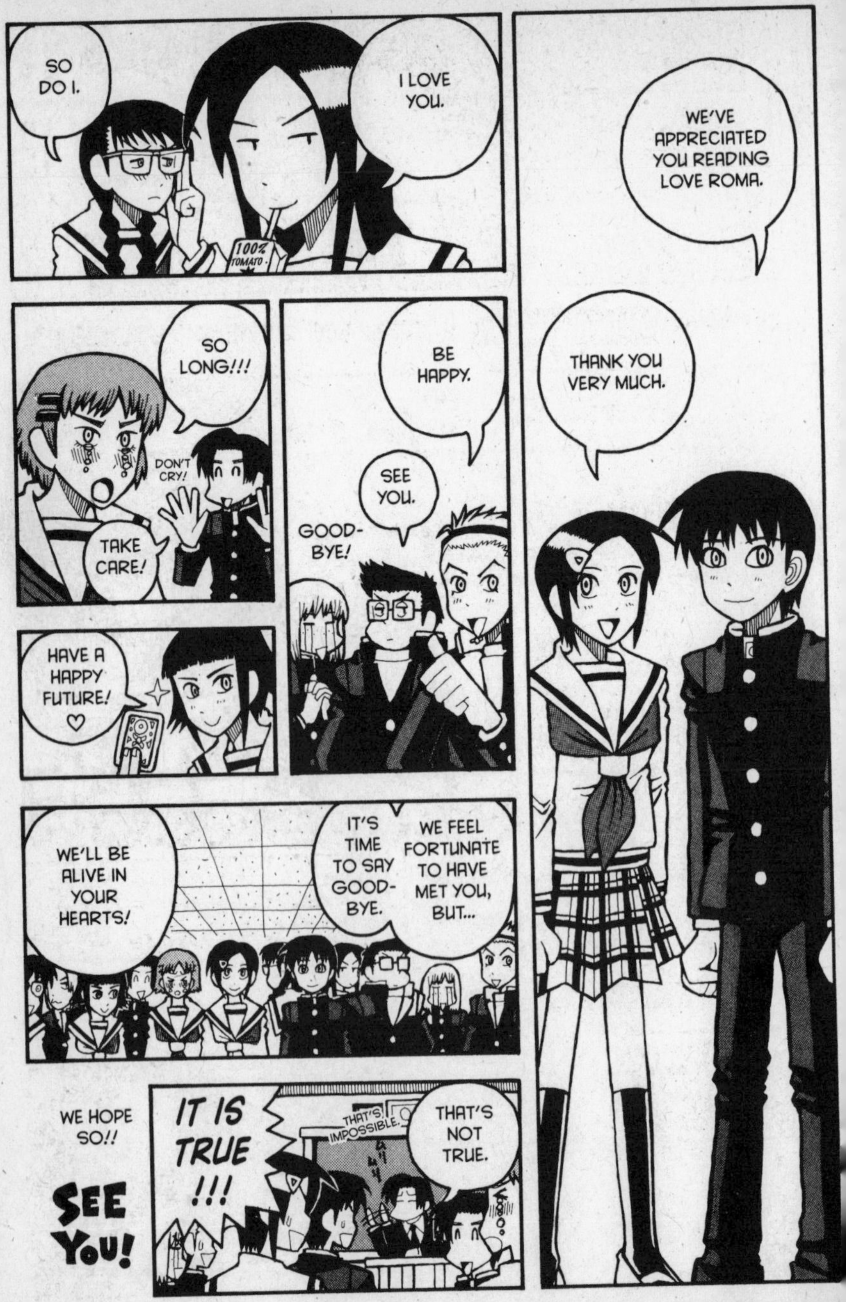
WE'VE APPRECIATED YOU READING LOVE ROMA.
THANK YOU VERY MUCH.
I LOVE YOU.
SO DO I.
BE HAPPY.
SEE YOU.
GOOD-BYE!
SO LONG!!!
DON'T CRY!
TAKE CARE!
HAVE A HAPPY FUTURE! ♡
WE FEEL FORTUNATE TO HAVE MET YOU, BUT...
IT'S TIME TO SAY GOOD-BYE.
WE'LL BE ALIVE IN YOUR HEARTS!
THAT'S NOT TRUE.
THAT'S IMPOSSIBLE.
IT IS TRUE!!!
WE HOPE SO!!
SEE YOU!

Translation Notes

Japanese is a tricky language for most Westerners, and translation is often more art than science. For your edification and reading pleasure, here are notes on some of the places where we could have gone in a different direction in our translation of the work, or where a Japanese cultural reference is used.

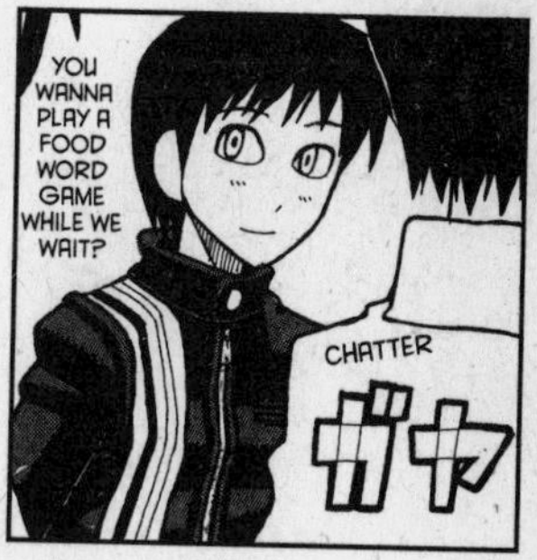
YOU WANNA PLAY A FOOD WORD GAME WHILE WE WAIT?
CHATTER
ガヤ

Food word game, page 11

While waiting in line for the ride, Negishi comes up with the idea to play a "food word game" to pass the time. This is a word game played in Japan (though "food" doesn't necessarily have to be the theme) in which one player says a word that has two syllables or more. Then the next person must say a word beginning with the last syllable of the word you just said. Hoshino chose "apricot" so now Negishi is trying to think of a food that starts with "cot."

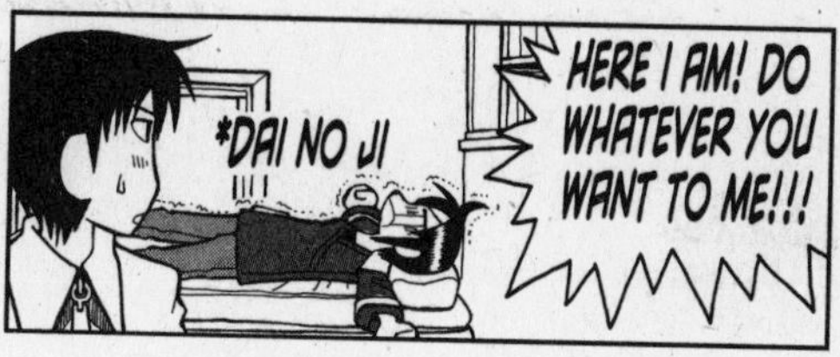
HERE I AM! DO WHATEVER YOU WANT TO ME!!!
*DAI NO JI

Dai no ji, page 48

The Japanese character on the left that looks like someone standing with extended arms means "big." The Japanese have an idiom, *dai no ji,* that is usually used to refer to the shape of a body when someone is lying down with arms and legs spread apart. In this case it is referring to the shape of Negishi's body as she offers herself to Hoshino.

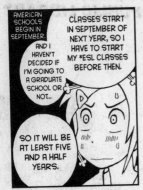

CLASSES START IN SEPTEMBER OF NEXT YEAR, SO I HAVE TO START MY *ESL CLASSES BEFORE THEN.
AMERICAN SCHOOLS BEGIN IN SEPTEMBER.
AND I HAVEN'T DECIDED IF I'M GOING TO A GRADUATE SCHOOL OR NOT...
SO IT WILL BE AT LEAST FIVE AND A HALF YEARS.

ESL, page 148

ESL stands for English as a Second Language.

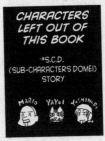

CHARACTERS LEFT OUT OF THIS BOOK
*S.C.D. (SUB-CHARACTERS DOMEI) STORY
MARIO
YAYOI
YOSHINORI

Domei, page 149

Domei means "alliance" in English. In the acronym S.C.D., Toyoda chose to use the English words "Sub-Characters," for the S and C, then used Japanese for the D.

Comike, page 150

Comike, or Comic Market, is a large comic convention held in Japan twice a year. The admission to the event is free and over 100,000 people visit the exhibition per day. Cosplay (dressing in costumes) is abundant and for die-hard collectors and fans alike, there's something there for everyone.

Shei shei, page 150

When Toyoda was in Taiwan, he said the only words he knew to reply were *shei shei.* A good choice, because in Chinese this means "Thank you."

STOP!

YOU'RE GOING THE WRONG WAY!

MANGA IS A COMPLETELY DIFFERENT TYPE
OF READING EXPERIENCE.

TO START AT THE BEGINNING,
GO TO THE END!

THAT'S RIGHT!

AUTHENTIC MANGA IS READ THE TRADITIONAL
JAPANESE WAY—FROM RIGHT TO LEFT. EXACTLY THE OPPOSITE
OF HOW AMERICAN BOOKS ARE READ. IT'S EASY TO FOLLOW:
JUST GO TO THE OTHER END OF THE BOOK, AND READ EACH PAGE
—AND EACH PANEL—FROM RIGHT SIDE TO LEFT SIDE,
STARTING AT THE TOP RIGHT. NOW YOU'RE EXPERIENCING
MANGA AS IT WAS MEANT TO BE.